Circumventing the Law

JEWISH CULTURE AND CONTEXTS

Published in association with the Herbert D. Katz Center
for Advanced Judaic Studies of the University of
Pennsylvania

Series Editors

Beth Berkowitz,

Shaul Magid,

Francesca Trivellato,

Steven Weitzman

A complete list of books in the series
is available from the publisher.

CIRCUMVENTING THE LAW

Rabbinic Perspectives on Loopholes
and Legal Integrity

Elana Stein Hain

UNIVERSITY OF PENNSYLVANIA PRESS

PHILADELPHIA

Copyright © 2024 University of Pennsylvania Press

All rights reserved. Except for brief quotations used for purposes of review or scholarly citation, none of this book may be reproduced in any form by any means without written permission from the publisher.

Published by
University of Pennsylvania Press
Philadelphia, Pennsylvania 19104-4112
www.upenn.edu/pennpress

Printed in the United States of America on acid-free paper
10 9 8 7 6 5 4 3 2 1

Hardcover ISBN: 978-1-5128-2440-7
eBook ISBN: 978-1-5128-2441-4

A Cataloging-in-Publication record is available from the Library of Congress

For Yonah, Azzan, and Navon,
with love

Contents

Introduction	1
Chapter 1. (When) Do Circumventions Disrespect the Law?	10
Chapter 2. Being Explicit About Legal Values and Integrity	31
Chapter 3. Romans as Jurists, Rabbis as Lawyers	53
Chapter 4. *Ha'aramah* and Intention	65
Chapter 5. *Ha'aramah* in the *Bavli*: Discomfort with Ritualized Intention	78
Chapter 6. *Ha'aramah* and Contemporary Legal Theory	107
Epilogue. *Ha'aramah* and *Takkanot*	135
Appendix. Comparing the *Yerushalmi*'s and the *Bavli*'s Use of *Ha'aramah* Terminology and Concept	145
Notes	147
Bibliography	199
Index	217
Acknowledgments	227

Introduction

American law recognizes the difference between illegal tax evasion and legal tax avoidance. But there is also a third space: the fuzzy category that was coined in the 1970s anti-taxation movement called "avoision," which does not seem to stand clearly on one side of the line or the other.

Avoision is everywhere, from formal legal machinations to daily mundane interactions. For example, children might practice avoision when directed by their parents not to read after lights out: instead, they play video games under their covers. Technically, they have not violated their parents' directive. In the legal sphere, avoision can appear as taking advantage of legal provisions in ways that were not previously anticipated. For instance, one might purchase an expensive new villa just before filing for bankruptcy because, by law, one can keep their home even if the filing takes place immediately following the purchase. Thus, one gets a new start living the high life without having to pay off any debt.

In this book, we will consider examples of avoidance, evasion, and avoision within Jewish law. Known for its subtle legal distinctions, the legal system developed by rabbinic Jews in Palestine and Babylonia from the second to seventh centuries contains many examples of such circumventions.

But the phenomenon of loopholing is certainly not a rabbinic invention. It is so ancient that it is used as a literary plot device in the ancient Near Eastern Epic of Gilgamesh: the gods are sworn to secrecy about the impending flood; they take an oath not to reveal the coming doom to any mortal, lest he or she escape. The god Ea circumvents his oath; rather than reveal the information directly to the mortal Utnapishtim, Ea shares what is coming, as well as a plan of action, with the walls of Utnapishtim's house in his presence:

> Far-sighted Ea swore the oath (of secrecy) with them,
> So, he repeated their speech to a reed hut,

> "Reed hut, reed hut, brick wall, brick wall,
> Listen, reed hut, and pay attention, brick wall:
> (This is the message:)
> Man of Shuruppak, son of Ubara-Tutu,
> Dismantle your house, build a boat.
> Leave possessions, search out living things.
> Reject chattels and save lives!
> Put aboard the seed of all living things, into the boat . . ."
> I realized and spoke to my master Ea,
> "I have paid attention to the words that you have spoken in
>   this way,
> My master, and I shall act upon them . . ."[1]

By circumventing his oath, Ea foils the gods' plans to wipe out humanity.

Loopholing is so pervasive throughout history that it finds its way into the later Western literary canon as well. In the climactic court scene in Shakespeare's *Merchant of Venice*, a vengeful Shylock plans to remove a pound of Antonio's flesh as interest on a defaulted loan, per their contract. But Portia enters, disguised as a lawyer, and offers a quite literal reading of the contract:

> Tarry a little; there is something else.
> This bond doth give thee here no jot of blood;
> The words expressly are "a pound of flesh":
> Take then thy bond, take thou thy pound of flesh;
> But, in the cutting it, if thou dost shed
> One drop of Christian blood, thy lands and goods
> Are, by the laws of Venice, confiscate
> Unto the state of Venice. (Act IV, Scene i)

Portia argues that the agreement for a pound of flesh as interest excludes any taking of blood. Surely Shylock had intended to include blood in the agreement. Yet, a very literal interpretation of the contract precludes it. Her reading saves Antonio's life, marking the beginning of Shylock's steep and sweeping decline.

My own early experience with loopholes, and specifically what felt like avoision, came annually in the springtime during my childhood. Although often falling in tax season, it was not related to taxes but to Passover. Because owning leavened foods (*ḥametz*)—bread, cookies and the like—on Passover is forbidden, we would search the house for *ḥametz* before Passover. The goal was to find the *ḥametz* and get rid of it. "Come downstairs to search for *ḥametz*," we were invited on the night before Passover. My father held a candle, as we playfully hinted where he could find the pre-placed pieces of bread throughout the house. As he found each piece, we would scoop it into a brown paper bag. The next morning, he would burn the bag of *ḥametz* in a safe and contained fire in our synagogue parking lot. And with that, our *ḥametz* was gone, and we were ready for Passover.

Well, sort of.

"But what about the boxes of *ḥametz* cereal and snacks we left in the cabinets?" I would ask. My parents' response: "Those have been sold for the duration of Passover to someone who is not Jewish so that we will not own *ḥametz* during Passover." "Will we get them back?" I would ask, concerned for my favorite foods. I was assured that we would, as the rabbi who sold the *ḥametz* on our behalf to a local gentile would buy it back immediately after Passover.

We sold most of our *ḥametz* to a gentile as a way of "getting rid of it," but we knew we would get it back after Passover because we would "repurchase" it. And, in the meantime, we participated in the rituals of searching for and burning our *ḥametz*, the ten pieces of bread that we had placed around the house specifically for the search.

I was confused: If we are meant to rid ourselves of *ḥametz*, why did we not *really* do that by fully giving it away rather than knowing we would buy it back? This felt like avoision, a term I would not know for many years: how legitimate is a sale that implicitly anticipates its countersale? As I got older and began to analyze my Jewish life, I became more confused not just about avoision but about all legal workarounds. Though the sale of *ḥametz* is perhaps the most famous Jewish legal circumvention, *halakhic* (legally observant) Jewish life is full of such elusions: loans between Jews are meant to be remitted by the sabbatical year (that is, every seven years), but there is a legal way around that (called *prosbul*); Jews may not take interest on loans made to other Jews, but the loan may be transformed into a business partnership, which allows the same money to be exchanged (called *heter 'iska*); one may not carry items outside on the Sabbath, but use of a string, poles, and a box of food (known as *'eruv*) can render that space a shared private domain where carrying is allowed; the list goes on.

Whether in secular or religious contexts, loopholes can serve to make the law viable as time passes and/or when challenging situations arise. But just because the law contains the tools for its own undoing does not mean that loopholes make sense as a strategy for those who respect law. After all, if a legal system is authoritative, why cheapen it through circumvention? Even the word "loophole" is understood as derisive: loopholing mocks the very law whose letter it claims to uphold. And if a law leads to a bad outcome, why hide that fact by using a clever dodge? Why not just call out the problematics in the law and change it outright? Why not opt for repeal and replace? Thus, loopholes either mock law or mock ethics. Or, at least, that is what people often think about them.

When it comes to religious law, these questions take on the added urgency of religious integrity. For the more conservative, loopholes are an affront because they attempt to fool an omniscient God and to undermine the ultimate Commander. If God knows about the ruse, why perform it? And furthermore, how can one dare circumvent God's law? For more liberal religious interpreters, loopholes do not go far enough: religion should lead to good outcomes. How can religion represent good values if it is stuck betwixt and between? Better to replace the law or change it explicitly than to simply maneuver around it.

With these questions in mind, we will explore Jewish claims—and specifically late antique rabbinic claims—about the function and significance of legal loopholes in religious law. How did these ancient scholars think about the categories of avoidance, evasion, and avoision? When, how, and why did they justify the use of loopholes? And what do their justifications reflect about how they understood their own religious legal system?

Rabbinic Mechanisms for Legal Change

In rabbinic literature from late antiquity, Jewish law evolves through various means. Sometimes the law changes through an explicit repeal and replace model, indicated by the rabbinic terminology of *ba-rishonah* (lit. "at first"); or through the creation of a new law where none existed before, as captured by the terminology of *takkanah* (regulation) and *gezerah* (restrictive law).[2] But there are also mechanisms for changing law that are more subtle, which do not declare themselves to be making change. For instance, sometimes the rabbis employ scriptural interpretation (exegesis) to limit or to expand the scope of an existing law.[3] Legal loopholes, which can also involve scriptural interpretation, are part of that same family of legal change. They involve taking advantage of an ambiguity, omission, or exception that provides a way to avoid a rule without violating its literal requirements.[4] Like exegesis, they purport to uphold the law, and do so in its letter, while defeating what seems to be the statute's obvious intent.[5]

In addition to exegesis and loopholes, there is another method for altering law: employing legal fiction. Legal fictions are assertions about reality that are partially or fully known to be false, such as claiming that a litigant is a Roman citizen when he is not.[6] Using legal fictions, one can extend the application of a law to a new situation without having to legislate a new rule.[7] Sometimes legal fictions are used to make new situations "thinkable" by analogizing them to familiar legal paradigms, for example, a corporation is a person, and so on.[8] One clear example of the rabbis using legal fiction to achieve a desired legal outcome is as follows: two witnesses testify that a husband who has been away is dead, and his widow remarries based on their testimony. According to Rav, if the first husband returns, the court should refuse to recognize him: "we say: It is not him." This is clearly false, and everyone knows it. And yet, Rav does not want to ruin the woman's life: any children from her new marriage would be considered legally illegitimate (and unable to marry anyone of credible Jewish pedigree), and she would be unable to remain married or to return to her previous marriage because of her "adultery."[9] So Rav suggests that the court use a legal fiction and declare that this man is not the original husband.

As a relevant aside, scholars disagree about the extent to which legal fictions are used within rabbinic literature for functionalist goals. Leib Moscovitz argues that functionalist fiction is the exception in rabbinic literature, proving the rule that rabbinic legal fictions are generally not used to achieve desired legal outcomes. Instead, rabbinic fictions are generally used in legislation (rather than adjudication) to extend or explain a base law.[10] For instance, while the shewbread in the Temple was meant to be arranged in two rows of six loaves, if one set out two rows of fourteen loaves, "Rabbi says: We consider the upper [loaves] as if they do not exist, and the lower ones are acceptable."[11] Considering the upper loaves as nonexistent is technically a legal fiction, but without any obvious functionalist legal change in mind. Instead, it merely extends the possibilities of the base law. Others claim that functionalism motivates many rabbinic fictions by defining the use of fiction more expansively. They define legal fiction as instances where law may override empirical fact. For example, when R. Gamliel accepts witnesses who testify to seeing the "old" moon (signifying the continuation of the previous lunar month) in the east in the morning and the "new" moon (signifying the start of the new lunar month) in the west in the evening (*mRH* 2:8), he is resorting to legal fiction, as such a phenomenon is physically impossible.[12] Or when R. Elazar tries to ameliorate the problem of the offspring of an illegitimate child (in Hebrew *mamzer* for males and *mamzeret* for females) being barred from marrying a pedigreed Jew, some argue that he does so through a fiction, stating: "Let someone bring me the third generation and I shall purify it." The Talmud goes on to explain, "It is because the *mamzer* does not live a long life."[13] Do the rabbis truly believe that a *mamzer/et* never lives to the age of having children of their own? Probably not. Instead, they utilize a fictional assertion to resolve a social and moral problem.[14]

The relationship between legal fictions and legal loopholes is layered. Both legal fictions and legal loopholes can be classified as legal circumventions, from the Latin *circumvenīre*, meaning, "to come around, surround, oppress or defraud." They represent an attempt to get "around" the law rather than changing it outright. Both reflect formalistic legal thinking in which rules and the way they are expressed carry great significance.[15] But some have argued that their main difference lies in what they seek to change: legal fictions change the *law* by stipulating that the court treat situation B like situation A while legal loopholes merely change the *facts* of a scenario.[16] However, making this stark distinction ignores the rhetoric of legal fictions. Legal fictions also focus on facts: the methodology asserts that the facts are A - whether or not they are - which allows for a certain legal outcome or rule to apply. Thus, both legal fictions and legal loopholes focus (even if only rhetorically) on changed facts rather than on changed rules.[17] Legal fictions assert facts (though untrue) that cause a desired legal outcome, and legal loopholes rely upon either actively changing the facts of a scenario or pointing out factual differences between one scenario and another to avoid the application of a law. Both are functions of a legal system in which it is easier or more desirable to change the facts of a case than to change the law.

Nonetheless, it remains true, as stated above, that even within this shared focus on changing facts, these two circumventive methods diverge in a significant way. Legal fictions assert new facts but do not in actuality change any facts "on the ground," that is, outside the courtroom. Legal loopholes, however, rely upon and/or create new facts "on the ground," concrete changes in perceptible reality, to circumvent a law. For instance, while in the aforementioned case of legal fiction, the court simply asserts that the "widow's" husband is not the man in the courtroom, in the introductory Passover example, my family did not rely on assertions. We did not simply claim that our ḥametz was sold; we actually sold it. There was a formal procedure by which we appointed our rabbi as an emissary, and there was another formal procedure by which he sold our ḥametz to someone who was not Jewish. And then there was a third formal procedure by which he repurchased that ḥametz after Passover. We changed the facts on the ground so that the transgression of owning ḥametz would no longer apply.

Taking both their convergence and divergence into account, legal loopholes and legal fictions appear to exist on a methodological continuum. In fact, one might challenge whether there is truly a qualitative difference between the assertion of facts and the creation of facts where everyone knows that the latter technical "change" in the facts is both provisional and symbolic, done only for the purpose of circumventing the law. True, the sale of our ḥametz was technically a sale. But socially speaking, did anything *really* change? The food remained in our home, and everyone knew that the new owner of the food was unlikely to stop by for a bite. And, as I was reassured, that new owner would definitely sell the food back after Passover. Nonetheless, I distinguish between loopholes and fictions within this book because rabbinic literature appears to distinguish between them: the technical difference between them results in a legal difference. Additionally, some rabbinic negotiation about loopholes (especially in the Babylonian Talmud) relates to differentiating loopholes from fictions.

The Focus of This Study

Legal circumventions are a hallmark of rabbinic jurisprudence. This book focuses on a category of circumventions within rabbinic law that appears similar to fictions and loopholes: *ha'aramah*. The word itself means cunning or subtlety, and its use in rabbinic legal discourse roughly conforms to the classic legal dodge.[18] This study has two goals: to examine the evolution of rabbinic attitudes toward *ha'aramah* and to compare these attitudes phenomenologically and historically to other jurisprudential cultures, past and present. This study yields insight into how rabbinic and other legal cultures thought/think about the relationship between rules, facts, and values, and how rabbinic approaches changed over time and place in response to, among other issues, interiority, intention, and an evolving understanding of the self.

Chapter 1 contains an analysis of *ha'aramah* in *tannaitic* literature, reflected in examples of avoidance, evasion, and avoision. I argue that the goals of a given *ha'aramah* determine whether it is rabbinically accepted. Chapter 2 reviews *ha'aramah* discourse within the Palestinian Talmud. This discourse makes explicit that both noble goals and procedural integrity determine whether *ha'aramah* may be used. Chapter 3 compares early rabbinic discourse to Roman discourse about circumventions, especially loopholes that use *ha'aramah*'s methods. Comparing them reveals significant differences regarding the relationship between the letter and the spirit of the law. It also suggests a difference in how Roman jurists and rabbis position themselves within the legal infrastructure. Chapter 4 studies so-called "fiction-like" *ha'aramah* in Palestinian corpora. I theorize that this type of *ha'aramah* is not actually fictional but instead reflects rabbinic ideas about the nature of the self and of intention. Chapter 5 then traces Babylonian discomfort with this type of *ha'aramah* in the context of developments in rabbinic thought regarding human subjectivity. This chapter also considers how a growing sense of subjectivity indeed turns *ha'aramah* more fiction-like, entailing gaps between law and reality, making *ha'aramah* seem more radical and potentially corrosive of legal observance. The chapter also considers the Persian context of such developments. And finally, Chapter 6 considers modern legal paradigms for thinking about *ha'aramah*. Here, I examine thought related to legal circumvention per se as well as more general issues such as legal interpretation and the roles that ambiguity and flexibility play in both maintaining and straining relationships.

The Limits of This Study

The term *ha'aramah* does not exhaust every legal circumvention found in rabbinic law. In fact, there are many examples of legal circumvention using other terms or no specific terminology at all.[19] Moreover, *ha'aramah* is most often used to describe loopholes that are lay performed to resolve ad hoc issues rather than addressing ongoing public policy concerns. Perhaps for this reason, the term *takkanah* (decree) is seldom used in the case of *ha'aramah*, again emphasizing its mostly private and piecemeal nature. In fact, rabbinic *takkanot* that circumvent laws—for example, *prosbul*, *'eruv*, and so forth—are not referred to as *ha'aramah* in early rabbinic literature. Nonetheless, examining the evolution of the term *ha'aramah*, used throughout early rabbinic literature for many circumventions, lays the groundwork for further exploration. Understanding explicit rabbinic choices regarding *ha'aramah* suggests patterns that may apply to other circumventions where the term is not used.[20] Consequently, this study will occasionally reference and/or describe some non-*ha'aramah* circumventions—whether formal *takkanot* or otherwise.[21] Furthermore, outlining *ha'aramah* patterns yields a model for comparative jurisprudence with other legal systems, both religious and secular.

A Note About Translation and Transliteration

Because *ha'aramah* can be considered avoidance, evasion, or avoision, I translate the term differently throughout the book. I translate it as prudence, circumvention, or strategy when it is affirmed as proper avoidance, as cunning or subterfuge when it is rejected as improper evasion. Where relevant to the sense of the text, I simply transliterate the word *ha'aramah* to maintain ambiguity.

As this book is meant for both academics and non-academics, I employ a modified version of the "general-purpose style" guidelines provided by the *Journal of Jewish Studies*, bringing the transliterations close to those used in Jewish communities today.[22] My intention is to promote interaction between the cultural milieu of lived Jewish practice and the academic study thereof. For the same reason, I do not anglicize Hebrew or Aramaic names of rabbis, not do I use diacritical marks in their transliteration.

Chapter 1

(When) Do Circumventions Disrespect the Law?

This chapter introduces two claims about the earliest rabbinic discussions of *ha'aramah*. First, that the rabbis have their own versions of avoidance, evasion, and avoision. They reject some uses of *ha'aramah* out of hand, endorse others, and argue about others. Second, that rabbinic parameters for *ha'aramah* reflect rabbinic values rather than mere formalism: in early *tannaitic* literature, rabbis endorse *ha'aramah* mainly when it upholds a principle or value of the Jewish legal system more generally. In the pages that follow, we will analyze several *tannaitic* examples of *ha'aramah* in both *Mishnah* and *Tosefta* to substantiate these claims.

The Term *Ha'aramah*: Both Cunning and Prudence

The multilayered approach to *ha'aramah* reflected in the *tannaitic* material inheres in the very word *ha'aramah* when traced back to its biblical roots. On the one hand, the root *'.r.m.* appears in Genesis 3:1, regarding the cunning serpent; in Exodus 21:14, regarding premeditated murder; in Joshua 9:4, about the deceptive Gibeonites; and in Job 5:13, regarding those who cause their own downfall through craftiness.[1] Alternatively, the term *'ormah* maintains a consistently affirmative character throughout the Book of Proverbs.[2] As Robert Alter explains, "Such usage fits with the pragmatic curriculum of Proverbs.[3] Intelligence of the most practical sort, involving an alertness to potential deceptions and seductions, is seen as an indispensable tool for the safe, satisfying, and ethical life, and a fool is repeatedly thought of as a dupe (*peti*)."[4] In fact, the Book of Proverbs (1:4) opens by promising that its teachings will afford that dupe prudence (*'ormah*).[5]

That theme recurs (8:5, 19:25). It is only the *'arum* (prudent one), and not the *peti* (dupe), who can truly recognize sin (22:3, 27:12). Moreover, "Lady Wisdom attests to the respectability of *'ormah* by declaring her own proximity to it" (8:12).[6] She lavishes praise upon the *'arum*: he can scheme to achieve his goals (14:8, 15); he is able to ignore insults (12:16); he looks where he is going (14:15); he sees and consequently avoids danger (22:3, 27:12). He acts with knowledge (13:16, 14:18) but does not show it off (12:23).[7]

While Alter defines *'ormah* as an ability to *detect* craftiness, Michael V. Fox asserts that *'ormah means* craftiness, as it does throughout the Bible: "the ability to devise clever, even wily tactics for attaining one's goals, whatever these may be."[8] Fox observes what "an audacious move" it was for Proverbs to appropriate cunning as a virtue (1:4, 2:11, 5:2).[9] In his words: "The Prologue wants the reader to know that the book of Proverbs (rather than, say, the wise guys down the street) is the place to turn if you want the prestigious skills of cunning and shrewdness. As Proverbs sees it, the promised skills must be applied to worthy ends."[10]

The term *ha'aramah* (pl. *ha'aramot* הערמות, active forms: מערימים, מערימין, יערים, תערים, הערים, etc.) in rabbinic literature refers to both *solomonic* and *serpentine* circumventions.

Which Values Matter?

The fact that *ha'aramah* can be serpentine or solomonic introduces the question of how to determine which it is in a given case. In the *tannaitic* scenarios outlined in this chapter, the recurring themes are financial hardship and ritual purity law. The rabbis endorse the use of *ha'aramah* where it can prevent financial loss that might result from following a particular law. The texts do, however, differentiate between preventing financial loss and exploiting someone for profit: in the latter case, *ha'aramah* is rejected as (serpentine) evasion. Contra cases of financial hardship, the rabbis consistently reject the use of *ha'aramah* to avoid the implications of ritual impurity. There is something objectionable about avoiding ritual impurity through *ha'aramah*, which I will explore below. These two poles in *tannaitic* corpora—supporting *ha'aramah* to prevent financial loss while forbidding it to evade ritual impurity—already begin to tell a story about early rabbinic priorities.

Ha'aramah in the *Mishnah*: Endorsement (with Reservation)

There are three uses of the root *'.r.m.* in all of *Mishnah*: two of them endorse (or at least allow) the use of *ha'aramah* to reduce the financial costs of following the law. The third refers to the "cunning scoundrel" without explaining what that person has done to earn the epithet. I will examine these instances below.

Relieving Financial Burden: The Case of Redeeming Tithes

According to biblical law, when a farmer reaps the harvest, some produce must be set aside as tithes. And in the first, second, fourth, and fifth year of every seven-year sabbatical cycle, one of these tithes is known as *ma'aser sheni*, "secondary tithes." *Ma'aser sheni* must be eaten in Jerusalem. If the produce is too burdensome to transport to Jerusalem, one may redeem it with money and spend the redemption money in Jerusalem instead. But monetary redemption has its drawbacks. According to biblical injunction, one who redeems *ma'aser sheni* must pay 125 percent of its value.[11] However, the rabbis affirm the use of *ha'aramah* to avoid paying the extra 25 percent for redeeming one's *ma'aser sheni*:

Mishnah Ma'aser Sheni 4:4 (MS Kaufmann)

מערימים על מעשר שני[12] כיצד או' אדם לבנו ולבתו הגדולים לעבדו ולשפחתו
העברים הילך את המעות האילו ופדה לך[13] את המעשר הזה אבל לא יאמר כן
לבנו ולבתו הקטנים לעבדו ולשפחתו הכנענים מפני שידו כידו

[We/they may/do/should] act prudently regarding the secondary tithe.[14] How so? One says to his adult son or daughter or to his Hebrew manservant or maid,[15] "Take these coins and use them to redeem this tithe." However, one may not say this to one's minor son or daughter, or to one's Canaanite manservant or maid, for their hand is like his.[16]

The *mishnah* suggests that the produce owner may enlist the help of an economically independent adult to avoid the extra 25 percent redemption tax. While the Bible stipulates a tax for redeeming one's own produce, it does not demand a tax for redeeming someone else's produce. Moreover, the Bible is silent about the prospect of giving someone else money and asking them to redeem the produce in order to avoid the tax. So long as the person who owns the redemption money does not own the produce (and is not explicitly declared the emissary of the person who does), there is no 25 percent tax.[17] Thus, this *ha'aramah* employs a "straw person" to change the facts of the case rather than changing existing rules or legislating new ones.[18]

The following *mishnah* offers a slight variation on this circumvention:

Mishnah Ma'aser Sheni 4:5 (MS Kaufmann)

היה עומד בגורן ואין בידו מעות אומר לחבירו הרי הפירות האילו נתונים לך מתנה
וחוזר ואומר הרי הן מחוללין על המעות שבבית

If he was standing on the threshing floor and had no coins with him, he says to his fellow: behold this produce is yours as a gift, and then he says, the produce is desacralized upon the coins that I have at home.

In this second version, when money is not available for transfer to an outsider to redeem the *ma'aser sheni*, one may transfer the produce to another party. Then the original owner of the produce can redeem that produce with his own money even if he is not carrying the money with him. This accomplishes the same goal of changing the facts of the case—ensuring that the redemption money and the produce are not owned by the same person at the time of the redemption—so that the 25 percent tax can be avoided.

This second strategy appears in the *Tosefta* in a slightly different way.[19] Rather than transferring ownership of produce instead of money because one is not carrying money, the transfer of produce is described as a way of ensuring that the "straw person" will not walk off with the money. Apparently, having "straw people" abscond with the money had become a problem for those trying to use this tactic:[20]

Tosefta Ma'aser Sheni 4:3 (MS Erfurt)

אמ' ר' יהושע בן קרחה בראשונה היו נוהגין כך משרבו הרמאין אומ' אדם לחבירו הרי פירות האילו נתונין לך במתנה וחוזר ואומר לו הרי הן מחוללין על פירות שיש לי בבית ובלבד שלא יאמר הרי הן מחוללין על מעות שיש לי בכיס עד שיזכם לתוך ידו או עד שישכיר לו את מקומו

> R. Yehoshua son of Korhah said: At first, they behaved thus. Once the defrauders increased, one would say to his fellow, "Behold, this produce is given to you as a gift," and then he would say to him, "Behold they are desacralized by produce which I have in the house," so long he does not say, behold they are desacralized by the coins that I have in my pocket until he places them (the produce) in his hand, or until he rents the land where the produce is to him.

When defrauders began to run off with the money that they should have used to redeem the *ma'aser sheni*, field owners made the circumvention more foolproof: rather than handing over money, which is easily stolen, field owners gave their produce to the other party as a gift. Then, field owners could redeem the produce with their own possessions. Transferring produce rather than money was likely more effective because the produce was useless to the second party: legally, the produce could not be eaten outside of Jerusalem, and it had to be eaten in a state of ritual purity.[21] Additionally, according to some, the owner handed over not only the *ma'aser sheni* produce, but the larger bundle of produce that it was part of, which has not yet been tithed.[22] Consequently, the straw person was not permitted to eat any of the produce before separating tithes. This might serve as motivation for following through on the transaction. And lastly, as produce is more cumbersome than money, it would be more difficult to run off with it after it was redeemed.

Within this version of the dodge, though, the original owner of the produce had to ensure that the transfer of produce met the proper legal standards. If the field owner had the redemption money in his pocket, he would have to do more to show that the money and the produce belonged to different people. He would physically place the produce in the second party's hands or rent the piece of land that the produce was on to the second party. Doing so would trigger a full acquisition of the produce by the second party, so there would be no illusions that the produce still belonged to the field owner.[23]

The rabbinic endorsement of *ha'aramah* comes through clearly in the language of this passage, as it pits the "defrauders" portrayed as bad actors *against* those using the circumvention. The terms for defrauders—רמאין (*rama'in*)—and for those who act prudently—מערימין (*ma'arimin*)—are phonetically similar yet conceptually contrasted.[24] The rabbis side with those who act prudently rather than with those defrauders who try to undermine the circumvention by stealing.

The *Yerushalmi* (Jerusalem Talmud) further defends this circumvention in two ways: first, by asserting that the *ha'aramah* was reinvented not once but twice (!), and second, by asserting that the reinvention was instituted *by the rabbis* themselves:

Yerushalmi Ma'aser Sheni 4:3, 55a (based on MS Leiden)

בראשונה היו עושין כן במעות היו נוטלין אותן ובורחין התקינו שיהו עושין בפירות
א'ע'פ'כ' היו נטלין אותן ואוכלין אותן התקינו שיהא מזכה לו אחד מעשרה
לקרקע ר' איניייא בר סיסי סלק גבי ר' יונה אמ' ליה אפרוק לך בהדא סילעא אמ'
אי בעא מינס נסא חזר ונסתה מיניה אמ' ר' יונה כד שערית דעתיה דאילו נסתה
לא הוה אמ' לי כלום לפום כן יהבת יתה לה

Originally, they would do this with coins. But they (= the other party) would take [the coins] and run away [instead of redeeming].[25] They *instituted* that they would do this with produce (= give the other party the *ma'aser sheni* produce), yet they would take the produce [following the redemption] and eat them [rather than returning them]. So, they instituted that he would give him ownership over one-tenth of the land [where the produce was located]. R. Inya b. Sisi went to R. Yonah. He (R. Inya) said to him (R. Yonah): Would you like me to redeem [your *ma'aser sheni*] for you with this coin? He answered: If you'd like, take it. [Afterward, R. Yonah] went back and took it from him. R. Yonah said: Because I understood R. Inya's attitude to be that he would not say anything if I took it (the money) back, therefore I gave it to him [in the first place].

This version adds further stages to the evolution of this *ha'aramah*. Originally, the field owner would transfer money to an *interposita persona*, another party. But bad actors would run off with the money. Then, a new method was devised: the field owner would give his cumbersome produce to the *interposita persona* so that the latter could not run away with it. But then these bad actors would simply eat the produce, likely after it was redeemed (but possible even before the redemption). A third method developed (presented in the *tosefta* as coextensive with the giving of the produce but here presented as a separate step): field owners would give rights to the *interposita persona* over the land where the produce was located instead of handing over any produce at all. Presumably, this land was out of sight from where the two people stood, so the field owner could redeem the produce before the second party could run off with it.

All versions of this *Yerushalmi* passage, both MS and printed editions, include the verb *hitkinu*, "they instituted": it seems rabbinic authorities themselves went to great lengths to preserve this *ha'aramah*. This is, in fact, one of the very few examples, if not the only example, in which an aspect of *ha'aramah* is described explicitly as a *takkanah*. Moreover, the passage describes two rabbis—R. Yonah and R. Inya—employing this *ha'aramah*. R. Yonah explains why he was willing to use the original method of giving money for the dodge: because he knew that R. Inya would not steal his money. R. Yonah likewise indicates that he made a full gift of the money to R. Inya, telling him that he could take it for himself, perhaps to explain what is necessary to effectuate this *ha'aramah*. On the one hand, the rabbis do not want defrauders to steal the money; on the other hand, the money must be fully transferred to the second party to effectively avoid the redemption tax.[26]

This becomes the classic case of *ha'aramah* as legitimate avoidance: the rabbis endorse it and even protect it over the course of generations. Clearly, the rabbis approve of circumventing the law to prevent financial loss in this instance. But adding historical context may explain why this particular financial loss was important to them. The *mishnaic* and *toseftan* corpora are both early third-century compilations, and they describe life when the second Temple stood as well as after it was destroyed in 70 CE.[27] Consequently, it can be difficult to tell when these corpora refer to life during Temple times and when they refer to life after Temple times. It is possible that this *ha'aramah* used to avoid the 25 percent redemption tax either developed or became more consistently accepted after the fall of the Temple. According to the majority of rabbinic opinions, people were no longer supposed to bring their secondary tithes to Jerusalem after the Temple was destroyed:[28] the produce was still sacred, but in recognition of the fall of the Temple, the practice of bringing the secondary tithes to Jerusalem and eating the produce there ended. However, the produce itself could not be eaten outside of Jerusalem either. This created a problem: if people could not eat their *ma'aser sheni* in Jerusalem (because they were no longer supposed to), and they could not eat it outside Jerusalem (because it is biblically forbidden), the produce would be left to rot. The alternative was to redeem the produce with money, but this could cause financial burden, especially with the excess 25 percent redemption tax.

Enter *ha'aramah* to at least relieve the 25 percent tax. While people would still have to redeem the produce at its value to save it, at least they would not have to pay the extra 25 percent.[29] To ease their burden, the rabbis endorsed a way to redeem the produce without the added expense.[30]

Relieving Financial Burden: The Case of Offering Firstborn Animals

The only other *ha'aramah*-as-circumvention in all of *Mishnah* relates to the sanctity of a firstborn kosher animal, *bekhor behemah tehorah*.[31] Per biblical law, one must give one's firstborn kosher male animals to a *kohen* (priest). If the animal is unblemished, the priest sacrifices it and eats parts of the offering.[32] Rabbinic sources state that if the firstborn animal is permanently blemished, the priest may eat it as non-sacred food (*ḥullin*) without offering any of it upon the altar: the permanent blemish makes the animal unfit for sacrifice.[33] In the following passage, the animal's owner would rather use the firstborn for his own private offering than as a gift to the priest. Consequently, the *mishnah* acknowledges (or affirms) the practice of preempting the firstborn status by designating the animal as a private sacrifice while it is still in utero.[34] This nominal reclassification of the animal is considered binding:[35]

Mishnah Temurah 5:1 (MS Kaufmann)

כיצד מערימין על הבכור מבכרת שהיתה מעוברת אומ' מה שבמעיה שלזו אם
זכר עולה ילדה זכר יקרב עולה אם נקבה זבחי שלמים ילדה נקבה תקרב שלמים
אם זכר עולה אם נקבה זבחי שלמים ילדה זכר ונקבה זכר יקרב עולה והנקבה
תקרב שלמים

How do/should we/they act prudently with regard to the firstborn? [When] an animal [is] pregnant with its first offspring, he says, "What is inside this, if it is male, it is a burnt offering." If she birthed a male, it shall be sacrificed as a burnt offering. "And if it is female, it is a peace offering."[36] If she birthed a female, it shall be sacrificed as a peace offering. "If it is a male, a burnt offering, and if a female, a peace offering,"—if she birthed both a male and female, the male shall be sacrificed as a burnt offering, and the female shall be sacrificed as a peace offering.

Traditional commentators suggest the following context: the owner has already committed to offering an animal sacrifice, and around the same time, one of his animals is due to birth a *bekhor*.[37] Rather than losing two animals—one as the promised sacrifice and another as a *bekhor* to the priest—he tries to save money by turning the would-be *bekhor* into the sacrifice. Ephraim Urbach reads the rabbinic affirmation of this practice as capitulating to a community that is already doing it: "It may be assumed that owners of cows bearing for the first time who felt an obligation to offer a whole offering in the Temple, used the evasion described to fulfill two obligations at once. The Sages accepted this situation because it at least preserved the commandment of the firstling of a clean animal."[38] Urbach's reading suggests that the rabbis accepted the ways that people were already cutting corners to save expenses. By endorsing this *ha'aramah*, the rabbis at least technically preserved the law of the *bekhor* animal. However, rabbinic literature does not indicate whether this circumvention comes from "the people" or from the rabbis. Rather than a capitulation, perhaps the rabbis are being thoughtful about how to save people money.

Additionally, despite the language of sacrifices, it is possible that this *ha'aramah* also reflects the financial difficulties of observant life after the fall of the Temple. Like *ma'aser sheni*, the *bekhor* was still considered sacred after the Temple, but it could not be eaten in its usual manner by the *kohen*.[39] During Temple times, the *kohen* would offer part of the *bekhor* as a sacrifice and eat the rest, but this was no longer an option after the fall of the Temple. In fact, relating to a biblical verse (Deut. 14:23), which cites the need for both *bekhor* and *ma'aser sheni* to be eaten "before God in the place that God will choose," which generally refers to Jerusalem and/or the Temple, R. Yishmael draws a parallel for the fate of both *ma'aser sheni* and *bekhor* after the Temple's destruction:

Tosefta Sanhedrin 3:3 (MS Erfurt)

ר' ישמעאל אומ' יכול יהא אדם מעלה מעשר שיני בירושלם בזמן הזה ואוכלו
ודין הוא הבכור טעון הבאת מקום ומעשר[40] שיני טעון הבאת מקום מה בכור אינו
נאכל אלא בפני הבית אף מעשר שיני אינו נאכל אלא בפני הבית ... תלמ' לומ'
ואכלת לפני י-י א-להיך מע' דג' ותיר' ויצ' ובכורות מה בכור אין נאכל אלא בפני
הבית אף מעשר שיני אין נאכל אלא בפני הבית

> R. Yishmael says: Perhaps a person should bring secondary tithe produce to[41] Jerusalem these days and eat it [there]? But[42] it stands to reason: the firstborn animal requires being brought to the place (= the Temple), and *ma'aser sheni* requires being brought to the place (= Jerusalem). [Therefore] just as the firstborn animal is not eaten except when the Temple stands, so *ma'aser sheni* is not eaten[43] except when the Temple stands... This is what is meant by the verse: "And you shall eat before the Lord your God [in the place that God shall choose for God's Name to dwell there] the tithes of your grain, your wine, your oil and your firstborn [animals] (Deut. 14:23)": just as the *bekhor* is not eaten except when the Temple stands, so the *ma'aser sheni* is not eaten[44] except when the Temple stands.[45]

After the fall of the Temple, just as people no longer ate their *ma'aser sheni* (secondary tithes) in Jerusalem, the priests no longer sacrificed and ate the *bekhor*, as they had when the Temple stood. Instead, the animal would be given to the *kohen* and left to graze. It could not be used for labor nor shorn for its wool. It was essentially useless unless it became permanently blemished, in which case the *kohen* could eat it without sacrifice.[46] Thus, a *bekhor* in the post-Temple period would likely never even be eaten by a *kohen* or by anyone else. The law of the firstborn had lost the practical value that it once had of supporting the priestly class and had turned instead into an animal sitting service. It is no wonder that, within the *mishnaic* tractate about firstborn animals (*mBekhorot*), the rabbis discuss the prominent role of experts in determining whether a firstborn was blemished in the "right" way to render it edible, as well as some of the (failed) attempts at dealing with rampant waste of animals.[47] Being able to render the *bekhor* edible was likely a great relief and thus a weighty responsibility.

The Talmud later offers a loophole for dealing with this problem: blemishing the animal in utero before it ever gains the legal status of a firstborn.[48] Additionally, in the Middle Ages, R. Jacob ben Asher suggests another avoidance tactic: he states that it is a *"mitzvah"* to evade firstborn status by selling partial ownership of the mother to a non-Jew so that the laws of the firstborn will not apply to her offspring.[49] The aforementioned *mishnah*, however, may be the earliest step in the process of conceiving of what to do with the firstborn animal: have the animal's owner commit the animal as a sacrifice while in utero to keep the animal rather than give it away. Still, the owner would be unable to eat it because it is considered sacred as a promised sacrifice. However, if the animal becomes blemished, the owner himself can redeem it with money (like *ma'aser sheni*) and use or eat the animal. This might give the animal's owner a chance to use it.[50]

This affirmed *ha'aramah* differs from the practice of having a non-Jew or a child purposely blemish a firstborn animal so that it could be eaten. *MBekhorot* 5:3, for instance, describes a Roman quaestor (public official) who finds old and unshorn firstborn animals belonging to Jews and actively blemishes them so that they can be eaten. When the official first does this on his own, the rabbis permit consumption of the *bekhor*; when he starts doing this to the many *bekhorot* he finds, the rabbis forbid all from eating them. The same occurs with children who are innocently playing with animals, causing a blemish to a *bekhor*: the first time it happens accidentally, the rabbis permit the blemished animal to be eaten, but when they see that having a child play rough with animals to "accidentally" blemish them becomes the new trend, they forbid all from eating such blemished animals. The rabbis do not approve of even tacit encouragement by Jews of non-Jews or Jewish minors to blemish a living *bekhor*.

On the other hand, declaring an animal to be a sacrifice in utero is permitted. But whether the affirmation of such *ha'aramah* takes place in the context of post-Temple life or while the Temple stood, the rabbis clearly recognize the financial toll that observance can take. And they respond by allowing or perhaps even actively endorsing *ha'aramah*.

Condemning "Cunning Rogue"

Alongside the two affirmative cases of *ha'aramah*, the corpus of *Mishnah* also contains a clear condemnation of cunning, though without explicating what is meant by it. *Mishnah Sotah* 3:4 (MS Kaufmann) asserts that the *rasha 'arum*, the cunning rogue, erodes the world:

ר' אליעזר אומר המלמד את בתו תורה מלמדה תיפלות ר' יהושע אומר רוצה
אשה בקב תיפלות מתשעת קבים ופרישות הוא היה אומר חסיד שוטה רשע ערום
אשה פרושה מכת פרושים הרי אלו מכלי העולם

R. Eliezer says: Anyone who teaches his daughter Torah teaches her frivolity.
R. Yehoshua says: A woman prefers one *kab* (= approx. 2.17 liters) of/and frivolity to 9 *kab* and abstinence. He would say: A foolish pietist, a cunning rogue, an abstinent woman,[51] and the wound of celibate men,[52] these bring destruction upon the world.[53]

This passage does not explain what makes someone a cunning rogue; perhaps not everyone who is cunning is wicked. However, the Talmuds offer their own glosses. According to a number of opinions in *bSotah* 21b, a *rasha 'arum* is one who suggests doing legal but ethically suspect activities. One such example is giving a pauper just enough money to make her ineligible to take charity from the collection plate. Rather than helping the poor, the *rasha 'arum* uses a technicality of the law—that one may only receive charity from the public collection plate if one has less than a certain amount of money—in order to undermine the goal of charity! This bears resemblance to evasion, doing what the law disapproves of by manipulating the law itself.[54] According to *ySotah* 3:4, 19a, the *rasha 'arum* is one who rules leniently for oneself but strictly for others. While this is less like loopholing, it still suggests an opportunistic way of applying law. Regardless of these later talmudic glosses, the *mishnah* itself does not appear to speak about *ha'aramah* as a legal mechanism. After all, the affirmative cases of *ha'aramah* in the *Mishnah* are introduced with a heading about performing *ha'aramah* followed by a description of how it is done.[55] Nothing similar appears in this *mishnah* about the *rasha 'arum*. Nonetheless, the fact that the corpus of *Mishnah* contains the use of root '.r.m. affirmatively and negatively speaks to the duality that the word itself offers.

Ha'aramah in Roman Context

The rabbinic approach to *ha'aramah* differs from the orientation of Roman jurists in the same period. This approach is preserved most poignantly in Justinian's *Digest*, a sixth-century collection and summary of the writings of classical

Roman jurists. The second-century jurist Paul is credited with introducing terminology for technical legal circumventions, only to call such dodges fraudulent. He defined the concept of *in fraudem legis*, a phrase used to challenge strictly formalistic arguments.[56] His definition of *in fraudem legis* is preserved in Justinian's *Digest*: "To do what the law prohibits violates the law, and anyone who evades the meaning of the law without disobeying its words, is guilty of fraud against it."[57] The concept of *in fraudem legis* was meant to empower judges to use their discretion to prevent the abuse that such literalism might afford. In the second century, Roman jurists began using the categorization of *fraus legi* for adjudication rather than relying on legislators to close loopholes.[58] It is certainly noteworthy that, in the same general period that saw the creation of a negative legal term for loopholing, rabbinic texts introduce the terminology of *ha'aramah* to explicitly affirm its use even if the word *'arum* may carry negative connotations as well. And while Paul is cited as the originator of the Roman terminology of *fraus legi*, I will show in Chapter 3 how deeply rooted this concept was in Greco-Roman thought as it developed over the prior centuries.

When *Ha'aramah* is Serpentine: *Tannaitic* Cases of Evasion

While *ha'aramot* (pl.) for *bekhor* and *ma'aser sheni* are supported in the *Mishnah*, other *tannaitic* texts detail *ha'aramah* cases that are rejected as "evasion." We discuss two examples of *ha'aramah* as evasion found in the *Tosefta*. The *Tosefta* contains at least eight examples of explicit *ha'aramah*, considerably more than the *Mishnah*. The *toseftan* discussion of *ha'aramah* differs qualitatively from that of the *Mishnah*: the *Tosefta* cites rejected *ha'aramot*, setting precedent for later rabbinic law; it also presents a type of *ha'aramah* that relies upon changed intention rather than external empirical change (to be examined more fully in Chapter 4); and it applies *ha'aramah* to more periodic situations such as random house fires in addition to systemic situations such as *ma'aser sheni*. The *toseftan* examples of evasion reflect rabbinic awareness of the hazards of *ha'aramah*.

Rejecting Ha'aramah *as Evasion: The Case of Ritual Impurity*

Within the *Tosefta*, rabbis consistently reject using *ha'aramah* to evade the contraction of ritual impurity.[59] Ritual impurity was a central concern when the Temple in Jerusalem stood.⁶⁰ Anyone who wished to enter the Temple precincts or eat any food associated with the Temple had to be in a state of ritual purity. But once the Temple was destroyed, ritual purity (besides corpse impurity, still relevant to those of priestly lineage today) became the concern of a select few—known as the associates (*ḥaverim*). This group chose to eat only ritually pure food, and only in a state of ritual purity themselves.⁶¹ Below is one example among many in which the rabbis forbid the use of *ha'aramah* to stave off impurity. However, like the *ma'aser sheni* and *bekhor* examples, these texts do not reveal whether they discuss Temple times, post-Temple times, or both:

Tosefta Kelim Metzi'a 5:9 (MS Vienna)

... כלי נצרין שלא קינבן ומשתמש בהן עראי טמאין היה עתיד לחסם ולקנב אע'פ שהוא משתמש בהן עראי ומשליכן טהורין ובלבד שלא יערים ואם הערים הרי אילו טמאין

> ... Vessels of twigs which one has not smoothed out and which one uses at random are susceptible to impurity. [If] one planned to make a rim and to smooth it (= the rim),⁶² even though one may [nonetheless] make use of them at random and throw them away, they are unsusceptible to impurity.⁶³ And [this rule applies] solely [on condition that] one not commit subterfuge. But if one did commit subterfuge, these are susceptible to impurity.

This passage defines when a receptacle like a basket officially becomes a vessel. Having the status of a vessel in Jewish law means the object can contract ritual impurity. Determining when this receptacle becomes a vessel is somewhat subjective because it can be made either with a smoothed rim or without one. If one plans to make such a rim, an unrimmed basket is considered incomplete and thus not yet susceptible to ritual impurity. Handling this basket with ritually impure hands or putting anything ritually impure into it does not impact its status. Thus, one might consider using a *ha'aramah* to prevent the basket's susceptibility to impurity by "intending" to add a rim to the basket (whether or not one plans to do so in fact) so that the basket will not contract ritual impurity as long as the rim has not been added. Using *ha'aramah* could be helpful to those concerned about ritual impurity. This text, however, rejects the use of *ha'aramah*, as do a handful of other *toseftan* texts involving ritual impurity.[64]

There are several reasons why the *Tosefta* might prohibit using *ha'aramah* to prevent ritual impurity, and each relates to not wanting to undermine the law. First, there is no convincing reason offered to permit *ha'aramah* in these situations. There is no clear value that such *ha'aramah* would champion. It appears that people are trying to make life just a bit simpler for themselves, but there is no real burden to be relieved. There is no monetary loss or other significant loss in this case nor in the other *toseftan* examples.

Second, perhaps the *Tosefta* objected to such *ha'aramah* because it involves manipulating one's intentions. After all, it seems suspect to "intend" to make a rim if one does not actually plan to do so. Perhaps such nominal intention is simply incompatible with the laws of ritual impurity. As Vered Noam notes in her study of ritual impurity, the *tannaim* (= second- and third-century rabbis) understood ritual impurity as primarily "an entity in nature that bears quasi-physical characteristics of movement, spreading out, flowing, and the like," with the role of human intention as mere "footnotes."[65] Thus, fabricating untrue intentions about an object does not make them true and cannot prevent the very real spread of impurity.

Third, if this text does refer to a post-Temple context, rabbinic strictness may be animated by the potential (and actual) atrophy of purity law in the rabbis' own day. As both archaeological and textual evidence indicate, following the loss of the Temple, observance of purity law waned.[66] Moreover, early Christian doctrine implicitly challenged physical, ritual notions of impurity as it replaced ritual notions with metaphorical ones, such as purity and impurity of heart and mind.[67] Perhaps the rabbis felt that they had to preserve purity law more forcefully as a result.

Or maybe this *ha'aramah* of intention is rejected specifically because of the way ritual impurity was reshaped by rabbinic thought. Mira Balberg posits that after the fall of the Temple, rabbinic tradition manifests a radical reinterpretation of ritual purity as relating deeply to personal subjectivity rather than to community or to the Temple. This transformation gave meaning to ritual purity law even without a Temple.[68] If ritual purity had become anchored in subjective self-formation, perhaps all intentions that impact ritual im/purity must be subjective and not formed for the purpose of circumvention. I will discuss each of these possibilities in further depth in Chapter 4. At this point, however, it is sufficient to note that ritual purity law stands out as a major exception to the use of *ha'aramah*.

Rejecting Ha'aramah *as Evasion: Not Taking Interest*

Another *tannaitic* example of evasion relates to finances. Jewish law forbids Jews to collect interest from one another.[69] This means that when a loan is given, the lender may not pay more than the amount of the loan to their creditor.[70] The following passage describes and rejects certain practices that (appear to) circumvent the law of taking interest:

Tosefta Bava Metzi'a 4:2 (Lieberman Ed., See also Yerushalmi BM 5:1, 10a)

יש דברים שאינן רבית אבל אסורין מפני ערמת[71] רבית כיצד א"ל הלויני מנה א"ל אין לי מנה טול לך מאה[72] של חטין אע"פ שחזר ולקח ממנו עשרים וארבע אינן רבית אבל אסורין משום [ערמת][73] רבית

> There are matters which are not usury de jure but are nonetheless prohibited due to being cunning forms of de facto collecting usury. How so? [If] one party said to another, "Lend me a one hundred *zuz*,"[74] and the other party responded, "I don't have money, but take instead one-hundred-*zuz*-worth of grain." If the original owner of the grain then purchases it from the other party at a discount [for] 24 [*sela*] (= 96 *zuz*)[75] this is not de jure usury. Nonetheless, it is prohibited as a cunning form of de facto collecting usury.

A gives B an advance of 100 *zuz* worth of grain, allowing B to pay for it later. It is a sale, but the buyer need not pay for the item immediately. Thus, the money due for the item is considered a loan. Effectively, B received a loan of 100 *zuz* and will eventually have to pay A back the 100 *zuz*. In the meantime, A asks B if, instead of selling the grain to someone else to make money, he would sell it to A for a little less than its value, only 96 *zuz*. Technically, there is nothing wrong with this because A may have been able to purchase the same amount of grain for this cheaper price from someone else by haggling, and B may have had to sell to someone else for the same cheaper price if someone else bargained with him. However, the rabbis are still concerned that perhaps B is giving A a special deal on the grain because of the original loan, and A is saving four extra *zuz* in the process. Hence, A is receiving something extra for lending money to B. Some suggest that this constitutes rabbinically prohibited interest, echoing the biblical version of the prohibition of interest, where the borrower pays back more than the loan was worth.[76] Others think the activity only looks like usury because A gave 96 *zuz* right now and will receive 100 *zuz* from B later. However, it is not actual usury, as A originally gave 100 *zuz* in the form of grain and will receive 100 *zuz* back in the form of coins.[77] In either case, the rabbis do not approve of a transaction that allows for (the appearance of) taking interest.

In other *tannaitic* examples about money—avoiding the tax on *ma'aser sheni* or easing the burden of having a *bekhor*—*ha'aramah* prevents financial loss. But, here the lender simply exploits the borrower to save a few bucks. Nothing here evokes necessity for the lender or extenuating circumstances. Thus, it is evasion.

Just as the rabbis advocate *ha'aramah* to uphold important values, they reject it to uphold important values. They do not want *ha'aramah* to be used to undermine and weaken Jewish law.

A *Toseftan* Innovation: *Ha'aramah* as Avoision

Thus far, I have described *tannaitic ha'aramah* cases that are considered either solomonic avoidance or serpentine evasion. However, the *Tosefta* introduces cases of avoision. In such cases, the verdict is not unanimous: rabbis debate whether or not *ha'aramah* may be used. Interestingly, the avoision cases tend to relate to unexpected incidents rather than consistent patterns in Jewish life like redeeming *ma'aser sheni*, letting firstborn animals remain unused, contracting ritual impurity, or common business transactions. Instead, many focus on what seem to be random accidents that occur on the Sabbath or festival that result in potential loss for the observant Jew.

Saving Extra Bread from a House Fire on the Sabbath/Festival: Yes or No?

One *toseftan* case describes a house fire breaking out on the Sabbath or festival.[78] According to Jewish law, one may only extinguish a fire during the Sabbath or festival to save human lives. But if a house fire breaks out and no one is in danger, the homeowner may not extinguish the fire. The homeowner may, however, retrieve a limited amount of food from the house, though not more food than is needed for the Sabbath or festival itself.[79] Although the homeowner's options are limited, she still has a degree of choice.

If she accidentally retrieves coarse bread first, she may return to the house to retrieve fresh bread. This qualification opens the door to *ha'aramah*:

Tosefta Shabbat 13:6–7 (MS Vienna)

מצילין מיום טוב לשבת זו לשבת אחרת ולא משבת ליום טוב ולא
משבת ליום הכפורים[80] ולא מיום הכפורים לשבת[81] ואין צורך לומ' מיום טוב
לחול ולא יציל ואחר כך יזמין[82] אלא יזמין ואחר כך יציל הציל פת נקייה אין
רשאי[83] להציל פת הדראה פת הדראה רשאי להציל פת נקייה ואין (מערבין)
מערימין בכך[84] ר' יוסה בי ר' יהודה אומ' מערימין בכך

[People may] save on the festival for the Sabbath but not on one Sabbath for another Sabbath, and not on the Sabbath for a festival, and not on the Sabbath for the Day of Atonement, and not on the Day of Atonement for the Sabbath, and certainly not on the festival for a mundane day. One should not save and afterward invite, but invite and afterward save.
[If] one saved bread of fine flour, one may not save bread of coarse flour. If one saved bread of coarse flour, one may save bread of fine flour. But people may not practice cunning in this R. Yose b. R. Yehuda says, "People may practice prudence in this matter."

Rabbinic permission to correct a retrieval error might prompt a shrewd homeowner, looking to save extra food, purposely to retrieve coarse bread first and then go back to save fine bread. This circumvention is subject to disagreement. May one purposely save the coarse bread first and then save fine bread in order to save beyond what is needed for the festival or Sabbath?[85] The argument may also relate to saving extra food for guests even if one has not invited them yet. In fact, MS Erfurt reads the debate as being about whether מערימין בהן, practicing prudence in *these* matters rather than *in this* matter (בכך), per MS Vienna. "These matters" would refer to both using the possible invitation of guests to save more food and intentionally saving coarse bread first in order to then save fine bread.

This case is both similar and dissimilar to the avoidance cases above. Once again, the protection of property (i.e., saving money) may justify *ha'aramah*.[86] But unlike the cases that relate to systemic societal issues, it is hard to detect the social urgency in these cases at all. Were house fires a systemic problem? Rather, cases like this one introduce the new element of private financial difficulty rather than ongoing social issues. Could that explain why one side of the debate rejected it? The text does not clarify.

Retrieving Animals from a Pit on the Festival: Yes or No?

These same elements are reflected in a second *toseftan* case. In this scenario, the prohibition at issue is *muktzeh* (lit. "marginalized"), referring to items—including livestock—that may not be handled during Sabbath or festivals. However, festival days have more permissive rules than Sabbath regarding food preparation. One may prepare food on a festival for that day even by using some of the thirty-nine categories of labor that are otherwise prohibited on Sabbath and festivals. This means that one may slaughter animals for that day's meal. Consequently, one may handle livestock on a festival for the purpose of slaughtering it for the day's meal. (This differs from the Sabbath when one may not employ any of the prohibited categories of labor, even for food preparation for the day.)[87]

In the avoision case cited below, two animals fall into a pit on a festival, and their owner is concerned about losing the livestock to heatstroke, predators, or the like. These would cause pain for the animals and financial loss for their owner. Nonetheless, because animals are *muktzeh*, the owner may not handle the animals even to retrieve them. The owner may only retrieve them to slaughter them for consumption that day. While retrieving the animals and slaughtering them may "save" these animals, the particulars of the scenario present a further complication: the two animals in the pit are a parent-offspring pair, and, per biblical law, one may not slaughter an animal and its offspring on the same day.[88] Thus, it seems the owner has only one choice: to retrieve one animal from the pit and slaughter it for the day while leaving the other animal in the pit until nightfall when the festival day ends. This is where the debate about avoision begins:

Tosefta Betzah 3:2 (MS Vienna)[89]

אותו ואת בנו שנפלו לבור ר' אליעזר אומ' מעלה את הראשון על מנת לשוחטו ואינו שוחטו והשיני עושה לו פרנסה במקומו בשביל שלא ימות ר' יהושע אומ' מעלה את הראשון על מנת לשוחטו ואינו שוחטו ומערים ומעלה את השיני[90] רצה שלא לשחוט את אחד מהם הרשות בידו[91]

An animal and its offspring that fell into a pit on a festival day, R. Eliezer says, "One raises up the first on condition to slaughter it, but does not slaughter it, and, for the second, one provides food while it is in its present location, so that it does not die." R. Yehoshua says, "One raises up the first on condition to slaughter it, but does not slaughter it, and, acting prudently, one then raises up the second. [If] he wanted to slaughter neither one of them, he has the right [to refrain]."

R. Eliezer accepts the limitations, somewhat: the owner may retrieve only one animal from the pit because only one is eligible for slaughter. However, the owner need not slaughter the animal in the end. Mere potential for slaughter suffices. It is puzzling that R. Eliezer does not use the term *ha'aramah* for his position: after all, is it not a circumvention to raise an animal from a pit "on condition to slaughter it" and then not slaughter it? R. Yehoshua's position, however, is presented as *ha'aramah*. He allows the owner to use R. Eliezer's trick twice. After all, if one may retrieve one animal from the pit for slaughter and then decide not to eat it, why not do it twice? R. Yehoshua suggests that one pull each animal out of the pit, ostensibly for slaughter, and "change one's mind" after each animal has been retrieved. This *ha'aramah* functions to circumvent the laws of *muktzeh* while protecting the owner of the animal from financial loss and possibly protecting the animal from extended suffering.

This debate focuses on a *ha'aramah* that can prevent financial loss and/or animal suffering. Like the house-fire scenario, the discussion centers on a random private occurrence rather than a systemic issue. It is not clear why R. Eliezer and R. Yehoshua disagree. Perhaps it is because this is a private matter and not a public one, so it warrants less flexibility. Perhaps the potential for financial loss is not imminent enough. Perhaps it is because the "on condition to slaughter" is impossible for both animals, given that they may not both be slaughtered on the same day. Or perhaps R. Eliezer objects because the ruse is too obvious, given that neither animal will be slaughtered. The text does not say.[92]

The *tannaitic* examples in this chapter tell a story of carefully walking the line between circumventing the law for noble ends and undermining the law. But the cases of avoision are still left somewhat unexplained: why, even where *ha'aramah* is permitted by some, do other *tannaim* demur? This chapter has inferred some factors that determine which are accepted as solomonic and which are rejected as serpentine. And yet, these early texts are not explicit about what these factors are. The *Yerushalmi*, however, begins to delineate these factors explicitly. I will discuss the *Yerushalmi*'s contribution in the following chapter.

Conclusion

Tannaitic texts reflect neither carte blanche acceptance nor rejection of *ha'aramah*. Like avoidance, evasion, and avoision, sometimes rabbis reject *ha'aramah* (e.g., taking interest), sometimes they embrace it (e.g., *ma'aser sheni*), and sometimes they debate it (e.g., retrieving extra bread from a house fire on the Sabbath). I have argued that the decision to accept or reject *ha'aramah* is not mere formalism or capitulation to laxity; instead, it depends on the worthiness of the purpose of the circumvention. For example, *ha'aramah* could be used to keep people from needlessly spending money on rituals that were too expensive for them and even defunct after the fall of the Temple. But it should not be used just to get around an inconvenient rule or to profit off someone else.

This multifaceted view of *ha'aramah* can be understood by the legacy of the word itself, echoing both the cunning of the snake in the Garden of Eden and the prudence offered in the Book of Proverbs. What is more, this multifaceted view contrasts clearly with the direction of contemporaneous Roman legal thought. Within a century of Roman jurists coining a discouraging term for legal dodges—*fraus legi*—and trying to eliminate them, the rabbinic texts introduce their own term—*ha'aramah*—which allows a differentiated (including affirmative) approach to their use.

Nonetheless, my suggestions in this chapter about when the rabbis dis/allow *ha'aramah* remain inductive: neither *Mishnah* nor *Tosefta* makes the parameters of *ha'aramah*'s use explicit. That discussion emerges in the next phase of the development of *ha'aramah*, in the *Yerushalmi*.

Chapter 2

Being Explicit About Legal Values and Integrity

In Chapter 1, I argued that rabbinic justification of *ha'aramah* is not defined exclusively by legal formalism but by upholding important values. Therefore, rabbinic texts do not allow *ha'aramah* to be used in every case. Sometimes they reject the use of *ha'aramah* (evasion), sometimes they accept it unanimously (avoidance), and sometimes they record debates about it (avoision). In *tannaitic* sources, both avoidance and avoision cases are marked by values that are generally relevant to Jewish law, such as preventing financial loss. Thus, *ha'aramah* should be used selectively, employed only in cases where there is some important value that warrants it. But this suggestion remains tacit in *tannaitic* discussions about *ha'aramah*. Interestingly, the controversial cases in *tannaitic* literature are left unexplained. And it is the controversial cases that are the most surprising because they reflect situations that should justify the use of *ha'aramah* based on the important values, yet some rabbis still reject it.

This chapter explores how passages in the Jerusalem Talmud, the *Yerushalmi*, analyze avoision cases to delineate parameters for *ha'aramah* while offering new examples of *ha'aramah* as well. This investigation yields a focus both on values as an important variable and on the integrity of the legal process itself. Thus, I focus on two types of variables offered within the *Yerushalmi*: substantive and procedural. Some *ha'aramah* parameters relate to the substantive goals of the circumvention while others convey limitations on which laws can be circumvented in the first place. Both the substantive and the procedural variables underline a need to respect the broader legal system, even when circumventing a law.

Chapter 2

Developing the Parameters of *Ha'aramah*

A passage in the *Yerushalmi* analyzes two arguments between R. Eliezer and R. Yehoshua about avoision cases, which then leads to a discussion of *ha'aramah*'s parameters. One case is about setting aside a portion of one's raw dough on Passover for a priestly gift, and the other is the animal-offspring avoision case discussed in the previous chapter. In both scenarios, following the law in the conventional way raises a conundrum. And yet, the passage argues that neither R. Eliezer nor R. Yehoshua is consistent regarding *ha'aramah* in these cases. Each approves of *ha'aramah* in one case but not in the other. This leads to theorizing about what would make *ha'aramah* worthy in one case but not in the other, and vice versa. The first case is about the portion of dough on Passover:

Yerushalmi Pesaḥim 3:3, 30a/Betzah 3:4, 62a (MS Leiden)

משנה: כיצד מפרישין חלת טומאה ביום טוב רבי אליעזר או' אל תקרא לה שם עד
שתיאפה בן בתירה או' תטיל לצונים אמר יהושע לא זה הוא חמץ שמוזהרים עליו
בל יראה ובל ימצא אלא מפרשתה ומנחתה עד הערב ואם החמיצה החמיצה

Mishnah (MS Kaufmann): How, on the festival [of Passover], do we set apart the dough offering (*ḥallah*) [if the dough is in a state of] impurity [and thus must be burned rather than given to a priest]? R. Eliezer says: She should not designate [the dough offering] until it is baked. Ben Beterah says: She should put the dough into cold water (so that it will not rise). Said R. Yehoshua: This is not the sort of leaven concerning which people are warned under the prohibitions, "Let it not be seen" (*bal yera'eh,* Exod. 13:7), and "Let it not be found" (*bal yimatze,* Exod. 12:19).[1] Rather, she separates the dough offering and leaves it until evening, and if it ferments, it ferments.

גמרא . . . כיצד יעשה על דר' אליעזר? מערים ואו' (וזו אני רוצה לוכל וזו אני
רוצה לאכול) ואופה את כולה וכשהוא רודה מערים ואו' זו אני רוצה ליישן זו
א{י}ני[2] רוצה ליישן ומשייר אחת. אמר לו רבי יושוע לא נמצאת כשורף[3] קדשים
ביום טוב?! אמ' לו ר' אליעזר מאיליהן הן נשרפין! אמ' לו ר'[4] יושוע לא נמצאת
עובר על בל יראה ובל ימצא. אמ' לו מוטב לעבור מצוה בלא תעשה שלא באת
לפניו ממצוה בלא תעשה שבאת לפניו.[5] . . .

Gemara:[6] How should one act according to R. Eliezer (who says one can handle the dough until it is baked, when it is designated and then properly left till the evening for burning)?
One acts with prudence and says: "This [portion] I want to eat and this [portion] I want to eat"; and one thus bakes all of the dough; then, when one removes it [from the oven, one] acts with prudence and says: "This [portion] I want to store away, and this [portion] I want to store away" and one leaves a single [piece in the oven which is then designated as *ḥallah*].
Said R. Yehoshua to him [R. Eliezer], "Do you not end up like one who burns consecrated items on the holiday [by leaving the dough offering to burn in the oven after baking the dough, which is a distinct violation]?" R. Eliezer said to him, "They burn on their own (i.e., without a separate act of burning, for the dough offering remains in the oven after it and the rest of the dough are baked)." Said he to R. Yehoshua, "Do you not end up violating the ban on seeing and finding leaven [on one's premises by allowing the dough to rise]?" [R. Yehoshua] said to him, "It is preferable to violate a negative commandment passively [by leaving out dough which will become leaven on its own], rather than actively [by placing the dough in the oven, even if ultimately it burns "on its own."]"[7] . . .

Although the word *ḥallah*, or "challah," as colloquially spelled, has become popularized as a type of Jewish bread, it has a distinct meaning in Jewish law. *Ḥallah* is the portion of dough set aside for priests, taken from both ritually pure and ritually impure dough. However, only *ḥallah* that is ritually pure may be eaten by the priest.[8] Impure *ḥallah* is burned instead to keep anyone from eating or otherwise using it. This *mishnah* addresses taking *ḥallah* from ritually impure dough on a festival day of Passover.[9] Because the dough is ritually impure, the priest may not eat it. And because no one will eat this dough on the festival day, it may not be placed into the oven on the festival, for only food that will be consumed that day may be cooked or baked.[10] So the dough will be left out until after the festival day is over.[11] But on Passover, this poses a problem: if the dough rises while it sits out, the person who owns it will violate the prohibition of owning *ḥamets* on Passover (Exod. 12:19, 13:7).[12] This means that one is effectively caught between the violation of owning leavened dough on Passover and the violation of burning dough on the festival.

There is one hope, however. In the *mishnah*, R. Yehoshua suggests that possession of the priest's portion of risen *ḥallah* dough does not violate *ḥametz* ownership perhaps because it is not considered owned by the person baking.[13] Ben Beterah and R. Eliezer, however, do think possession of the risen *ḥallah* dough on Passover is transgressive, so each suggests a way to keep the dough from rising: Ben Beterah uses chemistry, while R. Eliezer suggests a legal workaround to burn the dough instead of leaving it out to rise. R. Eliezer recommends not designating the *ḥallah* portion until the entire dough has already been baked in the oven and then passively leaving only the *ḥallah* portion in the oven to burn further.

While the *mishnah* reads like an argument over whether possession of risen *ḥallah* on Passover violates the prohibition of owning *ḥametz*, the talmudic debate centers on *ha'aramah*. Based on the *toseftan* parallel of this dispute (*tPes.* 3:7), which offers a different version of R. Yehoshua's position, the *Yerushalmi* passage proceeds as though both rabbis believe that owning this risen dough is problematic. What they argue about, however, is whether *ha'aramah* is permitted to prevent the dough from rising: R. Eliezer permits it whereas R. Yehoshua rejects it. R. Yehoshua would rather let the dough rise and thus violate the prohibition of owning *ḥametz* than have someone place the dough in the oven, knowing it is not food for the day.

Focusing R. Yehoshua and R. Eliezer's conflict on *ha'aramah* allows the text to compare it with another debate between them about *ha'aramah*, the case discussed in the previous chapter about the livestock pair that falls into a pit on the festival. R. Eliezer and R. Yehoshua seem to switch positions in the livestock case—with R. Eliezer rejecting *ha'aramah* for the animals even though he embraced it for the dough, and R. Yehoshua advocating *ha'aramah* for the animals even though he rejected it for the dough. The text analyzes why they switch positions, and in so doing, when and why *ha'aramah* should be considered evasion or avoidance. The text continues:

אותו ואת בנו שנפלו לבור ר' אליעזר או' יעלה את הראשון על מנת לשחוט וישחוט והשיני עושין לו פרנסה שלא ימות. ר' יושוע או' יעלה את הראשון על מנת לשחוט ולא ישחוט ויערים ויעלה את השיני א'פ' שחישב שלא לשחוט אחד מהן[14] מותה. ר' בון בר חייה בעי מחלפה שיטתיה דר' אליעזר תמן הוא אמ' אסור להערים והכא הוא אמ' מותר להערים? הכא משום בל יראה ובל ימצא תמן מה אית לך? מחלפה שיטתיה דר' יהושע תמן הוא אמר מותר להערים והכא הוא אמר אסור להערים? אמ' ר' אידי כאן שבות וכאן חיוב[15] חטאת. א'ר יוסה ביר' בון תמן כדי לחוס על ניכסיהן שליש' הכא מה אית לך?!

An animal and its offspring that fell into a pit [on a festival]—R. Eliezer says, "[One] should raise up the first on condition to slaughter and slaughter it, and the second; they feed it so that it does not die." R. Yehoshua says, "[One] should raise up the first one on condition to slaughter but not slaughter [it] and one should act prudently by raising up the second. Even though [one] intended/decided not to slaughter either one of them—this is permitted."

R. Bun bar Hiyya asked: "Is not R. Eliezer's logic reversed? There (in the case of the animals) he said it is forbidden to act with *ha'aramah*, yet here he said it is permitted to act with *ha'aramah*."

[The different positions do not contradict each other:] Here [he so rules] because of the ban on seeing and finding leaven [which justifies *ha'aramah* to remove the leaven]. There, is there any comparable justification?

R. Yehoshua's logic is reversed. There (in the case of the animals) he said it is permitted to act with *ha'aramah*, but here (in the case of dough) he said it is forbidden to act with *ha'aramah*.

Said R. Idi, Here (in the case of the animals) it is only a matter of a *shevut* (an added prohibition on not doing certain activities on the Sabbath or festival which, though not biblically constituting prohibited labors, are a violation of the "rest" appropriate for a Day of Rest), whereas here [where the individual bakes the impure dough, if it were the Sabbath, it would be a violation entailing] a liability for a sin offering.[16]

Said R. Yose b. R. Bun, "There [in the case of the animal caught in the pit, one can employ prudence] to have compassion on the property of Israel, whereas here [regarding the impure dough offering which is to be burned and which benefits neither an Israelite nor a priest], is there comparable justification?

What emerges from this comparison is that the same rabbi might reject *ha'aramah* in one case and embrace it in another. The Talmud offers three reasons why, and these reasons are either substantive or procedural in nature. I will review them one by one.

The first justification relates to substance: the goal of the *ha'aramah* is to avoid sin. In the *ḥallah* case, avoiding the sin of owning *ḥametz* on Passover is both necessary and sufficient for employing *ha'aramah*. In the case of the livestock pair, however, *ha'aramah* is unjustified because it is not used to prevent transgression but "merely" to protect one's possessions.[17] This approach is narrower than other cases so far: unlike the cases of *ma'aser sheni* and *bekhor*, this opinion rejects financial loss as a sufficient reason to employ *ha'aramah*. Instead, only preventing transgression validates the use of *ha'aramah*. In other words, legal circumvention should only be used to keep someone from violating another law: better to circumvent than to directly transgress. This view of *ha'aramah* is narrow: *ha'aramah* may only be used to protect legal observance.

The second variable, articulated by R. Idi, is the severity of the transgression being circumvented: in the livestock case, the violation being circumvented is handling animals on the festival, a violation not stipulated by the Bible.[18] In the *ḥallah* case, however, the violation being circumvented is based explicitly on a biblical verse warranting cooking only for the festival day itself. Regardless of the noble goals of the circumvention (such as preventing transgression), one may not use a workaround against an explicit biblical prohibition. This approach decenters the question of the substantive goals or values that one seeks to uphold and focuses on the procedural aspects of *ha'aramah* instead: there are limits to which laws one can stretch with integrity even when one's goals are noble.

The third approach, attributed to R. Yose son of R. Bun, returns to the substantive goals of the circumvention. His opinion reflects the logic of the avoidance cases in both *Mishnah* and *Tosefta*: the need to prevent financial loss justifies the use of *ha'aramah*. This aligns with the classification of preventing financial loss as a legal value elsewhere in the *Yerushalmi*: התורה חסה על ממונם של ישראל, the Torah spares Israel's money.[19] Not only do rabbinic texts attribute significance to preventing financial loss, but they assert it as a principle of Jewish law itself. *Mishnah Nega'im* 12:6 describes the process of clearing out a house that has been afflicted by the disease of *tzara'at* before the priest declares it impure.[20] If the house is pronounced impure, any items inside it become impure as well. The rabbis explain that the biblical injunction to clear out everything from the house before the priest proclaims it impure is done to minimize financial loss:

Mishnah Nega'im 12:6 (MS Parma 3173 (De Rossi 138))

וצוה הכהן ופינו את הבית—אפילו חבילי עצים ואפילו חבילי קנים דברי ר' יהודה.
רבי' שמעון או' עסק לפינוי אמ' ר' מאיר וכי מה מיטמא לו אם תאמר כלי עצו

ובגדיו ומתכתו מטבילן והן טהורין ועל מה חסה התורה? על כלי חרסו ועל פכו ועל תופיו[21] ואם כך חסה התורה על ממונו הבזוי קל וחומר על ממונו החביב אם כך על ממונו קל וחומר על נפש בניו ובנותיו ואם כך על שלרשע קל וחומר על של צדיק.

"And the priest shall command, and they shall empty the home" (Lev. 14:36)—[they empty the home] even [of] bunches of twigs, even of bunches of reeds, according to R. Yehudah. R. Shimon says: One should be busy in the emptying out for its own sake [i.e., even though most of the items in the house can be purified and thus will not be rendered useless by being declared ritually impure.] R. Meir said: Which items [will] become impure [if they remain in the home when the home is declared impure]? If you say his wooden vessels, his clothing and his metal [items], he can immerse them, and they will be purified. [So why not just leave them in the house and let them become impure and purify them later?] What did the Torah protect [by commanding that the house be emptied of everything before declaring it impure]? His [cheap] earthenware vessels, his flask and his small dripper [all of which must be broken if they become impure, as they cannot be purified through immersion]. If the Torah spares such cheap possessions, a fortiori it would protect more beloved (= valuable) possessions; and if thus, regarding his possessions, a fortiori [would the Torah protect] the lives of his sons and daughters. And if thus regarding a wicked person [who was deserving of a diseased house because of his own sinfulness], a fortiori regarding a righteous person.

Sparing people's money is presented as part of the logic *of the law itself*. The Torah protects Jewish possessions. While the discussion about *ha'aramah* does not specify whether the prevention of financial loss is a value internal to Jewish law or being brought into it by the rabbis, the fact that it is upheld as a principle of the law elsewhere is telling. Consequently, even if *ha'aramah* undermines the spirit of the specific law of not handling animals on the festival, it simultaneously upholds a general principle of the law: minimizing the financial loss caused by religious observance.

Each of these variables—preventing sin, respecting a weighty law, and protecting people's possessions—reflects that the use of *ha'aramah* is not a purely formalistic endeavor. The rabbis use *ha'aramah* as a tool for upholding principles that apply generally within Jewish law. Moreover, they draw a line when the integrity of the law is undermined by illegitimate goals or problematic processes (i.e., some laws may not be circumvented). And though different rabbis do not agree on which variable(s) is/are definitive, each approach reflects reverence for the Jewish legal system.[22]

Procedural Concerns: Temporary Betrothal

In addition to the discussion explored above, the *Yerushalmi* also contains at least one example where a different procedural aspect is explicitly cited as a reason for outlawing *ha'aramah*, even where the ends are noble. In the following example, a man wishes to betroth but not marry multiple women in order to support them financially.[23] While the goal is admirable, the *ha'aramah* is dismissed on procedural grounds:

Yerushalmi Yevamot 4:11, 6b (MS Leiden)

ומהו להערים? וכי ר' טרפון אביהן שלכל ישׂ' לא הערים? קידש שלש מאות נשים בימי רעבון על מנת להאכילן בתרומה תמן אין[24] כל אחת ואחת ראויה לוכל בתרומה ברם הכא כל אחד ואחד ראוי לייבם? ר' יודן ביר' ישמעאל עבדין ליה כן

> Is circumvention permissible [in the case of levirate marriage]?[25] Did not R. Tarfon, the father of all of Israel, practice circumvention with regard to marriage? Being of priestly lineage, he betrothed three hundred women during a famine to feed them priestly foods.
> There, each of the women could eat *terumah*; but here, can he marry each of these women?[26] R. Yudan the son of R. Yishmael, they did this to/for him.[27]

According to biblical law, if a husband dies without children, his brother should marry his widow to carry on the name of the deceased.[28] But the brother (the *levir*) may marry only one of his brother's wives. The question here is whether the *levir* can betroth all the wives (though he cannot and will not marry them all) to support them financially.[29] The text adduces precedent: during a famine, R. Tarfon betrothed many women (whom he did not plan to marry) to support them financially. As a *kohen*, R. Tarfon could only feed his priestly food to members of his family, including his betrothed, even if they were yet unmarried.[30] So he betrothed three hundred women to provide them with food that was otherwise unavailable to them.[31]

Ultimately, however, at least one voice in the text distinguishes between R. Tarfon's case and the case of the *levir* on grounds of whether the *ha'aramah* is procedurally legitimate. While R. Tarfon theoretically could have married all the women he betrothed, the *levir* cannot. Because the extra betrothals can never result in marriage, the *ha'aramah* is invalid. Perhaps the betrothal will only seem genuine if he can legally marry the women; otherwise, the ruse is too obvious.[32] Or perhaps betrothal simply cannot take effect if the couple may not marry.[33] Regardless, the litmus test for this approach to *ha'aramah* is not the nobility of the goal but the legitimacy of the process. Simultaneously, it seems that not everyone agrees with this logic, given the example that follows about employing *ha'aramah* in the levirate marriage of R. Yudan.

Biblical Justification for *Ha'aramah*

While the discussion of goals in the first case of this chapter relates to general legal principles, at least one passage in the *Yerushalmi* appeals to *ha'aramah* upholding the values of the specific law being circumvented. It records an opinion that *ha'aramah* may or should be used to save money in the case of *ma'aser sheni* because the Bible itself states that *ma'aser sheni* should be a blessing, that is, a source of abundance:

Yerushalmi Ma'aser Sheni 4:4, 55a (MS Leiden)

ר' אבון[34] אמ' איתפלגון ר' לעזר ור' יוסי בר חנינה חד אמ' למה מערימין עליו
מפני שכתוב בו ברכה

R. Avun said, "R. Elazar and R. Yose bar Haninah disputed [over the meaning of Deut. 14:24's claim that secondary tithe produce constitutes a 'blessing,' as follows]: One said, 'Why is it that people may practice circumvention [regarding the added 25 percent]? [We may infer that Scripture intends this money-saving leniency], because [second tithe produce] is described [in Deut. 14:24] as a blessing.'"

Deuteronomy 14:24–25 states that if one's *ma'aser sheni* produce is too abundant because God has blessed the farmer, the farmer may redeem the produce instead of hauling it to Jerusalem. In context, the "blessing" refers to having too much produce to bring to Jerusalem, yet the rabbis suggest that blessing characterizes the obligation of *ma'aser sheni* generally. Thus, circumvention of the 25 percent tax is warranted to bring the blessing of saving money. This text suggests that *ha'aramah* upholds the value of *ma'aser sheni* itself. Resorting to the use of decontextualized biblical phrasing to ratify a circumvention, however, should alert the reader to some anxiety over its use: circumventions are not justified based on abstract values of the legal system as a whole. Rather, they require express biblical validation. This approach is innovative within rabbinic literature: the need for biblical permission seems not to appear earlier in *Mishnah* or *Tosefta*.[35]

When Values Are Implicit

However, biblical validation for *ha'aramah* is not the norm within the *Yerushalmi* either: legal values and procedural integrity determine what is considered avoidance, evasion, or avoision. This is true both where the *Yerushalmi* cites earlier *mishnaic* or *toseftan* cases and for completely new *ha'aramah* scenarios.[36] However, many of the *Yerushalmi* texts do not make the reasoning as explicit as in the aforementioned examples. Below are cases that implicitly reflect the question of values in determining the use of *ha'aramah*.

Sidestepping the Law or Saving Money: Food on the Festival

Comparing two cases in the *Yerushalmi* from the same legal arena illustrates principled approaches to *ha'aramah*. Both situations involve food preparation during a festival. In one case *ha'aramah* is permitted, and in the other it is forbidden:

Yerushalmi Betzah 2:1, 61a (MS Leiden)

משנה: יום טוב שחל להיות ערב שבת לא יבשל בתחילה מיום טוב לשבת אבל מבשל הוא ליום טוב ואם הותיר הותיר לשבת ועושה תבשיל מערב יום טוב וסומך עליו לשבת. בית שמי אומ' שני תבשילים ובית הלל או' תבשיל אחד. מודים בדג

ובביצה שעליו שהן שני תבשילין. אכלו או שאבד לא יבשל עליו בתחילה. שייר ממנו כל שהוא סומך עליו בשבת.

גמ׳: . . . ר׳ כהנא בריה דר׳ חייה בר בא[37] אמ׳ ובלבד שלא יערים

Mishnah (MS Kaufmann): On a festival which fell on a Friday: one should not cook to begin with on the festival day [Friday] for the purposes of the Sabbath. Rather, one may prepare food for the festival day, and if one happens to have leftovers s/he may use it for Sabbath. One may, however, cook before the festival and rely upon it for the Sabbath. Bet Shammai says: two cooked items, and Bet Hillel says: one cooked item. They agree about fish and the egg on it that they are two cooked items. If one ate it (= the item that one cooked before the festival), or if it got lost, one may not begin cooking [on the festival for the Sabbath] by relying on it (= the cooked items that are gone). If one left over any amount of it (= the item that one cooked before the festival), one may rely upon it [to cook on the festival] for the Sabbath.

. . .

Gemara (MS Leiden): . . . R. Kahana bar R. Hiyya bar Ba said, "This is on condition that one not practice cunning [by baking or cooking a great deal of food, ostensibly for the festival itself]."

Because Jewish law allows cooking on a festival for consumption on the day itself but not for consumption on a different day, when the festival falls on a Friday, one may not cook on Friday even for the Sabbath.[38] If, however, one cooked for the festival day itself and somehow ended up with leftovers, one may eat those leftovers on the Sabbath. However, the *mishnah* explains that there is no reason to rely on accidental leftovers for the Sabbath meal. Instead, start cooking for the Sabbath before the festival by setting aside one or two cooked items. Various explanations for why this is considered more legitimate than starting to cook for Sabbath on the festival day have been offered, but regardless of the rationale, this is the clear ruling of the *mishnah*.[39] This strategy comes to be known as the *'eruv tavshilin*, the combination of foods, and it is still practiced in observant Jewish homes today.

In the talmudic discussion of this issue, R. Kahana bar Hiyya bar Ba forbids making extra food on the festival day to "accidentally" have leftovers for the Sabbath. Presumably, he disapproves of this because there is already a correct way to deal with cooking for the Sabbath when the festival falls on Friday: by starting the cooking prior to the festival. Ignoring this ruling and using one's personal circumvention instead is unacceptable. Such a *ha'aramah* is not about upholding virtue but about conveniently sidestepping the law.[40] Thus, he rejects the *ha'aramah*.

That said, the *Yerushalmi* does cite permission to use *ha'aramah* in other food preparation on a festival. Though Jewish law permits slaughtering an animal on the festival day for that day's meal, leftover meat will spoil unless it is salted. However, salting food on the festival for a non-festival day is forbidden. The solution to this problem is debated among various people citing Rav:

Yerushalmi Betzah 1:5, 60c (MS Leiden)

...חברייא בשם רב מולח הוא אדם דבר מרובה א'ע'פ' שאינו יכול לוכל ממנו אלא דבר ממועט ר' אחא בשם רב מולח ומערים מולח ומערים מלח הכא ומלח הכא עד דו מלח כוליה

> ... Associates [said] in the name of Rav: "One may salt a sizable piece [of meat on the festival], even though one is able to eat only a small part of it [on the festival day itself]." R. Aha in the name of Rav [said]: "One may put on a little salt and act prudently and salt, act prudently and salt, salting here and there until one has salted the entire piece."

Some cite Rav as permitting one to salt the entire large piece at once, even if the plan is to eat only part of it, perhaps because salting the full piece is basically one action.[41] However, R. Aha cites Rav as requiring the use of *ha'aramah* by salting each section of the large piece of meat under the pretense of "planning" to eat it that day. In this case, it seems that the use of circumvention is the stricter position of the two.[42] Nonetheless, this *ha'aramah* still allows one to salt all the meat. There are two reasons to endorse *ha'aramah* in this case. First, there is the value of not losing money while trying to celebrate the festival. And second, perhaps requiring the meat to spoil will prevent people from fulfilling their obligation to eat festive meals in the future to celebrate the holiday.[43] If one must leave the extra meat to spoil, one might choose not to eat meat on the festival at all, which would result in a lackluster celebration.[44]

These two examples exhibit, yet again, that when *ha'aramah* is used to uphold a value, or even an obligation of the legal system, it is likely to be approved, but when it is used simply to undermine the law, it is likely to be forbidden.[45]

Outlawing Economic Exploitation: Loan Fraud

Just as a *tosefta* outlawed *ha'aramah* used to take (apparent) interest from a borrower, the *Yerushalmi* cites a case outlawing *ha'aramah* to cheat a lender. While saving money is a rabbinic value, financial exploitation is not:

Yerushalmi Kiddushin 3:5, 64a (MS Leiden)

ר' יעקב בר אחא בשם ר' אימי ראובן חייב לשמעון סמכיה גבי לוי. איפרסן לוי. לית ראובן חייב לשמעון. הדא דאת אמר בשלא עשו בהערמה אבל עשו בהערמה חייב.

R. Aha in the name of R. Immi, "If Reuven owed money to Shimon, and assigned the debt to Levi; and Levi lost his money, Reuven does not owe Shimon money." That which you said applies when they did not practice cunning [to conspire against Shimon]. But if they practiced cunning, he (= Reuven) remains liable.

Here is the perfect dodge: a debtor names his bankrupt friend as the guarantor of his loan.[46] The contract requires a guarantor, so he presents one whom the lender thinks has means while the debtor knows otherwise.[47] When the lender comes to collect, and neither the debtor nor his guarantor has any money, the debtor will be off the hook. If this happens accidentally—namely, a debtor assigned a solvent guarantor who went bankrupt after the loan was made—it is legitimate. But if the debtor chose a bankrupt guarantor on purpose, it is evasion, and it is forbidden. Defrauding a lender is not how *ha'aramah* should be used. Following the law is not just about technicalities; it is also about values.

Suspecting Possible Misuse of *Ha'aramah*

In addition to the aforementioned examples of evasion, avoidance, and avoision, *Yerushalmi* texts highlight a new element reflecting concern for the law: rabbis prohibit certain activities if they suspect *ha'aramah* as a motivating factor. This is known as "suspicion of subterfuge" (חשש ערמה, *ḥashash ha'aramah*), and its appearance suggests that people may have been exploiting the strategies of *ha'aramah* in problematic ways.[48] Below are examples that demonstrate this concern.

Suspicious Activity: A Temple Treasury Refund

The first example is a case of potentially cheating the Temple treasury. A man consecrates his assets while his wife's marriage settlement has a lien on those assets. Then, he divorces her.[49] This is suspicious, as he may be divorcing her so that she can get the money back from the Temple treasury for him as payment of her marriage settlement. R. Eliezer says that when they divorce, the husband must vow never to allow her to enjoy benefit from his property. R. Yehoshua does not require such a vow, however.[50] R. Mana analyzes their debate as hinging upon the potential for *ha'aramah* as evasion:

Yerushalmi Nazir 5:1, 54a (MS Leiden)

אמ' ר' מנא ר' ליעזר חשש על הערמה רבי יהושע לא חשש על ה()[ע]רמה

> R. Mana said, "R. Eliezer suspects the possibility of cunning [between the husband and the wife to defraud the Temple]. R. Yehoshua does not suspect the possibility of such cunning."

When one designates funds to the Temple treasury, one cannot get them back. Thus, this man may be looking for a workaround to get his money back.[51] The possible evasion goes as follows: there was a lien on the man's donation to the Temple treasury for his wife's marriage settlement (*ketubah*); if he divorces her, she may retrieve the money from the Temple treasury for her *ketubah* payment; the man might then remarry her and regain possession of the money.[52] Thus, R. Eliezer makes the man forswear future benefit from his ex-wife so that they will not remarry, yet R. Yehoshua is unconcerned. R. Eliezer safeguards against a potential attempt to steal from the Temple treasury while R. Yehoshua does not. Perhaps R. Yehoshua thinks it is unlikely that a couple would do this. Perhaps he thinks that keeping them from remarrying in every case where a husband had given money to the Temple treasury is bad public policy.[53]

Suspicious Activity: *Where Do People Misuse* Ha'aramah?

The *Yerushalmi* also contains text indicating rabbinic awareness of where people were likely to misuse *ha'aramah*. In the following passage, the *Yerushalmi* compares people's treatment of the restriction against working their land during the intermediate days of a festival (*ḥol ha-mo'ed*) and the restriction against working their land during their seven days of mourning (*shiv'ah/shiva*, meaning, "seven") for immediate family members.[54] During both periods, farming is restricted to honor the status of these days. And yet, *ḥol ha-mo'ed* is ripe for trying to circumvent the law of minimizing labor.

Yerushalmi Mo'ed Katan 2:1, 81a (MS Leiden)

משנה: מי שהפך את זיתיו ואירעו אבל או אונס או שהטעוהו טוען קורה ראשונה ומניחה לאחר המועד דברי ר' יהודה. ר' יוסי אומר זולף וגומר כדרכו.

גמרא: . . . ר' יודה או' יאבד דבר ממועט ואל יאבד דבר מרובה. ר' יוסה או' אל יאבד דבר כל עיקר. ר' יודה בר פזי בשם ר' יוחנן כשם שהן חלוקין כאן כך הן חלוקין בהילכות אבל: דתני אילו דברים שעושין לאבל בימי אבלו דורכין את עבטו וזולפין את יינו וגפין את חביותיו וזיתיו הפוכין ושנויין טוחניןו(י)ן כדרכן ומשקין בית השלחין שלו בשהגיע זמנו לשתות וזורעין את נירו פשתן ברביעה דברי ר' יודה. אמרו לו אם אינה נזרעת פשתן תזרע מין אחר אם אינה נזרעת בשבת זו תזרע[55] בשבת אחרת. מנו "אמרו לו"? ר' יוסה. מחלפה שיטתיה דר' יודה תמן הוא אמ' יאבד דבר ממועט ואל יאבד דבר מרובה וכא אמ' הכין. שנייא [היא] תמן שדרכו להערים.[56] וכל שכן מחלפה שיטתיה דרבי יוסה מה אית תמן שדרכו להערים את אמר מותר כאן שאין דרכו להערים לא כל שכן? אמ' ר' חיננא מנו "אמרו לו"? חכמ' שהן בשיטת רבי יודה במועד

Mishnah: He who [prior to the festival] had turned his olives (to prepare them for pressing), and then an occasion for mourning or some accident befell him, or workers proved unreliable (so that he could not complete the processing prior to the festival): "[during the intermediate days of the festival] applies the pressing beam [to the olives] for the first time, but [then] leaves it (that is, does not squeeze out the oil) until after the festival," [thus are] the words of R. Yehudah. R. Yose says, "He squeezes out the oil entirely and seals it in a jar in the usual way."

. . .

Gemara: [Explaining the dispute in the *mishnah*], Rabbi Yehudah says: One should lose a little and not a lot. Rabbi Yose says: One should not lose anything. Rabbi Yehudah b. Pazzi in the name of R. Yohanan: Just as they (= R. Yehudah and R. Yose) argue here, so they argue with respect to the laws governing the mourner.

For it has been taught: "These are the things that they do for a mourner during the period of his mourning: they press his olive-mass, empty out his wine, and seal it in jars. As to his olives, if they have turned over once and then a second time, they press them in the usual way. And they irrigate his field that requires it when its turn has come to receive water. And they sow his furrow with flax at the rains," thusly the words of R. Yehudah. They said to him, "If it is not sown with flax, it may be sown with another species. If it is not sown this week, it may be sown in some other week [and hence, that may not be done for him]." Now who was it who said this to him? It was R. Yose. The opinions assigned to R. Yehudah are at variance with one another. There he said that one may lose a small volume, but not a large volume, while here has said this (i.e., that to avoid any loss at all, others may on his behalf press olives in the usual way).

There is a difference between the two cases. There (= regarding the intermediate days of the festival) it is common to practice cunning [and hence he is stricter about the intermediate days of the festival]. All the more so, are the opinions assigned to R. Yose reversed. If there [with respect to the festival] cunning is common, yet R. Yose says that it is permitted [to squeeze out the oil in the usual way so as not to lose anything], here [in a case of mourning], where cunning is uncommon, should he not [be permissive] that much more so? Said R. Hinenah: Who are they who "said to him"? They are the sages who concur with the view of R. Yehudah with respect to the intermediate days of the festival, [and are challenging him that the loss that the mourner would incur is minor and should not impact the ruling].[57]

This passage draws a distinction between the two arenas—mourning and the intermediate festival days—with regard to suspicion of evasion.[58] In the case of the seven days of mourning, the rabbis do not suspect a person of exploiting *ha'aramah*, though in the case of the intermediate days of the festival they do. This is easily explained by the difference between these two periods: the holidays occur annually whereas one's family member may die suddenly. Thus, the farmer knows that the holiday is coming, and if he does not complete the oil preparation beforehand, he may be intentionally leaving the work for *ḥol ha-mo'ed*.[59] Because the farmer should and can perform these tasks before the holiday begins, *ha'aramah* is unacceptable. On the other hand, because the timing of death and mourning is less predictable, the likelihood of orchestrating a situation in which one purposely performs labor during the seven days of mourning is low. Additionally, the mourner's emotional state makes it less likely that legal evasion is the goal.[60] Consequently, in this case, the rabbis see the real pathos of someone who does not want their olives to go to waste when confronted suddenly by the restrictions of *shiv'ah*.

In these examples, the rabbis are wise to people's abuse of *ha'aramah*, and they try to prevent it. While they do not always agree on how suspicious they should be of possible subterfuge or how to respond to that suspicion, they negotiate what to do about possible exploitation of *ha'aramah*.

Lamenting the Misuse of *Ha'aramah*, but Not Preventing It

At the same time, the *Yerushalmi* suggests that rabbis could not or would not close all loopholes even if they suspected misuse. In at least one instance, rabbis lament the overuse/misuse of a loophole, yet they do not close the loophole. The case relates to the tithe given to the Levite before partaking of one's produce. According to rabbinic law, a farmer is obligated to tithe their produce only once it has grown a certain amount.[61] If the food is not tithed once it has grown that amount, even if the food is not yet fully processed, the farmer and their associates may only snack on it; they may not consume it as a meal.[62] Once it is fully processed, if it will be sold at market, one may not even snack on it until it has been tithed. But if it will be brought into the harvester's house or guarded courtyard, it may still be eaten as a snack prior to tithing. The prohibition against eating it even as a snack unless it is tithed only applies once the produce reaches the house or courtyard.[63] One potential for circumvention lies in defining what it means to bring the produce into the house or courtyard. *Mma'aserot* 3:6 rules that the roof of the house—unlike the front door or the courtyard—does not catalyze the requirement for tithing, which means that one might theoretically put produce on the roof to continue to snack on it without tithing it. The *Yerushalmi* records that even some rabbis used this loophole:

Yerushalmi Ma'aserot 3:1, 50c (MS Leiden)

רבי עולא בר ישמעאל בשם ר' לעזר ר' ור' יוסי בי ביר' יהודה היו מכניסין את הכלכלה לאחורי הגנות. ראה אותן ר' יודה ביר' אלעאי אמר להן ראו מה ביניכם לראשונים! ר' עקיבה היה לוקח שלשה מינין בפרוטה בשביל לעשר מכל מין ומין, ואתם מכניסין את הכלכלה לאחורי הגנות!

R. Ulla son of Yishmael said in the name of R. Lazer: Rebbe and R. Yose son of R. Yehudah would bring their food basket to the back of the roofs. R. Yehudah son of R. Ilai saw them. He said to them: See what the difference is between you and the earlier ones! R. Akiva used to buy three different kinds of grain, each for the smallest unit of currency (= *perutah*), just to tithe each type [as tithing is only required on produce worth more than a *perutah*], whereas you bring your baskets in behind the roofs [to avoid tithing]!

R. Yehudah bar Ilai sees his son bringing produce to the roof to be able to eat from it without tithing. (Note: we read גגות, roofs, rather than גנות, gardens, per *mMa'as.* 3:6 and *bBer.* 35b.) R. Yehudah is disappointed. His own teacher, R. Akiva, would buy different kinds of grain to tithe more, while R. Yehudah's own son is trying to avoid tithing all together. Nonetheless, R. Yehudah does not prohibit the loophole. In fact, elsewhere in the *Yerushalmi*, there is explicit prescription for *ha'aramah* (albeit a different one) regarding tithing:

Yerushalmi Berakhot 5:1, 8d (MS Leiden)

רב ירמיה אמר לא יעמוד אדם ויתפלל אלא מתוך דין שלהלכה . . . תני ר' הושעיה מרבה אדם דגן בתבן ומערים עליו לפוטרו מן המעשרות[64]

R. Yirmiyah said: A person should stand for prayer only from [learning] a ruling of the law . . . R. Hoshayah taught: One (should? may?) increases one's grain with straw and act prudently to exempt it from tithes.

This passage is about the importance of learning Torah immediately prior to prayer. R. Yirmiyah states that one should study succinct legislation before prayer rather than more involved Torah discussion. The redactor(s) suggest the teaching of R. Hoshayah as such straightforward legislation: one may (should?) add straw to their grain to exempt it from tithing.

This circumvention engages a different aspect of the tithing requirement, that the grain be fully processed before requiring tithing. R. Hoshayah may be suggesting that one keep the wheat in its chaff so that it is not fully processed.[65] Alternatively, he may be suggesting that one add straw to fully processed grain, thus returning it to a less processed state.[66] Commentators argue over whether the purpose of this circumvention is to allow people to eat the grain without tithing it or to allow only animals to do so.[67] It is also unclear what warrants the use of legal circumvention in this case, but the Talmud presents it as settled law. Moreover, suggesting that one recite this passage prior to prayer casts this circumvention in a positive light. These two passages about dodging the requirement to tithe grain stand in tension with one another: should people avoid tithing or not?

Perhaps these two examples reflect different schools of thought in the *Yerushalmi* about the legitimacy of *ha'aramah*. Or perhaps they reference the responsibilities of different classes of people: the common person can use R. Hoshayah's leniency while rabbis should be more generous in their observance.[68] Alternatively, only those in financial need should avail themselves of circumvention, and R. Yose and his colleague were not in need. Regardless of how to resolve these two comments about tithing, they make clear that open loopholes may be used for virtue by some and for vice by others. Once they are open, they can be abused. It is hard to know the point when a loophole tips into improper use from proper use, such that authorities might try to close the loophole. Perhaps, so long as there are people whose need for a given loophole is virtuous, it may be unfair to close that loophole because of those who misuse it. Or, perhaps, vice versa.

Are "Legal Values" Internal or External to the Law?

Before concluding this chapter, I wish to address an important debate about legal values and Jewish law. These first two chapters named principles that are applicable to the legal system generally, such as saving money and avoiding sin. Moreover, some values are described in rabbinic texts as principles of the legal system itself. However, it is difficult, if not impossible, to truly determine internal or external origins: the extent to which rabbinic interpretation discovers what is in the text versus projecting the interpreters' own values onto the text. One cannot fully know why rabbinic texts emphasize certain principles as central to the law while downplaying others because the relationship between reader and text is always somewhat circular.[69] Additionally, it is unclear how much (different) rabbis see themselves as bringing values into the law because, as authoritative figures, this is their mandate. It is equally difficult to determine how much (different) rabbis require that values emerge from earlier legal corpora, and specifically the Bible, in order to be authoritative.

Scholars debate this question, especially in context of rabbinic revisions of biblical laws that seem to result from ethical considerations held by the generation of the rabbis themselves. For example, while the Bible describes the permission/mandate of parents to have their wayward son killed (Deut. 21:18–21), the rabbis narrow the applicability of this situation to such an extent that it is basically impossible to carry out.[70] Perhaps this change, though transformative, is not functionalist at all. They may have had traditions about these interpretations. Or their textual hermeneutics may simply force this reading from a technical standpoint. But it is also possible that the rabbis have functionalist goals relating to morality in narrowing the applicability of this law.[71]

And here is where an important debate begins: what is the source for morality that can allow the rabbis to read the wayward son case out of application? Some argue that the rabbis see the moral values pushing them to narrow the wayward son case as internal to the *halakhic* system: they are following God's own morality. Given that God is moral, the best legal interpretation of the law is one that respects the perfectly moral nature of its Author.[72] Others argue that the rabbis see their own authority as allowing them to revise the law (to a degree) based on their own moral concerns.[73]

I remain uncertain about the degree to which the rabbis saw such a clear distinction between internal and external values when it comes to the interpretation of law, especially in light of their understanding of the role of rabbinic authority in interpretation. As a result, when I refer to these principles or values as principles or values of the legal system, I do not mean to suggest that we know whether they arise purely from within the legal system or that the rabbis apply them to the legal system. I simply mean that these values are seen by the rabbis themselves as relevant to the application of Jewish law generally and not only in the instance at hand. As such, while they may not be the values of the particular law being circumvented, they may be considered principles of the rabbinically understood legal system as a whole.

Conclusion

This chapter examined the *Yerushalmi*'s contributions to the development of *ha'aramah*: texts therein make explicit some of the variables that determine when *ha'aramah* may be used. Some variables relate to the purpose for which the *ha'aramah* is being done, hearkening back to Chapter 1's analysis of *tannaitic* material, where values are paramount. One may use *ha'aramah* to avoid transgression or to save money, for example. But the *Yerushalmi* also contributes the procedural aspect to the *ha'aramah* debates: it is not only the goal of a *ha'aramah* but also its process that matters. Some laws are too weighty to evade, such as those written explicitly in the Bible; sometimes a circumvention hollows out an action too much, like betrothing people whom one may not marry. These procedural concerns also reflect reverence for the law as definitive for *ha'aramah*.

Additionally, a *Yerushalmi* text introduces for the first time the suggestion that a biblical text about the law being circumvented may be just what warrants the circumvention. This is a unique contribution that may manifest concerns about the legitimacy of *ha'aramah* in general.

In addition to making *ha'aramah*'s parameters explicit, the *Yerushalmi* also cites new examples of avoidance, evasion, and avoision, which implicitly suggest which purposes justify *ha'aramah* and which do not. Thus, one may not avoid one's legal obligations such as the laws of *ḥol ha-mo'ed* or ignore the rabbinic strategies for cooking on the festival for the Sabbath. One may not defraud the Temple treasury or exploit a creditor. On the other hand, one should (or may) consider using *ha'aramah* to save money or to ensure one's ability to celebrate the festival.

Beyond delineating and diversifying the parameters for *ha'aramah*'s use, the *Yerushalmi* contains text that openly suspects the misuse of *ha'aramah*. Some rabbis are also cited as lamenting the use of *ha'aramah* by the wrong people for the wrong ends. There are active attempts to prevent its misuse by being on the lookout for potential *ha'aramah*. When rabbis suspect wrongful use of *ha'aramah*, they may bar otherwise legitimate action. And yet, they recognize that shaping policy out of concern for possible *ha'aramah* may have negative consequences.

After investigating early Palestinian rabbinic discussions of *ha'aramah* in *Mishnah*, *Tosefta*, and the *Yerushalmi*, I will return in the coming chapter to the distinction between rabbinic and Roman approaches to legal dodges. Chapter 3 examines the contemporaneous (Greco-)Roman approach more closely and theorizes what the contrast between the rabbis and the Romans reveals about their respective understandings of their legal projects.

Chapter 3

Romans as Jurists, Rabbis as Lawyers

The first two chapters argue that the rabbis view *ha'aramah* as a mechanism that can be used well or poorly. This dual view differs from (Greco-)Roman rhetoric about technical legal loopholes similar to *ha'aramah* from around the same time. Contemporaneous with rabbinic discussions of *ha'aramah*, Roman jurists developed and articulated their own attitudes toward legal loopholing strategies. The contrast between Greco-Roman and rabbinic thought about legal dodges reflects how Roman jurists and rabbis understood their own roles within their legal frameworks.

Roman Approaches to Legal Circumventions

Roman treatment of legal circumventions is layered and evolved over time. For one thing, Roman jurisprudence is well known for its embrace of legal fiction as a strategy for circumventing law. While legislation was a foundational source of Roman law, in the second century BCE, a new source of law was introduced: the praetor was empowered to make new legal actions to supplement statute law, usually as a way of keeping law relevant and effective in light of changing economic and social realities. The praetor often introduced legal fictions, many of which were designed to change the standing of a litigant from one status to another, such as from alien to citizen, from possessor to owner, or from purchaser to heir. For example, through the *actio Serviana*, the praetor allowed one who had purchased goods from someone now deceased to have the rights of an heir to retrieve those goods: the purchaser could sue holders of the decedent's property, including those who owed the decedent money, to retrieve their purchase. Statute law gave the purchaser no such rights, but the legal fiction of treating him as an heir arrogated those rights to him.[1] This is one example among many. Moreover, Clifford Ando writes that he knows of no contested legal fiction in ancient Roman literature. He explains the embrace of fiction as a need of an expanding empire, which inevitably faced new economic, social, and even ecological realities that the early Roman legislators could never have envisioned. Fictions became a useful tool for traversing such gaps and manifested a constructivist approach to the power of legal language.[2]

Another well-known Roman circumvention is what later became known as "conversion." To uphold the validity of a transaction, sometimes jurists would transform one legal act into another. For example, a soldier may have intended to leave a will that conformed to certain requirements, such as witnesses' signatures, but died before it was completed. In such cases, rather than deeming the will invalid, the jurist would validate it as a different category of transaction, something known as a *testamentum militis* (soldier's testament), which had no formal requirements such as signatories. Thus, even though the soldier had intended to write a certain type of will and did fulfill its requirements, the court could "convert" it to a different form of transaction that would be valid.[3] Both legal fictions and the conversion method indicate that there was ample room in Roman legal thought and practice for the use of circumventions to change the outcome of a situation without new formal legislation.

However, when it comes to litigant loopholing that parallels the *ha'aramah* examples examined thus far, the classical period of Roman law (100 BCE–250 CE) yielded a growing distrust of relying upon the letter of the law over its intention. This marked a change from earlier jurisprudential thought. While there had long been an awareness of the gap between the wording (*verba* or *scriptum*) and the intention (*voluntas* or *sententia*) of a statute within Roman rhetorical tradition,[4] prior to the classical period, Roman interpretation of law tended to be narrowly literal. This left jurists less able to reject the use of loopholes without specific legislation against them.[5] As a result, legislators of the Roman Republic tried to write statutes that were as specific and comprehensive as possible, knowing that people could easily loophole if there were gaps in the letter of the law.[6]

The following are well-attested loopholing methods from ancient Rome:

(a) replacing prohibited transactions with nearly identical, but permitted, transactions, for example, a permissible gift and counter gift would replace a prohibited sale;
(b) engaging an *interposita persona*, a "straw person," who performs a transaction on behalf of someone who is legally barred from doing so;
(c) granting new legal status in name only, that is, without substantive change, for example, two people who are not domestic partners adopting marital status;[7] and
(d) removing oneself from a legal category to avoid the restrictions attendant thereto, for example, alienating some assets before tax season to move to a lower tax bracket.[8]

In the first century BCE, however, jurists begin to challenge the hegemony of a letter-of-the-law orientation to the interpretation of law. The *Causa Curiana* (92 BCE) served as a watershed case in which jurists chose to uphold the *intention* of a testator rather than the wording of his will. Coponius, a Roman citizen who died childless, had stipulated in his will that: (a) should he have a son, his son would inherit him; and (b) should his son die prior to adulthood, a man named Manius Curius would inherit him. When Coponius died childless, distant family members challenged Curius's claim to the inheritance. They argued their rights based on the wording of the will: Manius Curius was to inherit only in the event of the *death* of Coponius's son. But Coponius never had a son, so they argued that the arrangement was irrelevant. Curius's pleader, Cassus, defended Curius's rights to the inheritance with a speech that would become canonical within the annals of Roman legal thought. The crux of his message was that the testator's intention should take priority over the wording of the will. And the intention of the testator, he argued, was that Curius would inherit him if Coponius died with no son to inherit him. Cassus won, and the case was decided by the intention rather than the literal reading of Coponius's stipulation.[9]

Other jurists of that era likewise contested the dominance of fealty to the letter over the intention of the law: in his political and ethical treatise *De Officiis* (*On Duties*), the Roman lawyer, scholar, and statesman Cicero (106–43 BCE) writes that "summum ius summa iniuria" (lit. "more law, more injury"); that the extreme application of the literal law leads to injustice is a well-known adage.[10] Applying a literal interpretation rather than the most sensible interpretation of a statute could lead to immoral outcomes:

> Injustice often arises also through chicanery, that is, through an over-subtle and even fraudulent construction of the law. This it is that gave rise to the now familiar saying, "More law, less justice." Through such interpretation also a great deal of wrong is committed in transactions between state and state; thus, when a truce had been made with the enemy for thirty days, a famous general went to ravaging their fields by night, because, he said, the truce stipulated "days," not nights . . . Now that is swindling, not arbitration. And therefore, such sharp practice is under all circumstances to be avoided.[11]

In the first century CE, Roman jurists are recorded as rejecting the use of certain circumventions by litigants who came before them. For instance, when a twenty-year-old slave owner, too young to legally grant manumission, gave his slave as a gift to someone older to have him freed, Proculus invalidated the manumission, declaring that it constituted a "fraud on the law."[12] Roman legislators also did their part to close unwanted loopholes:[13] a senate decree under the Emperor Tiberius (14–37 CE) removed immunity from women who became procuresses or actresses to avoid punishment for adultery;[14] a senate decree in 62 CE declared that childless men could not avoid the political disadvantages attendant to their status by "adopting" children.[15]

But the approach to legal circumventions remained inconsistent. Some circumventions were still upheld.[16] Emperor Augustus (62 BCE–14 CE) legally enforced a circumvention known as the *fideicommissum*, first documented in 200 BCE. This workaround went as follows. According to Roman law, only Roman citizens could inherit a testator.[17] However, *fideicommissum* was a set of instructions that a testator could leave for his heir to grant property to non-family or to women.[18] While it had not been binding a century earlier, Augustus made the *fideicommissum* enforceable: if the heir refused to comply, the intended beneficiary could sue him to recover the property. Augustus also proposed a loophole to allow a slave to testify against his master in criminal cases: the slave should be sold to a state agent.[19] The emperor Tiberius (42 BCE–37 CE) later availed himself of this strategy to prosecute someone whom he believed to be conspiring against him.[20]

The second century of the Common Era—one century prior to the redaction of both *Mishnah* and *Tosefta*—marked the most sweeping change to formalistic Roman tendencies in interpreting and adjudicating the law. Considered the golden age of the Roman Republic and its most creative period in both writing and legal interpretation, ideas that had been germinating came of age.[21] Celsus (67–130 CE) defined Roman law by its moral values rather than by its posited law, declaring: *ius est ars boni et aequi*, "Law is the art of the good and the equitable."[22] He likewise asserted, "To know the laws is not to be familiar with their phraseology, but with their force and effect."[23] In other words, the mechanical enforcement of norms is not the sum total of what the law is. Regard must be given for the impact of applying the law.[24]

And it was during the second century that the Roman jurist Paul officially defined the concept of acting *in fraudem legis*.[25] His definition of acting *in fraudem legis* is "To do what the law prohibits violates the law, and anyone who evades the meaning of the law without disobeying its words, is guilty of fraud against it."[26] This concept marked further evolution in the Roman approach toward loopholes, from legislation to jurisprudence: instead of trying to write potential loopholes out of existence, recognition of actions done *in fraudem legis* empowered judges to use their discretion to close the loopholes that legislation had left open.[27] Consequently, in this century, jurists began using the categorization of *fraus legi* for adjudication rather than relying on legislators to close loopholes.[28]

The Roots of *Fraus Legi*: Greek Rhetoric of Equity

The concept of *fraus legi* was born of an assertion of the gap and even tension between the "letter" of a particular law and that law's "spirit," or intention. The Romans inherited this duality from Hellenistic rhetoric.[29] Among the Greeks, this dichotomy was not about circumventions per se but about the general relationship between law and justice. Though the distinction between letter and spirit was made most famous by Paul (2 Cor. 3:6; Rom. 7:6), Aristotle was among the earliest and most influential to discuss λόγος (word) and διάνοια (intention, meaning).[30] He understood that in exceptional cases where the letter of the law would lead to injustice, a judge must try to decide as the lawgiver himself would have decided rather than simply following the letter of existing law.[31] Aristotle referred to this as equity:

The source of the difficulty is that equity, though just, is not legal justice, but a rectification of legal justice. The reason for this is that law is always a general statement, yet there are cases which it is not possible to cover in a general statement. In matters therefore where, while it is necessary to speak in general terms, it is not possible to do so correctly, the law takes into consideration the majority of cases although it is not unaware of the error this involves. And this does not make it a wrong law; for the error is not in the law nor in the lawgiver but in the nature of the case: the material of the conduct is essentially irregular. When therefore the law lays down a general rule, and thereafter a case arises which is an exception to the rule, it is then right, where the lawgiver's pronouncement because of its absoluteness is defective and erroneous, to rectify the defect by deciding as the lawgiver would himself decide if he were present on the occasion and would have enacted if he had been cognizant of the case in question. Hence, while the equitable is just, and is superior to one sort of justice, it is not superior to absolute justice, but only the error due to its absolute statement. This is the essential nature of the equitable: it is a rectification of law where law is defective because of its generality.[32]

Because law is general and cannot anticipate every situation, there will be cases where the law, if applied, will necessarily cause injustice. Should the law still be applied to its letter in such circumstances? Aristotle says that it should not, and instead one should rule as the lawgiver would have ruled in such an exceptional case. He argues that one should do what will lead to the just outcome intended by the lawgiver, not simply what fulfills the existing statute. Aristotle assumes that the lawgiver would never have wanted the statute to apply in such a situation.[33] Greek rhetoricians furthered Aristotle's legacy by exploring the ῥητὸς καὶ διάνοια (spoken and intended) meaning of the law.[34]

The Roman rhetorician Quintilian (first century CE) cites early Greek rhetoricians in his *Institutes of Oratory* regarding this distinction.[35] He uses the Latin *scriptum* (written) and *voluntas* (will) or *sententia* (thought).[36] Roman rhetoricians engaged in legal dialectics, whereby each party had to advocate for a compelling reason to apply the letter or the intention of a statute. This activity was largely academic.[37] Nonetheless, Quintilian himself argues in favor of prioritizing the intention over the letter due to considerations of equity:

The majority of questions dealing with the *letter of the law* and *intention* are based on equity. (*Inst. Or.* III.6.43)

For every point of law, which is certain, is based either on written law or accepted custom: if, on the other hand, the point is doubtful, it must be examined in the light of equity. (*Inst. Or.* XII.3.6)[38]

What rhetoricians argued about for academic purposes, Roman jurists considered with regard to practical rulings. And the influence of Roman rhetoric on Roman law and procedure is well established.[39] For instance, Ulpian (later second century–early third century) uses the Greek rhetorical terminology of ῥητὸς καὶ διάνοια for juridical considerations: "Fraud is committed against the law when something is done which the law did not wish to be done but did not absolutely prohibit; and the difference between fraud against the law and violation of the same is that between ῥητὸς καὶ διάνοια."[40] Ultimately, the conflict between *scriptum* and *voluntas* became known as the conflict between *ius strictum* (strict justice) and *aequitas* (equity).[41]

No comprehensive study explains why Roman praetors and emperors tolerated certain "frauds on the law" and rejected others. Some suggest that they retained only those loopholes that were altruistic, fulfilling one's obligations to others.[42] Nonetheless, the overarching orientation of the classical period as distinct from its antecedents was to: (a) identify tension between the letter and the intention of the law; (b) favor the intention over the letter of the law; and (c) do so under the banner of equity—the just outcome that the lawgiver would have intended.

This approach implies that the formulation of statutes is an external cloak for the true essence of the law, the just aims of the lawgiver for regulating society. Thus, the letter of the law can undermine law's essence. How does this compare to rabbinic views?

Roman rhetorical and juridical rejection of the letter of the law as undermining its intentions stands in tension with rabbinic endorsement of *ha'aramah* to uphold the values of the legal system. Rather than dichotomizing law and viewing the letter as a threat or a hindrance to its intention, early rabbinic literature presents the letter of the law as a path to *upholding the very spirit* that the legal system should embody. That said, rabbis also recognize the dangers of *ha'aramah*, where the letter truly is used to undermine the spirit of the law. Nonetheless, as Roman legal rhetoric developed language to express the dangers of the letter of the law to its spirit—*fraus legi*—early rabbinic rhetoric developed language for a letter-of-the-law mechanism—*ha'aramah*—which carried both positive and negative connotations. And the rabbis endorsed its use in limited situations. Thus, the rabbinic establishment promoted the literal formulation of law as potentially redemptive.

To put the rabbinic approach into Roman terms: when it comes to the *voluntas* (will, intention, spirit) of the law, there are two registers: one local to the law in question and one more general to the legal system as a whole. While the letter of the law (*scriptum*) might undermine the intention of a particular law, it can simultaneously uphold the intentions and principles of the legal system more generally. Thus, the rabbis do not present *scriptum* and *voluntas* as primarily being in competition; instead, the *voluntas* of a particular law and the *voluntas* of the law generally jockey for dominance, and the *scriptum* might be the means for resolving the tension.

To be sure, there is at least one instance in which rabbis assert that using a letter-of-the-law orientation does in fact achieve the local intention of the law being circumvented: in the *Yerushalmi*, the rabbis justify circumventing the 25 percent redemption tax because the Torah itself declares that secondary tithing is meant to be a blessing. But generally, rabbis do not suggest that the intention of the local law being circumvented is upheld through *ha'aramah*. They are more likely to engage an intention or value from the broader legal system as the justification for using *ha'aramah*. This general approach aligns with Boaz Cohen's assertion that "paradoxically enough, the rabbis took deliberate advantage of the letter of the law to preserve its spirit . . . Often the rabbis resort to technicalities in interpretation."[43] But that was not only because the spirit of the law matters but because the *scriptum* of the law matters as well. However, the rabbis do have their limits: where the literal reading of the law undermines both the local and the global intentions of the law, they will not justify circumvention. Thus, there is a delicate balance between *scriptum* and *voluntas* in which both are valued.

Jurists or Lawyers?

The comparison between Roman and rabbinic legal cultures regarding loopholes yields both parallels and contrasts. On the one hand, both cultures developed terminology for letter-of-the-law loopholing around the same time, for the Romans, *fraus legi*, and for the rabbis, *ha'aramah*; additionally, both legal records evidence the retention of some loopholes and the rejection of others. Where the two cultures differ starkly, however, is in their express attitudes toward letter-of-the-law loopholes. The Romans develop rhetoric against such loopholing, and jurists reject the use of loopholes while legislators try to close them. Meanwhile, the rabbis introduce them as a mechanism that has the potential to manifest the spirit of the law, recognizing that they can be used well or poorly. Whether these similarities and differences reflect un/conscious interaction between the two cultures or simply a parallel development cannot be conclusively proven, but it certainly does highlight the peculiarity of the rabbinic stance.[44]

The rabbis choose to promote a mechanism that is both subversive and conservative at the same time. On the one hand, loopholes are subversive, in that they undermine the intention of a particular law. But on the other hand, they are conservative because even when the rabbis wish to uphold a value of the legal system, it must be done in a manner that adheres to the law's literal standards rather than overturning or legislating a new rule. Loopholing for positive ends appears to be a tool of those who recognize the need for legal change and exceptions but do not feel it possible or prudent to create new law whenever legal change is needed.

This conservatism is even more pronounced in the case of *takkanot* (rabbinic decrees) that use loopholing strategies. While *ha'aramah* is a term that usually covers more private scenarios (with possible exceptions such as *ma'aser sheni* and *bekhor* as discussed in Chapter 1), *takkanot* are clear expressions of rabbinic authority to make public policy enactments. However, these enactments often attempt to retain the form or the letter of the law even within a decree that changes the way the law is observed. For instance, the mechanism of *'eruv tavshilin* discussed in Chapter 2 does not simply permit people to cook on the festival day for the Sabbath. Instead, it attempts to redefine the prohibition of cooking on the festival for the Sabbath: do not *start* cooking on the festival day for the Sabbath. Start cooking the day before the festival and set aside the cooked food. Then the cooking on the festival for the Sabbath is not the beginning of the cooking but a continuation of it. And if one eats the cooked food (from before the festival), one may no longer cook on the festival for the Sabbath (*mBetzah* 2:1). In other words, the attempt is made to retain some of the original aspect of the prohibition of cooking on the festival for other days. Change is made through altering the facts of a scenario rather than officially changing a law on the books even where the rabbis are making an explicit *takkanah*.

This orientation toward manipulation of the law mirrors the role of lawyer rather than legislator or judge, even as rabbis are presented implicitly as adjudicating what to do in any given case of *ha'aramah*. This tracks theologically, as the rabbis may think of themselves more as lawyers arguing before God as the ultimate Judge and Legislator than as primarily judges or legislators themselves. Even when making legal change, rabbinic texts do not necessarily present rabbis as masters of the law but as legal practitioners who are bound by its statutes. The extent to which rabbis generally present themselves as lawyering rather than legislating or judging is debatable, but certainly the use of *ha'aramah* strongly reflects this orientation.[45] They use their understanding of the law—its rules and its values—to effect change.

A similar picture of rabbis as simultaneously judging and lawyering emerges from Richard Hidary's study of rabbinic judges as rhetors. On the one hand, rabbinic texts do not portray their courts as adversarial the way Greek and Roman courts were: rabbinic texts in fact forbid the use of lawyers in a courtroom.[46] Instead, judges were meant to hear the pleas and examine the witnesses themselves as in an inquisitorial model.[47] However, once the examination of witnesses was complete, the judges entered a deliberative stage among themselves. This stage of deliberation is described in *mSan.* 4:1–3 describes the judges as arguing different sides of the case against one another like lawyers would.[48] Even more strikingly, in capital punishment cases, deliberation protocols encouraged the judges specifically to argue on behalf of the defendant.[49] Thus, Hidary notes that the rabbinic court is described as both inquisitorial and adversarial.[50] The creativity needed to argue on behalf of the defendant in a capital crime perhaps led to a later rabbinic stipulation that a judge must be able to present a coherent argument based on Scripture itself that a reptile is ritually pure.[51] This would certainly be a rhetorical, lawyerly feat, given the plain declaration of Scripture that a reptile is ritually impure.[52]

In addition to the legal presentation of rabbinic judges as lawyering, both Hidary and Meira Kensky describe more homiletic (*aggadic*) rabbinic portraits of the Divine courtroom, where only God is the judge: the heavenly court is full of lawyers sometimes in the form of biblical characters who argue on behalf of the Jewish people.[53] Rabbinic tradition boasts a storied legacy of the role of an advocate and prosecutor in the heavenly court, beginning with biblical and Second Temple literature and continuing through *tannaitic* and *amoraic* material, as well as later *midrash*.[54] Hidary suggests that rabbis wanted advocates in the heavenly court "not in spite of the corruption . . . but precisely because of it. They feared that a heavenly court that followed strict justice and judged human actions according to the truth would issue impossibly harsh, even if justifiable, verdicts."[55] And Kensky points out that in the heavenly court, it was often God who was on trial for potential injustice against people rather than the reverse. Ironically, the human lawyer in the heavenly courtroom might prosecute God or at least call God to answer for possible injustice.[56] But rather than being considered disrespectful, Chapter 6 will show that this *midrashic* practice of lawyering with/against God constitutes a love language between God and the Jewish people.[57]

While much Roman juridical discourse about the letter of the law focused primarily on its threat to the law's integrity, rabbinic discourse included a more affirmative, even if mixed, character. Speaking more strictly as jurists and legislators, many Roman texts portray loopholes as deceptively exploiting the weaknesses of positive law, relying overly on form and validity over authenticity and truth. Rabbinic texts, however, present rabbinic authorities as both judges and advocates themselves for the average observant Jew: rabbis committed themselves to the letter of the law while attempting to use it to maintain both form and values. This approach will be further developed in Chapter 6 as a legal phenomenon that applies to other legal systems as well.

Conclusion

This chapter compared Roman and rabbinic views of letter-of-the-law circumventions. Inspired by Greek discourse about the tensions between the letter of the law and its intention, Roman legal thinkers emphasized the significance of the *voluntas* (will) of the law over its *scriptum* (literal meaning). In the second century CE, they even developed terminology for the problem of legal circumventions, *fraus legi*, in an evolving process of restricting or eliminating their use. Contemporaneously, the rabbis developed their own terminology for legal circumvention (*ha'aramah*) and constructed the relationship between the *scriptum* and the *voluntas* differently. They reflected an ideal of *voluntas* that is not about the local law being circumvented but about principles of the legal system as a whole. And they assessed *scriptum* itself as significant. Rather than presenting *scriptum* and *voluntas* as inherently threatening to one another, the rabbis suggest that sometimes *scriptum* can or should be used to attend to the general *voluntas* of the legal system. They championed these instances while being careful to maintain the legal system's respectability as a clear boundary.

While Roman texts betrayed the approach of a legislator or judge frustrated by the manipulation of the law, rabbinic texts reflect a lawyerly outlook: they are bound by the law but committed to advocating for their client to the extent possible. Rabbis were not just jurists or legislators; they were lawyers as well, with the Jewish people as their clients before God as the Judge. This accords both with the description of judgment in human-led rabbinical courts and with later portrayals of advocates in the heavenly court who twisted the law for the good of their client.

Previous chapters suggested how the rabbis would respond to the charge that legal circumventions undermine the law: the rabbis tried to limit the use of *ha'aramah* to those instances—of both ends and means—that would not disrespect the law but would uphold its virtues and integrity. This chapter suggests how such technical legal choreography may be considered valuable, given its craftiness. After all, it works to balance the technical continuity of a system while aiding clients who may be negatively impacted by that system.

These first three chapters have mapped out an overall early rabbinic approach to *ha'aramah*, which paints a picture of Jewish law and the rabbis' place within it. But the examples of *ha'aramah* examined thus far are not all the same: some appear closer to the classic legal loophole while others appear more like the classic legal fiction. The next chapter will delve further into the more fiction-like loopholes, suggesting that this subset reveals yet another dimension of rabbinic thinking about law and about legal subjects.

Chapter 4

Ha'aramah and Intention

Thus far, I have explored the rabbis' multipronged approach to *ha'aramah* and their own role as lawyering on behalf of the Jewish people. Rather than essentializing a dichotomy between the letter of the law and its spirit, the rabbis attempted to integrate the letter of the law and the spirit of the legal system. Thus, they sought *ha'aramah* as a means of circumventing Jewish law within parameters that could still be considered respectful of it. But they rejected circumvention where such harmonization was not possible.

Our analysis has not yet delved into distinctions between different types of *ha'aramah*. In this chapter, however, we will more closely examine how different types of *ha'aramah* work. As outlined in the Introduction, *ha'aramah* does not always entail the alteration of external, empirical facts. Sometimes it entails the alteration of intention. For instance, one may lift livestock from a pit on a festival if one has the intention to slaughter it. This type of *ha'aramah* has left scholars puzzled. Is this change in intention "true," or is it a legal fiction? Earlier scholars understood this type of *ha'aramah* as fiction-like;[1] some suggested that it is effective either because intention does not matter as much as action[2] or because one cannot truly know a person's intentions.[3] I take issue with this analysis. Rather than viewing *ha'aramah* of intentions as fictional, I argue that *ha'aramah* of intentions sheds light on a more ritualized and externalized possibility of what intentions mean, especially in early rabbinic jurisprudence.

I suggest that the rabbis offer the ritualization of intention as scaffolding for one's actions rather than as a reflection of one's internal subjective state. This may indicate that the rabbis understood intentionality along a sliding scale from highly personal and subjective to an objective performance akin to physical activity. Sometimes they employ a more performative version while at other times they require the more subjective intentionality. This aspect of *ha'aramah* has greater depth when understood in the context of contemporary scholarship about the degree to which the rabbis adopted Stoic understandings of the subjective self.

To begin the analysis of *ha'aramah* of intention, let us return to the livestock that fell into a pit on the festival:

Tosefta Betzah 3:2 (MS Vienna)[4]

אותו ואת בנו שנפלו לבור ר' אליעזר אומ' מעלה את הראשון על מנת לשוחטו
ואינו שוחטו והשיני עושה לו פרנסה במקומו בשביל שלא ימות ר' יהושע אומ'
מעלה את הראשון על מנת לשוחטו ואינו שוחטו ומערים ומעלה את השיני רצה
שלא לשחוט את אחד מהם הרשות בידו

An animal and its offspring which fell into a pit: R. Eliezer says, "One raises up the first on condition to slaughter it but does not slaughter it, and, for the second, one provides food while it is in its present location, so that it does not die." R. Yehoshua says, "One raises up the first on condition to slaughter it, but does not slaughter it, and, acting prudently, one then raises up the second. [If] he wants to slaughter neither one of them, he has the right [to refrain]."

To recapitulate: R. Eliezer says the owner can save only one of the animals whereas R. Yehoshua is willing to employ more human ingenuity to prevent loss. He sanctions what appears to be a new variation of *ha'aramah*, somewhat different in method from the *mishnaic* example of avoiding the *ma'aser sheni* tax through an *interposita persona*. Rather than changing the external, empirical facts of a case (e.g., alienating one's ownership of money or goods), this *ha'aramah* (ostensibly) concerns an internal, unverifiable element: one's intended purpose in performing an action. In this situation, *ha'aramah* entails (re)defining an action or object by having the "right intention," that is, an intention that can define one's actions as legal.

"Raise one up to slaughter it, but do not slaughter it; raise the other, but do not slaughter it." Why and how does this work? R. Yehoshua's ruling seems an obvious fiction. Most versions of R. Yehoshua's opinion present a definitive purpose for raising both the first and the second animal from the pit, namely, על מנת לשחוט ("*in order* to slaughter"), yet sincerity is improbable, given the owner's ultimate objective of saving the animals. Perhaps this explains why R. Yehoshua does not use the term *kavvanah* (intention), generally used to denote mental processes regarding Sabbath (and, by extension, festival) law, or *maḥshavah* (plan), the rabbinic term for one's intended plans for an object.[5] In fact, R. Yehoshua himself elsewhere advocates for the need for intention as mens rea in defining sin.[6] Perhaps in this case, he is not referring to one's subjective intention to slaughter. In fact, according to versions in both the *Tosefta* and *Yerushalmi*, R. Yehoshua does not require that either animal ultimately be slaughtered.[7] But *yPes.* 3:3, 30a (MS Leiden) offers the most radical version of this position:

ר' יושוע או' יעלה את הראשון על מנת לשחוט ולא ישחוט ויערים ויעלה את השיני א'ע'פ שחישב שלא לשחוט אחד מהן מותר

R. Yehoshua says: Raise up the first on condition to slaughter it, but do not slaughter it; and act prudently and bring up the second. Even if one planned not to slaughter either of them, it is permitted.

The word *ḥishev* (חישב) generally carries the connotation of *planning* in rabbinic literature.[8] According to the simplest reading of the passage, R. Yehoshua means that one may retrieve both animals "in order to slaughter" them even though one has no plan to slaughter either of them. While one may be raising the animal "on condition" to slaughter it, one's *maḥshavah*, that is, one's inner subjective plans, remains otherwise.[9]

Scholars have offered explanations for this version of *ha'aramah*, all of which leave something wanting. Samuel Atlas, for instance, downplays the role of intention in Jewish law: "One is using it to follow the law and *only* [emphasis added] transgresses in thought."[10] This position indicates that intention is not as important as action, and thus it may be falsified in this case.[11] Others emphasize the possibility of sincere intentions: because intention cannot be conclusively proven, it is *possible* that the person really wants to eat one of the animals, and R. Yehoshua uses this ambiguity to the animal owner's benefit.[12] Mere potential for one's intention to be genuine is sufficient in the eyes of the law. Both explanations—intention as less important and intention as ambiguous—do not satisfy. After all, these may be reasons not to prosecute after the fact, but they are hardly what judges or legislators should encourage beforehand.

Living in a Social World: *Mar'it 'Ayin*

Another explanation is that the falsified intention is a cover-up for the creation of an exception to the rule. Maybe *ha'aramah* of intention is simply about tricking potential onlookers. If so, R. Yehoshua is being conservative rather than innovative: one is indeed exempt from the laws of *muktzeh* where financial loss (or animal pain) ensues. Therefore, one should be permitted to retrieve the animal directly and with no ruse at all. And, in an ideal world, anyone who sees this will understand that this act is a justifiable exception. However, the world is less than ideal. In actuality, people are likely to misunderstand what they see or become lax because of one exception and start looking for reasons to override *muktzeh* where there is no justification for doing so. So, the owner must hide in plain sight by using *ha'aramah* and making people think that nothing exceptional is happening. *Ha'aramah*, then, is not about circumventing the law but about keeping leniencies private.[13] This approach replicates the rabbinic concern for what is known as *mar'it 'ayin*, the appearance of sin, even where no sin is committed.[14]

This explanation neutralizes any concerns about false intentions because the intention is only for show. And perhaps the condition of "in order to slaughter" indicates an audience. Who is one trying to convince? Oneself? God? An onlooker? A judge? Yet, this approach also has weaknesses. First, the term *mar'it 'ayin* appears at least eight times in the *Tosefta* and could easily have been mentioned with regard to *ha'aramah*, yet it is absent.[15] Second, *ha'aramah* does not read like a *mar'it 'ayin* case. *Mar'it 'ayin* is generally introduced in the following manner: X is permissible, but the rabbis forbade it due to *mar'it 'ayin*. For example:

Tosefta Yoma 4:1 (MS Vienna)

יום הכפורים אסור באכילה ובשתיה ברחיצה ובסיכה בנעילת הסנדל בתשמיש המטה אפי' באנפיליא של בגד קטנים מותרין בכולן ואסורין בנעילת הסנדל מפני מראית העין

On the Day of Atonement, it is forbidden to eat, drink, bathe, anoint, put on sandals, [and] have sexual relations. It is not permitted to put on even felt shoes. Minors are permitted to do all of them except putting on sandals, for appearance's sake.[16]

In this case, children may do any of the activities prohibited to adults on the Day of Atonement, but they may not wear leather shoes because of how it looks.[17] Action X is permitted in principle but then outlawed due to *mar'it 'ayin*. A phrase that encapsulates the prohibitive nature of *mar'it 'ayin* is found in *mKilayim* 3:5—כל מה שאסרו חכמים לא גזרו אלא מפני מראית העין, "All that the sages prohibited [here] is because of appearance to the eye." *Ha'aramah*, on the other hand, is presented as permissive in most cases: someone is stuck in a difficult situation and therefore may or should use *ha'aramah* to accomplish X. In other words, *ha'aramah* is presented as offering leniency while *mar'it 'ayin* is presented as a restriction. And in the case at hand, R. Yehoshua's *ha'aramah* is offered as the lenient position, in contrast with R. Eliezer's stricter position.[18]

And third, if *ha'aramah* is about being stricter than the law requires in principle (i.e., an additional requirement to convince onlookers), then the term *ha'aramah*, as it is used in rabbinic literature, has two completely different definitions: (a) changing the facts of a case in order to circumvent a law, and (b) putting on a good show so that witnesses do not realize that one is acting on an exception to the law. To be sure, legal terms are not always used consistently in the rabbinic canon, but the *mar'it 'ayin* analysis places the two basic uses of the term *ha'aramah* at odds with one other. The loophole version of *ha'aramah* obviates the need for an exception to the general rule while the cover-up version of *ha'aramah* implies an exception to the general rule that must be hidden. Hence, a loophole *ha'aramah* would be a leniency while a cover-up *ha'aramah* would be a stringency.

Living in a Social World: Ritual and Sincerity

Rather than suggesting that *ha'aramah* downplays intention, relies on the ambiguity of intention, or is just a smoke screen, perhaps there is a fourth possibility: that intention need not always be defined by internal subjectivity. Intention can be a constructed performance in the same way that physical actions are. If so, this type of *ha'aramah* is about constructing the proper intention rather than feeling that intention subjectively.

To understand this suggestion, I turn to the writing of Adam Seligman. Seligman advances the opposition between the "ritual self" and the "sincere self." Ritual is "not necessarily concerned with what we term sincerity" and is not simply "the nonessential husk of something else that is 'more' real (the visible sign of an invisible grace, as it were)."[19] Rather, the performance of ritual is a world of construction in which one is defined by outward performance. The world of ritual is social, interactive, shared.[20] This contrasts with the "sincere" model of self, which downplays social convention and emphasizes instead "individual soul-searching."

What if intention can be ritualized? Perhaps when one raises each animal "in order" to slaughter it and then "changes" one's mind, the criterion for intention is more outward than inward; the decision is not about what is in one's heart of hearts but about the intention one actively (and perhaps even externally) binds to the action.[21] Rather than suggest that *ha'aramah* works because the person is *merely* transgressing in thought, perhaps *ha'aramah* offers a different perspective on what legal intentionality is or can be for the early rabbis. Whereas Atlas claims that intention is not present, I suggest that intention is present but in a ritualized fashion. Intention may be more mechanical than organic: it defines the action rather than the actor. Whether or not *kavvanah* usually refers to performative intention, in the case of *ha'aramah*, where one actively seeks to avoid outright transgression, this is the type of intention (some) rabbis are looking for. After all, this performative intention constitutes a recognition of the law and thus may be sufficient for the purpose of avoiding sin.[22]

Deemphasizing subjectivity fits the way *ha'aramah* cases are generally described: the scenarios do not discuss the subjective feelings of the animal owner about potentially losing money. Instead, they describe the objective characteristics of the situation: animals have fallen into a pit, creating the potential for loss, with no mention of how the animal's owner feels. The situation is described from a more "objective" standpoint. Understanding this type of *ha'aramah as* performative intention rather than obstructing an onlooker's view also makes it more parallel to the other type of *ha'aramah*. There are two subsets of *ha'aramah*: those that use the mechanisms of general loopholing—for example, bringing a new party into a transaction—and those by which proper intentions are performed. In the loopholing type of *ha'aramah*, one changes a situation concretely to permit something that is otherwise forbidden. In performative intention *ha'aramah*, one likewise changes a situation concretely by ritualizing new intentions to permit something that is otherwise forbidden.

Thus, both types of *ha'aramah* accept a deeply performative view of reality. Consider the first example of loopholing *ha'aramah* in Chapter 1: avoiding the 25 percent redemption tax of *ma'aser sheni* by using an *interposita persona*. When the owner of the produce hands another adult money to redeem his produce, the fact that internally, subjectively, the owner of the produce is trying to get around the tax does not take center stage. Instead, once the rabbis determine that the use of the loophole is warranted, the performed actions matter most. The same is true for *ha'aramah* of performed intentions: once the rabbis determine that *ha'aramah* is justified, the performance of the right intentions is what matters. At their core, both types of *ha'aramah* rely upon performance rather than internal feeling. It is just that *ha'aramah* of intention is specific to those areas of Jewish law in which intention plays a definitive role, such as Sabbath/festivals and ritual purity law.[23] Because the two types of *ha'aramah* are indeed similar, neither the *Tosefta* nor the *Yerushalmi* makes any explicit distinctions between them. They are cut from the same conceptual cloth.

Intention in General

Some argue that *ha'aramah* is not an outlier at all. Rather, it reflects what the rabbis mean by *kavvanah* and *mahshavah* in general.[24] R. Yehoshua's only innovation is that he is willing to push this kind of construction to its limits. Ishay Rosen-Zvi has argued that rabbinic legal notions of intention as described in the *Mishnah* betray a notion of the self more related to performance than to unknowable subjectivity. He bases his thesis on the fact that *kavvanah* is consistently defined in the *Mishnah* with reference to external activity, such as the recitation of the *shema* or the blowing of the *shofar*. Likewise, the categories of *mahshavah* (plan) and *ratzon* (desire/will) in the realm of purity law indicate that the chief function of intention is to qualify and to define outward action. Additionally, *tannaitic halakhah* for the most part does not concern itself with thought or will that does not relate to action. Thus, he concludes that "the subject . . . formed by rabbinic *halakhah* is flat; its thoughts and deeds are on the same plane. There is no inner world which is fundamentally different from the outer one."[25]

Rosen-Zvi is correct that intention, as discussed in the *Mishnah*, is not personal or intimate. Regarding *shema*, for instance, there is clearly a requirement (*mBer.* 2:1) to read with the intention of fulfilling the commandment of reciting the *shema*, but there is no discussion of a requirement to understand or to identify oneself with the content of what one is reading.[26] This understanding of intention parallels the concreteness of rabbinic views of other concepts as well, such as time. Rather than viewing time as "a reified abstraction" or "an entity that flows on its own, independently from the rest of reality" as the Greeks did, the rabbis (following most ancient Near Eastern cultures) viewed time as "concrete, embedded, and process-linked." This explains why the rabbis often reference time in terms of human activity or natural phenomena such as when the sun sets or when the priests eat their *terumah* (*mBer.* 1:1).[27]

For Rosen-Zvi, the understanding of the self reflected in early rabbinic legal discourse diverges from contemporaneous cultures, specifically the Stoics and the early Christians.[28] Unlike Stoics and Christians, the rabbis did not perceive action and intention as existing in two different realms; both were more performative than subjective:[29]

> And so, while a mental world does indeed appear in the *Mishnah*, it is markedly different from the Hellenistic one. There is no "inner person", a soul or logos that stands in contrast to "external" parts of "me" such as my body or my appetites, as in Plato or Paul. The *Mishnah* does not feature a self that thinks itself into being, as in the Stoic asceticism studied by Pierre Hadot, or a confessional Christian self, celebrated by Foucault and Peter Brown as the birth of the subject. The Mishnaic truth cannot be found by looking inwards—as in Augustine—and there is no hidden "inner truth", known only to "me", of the type which created the modern radical dichotomy between inside and out, whether in the Cartesian rationalist cogito or in the Lockean empiricist camera obscura. The mental world discussed above is a far cry from all these inner realms. It is a simple world that merely replicates the outer one and is subject to its rules. This mental realm is built as part of the halakhic world and at its service: "thought" creates piggul, "will" fosters impurity, and "intention" is a requisite of prayer. The inner world is not one of truth and lies, as in Plato or Paul, but of commandments and prohibitions. This seems crucial to decoding the nature of the Mishnaic inner world. If it were a Platonic inner world, radically different from the outer one, law could not penetrate it. It would have been substantially different from the world of action, and halakhic logic would not apply to it. This is inconceivable for the rabbis. It is not simply a matter of style, thus, but of the most basic halakhic conceptualization of the world.[30]

This rabbinic legal definition of selfhood and intention justifies how and why *ha'aramah* of performative intentions could be viable. If intention and selfhood are truly continuous with external action, one might reasonably fashion an intention that defines an action as licit even if one's most subjective inner thoughts about that action are otherwise.

While Rosen-Zvi's observation about intention and action is illuminating, one need not accept such a rigid view of intention as solely internalized action to explain this type of *ha'aramah*. It is possible to understand intention on a continuum between the more subjective and the more performed, and *ha'aramah* is a situation in which the more performed intention is suitable. Understanding this sliding scale may be useful for explaining why rabbinic literature consistently rejects the use of *ha'aramah* in cases involving ritual impurity.

As mentioned in Chapter 1, human intention plays an important role in ritual purity law by defining everything from food to clothing to vessels and furniture, and more.[31] For instance, a food item or a crafted object might only be considered susceptible to ritual impurity if the one processing or crafting it plans to use it as is. Thus, one may be tempted to use performative intention *ha'aramah* by performing one's intention to plan to process a food item further or continue working on the vessel to prevent it from becoming susceptible to impurity. However, throughout *tannaitic* literature, the rabbis insist that *ha'aramah* has no effect. Let us return to the example from Chapter 1 to illustrate this phenomenon:

Tosefta Kelim Metzi'a 5:9 (MS Vienna)[32]

... כלי נצרין שלא קינבן ומשתמש בהן עראי טמאין היה עתיד לחסם ולקנב אע'פ שהוא משתמש בהן עראי ומשליכן טהורין ובלבד שלא יערים ואם הערים הרי אילו טמאין

... Vessels of twigs which one has not smoothed out, and which one uses at random are susceptible to impurity. If one planned to make a rim and to smooth it (= the rim), even though one may [nonetheless] make use of them at random and throw them away, they are unsusceptible to impurity. And [this rule applies] solely [on condition that] one not commit subterfuge. But if one did commit subterfuge, these are susceptible to impurity.

To recapitulate: this passage defines at what point a certain type of receptacle becomes a vessel from the perspective of Jewish law, such that it can contract ritual impurity. The reason to prevent one's vessels from contracting ritual impurity during Temple times would be particularly strong if one wished to keep pure certain foods, such as the priestly gift of *terumah* (heave offering), which could only be eaten in that state. Even after the fall of the Temple, one might wish to prevent food receptacles from becoming susceptible to impurity if one took on the voluntary practice of only eating one's foods in a state of purity. As mentioned above, after the fall of the Temple, there was a group of people known as *ḥaverim* who took on such a practice—commemorating the centrality of purity law for the Temple and for priests in particular.

In this case, someone crafting a basket can decide when the item becomes a vessel for the purposes of contracting impurity. Because people could use twig baskets either with a smooth rim or without one, if the basket weaver intends to make such a rim, an unrimmed basket is considered incomplete and is therefore not susceptible to ritual impurity. But if the basket weaver does not intend to make a rim, once the rest of the basket is crafted, even without the rim, it is considered a vessel and its contents are susceptible to ritual impurity. If priestly food became impure, it could not be eaten. And after the Temple, if the food of a *ḥaver* became impure, the *ḥaver* would not eat it. To avoid susceptibility to impurity, the basket weaver might use *ha'aramah* by constructing an intention to make a rim without any "true" subjective intention to do so. But the passage rejects this option. In no fewer than five cases—all related to intention-oriented *ha'aramah* to circumvent (susceptibility to) ritual impurity—the *Tosefta* rejects its use.

While one might explain why *ha'aramah* may be rejected in this or that case of ritual purity law, the carte blanche rejection of *ha'aramah* (labeled as such) in all ritual impurity cases is inconsistent with the rest of the *tannaitic* canon. It calls for explanation. I suggested in Chapter 1 that perhaps rabbinic strictness in this arena is animated by the potential (and actual) atrophy of purity law in the rabbis' own day. I also considered the possibility that the rabbis viewed ritual impurity as primarily "realistic," that is, as an immanent, naturalistic force, even though they also had nominalistic tendencies of emphasizing the role of human intention and awareness in shaping this area of Jewish law.[33] If impurity is primarily a force in nature that exists beyond the mind, perhaps it follows that even when impurity depends upon human intentions, performative intentions are insufficient to override the primary realist conception.[34]

However, in light of the discussion about how subjective or objective intention might be, here we might consider a third alternative. Perhaps ritual purity law specifically requires subjective intention not to combat the quasi-physical force of impurity but because the rabbis understood im/purity law as about the creation of a subjective self. Balberg argues that rabbinic ritual purity law exemplifies just the kind of Stoic subjective understanding of the self that Rosen-Zvi rejects. She argues that the centrality of *maḥshavah* (human intention, planning) and *ratzon* (human will) in defining ritual im/purity emerges from the gradual recomposition of ritual purity law from being mostly about the Temple and the community to focusing on the individual self.[35] Balberg sees ritual purity law as emphasizing the essential role that the subjective self must play in defining one's surroundings. She argues that it is precisely the internal awareness of individuals that defines what can and cannot become ritually impure:

> One must have personal stakes in the object in question in order to make it susceptible to impurity. Only an owner who decides to use an artifact, that is, who is personally interested in the durability, function, and performance of this artifact, can deem an artifact susceptible to impurity; only one who decides to consume some substance as food, and for whom thereby the smell, taste, texture, and so on of this substance make a difference, can deem it susceptible to impurity; and similarly, only body parts that humans identify with themselves, of which they are cognizant and aware, can partake in the realm of impurity. The rendition of an object as susceptible to impurity effectively means allowing this object to make a difference in the ritual sphere: a difference in the purity status of humans and objects that come into contact with it, and a difference in the way in which it is approached and handled in the course of everyday activities. By incorporating thought and intention into the determination of an object as susceptible to impurity, the rabbis put forth the notion that for an object to make a difference in the realm of purity and impurity, it must first of all make a difference to its owner on a day-to-day basis, that is, its owner must be invested in this object's existence and in its condition. According to the rabbinic

view, then, an object about which one does not care, which is inconsequential for its owner as a usable tool or as edible food, is by necessity also inconsequential in terms of purity and impurity.[36]

She notes that this is a major transformation from the biblical materials about ritual impurity, which do not engage questions of will or intention. Even beyond the role of intention in defining susceptibility to ritual impurity, Balberg sees ritual purity law as helping one fashion oneself into a subject. Specifically, one must constantly be vigilant to avoid becoming ritually impure.[37] This kind of ongoing attentiveness, or "mental dedication to the pursuit of purity," is part of molding oneself as a person who is dedicated to the all-encompassing nature of Jewish law. She compares this ongoing discipline to the Stoic ethical ideal of *askesis*, or self-training.[38]

Balberg's understanding of the role of subjectivity in ritual purity law explains that *ha'aramah* of performed intention cannot circumvent impurity. In ritual purity law, subjectivity matters, and performed intentions are insufficient. This may break down in the binary of whether the early rabbis understood the self as subjective. While Rosen-Zvi argues for an all-encompassing flattening of the subjective, Balberg points to an arena in which awareness appears more subjective. There are also those whose thesis about subjectivity is more expansive than Balberg's. Joshua Levinson, for example, cites the role of *kavvanah* in early rabbinic literature as indicating that subjectivity and "the reflective" self are essential to all of Jewish law.[39] However, perhaps one need not apply either of these poles to all legal arenas. Rather than accept all-encompassing views, maybe early rabbinic views of intentionality exist on a spectrum from the ritualized to the subjective.

Perhaps the question is not whether the rabbis understood the "inner self" concept but simply what role the inner self was meant to play in different legal situations. For the rabbis, action and thought are on a continuum, but the balance tips toward the internal in the realm of ritual im/purity law and toward the external in Sabbath and festival law. Alternatively, perhaps the notion of intention-oriented *ha'aramah* itself suggests that the rabbis view intention on a spectrum between the sincere and the performative, and it is the scenario that determines the kind of intention required. Thus, ideally, full subjectivity is generally required, but in a case that warrants a circumvention for reasons of preserving important principles and values, performative intention is enough.

Conclusion

This chapter presented a thesis about how *ha'aramah* of intention works. Such *ha'aramah* does not downplay the importance of intentionality but rather defines intention in a way that moderns may not always recognize. Consonant with the distinction between the "sincere self" and the "ritual self," *ha'aramah* offers a ritualized version of intention: one that is performed for the sake of defining action rather than reflecting the intimate truth known only to the person wielding that intention. This does not mean that the intention is insincere in the sense of being false; it simply means that legal intention need not be based on what is in a person's heart of hearts but by the purpose one chooses to bind to an action. This understanding of intention *ha'aramah* renders it parallel to the other type of *ha'aramah*, where one changes the external facts of a scenario, which then modifies the legal requirements or outcomes.

This understanding of intention may not be unique to *ha'aramah* but is perhaps an aspect of how the rabbis understand intention generally. In the ongoing debate between Mira Balberg, Joshua Levinson, and Ishay Rosen-Zvi over the extent to which the rabbis recognized the sincere, subjective self, I suggested that perhaps the rabbis are inconsistent in their definitions of intentionality.[40] They allow for a spectrum from the performative to the subjective. This may explain, for instance, why the rabbis always reject intention-based *ha'aramah* in *toseftan* cases of ritual impurity, as it may be an arena in which intention requires genuine subjectivity. In cases such as those of Sabbath and festival law, however, intention may be performative. It is also possible that intention should usually be subjective, but when *ha'aramah* is warranted, performed intention is sufficient.

The following chapter tracks what becomes of performative intention *ha'aramah* in the Babylonian Talmud, perceiving a repositioning of intention at the more subjective/sincere side of the spectrum.

Chapter 5

Ha'aramah in the *Bavli*
Discomfort with Ritualized Intention

The previous chapter discussed how intention-oriented *ha'aramah* works. I posited that this type of *ha'aramah* allows for ritualizing intention. The Babylonian Talmud, known as the *Bavli*, depicts a starkly different approach to this type of *ha'aramah*—and even sometimes to the first type of *ha'aramah*—than do the Palestinian materials. Throughout the *Bavli*, one finds increased emphasis on the "sincere self": one's external actions should not betray one's inner subjective intention to evade the law. In this chapter, I outline the various indicators and dimensions of this shift and offer three interrelated suggestions to account for it. I argue first that rabbinic ideas about intention evolved during this period to a more consistently subjective requirement. This may be a matter of philosophical evolution within rabbinic thought itself or may relate to ambient Zoroastrian and/or Christian ideas of the time about the centrality of intention and inner thought. Second, I discuss this orientation to *ha'aramah* in the context of general discomfort among later Babylonian *amoraim* with gaps between law and truth. And lastly, I discuss how the first two concerns explain a third dimension, which is attested to explicitly in the *Bavli*: the rabbis worry that *ha'aramah* will lead to a decline in observance of the law.

Ha'aramah: General Differences Between the Two Talmuds

Before concentrating on the *Bavli*'s increased focus on subjectivity in the context of *ha'aramah*, here are a few general findings about the *Bavli*'s treatment of *ha'aramah*. First, the parameters for when *ha'aramah* may be used generally mirror those of the *Yerushalmi*: though not identical to the *Yerushalmi*'s guidelines, the *Bavli* offers its own variations on: (a) avoiding sin, (b) saving money, and (c) limiting *ha'aramah* to the circumvention of a less severe law rather than a more severe law.[1] That said, the *Bavli* does focus more on using *ha'aramah* to avoid sinful behavior than to save money.[2] This is evident through new examples of *ha'aramah* as avoidance of some other direct sin (e.g., *bShab.* 65b) but also in the ways the *Bavli* redactors analyze R. Yehoshua's position in the animal/offspring pair case: the justification of the *ha'aramah* is avoiding the sin of causing the animal pain rather than saving the owner money (*bShab.* 117b). This indicates increased strictness for the parameters of what justifies *ha'aramah*. The *Bavli* also questions whether a given *ha'aramah* is necessary; might one accomplish the same goal without it?[3] If the rabbis do not permit *ha'aramah*, will the person in this bind do something worse, like commit an outright infraction?[4]

But the most obvious and consistent difference between the two Talmuds is that the *Bavli* uses *ha'aramah* terminology for loopholing less often than the *Yerushalmi* does, including not mentioning suspicion of *ha'aramah* unless it is clear and present.[5] Considering their respective lengths, the fact that the two Talmuds contain practically the same number of distinct *ha'aramah* circumvention cases stands out.[6] Sometimes the absence of *ha'aramah* is terminological: the *Bavli* describes circumventions but does not use the label "*ha'aramah*."[7] But sometimes the *Bavli* omits the circumvention phenomenon completely in its analysis.[8] Examining parallel passages within the *Yerushalmi* and the *Bavli*, where the latter does not use *ha'aramah* terminology at all to probe the same legal scenarios, is telling, though one cannot know conclusively whether the *amoraim* and redactors were aware of the Palestinian sources and consciously decided to depart from them.[9]

There are various ways to read the relative paucity of *ha'aramah* terminology in the *Bavli*. The first is to understand it simply as a change in nomenclature. While Roman jurists and Palestinian rabbis were preoccupied with classifying the phenomenon they called *fraus legi* and *ha'aramah*, respectively, perhaps for the Babylonian *amoraim* and redactors, circumvention was integrated enough into the legal machinery that it no longer warranted explicit terminology. And yet, in some instances, the pivot moves beyond terminology. Instead, it indicates rabbinic desire to narrow the use of *ha'aramah*. This is most obvious in the *Bavli* regarding the *ha'aramah* of performative intention. Thus, there may be two developments in the *Bavli* that stand in tension with one another: an increased comfort with the use of one type of *ha'aramah* and a decreased comfort with the use of another type, that is, performative intention *ha'aramah*.

Obvious Ruses

Unlike Palestinian rabbinic literature, the *Bavli* explicitly challenges the use of *ha'aramah* when there is a clear gap between one's performed intentions and one's subjective intentions. The following example illustrates negotiating this gap. The case relates to setting up a strainer to filter wine on the festival. Setting up a strainer is likely prohibited on a festival day because it looks too much like a weekday activity.[10] However, using a strainer to strain wine for the holiday if it has already been set up in a legally acceptable way is permissible:

Bavli Shabbat 139b (MS Munich)

אמ' רבה בר רב הונא מערים אדם על המשמרת ביום טוב לתלות בה (ל)רמונים ות[ו][ל]לה בה שמרים[11] אמ' רב אשי והוא שתלה בה רמונים

Rabbah b. R. Huna said: One may circumvent [the law by placing] a strainer [on a barrel] on the festival day to place pomegranates there, and place dregs there [instead]. R. Ashi said: And that is [only] if he [actually] places pomegranates there.

Rabbah b. R. Huna offers a way around the problem of setting up the strainer: set up the strainer "in order to" hold pomegranates, that is, as a basket of sorts rather than a strainer. Creating a resting place for pomegranates on the festival is acceptable. Once the strainer is set up this way, one may then use this "pomegranate holder" to filter wine. This is a typical case where performative intention should be sufficient, presumably whether or not one actually places any pomegranates there. R. Ashi, however, deems the mere ritualization of intention insufficient. He insists that one "prove" their intention to fashion a resting place for the pomegranates by first using the strainer to hold pomegranates before using it to filter the wine. Only once one has used it for its "original purpose" of holding pomegranates may one use it for this "secondary" purpose of filtering wine. In other words, one cannot simply construct an intention. It must be proven as one's subjective intention, borne out by an action. This demand for physical action is significant. Effectively, it undoes the concept of performative intention *ha'aramah* because it requires the kind of empirically verifiable change that loopholing *ha'aramah* requires. Just as one brings in an *interposita persona*, or declares an animal sanctified in the womb, one must use the object in a way that makes its construction licit. Ritualized intention is insufficient.

The redactors further analyze R. Ashi's statement. They compare the problem of making a strainer on the festival to brewing new beer during the *ḥol ha-mo'ed* for after the holiday. The beer-brewing case is presented as more permissive:

ומאי שנא מהא דתניא מטילין שכר במועד לצורך המועד [שלא לצורך המועד אסור] אחד שכר תמרים ואחד שעורים [[אסור]] וא'ע'פ שיש להם ישן מערים ושותה מן החדש

> How is this different from the following which is taught in a *baraita*: "One may produce beer on the intermediate days of the festival for the holiday, but if it is not for the purpose of the festival, it is prohibited. Whether date beer or barley beer, it is prohibited. And even if they [already] have old beer, one acts prudently and drinks from the new beer.

The *stam* contrasts the strainer case with brewing beer during *ḥol ha-mo'ed* for after the holiday, which is problematic because it involves doing unnecessary labor on the intermediate days of the festival. However, there is a workaround: one may brew beer for after the holiday and drink some on the holiday. Unlike the strainer case, where one has to physically place the pomegranates in the strainer first to "prove" one's intention, in this case, one need not prove the need for new beer before brewing it.[12]

The redactors contrast the cases of the beer and the strainer by dint of how obvious the circumvention is:

התם לא מוכחא מילת' הכא מוכחא מילתא

> There (= in the case of brewing beer), it is not obvious, here (= in the case of the strainer) it is obvious.[13]

The key difference is the transparency of the ruse. If one does not use the cloth for the pomegranates before using it as a strainer, it is too obvious that the cloth-as-pomegranate-basket was just a ruse to place a strainer on the festival. In the case of beer, however, perhaps people might think that one wants to drink new beer on the festival, or people might not know that one already has enough beer for the festival. Therefore, drinking some beer on the holiday is sufficient. Most important, what matters is whether people can tell that one is dodging the law. The concern of obviousness is either absent from or only implicit within the Palestinian material about *ha'aramah*.[14] This distinction between obvious and not obvious adds nuance to the discussion of *ha'aramah*: performative intention is insufficient. And even the type of concrete action needed— whether placing a strainer before or just drinking some after—differs depending on whether one's subjective intention to circumvent the law is obvious (as in the strainer case). The redactors do not want one's subjective intention to circumvent the law to be discernible.

And there are some instances in the *Bavli* in which even concrete actions cannot hide subjective intentions to circumvent the law. For instance, the case known as the "gift of Bet Ḥoron" is another situation in which the rabbis want to hide one's subjective intention to circumvent the law. The context for the case is as follows: the *mishnah* describes what to do when one forswears benefit to someone but that someone is later starving. The *mishnah* rules that the one who made the oath may give food to a third party, and the starving person may then eat from that food: the classic use of an *interposita persona*. The *mishnah* then describes a case that seems to follow that same ruling of using the *interposita persona* to navigate around an oath. This case, the gift of Bet Ḥoron, entails a man who forswore his own father from any benefit, but when the man was marrying off his son, he wanted his father, the groom's grandfather, to attend the wedding. So, apparently adhering to the previous ruling of the *mishnah*, the man gifted the wedding courtyard and feast to a third party so that his father could participate in the wedding celebration.

But something went wrong: his third party turned on him. Knowing that this was a legal dodge just to include his father in the wedding, the third party consecrated the courtyard and the food to the Temple treasury rather than using them for the wedding. When the father of the groom confronted his "straw person" for doing this, the man fired back: "You only gave me your possessions so that you and your father could eat and drink together and make amends, and I would be at fault for helping you break your vow!" The case was brought to the rabbis, who declared that any gift that cannot be consecrated to Heaven by the recipient is not a true gift. Here is the text:

Mishnah Nedarim 5:6 (MS Parma 3173)

המודר הנייה מחבירו ואין לו מה יאכל נותן לאחר משם מתנה והלה מותר בה. מעשה בבית חורון באחד שהיה אביו מודר ממנו הנייה והיה משיא את בנו[15] אמר לחבירו הרי החצר והסעודה נתונין לך במתנה והן בפניך עד שיבא אבא ויאכל עמנו בסעודה. אמר לו אם שלי הם הרי הם מוקדשים לשמים. אמר לו לא נתתי לך את שלי שתקדישם לשמים. אמר לו לא נתתה לי את שלך אלא שתהא אתה ואביך אוכלים ושותים ומתרצים זה לזה ויהא עוון תלוי בראשי וכשבא דבר לפני חכמ' אמרו כל מתנה שאינה שאם הקדישה תהא מקודשת אינה מתנה

One who is prohibited by vow from deriving benefit from another, and has nothing to eat, the one [from whom he is denied benefit] may give [food] to a third party as a gift, and this (= the one who is denied benefit) may partake of it. There was someone in Bet Horon whose father was prohibited by vow from deriving benefit from him. And he [the man in Bet Horon] was marrying off his son[16] and he said to his fellow, "The courtyard and the banquet are given over to you as a gift. And they are yours so that father may come and eat with us at the banquet." The other party said, "Now, if they really are mine, then lo, they are consecrated to Heaven!" Said he to him, "I did not give you what is mine so that you would consecrate it to Heaven!" He replied, "You did not give me what is yours except so that you and your father could eat and drink and be reconciled, while the sin [for violating the oath] could devolve upon my head!" And when the issue came before the sages they said: Any gift that may not be consecrated is not a gift.

The Talmuds try to explain why, if the *mishnah* allows gifting to a third party to circumvent a vow, the rabbis disapprove of the same in the Bet Horon case. The *Bavli*'s discussion of why the gift of Bet Horon is discredited focuses on the transparency of the ruse:

Bavli Nedarim 48a (MS Munich)[17]

מעשה לסתור? חסורי מחסרא והכי קתני ואם הוכיח סופו על תחילתו[18] אסור ומעשה נמי בבית חורון באחד דהוה סופו מוכיח על תחלתו

Would the *mishnah* bring an incident that conflicts with its own ruling? There must be a few words missing [in the *mishnah*], and this is how it should be read: "But if its ending proves [the motivations of] its beginning, it is prohibited. And there was likewise an incident in Bet Ḥoron with someone, where its ending proved [the motivations of] its beginning."

The problem with the gift of Bet Ḥoron is that the ruse is too obvious: the subjective intention of the man to get his father to the wedding is on full display. The passage continues with two versions of Rava's opinion on why the gift of Bet Ḥoron was discredited. Here is first version:

א' רבא לא שנו אלא דא'ל ואינן לפניך אלא כדי[19] שיבא ()[א][בא [אבל] א'ל והן בפניך כדי שיבא אב' מדעת' הוא דא'ל

Rava said: They only learned [that the Bet Ḥoron case is prohibited] if the man said to him (= the third party): And they are yours *only* so that father will come. If [however], he said to him: And they are yours so that father may come, then it is of his own accord.

Rava claims there is a difference between the man saying that the gift is *solely* so that his father can join the wedding feast and saying that his father *may* join the wedding feast. If he says, "*solely* so that father will come," it is a problem, perhaps because he is making the third party his direct emissary or because he is limiting the gift and thus it does not truly belong to the third party. But if the man says, "so that father will come," the circumvention works. The man is merely expressing that the gift is so complete that the man's father may eat of the wedding feast because the property has been fully alienated, so the vow no longer applies to it. But it is the third party's own decision to allow the father to benefit. Rava's opinion is about conditional gifts: gifts are invalid if they cannot be used however the recipient pleases.[20]

But the second version of Rava's explanation returns to the transparency of the ploy:

לישנא אחרינא אמרי לה א' רבא לא תימ' טע' דא'ל ואינן לפניך הוא דאסור אבל
א'ל והן לפני' כדי שיבא ויאכל אסור מאי טע' סעודתו מוכח' עליו

> They reported another version: Rava said: Do not say that the reason [the Bet Horon gift is prohibited] is that he said to him, "and they are *only* yours [so that father will come]," etc., but if he had said: "*so* that he will come and eat" [it is permissible.[21] Rather] it is forbidden [regardless]. Why? Because his meal proves it (i.e., his intention).

This second version of Rava demonstrates that a gift like that of Bet Horon is going to be discredited no matter what the man says when he gifts the courtyard and the meal. Why? Because the very fact that there is a special feast involved will always makes it too obvious that the gift is just a ploy to allow the father to attend the wedding.[22] It is too obvious that the man's subjective intention is to invite his father to the meal.[23]

According to the redactors and the second version of Rava, *ha'aramah* is not only about taking external steps to change the facts of a situation. What matters is how clear the subjective goal of the person is to circumvent the law. This reflects a shift from the Palestinian approach to *ha'aramah* that performed intentions or concrete changes of the external facts of a situation are sufficient. In these earlier discussions, a ruse being obvious does not appear to violate the integrity of the law, whether substantively or procedurally. In the *Bavli*, however, an overriding concern is whether the legal dodge is discernible. In fact, the *Yerushalmi*'s discussion of the Bet Horon case does not discuss transparency at all. Instead, it focuses on how conditions impact a gift: making conditions on how a recipient may use a gift undermines the legal status of the gift.[24]

Probing Subjective Intentions

Beyond concerns about whether a *ha'aramah* is too obvious, the *Bavli* also contains explicit discussion about the significance of one's subjective intentions.

While neither of the examples below use the term *ha'aramah*, both are cases of legal circumvention. And both describe a person being *gomer be-libo*, literally "concluding in their heart." The first example relates to the prohibition of cooking food on a festival day that will be eaten on a non-festival day. Rabbah and R. Hisda argue over whether a person can be lashed as punishment for cooking extra on a festival day, given that it is possible that guests might show up and eat the food on the festival.

Bavli Pesaḥim 46b (MS Munich)

איתמר האופה מיום טוב לחול רב חסדא אמ' לוקה לא אמרינן ליה הואיל ומקלעי ליה אורחין חזי ליה רבא אמ' אינו לוקה אמרינן הואיל . . .

It was said: One who bakes on the festival for a regular day, R. Hisda said: He gets lashes; we do not say, "Since guests come to him, it is [considered] fit [food for] him [to eat, and thus, to cook]." Rabbah[25] said: He does not get lashes; we say, "Since . . ."

R. Hisda rules that a person who cooks food on the festival for a non-festival day should be punished by lashes; the fact that guests might show up on the festival day and eat the food makes no difference. Rabbah, in contrast, thinks the fact that (even uninvited) guests might show up and eat the food that day classifies the food as fit for that day. The passage then challenges R. Hisda's position based on a *baraita*:

איתיביה בהמה מסוכנת לא ישחוט אלא אם כן יכול לאכול ממנה כזית צלי מבעוד יום כדי שיכול לאכול ממנה אע"ג דלא אכל בשלמ' לדידי דאמרינן הואיל ואיבעי למיכל מצי אכיל משום הכי שחיט אלא לדידך דאמרת לא אמרינן הואיל אמאי שחיט

. . . He challenged him from a *baraita*: "One may not slaughter [on the festival] an animal in danger [of dying] unless one can eat an olive's worth of roasted [meat] from it during daylight (= before the end of the festival day)." This indicates that one need *only have the potential* to eat from it to [permissibly] slaughter, even if *one does not eat* [from it that day]. This corresponds to my (= Rabbah's) opinion [which recognizes the *potential* to be eaten as legally significant], for we say, "Since if he wants to eat [from] it, he can [do so before sundown], therefore he may slaughter it." But according to your [opinion, R. Hisda, who does not recognize the *potential* to be eaten as legally significant], for you say, "We do not say 'Since,' why may he slaughter?"

A *baraita* allows one to slaughter food on the festival even if it only *might* get eaten. This challenges R. Hisda, who allows cooking for the festival only if the food *will* be eaten on the festival (not just if it might get eaten). On the other hand, the *baraita* corresponds to Rabbah's opinion, as he allows one to cook on the festival even if there is only the *potential* for the food to be eaten by guests. The passage attributes the following response to R. Hisda:

א"ל משום הפסד ממונו. ומשום הפסד ממונו שרינן איסורא דאורייתא? אין משום הפסד ממונו גמר בלבו לאכול כזית מבעוד יום ואי אפשר לכזית בשר בלא שחיטה...

He [R. Hisda] said to him [even though he will not eat it, he may still slaughter it], because of his financial loss [because the animal will die and not be used for meat]. [The redactors challenge that answer:] And because of financial loss we permit a biblical violation [of slaughtering an animal that is not for the festival]? Yes, because of his financial loss, *he concludes in his heart* that he will eat an olive's worth of meat during daylight, and one cannot eat [even] an olive's worth of meat without slaughter[ing the animal].

There is a difference between cooking and slaughtering an animal: one may only cook food on the festival if one knows it will get eaten, but one may slaughter an animal on the festival even if it *might* get eaten because if slaughtered meat becomes forbidden, the animal owner loses money. And if one stands to lose money, so long as there is enough time in the day to eat some of the meat, the owner subjectively intends to eat it so that he will not incur loss. If, in the end, he does not eat any of the meat that day, R. Hisda assumes that this is accidental and does not penalize him for it. Because one knows that the permissibility of the slaughter depends on consumption of the meat, one will accept the need to eat the meat to save money. The language of *gamar be-libo*, he has concluded in his heart, speaks not to performed intentions but to subjective intentions. In other words, the argument here is that the awareness of potential loss leads a person not simply to perform certain intentions in order to enable a ruse, but it actually leads to sincere intentions: when monetary loss it at stake, one will choose to eat meat that one otherwise would not want to eat. This activity becomes akin to placing pomegranates on the strainer. True, the person may not eat in the end, but he really wants to and plans to do so.

A second instance where the *Bavli* navigates a gap between subjective intention and performed intention relates to coerced consent. *M'Arakhin* 5:6 states that one may be coerced into saying "I want" and this counts as consent in the following two legal arenas: (1) when offering certain sacrifices that only expiate if one offers them of their own will, and (2) when a man gives a woman a writ of divorce, which must be done of the man's own free will.[26] To consider a coerced "I want to do this" as a legally binding statement of consent seems farcical, as one's subjective intentions are obviously otherwise. The *Bavli* discusses coerced consent in several places, trying to manage the gap between internally subjective intention and externally performed action.

One mode of navigation is to suggest that based on the compulsion, one's internally subjective intention has changed, known in Aramaic as *agav onseh gamar u-makneh*: due to his coercion, he has resolved to commit the transaction.[27] This is similar to the logic offered above regarding a person deciding to wish to eat meat that would otherwise be lost on the festival.

Elsewhere, the *Bavli*'s editors grapple with compelled consent by introducing the stakes of a given scenario. The Talmud discusses whether one's intentions about a transaction—*devarim she-ba-lev* (lit. "words in the heart")—are legally significant if one does not stipulate those intentions aloud at the time of the transaction. For instance, if one sells their possessions planning to move to Israel but never stipulates that reason for selling and if the move never materializes, is the transaction void? The *Bavli* connects this question of *devarim she-ba-lev*, itself an indication of a more subjective self, to the issue of compelled consent in both sacrifices and divorce:

Bavli Kiddushin 49b–50a (MS Munich)

ההו' גבר' דזבין לנכסי' אדעת' למיסק לארע' דישר' בעידנ' דזבין לא א' ולא מידי א' רבא הוי דברי' שבלב ודברי' שבלב אינן דברים מנליה לרבא הא אילימ' מיהא דתנן יקריב אותו מלמ' שכופין אותו יכול בעל כרחו ת"ל לרצונו הכיצד

כופין אותו עד שיאמ' רוצ' אני ואמאי והא בלביה לא ניח' ליה אלא לאו משו'
דאמרי' דברי' שבלב אינן דברי' דילמ' שאני הת' דאנן סהדי דניח' ליה בכפר'
אל' מסיפ' וכן את' או' בגיטי נשי' כופין אותו עד שיאמ' רוצ' אני ואמאי הא
בליבי' לא ניח' אלא לאו משו' דאמרי' דברי' שבלב אינן דברי' דילמ' שאני הת'
'משו' דמצו' לשמוע דברי חכמי

> One who sold his property with the intention of immigrating to Israel, but when selling said nothing [about that intention]. Said Rava: That is an internal stipulation (*devarim she-ba-lev*) and is not recognized [as legally definitive. Therefore, the sale is valid even if he does not move to Israel]. From where does Rava know this? Shall we say, from what we learn in the *mishnah*: "He shall offer it"—this teaches that they may force him [to offer it]. Perhaps they may do so against his will? Therefore, Scripture stipulates, "according to his will." How so? They force him until he says, "I want [to offer it]." Yet why is this [coercion] effective if in his heart he is unwilling? It must be because we say that internal stipulations are not recognized [as legally definitive]! But perhaps it is different there, for we ourselves are witnesses that he is pleased to gain atonement. Rather [it follows that internal stipulations are not recognized as legally definitive] from the second clause: "and you find it likewise in the case of women's divorce": they compel him, until he declares, "I am willing." Yet why [is this effective] if in his heart he is unwilling? Rather, is it not because we say that internal stipulations are not recognized [as legally definitive]. Perhaps it is different there because it is a religious duty to obey the words of the sages.[28]

While this passage entertains the possibility that compelled consent proves that subjective internal feelings carry no legal force in defining transactions, it is ultimately rejected. Instead, the redactors introduce the issue of what is best for the person being coerced. In a situation in which an action will help gain atonement (as in the case of sacrifice) or will constitute heeding the words of the sages (as in the case of divorce), coercion is effective. Perhaps this is indeed because it is presumed that the person's internal subjective will is to gain atonement and to heed the sages in these respective cases.[29] Alternatively, perhaps the coerced actor still does not wish to offer the sacrifice or to give the *get*. Nonetheless, the law ignores those internal intentions because they are self-sabotaging.[30] Regardless of which is the case, it is noteworthy that the *Bavli* redactors attempt to reconcile the problematic of one's internal subjective intentions not matching one's external actions.[31]

Analytical and Editorial Changes

There are also subtler indications of the *Bavli*'s focus on narrowing the gap between subjective intention and external action. Specifically, the *Bavli* recasts the earlier Palestinian material in ways that manifest the importance of not being obvious about one's intentions to circumvent the law. For example, in the classic livestock *ha'aramah* case, while Palestinian texts have R. Yehoshua allowing the owner not to slaughter either animal, the *Bavli* consistently cites a different version of R. Yehoshua: he always requires the owner to slaughter at least one of the animals:[32]

מעלה את הראשון על מנת לשוחטו ואינו שוחטו וחוזר ומערים ומעלה את השני רצה זה שוחט, רצה זה שוחט.

> One raises up the first on condition to slaughter it but does not slaughter it, and, acting prudently, one then raises up the second. If one wishes, he slaughters this one, or if he wishes, he slaughters that one.

While the Palestinian citation of this case does not seem to require the slaughter of either animal, the *Bavli*'s version of the case does.[33] Once again, the *Bavli* narrows the gaps between performed intention and subjective intention.[34] Slaughtering one of the animals authenticates one's intentions to slaughter an animal. The ploy is less obvious.

Another example of reshaping earlier material is where an *amora* analyzes a dispute that was previously understood as intention-oriented *ha'aramah* as being about something else entirely. One such instance relates to the argument between R. Yehoshua and R. Eliezer about whether to leave the *ḥallah* portion from impure dough in the oven on Passover so that it will not rise (see Chapter 2). In the *Yerushalmi*, this is understood as a case of intention-oriented *ha'aramah*, but the *Bavli* analyzes it as a question about the potential for each piece of dough to be eaten. While the *Yerushalmi* provides an elaborate piece-by-piece monologue about the bread, spelling out the *ha'aramah* strategy in detail, the *Bavli* does nothing of the sort:

Bavli Pesaḥim 48a (MS Munich)

אמ' רמי בר חמא הא דרב חסדא ורבה[35] מחלוק' ר' אליעזר ור' יהושע דר' אליעזר סבר אמרינן הואיל ור' יהושע סבר לא אמרינן הואיל אמ' רב פפא ודילמא לא היא עד כאן לא קא"ר אליעזר התם דאמרינן הואיל דבעידנא דקא עיילינהו לתנורא כל חדא וחדא חזייא ליה לדידיה אבל הכא דלאורחים הוא דחזי הא לדידיה [לא] חזי הכא נמי דלא אמרינן הואיל אמ' רב שישא בריה דרב אידי ודילמא לא היא עד כאן לא קא"ר יהושע אלא דאיכא חדא דלא חזיא לדידיה ולא לאורחים אבל הכא דחזי מיהת לאורחין הכי נמי דאמרינן הואיל

> Rami b. Hama said: This [argument between] R. Hisda and Rava [regarding "Since"—i.e., whether the potential for people to eat a food makes cooking it on the festival permissible] corresponds to the argument between R. Eliezer and R. Yehoshua: R. Eliezer held that we do say, "Since," and R. Yehoshua held that we do not say: "Since." R. Pappa said: But maybe this is not [correct]. Until now, R. Eliezer only said there (= in the case of *ḥallah* on Passover) we say "since" because when he puts them (= the pieces of dough) into the oven, each one is fit for him [to eat]. However, here (= in a case of cooking extra food on the festival for afterward because guests might arrive) while it is fit for guests to eat, it is not fit for him to eat [all of it], so we do not say, "Since." R. Shisha the son of R. Idi said: And maybe it is not [correct]. Until now, R. Yehoshua only said [no to "since" in the case of *ḥallah* on Passover] because there is one [piece] that is not fit for him [to eat] or for guests [to eat, as it is impure *ḥallah*], but here where [all of] it is fitting for guests to eat, we do say "since."

Instead of analyzing R. Yehoshua's and R. Eliezer's argument in terms of *ha'aramah*, Rami bar Hama analyzes it in terms of a different legal concept, examined earlier in this chapter, known as "since" (*ho'il*). "Since" is about the potential for something to be used even if it is not actually used. For instance, for Rabbah, so long as there is enough time left in the day that guests may stop by and eat the extra food that one prepared on the festival for after the festival, there is no penalty for cooking the extra food on the festival.[36] Rami b. Hama applies the same logic of "since" to R. Eliezer's permission to leave the *ḥallah* in the oven on Passover: "*since* it may potentially be eaten." Because each piece of dough may potentially be eaten that day—though they will not all be eaten because one will be designated *ḥallah*—R. Eliezer allows one to place all the dough in the oven and designate one piece as *ḥallah* once the dough has been baked.[37] This analysis differs from the *Yerushalmi*'s explanation of R. Eliezer's position.

The way the *Yerushalmi* presented R. Eliezer, one "plans" to eat each piece: R. Eliezer requires a person to have a "conversation" that suggests a desire to eat each separate piece of bread, saying about each piece, "This portion I want to eat and this portion I want to eat" to permit placing it into the oven.

Additionally, the *Bavli* explains R. Yehoshua's position not to place the *ḥallah* portion into the oven not as being anti-*ha'aramah* but as being against the principle of "since." For R. Yehoshua, the fact that a food might be eaten does not permit baking it on the festival. R. Pappa and R. Shisha challenge whether this analysis works, as there may be important differences between the case of baking extra food on the festival that guests might eat and the case of baking a piece of *ḥallah* dough that has not yet been designated as such.

Nonetheless, the use of the principle of "since" to analyze what was previously described as *ha'aramah* is noteworthy. "Since" is not about performed intentions or monologues; it is about legal definitions.[38] If an item might be eaten by someone on the festival, it is defined as festival food. This approach focuses on the status of the food rather than the machinations of the person preparing the food. The *Bavli*'s "since" explanation exemplifies the move away from performative intention.

Language: *Ha'aramah* as Deceit

Yet another indication of the *Bavli*'s discomfort with performed *ha'aramah* is the use of the root ʻ.r.m. to mean *lying* by the *Bavli* redactors and perhaps even some third- and fourth-generation *amoraim*. Thus, they relate the term *ha'aramah* not only to circumvention but to mendacity.³⁹ Here is one example among a handful of such instances:

Bavli Ketubot 79b–80a

משנה: המוציא יצאות על ניכסי אשתו הוציא הרבה ואכל קימעה קימעה ואכל הרבה
מה שהוציא הוציא ומה שאכל אכל הוציא ולא אכל ישבע כמה הוציא ויטול

Mishnah (MS Parma): One who spends money on his wife's possessions (which she brought into the marriage from her father's house),⁴⁰ whether he spent much and consumed little or the reverse, [when they divorce] that which he spent is spent and that which he consumed is consumed (i.e., he cannot reclaim the money he spent). However, if he spent money [to improve the possessions] but did not consume anything, he takes an oath as to how much he spent and takes [that amount in return when they divorce].

גמרא: . . . אמ' רב אסי והוא שהיה שבח כנגד הוצאה למאי הילכתא? אמ' אביי
שאם הייתה⁴¹ שבח יתר על הוצאה נוטל הוצאה בלא שבועה. א"ל רבא⁴² אתי
לאיערומי! אלא אמ' רבא שאם היתה הוצאה יתירה על השבח אין לו אלא הוצאה
שיעור שבח ובשבועה

Gemara (MS Munich): . . . R. Asi said: This is only the case (i.e., he only takes an oath as to how much he spent) when the improvement equals his investment. For what legal end [did R. Asi make his statement]? Abaye said: that if there was more improvement than money spent, he can retrieve the money that he spent without an oath. Rava said to him: [If so] he will lie [about how much he spent]! Rather, Rava said: if the money spent was more than the improvement, he only gets the amount of profit. And only with an oath.

Without getting into the details of the legalities of marital property law, it is worth noting that Rava, the fourth-generation *amora*, uses '.r.m. here to mean perjury.⁴³ While one cannot know if this was Rava's exact phrasing or the work of the redactors, in another passage in the *Bavli* Rava is said to use this same terminology when speaking to his student R. Nahman b. Yitzhak to suggest that someone was lying about being religiously rehabilitated.[44] Regardless of whether this is the language of Rava or of the redactors, the root of the word *ha'aramah* is being used here to mean deception, and this is one of several such cases in the *Bavli*.[45]

To be sure, there are uses of *ha'aramah* as deception that predate the *Bavli*.[46] But added to the other concerns about *ha'aramah* as a mechanism within the *Bavli*, the use of *ati le-i'arume* (אתי לאיערומי) to mean lying about past facts to avoid legal consequences stands out: examples include lying about purposely placing a pot on the stove on Friday afternoon for it to cook on the Sabbath (*bShab.* 37b–38a); lying about how much one owes their creditor to get out of having to take an oath (*bBM* 4b); or lying about how much *ketubah* payment one has received as her marriage settlement (*bKet.* 87b). In the redactional layers and perhaps as early as the fourth-century *amoraim*, the terminology of איערומי becomes a synonym for perjury about established fact.[47] Michael Sokoloff offers the connotation of the reflexive איערומי as "to deceive" while defining the simple verb form ערם as "to beguile."[48] This terminology indicates an attitude not simply about these particular cases but about *ha'aramah* itself as involving a denial of facts rather than simply the construction of "new" facts.

Why the Change?

This chapter has shown the *Bavli*'s changed attitude toward *ha'aramah* and specifically toward *ha'aramah* as ritualized intention. This includes increased emphasis on the legal status of internal, subjective intentions within transactions generally (*gomer be-libo*); rejection of performances that obviously betray intentions to dodge (*mukheḥa milta*) and a requirement for the performances to effect external factual change (using the filter cloth for pomegranates); using concepts other than *ha'aramah* to analyze cases previously understood as *ha'aramah* (e.g., *ho'il* for the *ḥallah* case); and using the root ʿ.r.m. to refer to lying.

What motivated this changed view of *ha'aramah*? There are at least three related possibilities for the *Bavli*'s conservatism regarding *ha'aramah*: (a) increased focus on subjectivity, (b) discomfort with gaps between law and reality, and (c) concern for how *ha'aramah* might lead to a decline in observance.

Increased Focus on Subjectivity

The *Bavli*'s approach to *ha'aramah* is a product of evolving rabbinic thought about intention and the interior self. The earliest *amoraim* cited as being suspicious of performing intention for *ha'aramah* date from the third and fourth generations of *amoraim*. It is well attested that these same generations of *amoraim* expanded the categories of intention and heightened their importance, especially to determine culpability in civil and ritual law.[49] But more than simply bringing the idea of intention to the fore, *Bavli* discussions of *ha'aramah* suggest a more subjective understanding of intention than the *tannaitic* material.[50]

Just as the Palestinian Talmud's treatment of *ha'aramah* should be viewed within its broader Greco-Roman context, the *Bavli*'s increased focus on interiority might be understood within its Persian cultural context. One aspect of this embeddedness involves a relationship with Zoroastrian thought and culture. In recent decades, many scholars, notably Yaakov Elman and his students, have deepened our understanding of the relationship between Zoroastrianism and Babylonian rabbinic thought.[51] Another aspect of Jewish life in the Persian Empire is its relationship with Christian thought and culture.[52] Michal Bar-Asher Siegal has argued that Jewish-Christian interactions in late antique Babylonia were about more than just exegetical polemics over Scripture. She identifies Egyptian monastic writings that circulated in the Persian Empire that may have been absorbed into rabbinic writings and used "for their own purposes and to promote rabbinic values."[53] Zoroastrian and Christian monastic texts in *amoraic* Persia do indeed reflect on the importance of internal, subjective thought and intention. Regarding Zoroastrianism, Shaul Shaked writes, "the Zoroastrian doctors regarded intention, either in the virtue of performing good deeds or in the sin which consists of desisting from such a performance, a meaningful factor, perhaps an essential one, in evaluating the religious merit of a person's ritual conduct."[54] Zoroastrian ideas of intention relate to the development of character:

AW (Ayādgār ī Wuzurgmihr) §84

The function of innate wisdom is to preserve the body from doing things that induce fear, from deliberate sin, and from fruitless effort, to hold in mind the transience of the things of this world and the finality of the body, not to diminish from the things related to one's future existence, and not to increase those that are related to one's passing away.

WZ (Wizīdagīhā ī Zādspram) 29.7

And the soul, the commander, which is the lord and administrator of the body, in which is its own chief and foundation, is similar to a fire-tender, who has among his functions (the duty) to keep the dome clean, proper, and under supervision, and to kindle the fire.

In these passages, the mind—the intimate "I"—is understood as the preserver of wisdom, and it supervises the body's activities. Additionally, Zoroastrian texts decouple thoughts from deeds, viewing thought itself as deserving of punishment or reward:

Dēnkard 6:227

Every person should be contrite and repentant to the gods for every sin he thinks he was guilty of that day in thought, speech, and action.

Dādestān ī dēnīg 13.3

And in the future body, on the completion of all accounts, the Creator Ohrmazd himself does the account, (the Creator Ohrmazd) to whom the account of all the thoughts, words, and deeds of the creatures . . . are known through his omniscient wisdom.

Dādestān ī dēnīg 19.2

It is said that the souls of the dead and departed are on the earth for three nights. The first night they receive comfort as a result of their good thoughts and sorrow as a result of their evil thoughts. The second night they receive pleasure as a result of (their) good words and trouble and punishment as a result of (their) evil words;

and the third night they receive help as a result of (their) good deeds and punishment as a result of (their) evil deeds.

Thought is not simply an extension of action. It stands apart from action, and people are held accountable for their thoughts.

Christian monastics also articulated a notion of thought being sinful separate from action:

Praktikos 48

Just as it is easier to sin by thought than by deed, so also is the war fought on the field of thought more severe than that which is conducted in the area of things and events. For the mind is easily moved indeed, and hard to control in the presence of sinful phantasies.

This approach to the importance of thought parallels Babylonian rabbinic thought. David Brodsky has observed that some Babylonian *amoraim*—predominantly Rav, Rav Nahman, Rava, and Ravina, known to be the most culturally Persian[55]—likewise introduce the possibility of thoughts being rewarded or punished even without action.[56] And Ron Naiweld argues that the rabbinic concept of *hirhur*, thought, functions the same way as the Christian monastic concept of *logismos*, as an obsessive evil thought that "can stir the disciple away from the normative virtuous behavior."[57]

Thus, it may be fruitful to consider Babylonian rabbinic attitudes about the internal self in the context of Zoroastrian and Christian contemporaries. While *tannaim* do not discuss the legal significance of intention outside the context of action, for some Babylonian *amoraim*, intention and thought matter on their own.[58] This corresponds to what we have seen regarding *ha'aramah*: earlier rabbinic material, both *tannaitic* and Palestinian *amoraic*, may be comfortable with a flatter version of intention that is more about defining action than about defining the self. But in the *Bavli*, the subjective self and subjective intention become the norm within rabbinic thought.

A Persian Loanword for Illegitimate *Ha'aramah*?

In addition to the consideration of interiority, it also interesting to note a citation of legal circumvention in the *Bavli* that uses a Persian loanword to refer to an excuse to avoid performing a ritual obligation, in other words, a case of evasion:

Bavli Menaḥot 41a (MS Munich 95)

דמלאכ(ה)[א] אשכחיה לרב קטינא דהוה מיכסי סדינא. א״ל קטינא סדינא בקייטא וסרבלא בסיתווא ציצית מה תהא עליה? א״ל ענשיתו אעשה? א״ל בזמן דאיכ' ריתחא ענשינן. אי אמרת בשלמ' גבר' הוא היינו דמיחייב דלא קא רמי אלא אי אמרת חובת טלית היא הא לא מיחייב. ואלא מאי? חובת גברא היא. נהי דחייביה רחמ' כי מיכסי טלית דבת חיובא היא לכסוייה מי חייביה רחמ'? הכי קא״ל טצדקי למיפטר נפשך מציצית

For an angel once found R. Katina [who was accustomed to] wearing a [linen] wrap.[59] He (the angel) exclaimed: "Katina, a [linen] wrap in the summer and a cloak in the winter, but what will happen with the *tzitzit* (fringes)?" (R. Katina) replied: "Do you punish a person for [omitting to perform] a positive precept [such as wearing *tzitzit*]?" He (the angel) said: "In a time of wrath we do." Now, if you hold that the law of *tzitzit* is an obligation relating to the person—then that is why he would incur guilt for not wearing a garment with fringes; but if you hold that it is an obligation relating to the garment, then [he should not incur guilt given that] he is not obligated. Rather what? It is an obligation incumbent upon the person. [Even if this is so], granted that the Torah holds him accountable if he is wearing a garment that is subject to fringes [but fails to put them on], but did the Torah also oblige him to cover himself [specifically with clothing that requires fringes]? This is what [the angel] said to him: "[It is] a means to excuse yourself from the law of fringes!"

This anecdote is part of a discussion about whether the biblical commandment (Num. 15:38–39; Deut. 22:12) to wear fringes (*tzitzit*) on the corners of one's garments is an obligation driven by the garment or by the person. The difference between the two positions is whether one must attach fringes to a four-cornered garment even if one is not wearing that garment. (A garment that does not have four corners does not require *tzitzit* whether or not one wears it.) In this story, R. Katina wears garments throughout the year that do not require *tzitzit* either because the garment does not have four corners (e.g., his winter cloak) or because the garment may not have *tzitzit* (i.e., the linen garment).[60] Consequently, he never fulfills the commandment of wearing *tzitzit*. He is chastised by an angel for this behavior. The redactors wonder why he is chastised: after all, even if one must wear *tzitzit* when wearing a four-cornered garment, who says one must ever wear a garment with four corners? The response offered is that the angel is accusing R. Katina of wearing clothes that are exempt from *tzitzit* specifically to circumvent the commandment of wearing fringes.

Scholars have suggested that the term used to refer to R. Katina's evasion, *tatzdeke*, should actually be read as *tatzreke*.[61] A. Kohut and J. N. Epstein, among others, have related this word to the Middle Persian word *čārag*. According to P. O. Skjaervo, this Pahlavi word means "a way out, a way to do." In other words, R. Katina is looking for any way out of wearing *tzitzit*.[62] What makes R. Katina's actions problematic are not the actions themselves but the unstated intention that animates those actions.[63] In light of the Zoroastrian focus on intentions, it is interesting that the term used to condemn R. Katina's evasion in the *Bavli* is a Middle Persian loanword. While inconclusive, this etymology is suggestive of some potential convergence between Zoroastrian and rabbinic thought about workarounds.

Discomfort with Gaps Between Law and Reality

In addition, the focus on the subjective self/inner thoughts intersects with another changing aspect of Babylonian rabbinic thought: growing discomfort with gaps between law and reality. Christine Hayes has observed regarding legal fictions, and Tzvi Novick has observed regarding implausible legal presumptions, that Babylonian *amoraim*, especially in later generations, limit the use of constructions that do not reflect empirical reality.[64] They understand the reasons for this discomfort differently. Novick argues that this change reflects a new level of rabbinic sophistication that "came to view the blatant legal fiction as inelegant and a violation of the rules of argumentation." And Hayes understands it as evidence of increasing rabbinic realism.[65] Referenced earlier with regard to im/purity law, realism and nominalism are two distinct philosophical approaches. Realism understands reality as independent of the mind while nominalism understands reality as based on the mind. When applied to law, realism expects law to align with a discoverable mind-independent reality while nominalism allows for law to create its own reality. Thus, nominalistic thinking tolerates a gap between law and what is true "out there in the world." Rabbinic literature contains a strong nominalist impulse alongside its realist impulse, but in the Babylonian Talmud, realism gains more traction than in earlier Palestinian material. While earlier rabbinic orientations to Divine law did not necessarily require law to comport with ontological truth, transformations within the *Bavli* suggest that it should. Thus, later Babylonian *amoraim* attempt to bridge the gap between law and reality through either rejection or redefinition of earlier rulings that allowed this gap to persist.[66]

Admittedly, the rise of subjectivity and rabbinic discomfort with obvious fictions are somewhat in tension. Emphasis on the activities of the mind, such as intention, is characteristic of nominalistic thinking; discomfort with obvious fictions is characteristic of realistic thinking. On the other hand, only once intention is understood as truly subjective does the gap between the actions that one takes and the truth of what intends to do—namely, avoid the law—matter. If not for a rise in subjectivity, one's performed intentions might in fact be considered one's "real" intentions in the eyes of the law.

This rise in realism intersects with rabbinic concerns about the use of radical human agency in the context of a Divine Law.[67] Thus, yet another prong of the earlier rabbinic orientation to Divine Law—its changeability—also declines during this period.[68] As Yitzhak Gilat points out, the *Bavli* first introduces explicit limitations on rabbinic authority to "abrogate" (לעקור) biblical law though their decrees.[69] It restricts this privilege only to (a) passive abrogation (e.g., not blowing the *shofar* when Rosh Hashanah falls out on the Sabbath); (b) temporary abrogation as an emergency measure (such as Elijah the prophet bringing sacrifices outside of the sanctum); and (c) finance law (though even that becomes justified through a biblical principle about the powers of the court).[70]

This departs from *takkanot* in *tannaitic* literature, which appear unconstrained in allowing rabbis to make decrees that abrogate Torah law.[71] Therefore, the *Bavli* interprets these *takkanot* in a manner that defangs them. For example, *mGit.* 4:2 cites R. Gamliel as decreeing that a man may not cancel a writ of divorce that is already en route to his wife who lives elsewhere, presumably because sometimes a woman would not find out that she was still married. This is a bold innovation, given the fact that biblically, the husband should be able to nullify the *get*. The *Yerushalmi* (*yGit.* 4:2, 45c) ratifies the authority of rabbis to "uproot a rule of the Torah." The *Bavli* (*bGit.* 33a), on the other hand, asserts that any man who betroths a woman does so at the will of the rabbinic establishment, and thus, if the rabbis say that he is not married, then he is not married. In other words, rather than suggest that R. Gamliel is limiting a man's freedom to divorce his wife, the *Bavli* says he does no such thing. Instead, because marriage is conditional on the support of the rabbinical establishment, the rabbis simply annul the marriage. The *takkanah* is not uprooting a rule from the Torah; it is merely allowing the rabbinic circumscription of Jewish marriage to take effect.[72] Gilat relates this growing conservatism to the further development of distinctions between rabbinic and Torah law. Hayes, on the other hand, suggests that earlier rabbinic boldness parallels the Roman legal phenomenon of the praetorian edict while the Babylonian rabbis think and work in a different legal milieu.[73]

Regardless of their origins, both the documented rise of realism and rabbinic anxiety about human agency comport with the evolution of *ha'aramah*. Both *tannaitic* and *amoraic* Palestinian texts allow performed intention to define situations of even obvious circumvention. The *Bavli*, however, attempts to narrow the gap between law and reality. If one sets up a strainer on the festival "in order to" hold pomegranates, the "strainer" must in fact hold pomegranates. If one may place all of one's dough in the oven on Passover, it is only because each piece may get eaten rather than because of one's performed intention to eat each piece. Additionally, *Bavli* texts reject the use of *ha'aramah* that is too obviously a manipulation of the law: where the gap between what is really happening and what one says is happening is transparent. This kind of obvious human agency to avoid a law will not pass. Some rabbis are even stricter in responding to misuse of *ha'aramah* than they are to cases of purposeful transgression.

Potential Deterioration of Observance

There is one final layer that can account for the *Bavli*'s discomfort with both types of *ha'aramah*: the rabbis worried about a decline in observance, at least for the one using the *ha'aramah* and perhaps for others as well. After all, the use of loopholes, especially those that are not subtle, can erode people's fealty to the law or simply confuse them about what the law is. Thus, if the self is more subjective and law should align with truth, it is reasonable to suspect that *ha'aramah* might easily undermine the law rather than help bolster it.

Consequently, when discussing *ha'aramah*, rather than asking only whether a *ha'aramah* is justified, the *Bavli* often expresses concern that *ha'aramah* could lead to future problems with adherence to the law. For example, in *bBetzah* 18a, women are permitted to immerse their ritually impure clothing on a festival by wearing it while immersing for their own bodily purity in a ritual bath (*mikvah*). However, the redactors worry that using this *ha'aramah* will lead women to forget that immersing impure clothing in a *mikvah* on a festival day is usually forbidden.[74] The redactors dismiss this worry only by arguing that immersing the clothing in a different manner than usual—by wearing it—will help her remember that *ha'aramah* is the exception and that usually she may not immerse impure clothing on the festival. This concern is new: the *Mishnah*, *Tosefta*, and *Yerushalmi* do not explicitly raise the possibility of forbidding a *ha'aramah* practice for fear that it might lead someone to break the law in the future.

Another example appears in *bBetzah* 11a. The Talmud relates a discussion about how to preserve the extra meat from an animal that was slaughtered on the festival but cannot be eaten that day. R. Yehoshua rules that on a festival, though one may not salt the extra meat fat, one may spread the fat out on pegs in the wind to prevent it from decaying. The redactors, however, explain that this leniency is rejected because it is too obviously a way to prevent decay.[75] The concern is that using such an obvious ruse to prevent decay will lead to the assumption that one might also perform prohibited actions such as salting extra meat to prevent it from spoiling. But it is unclear from the manuscripts whether the worry is that the person who hangs the meat or an onlooker will reach this erroneous conclusion.[76] In *bNed.* 23a–b, we find a concern regarding loopholing in general, as Rava admonishes a colleague not to teach a certain loophole related to vows publicly.[77] He worries that if people know about the loopholes, they may treat the laws of vows lightly. As he says, "the *tanna* made it unclear so that people would not treat vows lightly, and you wish to teach this at the public session?!"[78]

Additionally, several times in the *Bavli*, the use of *ha'aramah* is limited to Torah scholars, presumably because they will not become lax or confused about the law in the future. R. Ashi, a fourth-generation Babylonian *amora*, on *bShab.* 139b, addresses this issue in the continuation of the discussion about the strainer on the festival cited at the outset of this chapter:

Ha'aramah in the *Bavli*

אמרו ליה רבנן לרב אשי חזי מר האי צורבא מרבנן ורב הונא בר ר' חיון שמיה ואמרי לה רב הונא בר' חלוון שמיה, דשקל ברא דתומא ומנח בברזא דדנא ואמר לאצנועיה קמיכוינא ואזיל ונאים במברא ועבר להך גיסא וסייר פירי ואמר אנא למינם קמיכונא. אמר להו הערמה קאמרת? הערמה בדרבנן[79] היא וצורבא מרבנן לא אתי למיעבד לכתחילה.

> Said the disciples to R. Ashi: "We would call the attention of the master to this young scholar, R. Huna bar Hiyon or Hilvon by name, who takes the clove of garlic and stops up a hole in a wine barrel with it, saying that he intends merely to preserve the clove of garlic. He also goes and lies down on a ferry to sleep; in the meantime, he is ferried across the river, and on the other side he checks on his produce, saying, however, that he merely intended to sleep." Answered R. Ashi: "You speak of *ha'aramah*. All the acts mentioned by you are prohibited by rabbinical laws only, and in the case of a scholar, there is no danger that he will commit them *ante facto*."

The students ask R. Ashi what he thought about a fellow student's use of intention-based *ha'aramah* when that student's intentions were so obviously suspect. He circumvented the prohibition of repairing a barrel on the Sabbath by suggesting that his intention was otherwise.[80] Likewise, he managed to sail across a river on the Sabbath, also rabbinically forbidden, while suggesting that his intention was simply to sleep.[81] R. Ashi, however, permits the young scholar's actions precisely because he is a rabbinic scholar. This is surprising both because of how obvious this ruse is and because it involves the construction of intention.

The exact text and meaning of R. Ashi's comments are elusive: R. Ashi maybe be suggesting that *ha'aramah* is only rabbinically prohibited.[82] Or he may be stating that *ha'aramah* is permitted because the student is only circumventing a rabbinic law.[83] Or perhaps he is telling his students that *ha'aramah* is a tool that comes from the rabbis themselves, and so rabbinic scholars may avail themselves of it.[84] According to any of these readings, R. Ashi asserts that this scholar has the right and/or the scruples to use this *ha'aramah*. He is trusted not to use *ha'aramah* when he does not need to, or, alternatively, he is trusted not to allow this tool to erode his respect for the law and start sailing willy-nilly on the Sabbath for no reason and with no cover-up. A less learned and religiously committed person in the very same predicament would not be so trusted to distinguish between various situations.

This marks an important turn in the parameters of *ha'aramah*: it is meant for a person with a certain level of commitment to, and understanding of, Jewish law. Is this a local statement about this particular case or a general dispensation regarding *ha'aramah*?[85] There is at least one other source in the *Bavli* for permitting a particular *ha'aramah* specifically to a Torah scholar: in *'Arakhin* 23a, the redactors suggest that Abaye would make an exception for a *tzurba me-rabanan* (rabbinical student) to employ a circumvention that he usually thinks it is wrong to suggest.[86]

The orientation of treating a rabbinical student (*tzurba me-rabanan*), that is, a Torah scholar, differently than others is characteristic of Babylonian *amoraic* perspectives in general, whereby they secluded themselves from non-rabbis and looked down upon them.[87] This was quite pronounced, compared to Palestinian *amoraim*, who were much more integrated into general, non-rabbinic society.[88] Additionally, the distinction between the young Torah scholar and others is elsewhere attributed to fourth-generation *amoraim* to R. Ashi himself, and in the anonymous editorial layer of the *Bavli*.[89]

Another indication that the *Bavli* reflects worries about a decline in observance is the way R. Ashi talks about *ha'aramah* when it is juxtaposed to the use of the rabbinically created decree of *'eruv tavshilin*. If one chose not to set aside as *'eruv tavshilin*, one may not use *ha'aramah* by purposely making extra food and claiming it is leftovers:

Bavli Betzah 17b (MS Munich)

ת"ש מי שהניח ערובי תבשילין הרי זה אופה ומבשל ומטמין ואם רצה לאכל את ערובו הרשות בידו. אכלו עד שלא אפה עד שלא בישל עד שלא הטמי' הרי זה לא יאפה ולא יבשל ולא יטמין לא לו ולא לאחרים ולא אחרים אופין לו ומבשלין לו, אבל מבשל הוא ליום טוב ואם הותיר הותיר לשבת, ובלבד שלא יערים ואם הערים אסור. אמ' רב אשי הערמה קאמרת שאני הערמה דאחמירו בה רבנן טפי ממזיד

Come and learn: One who left an *'eruv tavshilin* (lit. "combined cooked foods") may bake, cook, and insulate, and if he wishes to eat his *'eruv* he may. If he ate it before baking, cooking, or insulating, he may not bake, cook, or insulate, neither for himself or others, and others may not bake or cook for him. He may, however, cook for the holiday itself, and if he had leftovers, he has them left for the Sabbath, so long as he does not practice cunning [to cook extra]. And if he did practice cunning [to cook extra], it is forbidden. R. Ashi said: You are comparing (the earlier case, not brought here) to *ha'aramah*? *Ha'aramah* is different, as the rabbis were stricter in its regard than in cases even of purposeful transgression!

One should use the rabbinic *takkanah* of *'eruv tavshilin* rather than using *ha'aramah*. This itself is understandable. But R. Ashi goes further, saying that the rabbis are stricter about the use of *ha'aramah* than about purposeful transgression. Perhaps the reason is that *ha'aramah* undermines the use of *'eruv tavshilin*. It is a personalized circumvention rather than using the public *takkanah*. By opting out of the rabbinic mechanism and using *ha'aramah* instead, one expresses disregard for rabbinic legal authority.[90]

The *Bavli*'s concern that *ha'aramah* might undermine observance of the law is an enhancement of the concern for legal integrity. While the *Yerushalmi* discussed maintaining procedural and substantive integrity of the laws by focusing on which laws could be circumvented and what values were worth circumvention of the law, the *Bavli* adds the concern for circumventions potentially leading to a decline in observance. This concern led to the development of new parameters for how, when, and by whom *ha'aramah* should be practiced.

Conclusion

This chapter posited a Babylonian turn in rabbinic attitudes toward *ha'aramah*, notably *ha'aramah* of performative intentions. Later *amoraim* and the redactors of the *Bavli* insist on narrowing the gap between one's performed intentions and one's subjective intentions. They do so by: (a) redacting bolder cases of performative intention *ha'aramah* (e.g., changing R. Yehoshua's opinion in the livestock case); (b) requiring that one authenticate performative *ha'aramah* through external factual change (e.g., placing pomegranates in the strainer); (c) barring *ha'aramah* that is too obviously a ruse; (d) rereading Palestinian cases of *ha'aramah* through lenses other than *ha'aramah* (e.g., using "since" to understand R. Yehoshua and R. Eliezer's debate about burning ḥallah dough on Passover); and (e) offering language for and asserting the importance of subjective intention, and even asserting that compelled consent relies upon it (as in the case of *gomer be-libo*). They do all this in addition to using the terminology of *ha'aramah* less often than the *Yerushalmi* and employing the root *'.r.m.* to mean deceit.

I suggested that this evolution in rabbinic thinking about *ha'aramah* may relate to any or all of the following phenomena: (a) the growing dominance of subjective intention in rabbinic thought, also indicated in neighboring Persian cultures, both monastic Christianity and Zoroastrianism; (b) general changes in rabbinic attitudes toward bold counterfactual legal claims and initiatives; and (c) concerns about the deterioration of observance of the law that *ha'aramah* might cause. Each of these plays its own role in the way that *ha'aramah* develops.

Now that I have surveyed the ancient material, including possible parallels from other cultures, in the following chapter, I will place my observations about *ha'aramah* in dialogue with contemporary legal theory.

Chapter 6

Ha'aramah and Contemporary Legal Theory

Now that I have examined the phenomenology of rabbinic legal circumventions in their ancient context, I return to today's jurisprudential paradigms. After all, legal circumventions emerge within legal systems ancient and modern, secular and religious, the world over. Placing our rabbinic exploration of *ha'aramah* in dialogue with contemporary paradigms will demonstrate both how tools of modern secular jurisprudence can be useful in analyzing even ancient religious law and what a study of ancient rabbinic legal dodges can contribute to contemporary secular legal thought.

Haim Tchernowitz: *Ha'aramah* as Historical Jurisprudence

Already in the nineteenth century, Rabbi Haim Tchernowitz, a scholar of rabbinics who used both traditional and critical methods, attempted to translate *ha'aramah* into the legal paradigms of the day.[1] He looked to the Historical School of jurisprudence founded in Germany by Friedrich Carl von Savigny.[2] The Historical movement applied Hegel's idea of the *Volksgeist*, the spiritual essence of a nation, to law. Instead of viewing institutional legislation as the primary source of law, this school of thought argued that law grows organically from among the people, and thus the law and its evolution reflect the evolving spirit of the people. Tchernowitz applied this concept to Jewish law, arguing that Jewish law also emerges from the unique essence of the Jewish people.[3] Consequently, he suggested that "[the Rabbis] were just as concerned with the outer shell and dressing [of the law] as they were with its inner core and substance. For sometimes the outer garb, too—to the extent that it takes on the national form—is also important for maintaining the existence of the nation."[4] Using this lens, he argued that *ha'aramah* endeavors to retain the "outer garb" of the law because of its connections to the spirit of the Jewish nation while making important changes to its substance.[5]

Using a legal framework of his time, Tchernowitz breathed new life into the understanding of *ha'aramah*. Specifically, by choosing Historicism as his model, he challenged the charges of dry legalism that were often leveled against talmudic law. In fact, he subverted the model: the letter *is* the spirit, the spirit of the Jewish people; that is, letter of the law reflects the essence of its constituency.

Like Tchernowitz, I too will use the tools of contemporary jurisprudence to discuss *ha'aramah*. And it is true that often using such tools can make a strange phenomenon like *ha'aramah* seem more palatable to the modern reader. However, I hope that what I have presented thus far has already made *ha'aramah* palatable on its own terms and in its own context. Unlike Tchernowitz, I will not use a single theory to try to explain the logic behind *ha'aramah*. Additionally, I will present here the ways that *ha'aramah* can contribute to contemporary legal debate, specifically in challenging the binary of legal formalism and legal realism.

Ancient and Contemporary Paradigms: Changing Facts, Not Rules

This book has distinguished between legal loopholes and legal fictions throughout, arguing that *ha'aramah* is the former rather than the latter. Unlike legal fiction, which asserts something that is clearly false without actually changing any facts on the ground, *ha'aramah* requires a change of concrete facts (and even intention may be thought of in more concrete terms within this model). Unlike the classical fiction, which is the province of a court, *ha'aramah* is most often presented as a loophole used by private citizens. Despite these differences, however, I also noted that loopholes and fictions both rely on manipulating facts rather than changing rules. And it is this similarity that makes contemporary jurisprudential theories about legal fiction relevant to *ha'aramah*.

Frederick Schauer, in trying to understand the prevalence of legal fictions in the Common Law tradition, discusses why manipulating facts may be preferable to changing rules.[6] In some legal systems, he argues, the idea of changing a rule is not palatable. Additionally, changing a rule will affect the entire web of the legal system in unpredictable and perhaps undesirable ways. Consequently, it is often better to keep the rules as they are but to engineer the facts of a situation for minimal disruption to the legal system. This allows for an equitable outcome without relying on an equity court, for example, where the rules would be set aside in favor of a just outcome

The analysis is useful for *ha'aramah*. The degree to which rabbis felt authorized to change the law is subject to debate among scholars.[7] But even where they did, it is possible that changing the law would be less palatable to practitioners. And what's more, their intervention in the law could cause unanticipated ripple effects in other situations. Take, for example, the original mishnaic case of *ha'aramah* to avoid the redemption tax on *ma'aser sheni*. It is fairly uncontroversial to suggest that the rabbis most likely did not believe they had the authority to directly repeal the rule requiring a 25 percent tax on redeeming one's own *ma'aser sheni* even if this would have helped people. However, even if they did believe technically in their own authority to repeal it, the change still may not have been received well within rabbinic circles, and this interference in biblical law would have raised other issues. One can imagine a slew of questions that would arise in the wake of trying to repeal the 25 percent redemption tax: for example, should the tax still apply to people who can afford it? And how does one determine who can afford it? If this was specifically done after the fall of the Temple, should the tax return when the Temple is rebuilt? And what of the notion of *ḥomesh*, adding 25 percent to a principal in general?[8] Would it be questioned in its other contexts as well? And would anything change about rituals and laws that are analogized to *ma'aser sheni* because of this new ruling?[9] Changing a rule brings in its wake new questions and effects. Giving people a workaround, on the other hand, has fewer ripple effects.

Eben Moglen suggests that the pervasiveness of legal fictions in the Common Law tradition reveals a provocative paradigm shift: while people think of legal systems as making law through legislation, the Common Law tradition more often used adjudication to make new law.[10] When manipulating facts is permitted—whether through fictions or loopholes—adjudication no longer entails simply applying statutes to the facts of a given case. Adjudication includes the possibility of shaping the case anew. Moglen's approach of seeing adjudication as a primary mode of making new law also shed light on *ha'aramah*. While the rabbis did legislate *takkanot* and *gezerot*, they also made new law through judging individual cases and allowing or disallowing *ha'aramah*. And beyond *ha'aramah*, the paradigm of adjudication as a primary source of law is relevant to much of rabbinic tradition.

Theorizing Legal Loopholes: Laws and Principles

While contemporary thought on legal fiction proves useful in considering *ha'aramah*, there is also interesting work that has been done specifically on the phenomenon of legal loopholing. Leo Katz, for example, takes up the question of why loopholes persist in a legal system. Many, he notes, suggest that the reason for loopholes is because all law is under- or over-inclusive: no system of law can possibly anticipate all outcomes or express itself in ways that will lead to its perfect application. Katz disagrees with this explanation, interestingly, precisely because of the persistence of loopholes within both rabbinic and Jesuit traditions. If the issue were simply over- or under-inclusivity of law, rabbis and Jesuits would have disallowed loopholes. After all, are people trying to fool God? Instead, Katz suggests a theory of multicritical decision making as the reason for loopholes' tenacity: so long as law has multiple principles involved, loopholes that uphold at least one legal principle cannot be stamped out.

He offers the following example: if someone is attacked, he may defend himself even by killing his perpetrator because people have the right to self-defense. This is a legal principle. If, however, the would-be victim can easily escape, he must run rather than kill the perpetrator because the law also requires not doing disproportionate harm. Not doing disproportionate harm is also a legal principle. If escape is an option, the law favors the principle of not causing disproportionate harm over the right to self-defense. But what if we complicate the scenario? Let's say this man actually wants to kill the attacker and devises a situation where he will be attacked in a place where he cannot easily escape. Would the law find him guilty of murder if he kills his attacker, even though the situation was purposely orchestrated this way? Katz argues that the law cannot find this man guilty of murder because of the legal principle of self-defense, which this person has exercised. Just because the person set up the situation with no option for escape does not mean that he has lost his right to self-defense if someone attacks him.

Katz applies this logic to other situations as well. Another example involves someone who wants to emigrate to America but has no legal recourse to do so. American immigration law entails both of the following principles: (1) America cannot absorb everyone, but also (2) refugees seeking asylum from other countries deserve protection from the United States once they are within its borders. These two principles can be at odds with each other. Katz asks his readers to imagine that someone who wishes to move to America enters the country illegally. According to the first principle, she should leave the country and go back to her country of origin. However, what if she decides to force the second principle by making comments that would lead to execution in her country of origin? Katz argues that she should not be deported, though she exploited a loophole: the legal principle of protecting asylum seekers still applies.[11] Katz's approach is relevant to *ha'aramah*. I too have argued that *ha'aramah* is not simply about taking advantage of the technical reading of the law but about claiming legal values. However, this is only a subset of cases.[12]

The Responsibility of Lawyers

Another fruitful dialogue with contemporary legal theory involves the responsibility and limitations placed on lawyers in employing legal dodges. I noted earlier that in advocating for and/or accepting the use of loopholes, the rabbis resemble lawyers. The function of lawyers, when it comes to clever interpretations of the law, is a matter of controversy among legal thinkers today. Bradley Wendel, for example, states that the most common position on this is too expansive: the role of a lawyer is to zealously defend their client's interests without breaking the law. This suggests that a lawyer can do whatever they can "get away with."[13]

Wendel and others consider this to be unethical "loophole lawyering."[14] Wendel thinks that the job of a lawyer is to "represent her client effectively within the bounds of the law."[15] This places the lawyer's fidelity to the law as a constraint upon what the lawyer can advise or argue on behalf of a client: one can only argue an entitlement of a client that is defensible with valid legal logic. He calls this an "internal point of view"—internal to the law, that is.[16] Once one sees the law as having a purpose, fidelity to the law means not trying to frustrate that purpose. Some suggest that context determines the degree to which one may manipulate the law. In the context of litigation, for example, some are more permissive regarding loopholing, whereas in non-adversarial contexts one should use more ethical self-restraint.[17] Rabbinic texts regarding *ha'aramah* parallel the approach that requires the "internal point of view" in the sense that the goals and procedures of *ha'aramah* should consider the values that have been attributed to the law itself.

Beyond Theories of Circumvention: Subverting the Formalism vs. Realism Binary

The examples above speak directly to the phenomenon of legal circumvention. They exhibit a relationship between the paradigms offered by legal thinkers today and those even of ancient times. However, this study of *ha'aramah* is also relevant to broader modern discussions about the character of law: whether it is formalistic or realistic. *Ha'aramah* actually disrupts this neat binary.

Legal Formalism *and* Legal Realism

This book has illustrated the ways that *ha'aramah* incorporates a willingness to use the formal reading of a statute while undermining the intended meaning of that statute. Nonetheless, I noted throughout the book the limits of formalistic thinking regarding *ha'aramah*. Palestinian texts—both *tannaitic* and *amoraic*—set limitations: rabbis accept *ha'aramah* where it promotes broad legal principles but reject it where it does not. Rabbis accept *ha'aramah* where it does not undermine the procedural integrity of the law but reject it where it does. And the *Bavli* too created its versions of these limitations: *ha'aramah* is rejected if it will lead to a decline in the observance of the law, whether because it is too obvious or because the wrong people are using it. These rabbinic approaches to *ha'aramah* challenge the neat distinction between legal formalism and legal realism. While it appears to be more realistic, focusing on functionalist outcomes, *ha'aramah* adopts some of the tools of formalism, a focus on the letter of the law.

The late nineteenth century and early twentieth century saw the development of a major debate between proponents of legal formalism and legal realism.[18] Legal formalists emphasized the importance and the comprehensiveness of rules in making law. They deemphasized gaps and ambiguity in the law and asserted that law could be deduced from the words of statutes with little recourse to judicial discretion or policy considerations. In other words, law is a science, and its materials are in law books.[19] As Thomas C. Grey explains in his outline of Christopher Columbus Langdell's formalism:

> The heart of the theory was the view that law is a science. Langdell believed that through scientific methods lawyers could derive correct legal judgments from a few fundamental principles and concepts, which it was the task of the scholar-scientist like himself to discover.[20]

And

> The heart of classical theory was its aspiration that the legal system be made complete through universal formality, and universally formal through conceptual order. A few basic top-level categories and principles formed a conceptually ordered system above a large number of bottom-level rules.... When a new case arose to which no existing rule applied, it could be categorized and the correct rule for it could be inferred by use of the general concepts and principles; the rule could then be applied to the facts to dictate the unique correct decision in the case. The system was doubly formal. First, the specific rules were framed in such terms that decisions followed from them uncontroversially when they were applied to readily ascertainable facts.... Second, at the next level up one could derive the rules themselves analytically from principles.[21]

In other words, most cases could be adjudicated uncontroversially by reference to general legal principles (e.g., "a contract cannot be formed unless there is a bargained-for consideration") and/or direct rules (e.g., "a contract that is sent by mail is not formed until it is received and read"). And new cases that arise can be comfortably assessed by reference to the general legal principles. Thus, there is little need for independent judicial ideas and little interest in considerations of external concerns, such as the social acceptability of the outcome in a given case.

Frederick Schauer argues for why formalism is important for society.[22] He asserts that the existing law is complete and that one must make decisions on the basis of limiting rules rather than other variables.[23] He defends the position of being a "slave to marks on a page," by arguing that a rule is only a rule if it stands independent of reason.[24] He writes, "If every application that would not serve the reason behind the rule were jettisoned from the coverage of the rule, then the decision procedure would be identical to one applying reasons directly to individual cases, with the mediation of rules. Under such a model, rules are superfluous except as predictive guides, for they lack any normative power of their own."[25] Thus, Schauer equates formalism with "taking rules seriously."[26] While he realizes that rules may lead to unjust consequences, he lauds their ability to inject stability into a system and to restrict misguided judges.[27]

However, there is another philosophy of formalism that does not just stress the authority of rules or their independence from reason but instead focuses on the logical coherence that is inherent to a given legal system. Ernest Weinrib defines formalism as insisting that (a) legal justification must emerge from a rationality that is less open-ended than political or ideological contest (what he calls "rationality"); (b) this rationality is internal to the materials of the law itself (what he calls "immanence"); and (c) there is an intelligible moral order to the legal materials (what he calls "normativity").[28] He emphatically does not believe that justification for legal decisions should come from some political goal outside of the law, such as solidarity or the like. As Suzanne Last Stone writes, "the characterization of rule application as mechanical is a polemical term invented by formalism's opponents. Formalism is evaluative, but, crucially, its evaluative criteria are internal to law, reflecting law's inner morality."[29] This view of formalism focuses less on predictability/stability of the law and more on the internal coherence of the law.

Legal realists, on the other hand, emphasize the "sociocultural dimensions" of the law—how lawyers and judges practice and decide law in real life—rather than simply the texts of the statutes themselves.[30] They argue that "law is a means to social ends . . . and . . . that one must go beyond legal doctrine to understand how law actually functions."[31] In other words, the social acceptability of legal outcomes matters, and judges use maximal discretion in the interpretation and application of law. As Karl Llewellyn, an early proponent of legal realism, wrote regarding judicial decision making:

> The traditional approach is in terms of words; it centers on words. If nothing be said about behavior, the *tacit* assumption is that the words do reflect behavior, and if they be the words of rules of law,

do influence behavior, even influence behavior effectively and precisely to conform completely to those words. Here lies the key to the muddle . . . Do I suggest that (to cut in at one crucial point) the "accepted rules," the rules the judges say that they apply, are without influence upon their actual behavior? I do not. I do not even say that, *sometimes*, these "accepted rules" may not be a very accurate description of the judges' actual behavior. What I say is that such accuracy of description is rare. The question is how, and how much, and in what direction, do the accepted rule and the practice of decision diverge? More: how, and how much, *in each case*? You cannot generalize on this, *without investigation*.[32]

Judges do not simply apply rules mechanically the way he would characterize (or mischaracterize?) the formalists' position. Instead, for Llewellyn, the focus of law is the practice of the courts in interpreting and applying the rules, which is neither automatic nor uncontroversial. And social acceptability is an important part of what impacts judicial decision making in this process of applying the rules:

Gone is the ancient assumption that law is because law is; there has come since, and remains, the inquiry into the purpose of what courts are doing, the criticism in terms of searching out purposes and criticizing means. Here value judgments reenter the picture, and should. . . . It seems patent that only a gain in realism and effectiveness of thinking can come from consistently (not occasionally) regarding the official formulation as a tool, not as a thing of value in itself; a means without meaning save in terms of its workings, and of results desired. In the terms used above: as *prima facie* pure paper until the contrary is demonstrated; and as at best a new piece of an established but moving environment, one single element in a complex of practices, ideas and institutions without whose study the one element means nothing. Hence, not the elimination of rules, but the setting of words and paper in perspective.[33]

Or, as Oliver Wendell Holmes writes: "Inasmuch as the real justification of a rule of law, if there be one, is that it helps to bring about a social end which we desire, it is no less necessary that those who make and develop the law should have those ends articulately in their minds."[34] Legal realists argue that law is fundamentally instrumental, and so one may use the law to accomplish proper ends, be those immanent to the rationality of the legal system or not.[35] The realistic orientation "stresses [law's] . . . manipulability over its certainty; and its instrumental possibilities over its normative contents."[36]

While many debate the precise definitions of the arguments of these two schools,[37] in broad strokes it is fair to say that formalists believe that law should be derived from statutes and precedent while realists believe that external concerns related to social desirability should shape law's interpretation. There are likewise those who argue that both formalism and realism are inadequate as comprehensive theories of law.[38]

So where does rabbinic law fit, and how might *ha'aramah* inform this debate?

There has been much discussion over the degree to which rabbinic law maps onto either realism or formalism, whether because of its religious nature, its ancient provenance, or its particular features.[39] I find myself most convinced by those who do not try to map rabbinic law onto one of these schools wholesale but instead find aspects of both formalistic and realistic thinking within rabbinic jurisprudence.[40] Chaim Saiman, for instance, points out that rabbinic law has a realist tendency because it considers the purposes of law and gives discretion to rabbis and/or judges. But it also has a formalistic tendency because it often ritualizes laws in ways that diverge from the original meaning or intention of a law, because it focuses on details that do not functionally matter, because it emphasizes the form of the law, and because a theological position describes our inability to change the law (even if in practice legal interpreters do so).[41] *Ha'aramah*, in fact, exemplifies how both formalism and realism play a role in rabbinic decision making. On the one hand, it is tempting to view *ha'aramah* as a formalistic tool that recognizes the importance of the rules and the way they are stated, yet the parameters that the rabbis place around *ha'aramah* indicate that rules are not everything.

One theory that captures this synthesis of activism and attentiveness to statutes is that of Ronald Dworkin. He rejects both conventionalism—the theory that law can only be made from preexisting statutes and precedents—and pragmatism—the theory that adjudication is constrained only by what is best for the community and not by existing law. Instead, he focuses on the coherence of the legal system and the role of interpretation. His theory of "law as integrity" describes judges as attempting to make law coherent through interpretation, which includes both rules and moral principles. Rules are "all-or-nothing. . . . If the facts a rule stipulates are a given, then either the rule is valid, in which case the answer it supplies must be accepted, or it is not, in which case it contributes nothing to the decision."[42] Principles, however, are moral values: "a standard that . . . is a requirement of justice or fairness or some other dimension of morality."[43] Principles must be taken into consideration when deciding whether to apply a given rule.

Dworkin likens this constructive, interpretive model of adjudication to authors writing a chain novel. Each judge is akin to an author writing the next chapter of a novel that has been cowritten by earlier authors. The new "novelist" must ensure that the narrative remains coherent, able to have been authored by one person, though in truth it is authored by many: this means that the novelist will be bound to the previous chapters while having their own perspective about the general principles and ideology that run through the story. This is necessarily an interpretive process because each novelist in the chain will have an opinion about what does and should animate the novel, and yet these ideas must adequately explain earlier chapters. The ideas that animate the novel are the principles, and the degree to which these principles emerge from the law or are imposed as organizing principles of the law is ambiguous.

Dworkin illustrates law as integrity by examining the 1882 New York Supreme Court case of *Riggs vs. Palmer*.[44] Elmer Palmer stood to inherit most of his grandfather's estate. Concerned that his grandfather might change the terms of the will in light of his recent remarriage, Palmer murdered his grandfather before he could alter the will. May Palmer inherit his grandfather's estate? Judge Gray, who wrote the dissenting opinion, argued that by literal interpretation of the statute of wills, which says nothing about restricting the rights of an heir who murders the testator, Palmer should inherit. However, the majority voted for Palmer not to inherit. Judge Earl, writing for the majority opinion, suggested two reasons why. The first regards the intentions of those who wrote the law of inheritance: "It is a familiar canon of construction that a thing which is within the intention of the makers of a statute is as much within the statute as if it were within the letter; and a thing which is within the letter of the statute is not within the statute, unless it be within the intention of the makers."[45] Clearly, the shapers of the doctrine of inheritance did not intend for murder to be a valid part of claiming one's inheritance. This sounds precisely like Aristotle's concept of equity, as discussed in Chapter 3: laws will always be imperfect, and when a difficult case arises, think about what the lawgiver(s) intended. But Gray's second reason is about general principles of law. Rather than reading the statute about inheritance in isolation from other legal texts, one should apply the statute in light of "principles of justice assumed elsewhere in the law."[46] As Gray writes: "Besides, all laws as well as all contracts may be controlled in their operation and effect by general, fundamental maxims of the common law. No one shall be permitted to profit by his own fraud, or to take advantage of his own wrong. . . . These maxims, without any statute giving them force or operation, frequently control the effect and nullify the language of wills." This expresses a view of law that is not only about the statute in question but about the principles of the legal system as a whole.

Dworkin believes that the Palmer case argument should be understood as being about the interpretation of law rather than about the clash between societal needs and legal statutes: "the dispute about Elmer was not about whether judges should follow the law or adjust it in the interests of justice. . . . It was a dispute about what the law was, about what the real statute the legislators enacted really said."[47] Dworkin suggests that the principles—the values that can be understood as coherent justifications for much of the legal system—must be part of one's interpretation of a given statute. As Bernard Jackson explains, "Dworkin's legal theory attaches supreme importance to the value of rationality in the form of consistent application of the morality of the community, and thus implementation of the rights which that community morality confers."[48]

Dworkin's schema suits *ha'aramah*.[49] Throughout this book, I have argued that, in context of *ha'aramah,* the rabbis manifest concern not only with technicalities of the law but with principles that matter to the legal system as a whole: for example, not losing money due to religious obligation, not cheating the Temple treasury, avoiding transgression, celebrating the festivals with food and drink, not cheating other people, not undermining people's respect for the law. Whether in cases where *ha'aramah* is permitted because of its value-laden aims or where it is disallowed, there are significant general legal principles at play. Rather than understanding *ha'aramah* as a narrow interpretation of the statute being circumvented, the rabbis introduce an expansive view of the legal system as a whole. They want the legal system to be "morally coherent."[50]

Dworkin's model is particularly apt for analogizing rabbinic legal circumventions because of its constructive/subjective approach. While Dworkin discusses the principles as being part of the legal system, he also recognizes that the judge projects the principles onto the law because of the judge's own subjective views about their explanatory power and their value. A judge understands the law to have a certain undergirding moral logic, but arguably a different judge might emphasize a different logic. In his description of how a chain novelist continuing to write the book decides how to proceed, Dworkin writes:

> Your assignment is to make the text the best it can be, and you will therefore choose the interpretation you believe makes the work more significant or otherwise better. . . . Is your judgment about the best way to interpret and continue the sections you have been given . . . a free or a constrained judgment? Are you free to give effect to your own assumptions and attitudes about what novels should be like? Or are you bound to ignore these because you are enslaved by a text you cannot alter? The answer is plain enough: neither of these two crude descriptions—of total creative freedom or mechanical textual constraint—captures your situation, because each must in some way be qualified by the other. . . . Both major types of convictions any interpreter has—about which readings fit the text better or worse and about which two readings make the novel substantively better—are internal to his overall schemes of beliefs and attitudes; neither type is independent of that scheme in some way that the other is not.[51]

This parallels the rabbinic case too. While the principles they uphold in *ha'aramah* are described elsewhere as emerging from within the legal system itself (e.g., *mNeg.* 12:6 about Torah sparing people's possessions), where these values originate is something of a chicken-and-egg question. Are the rabbis finding these values within the law because these values assert themselves, or are the rabbis constructively bringing out values in the law because these values resonate? It is impossible to know, and, in fact, most rabbinic rhetoric about *ha'aramah* never cites the values' origins.[52]

Rabbinic application of general legal principles to Jewish law is well attested beyond the realm of legal circumvention.[53] In fact, the very principle in the *Riggs vs. Palmer* case, that one should not profit from their misdeeds, is a principle attested in rabbinic literature:

Mishnah Ḥallah 2:7 (MS Kaufmann)

שיעור החלה אחד מעשרים וארבעה. העושה עיסה לעצמו העושה משתה לבנו אחד מעשרים וארבעה. נחתום שהוא עושה למכור בשוק וכן האשה שהיא עושה למכור בשוק אחד מארבעים ושמונה. מטמאת עיסתה שוגגת או אנוסה אחד מארבעים ושמונה מטמאת מזידה אחד מעשרים וארבעה כדי שלא יהא חוטא ניסכר.[54]

> The [minimum] measure of *ḥallah* is one twenty-fourth [of the dough]. If one makes dough for himself or for his son's banquet—one twenty-fourth. A baker who makes it to sell in the market, and so, too, a woman who makes it to sell in the market—one forty-eighth. If her dough was rendered ritually impure either unwittingly or by circumstances beyond her control—one forty-eighth. If it was rendered ritually impure deliberately—one twenty-fourth, so that a sinner should not profit.

Here we return to the obligation to set aside part of one's dough for consumption by the priest and to burn that portion (*ḥallah*) if it becomes ritually impure. The *mishnah* considers what to do if someone purposely made the dough impure. If dough becomes impure by mistake or accident, one may set aside less dough than usual for the *ḥallah* obligation so as not to waste extra now that no one can eat it. But if one purposely makes their dough impure, one does not get the same lenient dispensation, so the sinner will not profit. Where does this principle that a sinner should not profit originate? The rabbis do not say, but it does seem to be a logical way to apply the law. This concept becomes a legal principle that is applied elsewhere as well.[55] Rabbinic treatments of *ha'aramah* use this same methodology of navigating rules and principles.

Beyond Circumvention: Legal Flexibility

Another contemporary discussion that relates to *ha'aramah* is about legal flexibility versus legal rigidity. Allowing the use of loopholes involves flexibility, giving people license to interpret statutes creatively and even against their grain. On the other hand, when judges or legislators close off loopholes, they create boundaries and narrowness. In discussing American property law, Carol Rose describes the dynamics between legal rigidity and legal flexibility generally. She claims that the workings of legal systems betray an ongoing negotiation between what she calls "crystals" and "mud" in legal history. Crystals are "hard-edged rules" that do not buck exceptions. As she illustrates colorfully: "Default on paying your loan installments? Too bad, you lose the thing you bought and your past payments as well. Forget to record your deed? Sorry, the next buyer can purchase free of your claim, and you are out on the street. Sell that house with the leak in the basement? Lucky you, you can unload the place without having to tell the buyer about such things at all."[56] These rules are clear and sharp like crystal: everyone knows what to expect and what is expected of them.

"Mud," on the other hand, is described as "fuzzy, ambiguous rules of decision for what seem to be perfectly clear, open and shut, demarcations of entitlements."[57] For example, in property law, there was a crystalline rule called caveat emptor, which states that a purchaser is perfectly capable of inspecting property and deciding whether to buy it. Consequently, the seller need not disclose any defects to the buyer (though the seller may not deliberately mislead the buyer), and the buyer may not rescind the sale upon later discovery of defects.[58] However, the doctrine of "latent defects" provided an exception, and a muddy exception at that: the seller must inform the buyer about material problems with the property that are known to the seller but not reasonably discoverable by the buyer.[59] This doctrine produces mud: ambiguities that make the law less clear-cut. Now judges must define what defects are considered "material," what the seller "knows," and what "reasonably" means. This creates discretion, imprecision, and fluidity.

Rose argues that legal systems reflect a continuous cycle from crystals to mud and back to crystals. In the previous example, for instance, she notes that private bargainers try to install their own crystal rules such as a waiver of warrantees or the responsibility of disclosure on the part of the buyer. Likewise, the law itself might see such waivers and then ban them to return the crystal to mud once again.[60] Rose notes that people tend to favor one or the other—crystals or mud—but, in truth, we are stuck with both.[61]

Though not identical, *ha'aramah* suggests a similar pattern. The requirement to pay an extra 25 percent when redeeming *ma'aser sheni* is crystalline. The law clearly does not mean for farmers to alienate their produce or their money on purpose to avoid this tax. And yet permitting *ha'aramah* to do precisely that introduces some flexibility and ambiguity in the original terms.

What does ownership mean in the case of redemption? *Ha'aramah* expands the anticipated meaning of ownership by allowing a person to temporarily transfer money or goods to someone else solely for the purpose of redeeming the *ma'aser sheni*. Contrariwise, in the *Bavli* some of the mud is turned back into crystals, as less interpretive flexibility and ambiguity is allowed. For example, in discussions about intention-focused *ha'aramah*: one must place the pomegranates in the strainer or slaughter one of the two animals in the pit. And, on plenty of occasions, one may not use *ha'aramah* at all.

What is powerful about Rose's conceptualization of crystals and mud is the social relationships she asserts correspond to each. People need crystals when interacting with strangers because they do not trust others to come to agreement on their own. Strangers need transactions to be predictable. Mud, however, exhibits the flexibility of people who have a long-standing relationship and want to help each other in the context of that relationship:

> It is indeed the element of ongoing social interactions that mud rules focus upon. They attempt to introduce an element of continuing dialogue among persons who acted as if they were ordering their affairs as strangers. When a court introduces ambiguity into the fixed rules that the parties initially adopted, it in effect reinstates the kind of weighing, balancing, and reconsidering that the parties might have undertaken if they had been in some longer-term relationship with each other. Thus, if the mortgage can't be paid on time, the lender's expectation of prompt payment has to be weighed against the borrower's loss of the deal; if the house buyer discovers a leaky sewage line, perhaps he should get some concession from the seller to make up for this unexpected damage. But these judicial interventions are a crude substitute for dialogue, for talking things over and adjusting entitlements, as one would be likely to do in an ongoing trading relationship, or as one would in a family or religious community.[62]

This conception of mud resonates with *ha'aramah* as well. Within legal discussions of *ha'aramah*, rabbinic literature does not include mention of relationship: between God and the rabbis, God and legal adherents, or rabbinic authorities and legal adherents. However, the flexibility that *ha'aramah* offers to prevent the adverse effects of following the law certainly reflects a give-and-take relationship. The rabbis are not strangers to Jewish law or to God, nor are the practitioners. And the rabbis and their imagined practitioners are not strangers to each other. There are deep investments in all of these relationships. Circumventions leverage the generosity and trust of those long-standing relationships while allowing those relationships to continue to flourish.

Rabbinic Homiletics: On Dialogue and Relationship

The role played by relationships in legal manipulation is portrayed stunningly within later *aggadic* (homiletical) rabbinic discussion, as mentioned in Chapter 3. Later *aggadic midrashim* offer a picture of legal circumvention as part of the human-Divine dialogue. These evocative scenes manifest the significance of multiple relationships: between God and religious authorities; between God and the nation of Israel/the average person; between religious authorities and people in need; and simply among people themselves. The first of several such examples comes from the eighth- to ninth-century text Song of Songs *Rabbah*. It relates a story about the commandment to procreate, understood by rabbinic Judaism as an obligation incumbent upon every male Jew.[63] If a couple has been together for ten years and still cannot have children, the husband must increase his chances of having children by marrying someone else. In the following *midrash*, an infertile couple seeks divorce after ten years, and two of the characters collaborate to change the situation.

Song of Songs Rabbah 1:4:8 (MS Vatican 76)

אמ'"ר אדי מעשה באשה אחת בצידן ששש(ת)[ה]ת עשר שנים עם בעלה ולא ילדה אתון גבי ר' שמעון בן יוחאי בעיין למשתבקא דין מן דא. אמ' להון חיינון כש' שנזדווגתמ(ב)[ז]ה לזה במאכל ומשתה כך אין אתם מתפרשין אלא במאכל ומשתה. הלכו כדבריו ועשו להם יום טוב וסעודה גדולה. ושיכרתו יותר מידאי. כיון שנתיישבה דעתון עליו א?(ל)[ל]' מ' לה בתי ראי כל חפץ טוב שיש לי בבית·וטלי אותו ולכי לבית אביך. מה עשתה היא? לאחר שישן רמזה לעבדיה ולשפחתיה ואמרה להם שאוהו במטה וקחו אותו והוליכוהו לבית אבא. בחצי הלילה ננער משנתו. כיון דפג חמריה, אמ' לה בתי איכן אני נתון? אמרה ליה בבית אבא. אמ' לה מה לי ולבית אביך? אמרה לו ולא כך אמרת לי בערב כל חפץ טוב שיש בביתי טלי אותו ולכי לבית אביך? אין חפץ טוב לי בעולם יותר ממך! הלכו להם אצל ר'

שמעון בן יוחאי ועמד ונתפלל עליהם ונפקדו. מה הקב״ה פוקד עקרות אף צדיקים פוקדין עקרות. והרי דברים קל וחומר: ומה אם על בשר ודם על שאמר לבשר ודם שכמותו אין לי חפץ בעולם טוב ממך נפקדו, ישראל המחכין לישועתו של הב״ה בכל יום ויום ואומ׳ אין לנו חפץ טוב בעולם יותר ממך על אחת כמה וכמה! הוי נגילה ונשמחה בך.

R. Idi said: There was an incident with one woman in Tzidon, who was married to her husband for ten years and did not birth [children]. They came to R. Shimon ben Yohai and wanted to get divorced him from her. He said to them: By your lives! Just as you got married with food and drink (i.e., a party), so you shall not separate from one another except with food and drink (i.e., a party). They followed his guidance, and they made themselves a festive day and a great feast; and she got him excessively drunk. When his mind was settled, he said to her: My daughter, see any good item that I have in the house, and take it, and go to your father's house. What did she do? After he fell asleep, she hinted to her servants and maids, and said to them: Lift him in the bed and take him and bring him to [my] father's house. In the middle of the night, he awoke from his sleep. When his alcohol wore off, he said to her: My daughter, where am I? She replied: In [my] father's house. He said to her: What am I doing in your father's house? She said to him: Did you not tell me last night: Any good item that I have in my home, take it and go to your father's house? There is nothing greater in the world to me than you. They went to R. Shimon b. Yohai, and he stood and prayed for them, and they were remembered [with a child.] Just as God remembers barren women [to give them children] so to the righteous remember barren women [to give them children]. And behold these matters are a fortiori: if a person says about another person like themselves "there is nothing greater in the world to me than you" and they are remembered, [then surely] Israel who awaits God's salvation every day and says, "There is nothing greater in the world to us than You" (about God) how much more so! This is what is meant by, "we shall delight and take joy in You."[64]

The couple follows the letter of the law: they will divorce so that the man can fulfill his obligation to have children. But R. Shimon ben Yohai and the woman each take lawyerly steps to avoid the divorce, and God responds positively. R. Shimon b. Yohai does not allow the couple to divorce immediately, nor does he tell them not to divorce. Instead, with a wink and a nod, he sends them off to rediscover their love for one another, daring to hope that something might come of it. The woman makes the most of the opportunity by using the letter of her spouse's words in a hyper literal way. He had told her that she could take anything with her from the divorce. So, she takes *him*! In response to this touching display, R. Shimon b. Yohai prays for them to have a child, and God responds by granting her fertility. Moreover, the *midrash* ends by the woman's actions being compared valiantly to the aspiration of the people of Israel to be reunited with God from their exile. Clearly, her subterfuge is looked upon favorably.

The plot of this story indicates that the couple triumphs not *despite* their lawyering but because of it. Their fealty to the command of having children coupled with the wife's resourceful interpretation of her husband's offer places before R. Shimon b. Yohai and ultimately before God the pathos of the situation against the backdrop of their commitment to Jewish law: they have already shown their willingness to divorce but also their own distress. The woman's loophole and R. Shimon b. Yohai's wise counsel become the plea before God to recognize that they legitimately feel caught between, and loyal to, both the value of their marriage and the value of the commandment to have children. And Shimon b. Yohai does in fact plead before God in a manner of prayer. God responds by solving the problem. The story does not describe people trying to dupe God or cheapen the law. It describes people who desperately cling to both sides of a conflict, and each side matters, even to God. Consequently, they achieve a redemptive ending that the reader can only wish upon all those who experience such conflict.

The role of the religious leader matters here. R. Shimon b. Yohai actively recognizes the tragedy of the story, and so he tries to set the stage for avoiding this divorce by telling the couple to party together, hoping something might happen. When he hears of the woman's workaround, he brings the case before God. Ultimately, God saves them from the effects of the law altogether by granting them a child. There are so many precious relationships activated in this *midrash*: among the couple themselves, between R. Shimon b. Yohai and a couple in need, between God and the couple, and between God and R. Shimon b. Yohai. And all of these relationships are preserved or enhanced by the lawyering rather than undermined.

In the next example, from Exodus *Rabbah*, the stakes are collective. The *midrash* describes the aftermath of the sin of the golden calf, which threatens to undermine the covenant between God and the Jewish people.⁶⁵ Moses is described as an advocate (*sanegor*) arguing in the heavenly court, who, like a good Roman rhetor, offers any persuasive argument he can to save the Jewish people from destruction and restore their covenant with God.⁶⁶ Among the many arguments Moses presents, the *midrash* suggests a hyper literal reading to avoid punishment.

Exodus Rabbah 43:5 (MS Jerusalem 24 5977)

ד׳א׳ ״ויחל משה״ אריב״ל בשרשב״י.
פתח של תשובה פתח לו הקב״ה בסיני. ״אנכי י״י א-להיך.״ בשעה שעשו ישראל
אותו מעשה עמד משה והיה מפייס את האלי׳ם. ולא היה נשמע לו.
א׳ל איפשר שלא נעשה בהם מדת הדין על{שנטלו} ‹שבטלו› את הדבור?
א׳ל רבון העולם כך אמרת ״אנכי י-י א-להיך״ ולא אמרת ׳א-להיכם.׳ לא לי
אמרת ״אנכי י-י א-להיך״? שמא להם אמרת? ואני בטלתי את הדיבור? אתמהא!
{ד׳א. ויחל משה} אריב׳ל. לפי׳ חזר הדיבור בתורה בלשון רבים: ״אנכי י-י
א-להיכם.״ וכן בכל מצות: ״אנכי י-י א-להיכם.״⁶⁷ ולא אמ׳ עוד ״אנכי י-י א-להיך.״

Another explanation: And Moses beseeched [God] (Exod. 32:11). R. Yehoshua b. Levi said in the name of R. Shimon b. Yohai: God offered him an opening to argue at Sinai: "I am the Lord your (*sing.*) God." When the Israelites committed that act (i.e., made the golden calf), Moses stood and tried to appease God, but God would not accede. God said to him: Is it possible that We should not mete out judgment for nullifying the command? Moses said to God, Sovereign of the universe, You said thus: "I am the Lord your God" in the singular, and You did not say "your God" in the plural. Did You not say [specifically] to me "I am the Lord *your* God" [rather than to them]? Did You say it to them? And have I nullified the command? (Strange!)⁶⁸ {Another explanation: And Moses beseeched} R. Yehoshua b. Levi said: therefore, the command is repeated in the Torah in the plural: "I am the Lord your (*pl.*) God," and likewise regarding all commandments: "I am the Lord your (*pl.*) God," and no longer said, "I am the Lord your (*sing.*) God."

In his role as the Jewish people's advocate, Moses chooses to read the very foundation of the revelation of God at Sinai in a manner that defangs it. The opening line of revelation is God introducing Godself to the people of Israel: "I am the Lord your God who took you out of Egypt from the house of bondage" (Exod. 20:2). Moses notes, however, that the statement is in the singular, not only about God but about the people. While the use of the singular "your" is common practice in biblical Hebrew, Moses argues that God could not have been speaking to the multitudes of Israelites if "your" is in the singular! Instead, this statement of revelation does not apply to the people but only to the singular Moses himself. And because Moses has not done anything wrong, no one should be punished. God's hands are tied, so to speak, and all God can do is try to close the loophole in the future by changing the "your" in statements of "I am the Lord your God" elsewhere in the Torah to plural. But God "cannot" punish the current infraction because it is no infraction at all.

The farcical nature of Moses's reading of "I am the Lord your God" is obvious.[69] What is most intriguing, however, is that the *midrash* asserts that God opened the door to this creative loophole by stating the law in the singular in the first place. God is party to the plan to begin with through the formulation of the statute. God wants Moses to make this argument.[70] Moreover, the loophole that Moses uses to suggest that it is only he who has been commanded to treat God as his God emphasizes Moses's relationship with God. There is a tacit suggestion that the relationship between God and Moses should be a factor in God's decision: after all, Moses has been loyal.[71] The thread of relationship runs through this passage: between Moses and the Israelites, between God and Moses, and between God and the Israelites. The suggestion that God would place such a loophole into the Torah to begin with as a safety valve to stave off destruction or that God would accept such a spurious reading of the Torah after the fact bespeaks a desire to do whatever can be done to protect the Jewish people, even when they have done wrong.[72]

In the surrounding context of the Exodus *Rabbah midrash*, Moses uses several other rather technical stratagems to prevent the punishment of the people following the golden calf: tearing up the contract (the tablets on which the Ten Commandments are written); grabbing God's "pen" before God can write the decree of destruction; nullifying God's vow to punish those who practice paganism.[73] However, in another version of the very same scene in Numbers *Rabbah*, Moses's loophole is juxtaposed to appeals for Divine compassion. There, the loophole itself is less about a literal reading of the statute and more about whether God has set the foundations for monotheism and for a covenantal relationship with the people. Moses's argument is pedagogical in nature rather than nitpicking.

Numbers Rabbah 19:33 (MS Paris BN 150)

דבר אחר אז ישיר ישראל: זה אחד משלשה דברים שאמר משה לפני הקב"ה, וא"ל למדתני.
אמר לפניו: ריבונו של עולם מנין ישראל יודעין מה עשו, לא במצרים נתגדלו וכל מצרים עובדי ע"ז הם. וכשנתת את התורה, לא נתת אותה להם ואף לא היו עומדין שם, שנאמר (שמות כ): ויעמד העם מרחוק, ולא נתת אותה אלא לי, שנאמר (שם כד): ואל משה אמר עלה אל י'י, וכשנתת את הדברות לא נתתם להם, לא אמרת: "אני י'י א-להיכם" אלא (שם כ): "אנכי י'י א-להיך" לי אמרת, שמא חטאתי? אמר לו הקדוש ברוך הוא: חייך, יפה אמרת, למדתני. מכאן ואילך, אני או' בלשון רבים: "אני י'י א-להיכם".

Another reading: "Then Israel sang (Num. 21:17)"—This was one of three things that Moses said before God, and God said to him: "You have taught Me!"

Moses said before God: Sovereign of the universe, how do the Israelites know what they did [in committing the golden calf]?! Did they not grow up in Egypt, and all the Egyptians are pagans! And when You gave the Torah, You did not give it to them, and they were not even standing there, as is said, "And the nation stood at a distance (Ex. 20:18)." Rather, You only gave it to me, as it is said, "And to Moses [God] said, Ascend to the Lord (Ex. 24:1)." And when You gave the [Ten] Commandments, You did not give them to them (i.e., the Israelites). You did not say, "I am the Lord your (*pl.*) God" but "I am the Lord your (*sing.*) God." You said it to me. And have I sinned? God said to him: "By your life! You have spoken well. You have taught Me. From now on I will say it in plural language 'I am the Lord your (*pl.*) God (Lev. 25:38; Numbers 15:41).'"

We read here an excerpt from a *midrash* that enumerates three instances in which God learns (and changes) something as a result of a conversation with Moses: "You have taught Me!" goes the refrain. The refrain affirms a surprisingly bilateral relationship between God and Moses. Moses is permitted to argue with God. Notably, his argument in this *midrash* about why the people should not be punished for the sin of the golden calf is not simply linguistic or technical: it is a logical argument about what is realistic to expect from the Israelites at this point. Moses asks about the justice of holding the people accountable for idolatry given their coming of age in pagan Egypt and given the fact that they were not as intimately involved in revelation as Moses was. It is in relation to this argument—that God should not expect the people to be ready for full monotheism yet—that God accepts Moses's grammatical point about the phrasing "your God" being singular rather than plural. Moses, on the other hand, has a long-standing relationship with God. The interaction between Moses and God is not about a shrewd textual reading. It is about the newly minted relationship and religious identity of the Israelites that God wishes to encourage. And it is about the ongoing relationship between Moses and God as well as Moses and the Israelites. Consequently, the loophole argument of "your God" represents much more than a technicality.

In each of the aforementioned *midrashim*, circumvention invokes the flexibility inspired by long-term relationships that is also needed to maintain those relationships—whether between God and the infertile couple, the infertile partners themselves, God and the Jewish people, God and Moses, and so on. Sharp-edged rules will lead to disaster whereas some give, some generosity, allows, respects, and salvages ongoing relationships. Viewing circumventions in this way places them within a larger discourse of rabbinically narrated dialogue between God and the Jewish people. Within this discourse there exists a protest genre. In his book *Pious Irreverence*, Dov Weiss studies the phenomenon of rabbinic protest of the Divine, which he sees as an important facet of the evolving rabbinic understanding of the human-Divine relationship. His work illustrates that *tannaitic* corpora evince an anti-protest theology, while a protest-affirming theology "emerges in amoraic texts, such as Genesis *Rabbah* and Lamentations *Rabbah*, and reaches its fullest expression in the writings of the post-amoraic *Bavli* and the *midrashim* of *Tanḥuma-Yelammedenu* (seventh century midrash)."[74] His study relates mostly to narrative discussion in which the rabbis use "ventriloquism," challenging God's decisions through biblical characters to express their own misgivings.[75] Thus, the broader Numbers *Rabbah* citation above also challenges the propriety of God's punishing the righteous for the transgressions of their parents by placing this concern in the mouth of Moses. This makes the critique less disrespectful, as Moses is a character worthy of such dialogue with God.

Weiss's study can add texture to the conversation about *ha'aramah* even if the texts he examines come from a different time and place, with different redactors and rabbinic figures, from the *ha'aramah* passages presented throughout this book.[76] Nonetheless, rabbinic protest literature may offer a sort of commentary on the phenomenon of *ha'aramah*, a window into its character. After all, both protest and *ha'aramah* reflect honesty about the conflicts that can arise between human needs and Divine directives. At the same time, both protest and *ha'aramah*, as described in rabbinic literature, preserve reverence even while challenging the status quo. Weiss points out that rabbinic literature uses both prayer and the court of appeals as some of the main literary frames for protest. These arenas by definition preserve reverence for God even as they level critique; they offer "religious shelter for irreverent content."[77] Prayer, after all, is a pious activity, recognizing God as Sovereign. And in the courtroom scene, God is a litigant but is also the Judge. In other words, context matters for how protest is understood. Likewise, using *ha'aramah* indicates deep knowledge of and attachment to the Jewish legal framework. By not changing the law outright but instead using a workaround, the rabbis maintain the overall context that affirms Divine authority even while making practical, ethically motivated changes to its application. The entire activity is circumscribed by a sense of reverence for Divine rules.

Destructive Potential

The *midrashic* texts above offer a model of circumvention strengthening relationships, per Carol Rose's suggestion about the role of flexibility and ambiguity. But there are also *midrashic* models of circumvention sowing distrust and even destroying relationships.

One example comes from an *amoraic midrash* in which it is not human beings who use the legal dodge but God. The context is Abraham's pleading for Sodom and Gomorrah not to be destroyed (Gen. 18):

Genesis Rabbah 39:6[78] (Theodor-Albeck)

אמר ר' אחא נשבעת שאין אתה מביא מבול לעולם מה אתה מערים על השבועה?
אתמהא! מבול שלמים אי אתה מביא אלא מבול שלאש אם כן לא יצאת ידי השבועה

R. Aha said: You swore and said that You would not bring a flood to the world—why are You cunningly undermining Your oath? (Strange!)[79] You are not bringing a flood of water, but a flood of fire! If so, You have not fulfilled Your oath!

Much as the *midrashim* above enhance Moses's biblical pleading with God not to destroy the Israelites after the golden calf, this *midrash* enhances Abraham's pleading with God not to destroy Sodom and Gomorrah. Abraham and God are depicted in Scripture and in this *midrash* as having such a strong bond that Abraham can level his argument. Moreover, Abraham clearly feels so devoted to humanity that he is willing to confront God about the plan to destroy Sodom and Gomorrah.

Abraham accuses God of using a cheap loophole to destroy Sodom and Gomorrah: Genesis 9:11 records a Divine promise never again to flood the earth to destroy humanity, and yet God tells Abraham of a plan to destroy Sodom and Gomorrah (ultimately through raining down sulfurous fire upon the region; see Gen. 19:24). Identifying a tension between God's vow and God's current plan, Abraham argues that destroying these cities violates God's earlier oath. Just because God plans to rain down fire rather than water does not make this any less a destruction. This can be understood as an argument against collective punishment, against the absolute destruction of a sizable area of cultivated habitation, or perhaps against both. Significantly for our purposes, Abraham levels his argument by accusing God of following the letter of the law while hollowing out its true purpose.[80] He refuses to accept God's use of *ha'aramah*. This *midrash* mirrors the legal concern about *ha'aramah* being used in serpentine ways. *Ha'aramah* should not be used to create conflict or to hurt people. It is meant as a protective device for people in need. Thus, a *ha'aramah* that undermines God's relationship with humanity and God's standing as the faithful Judge of the universe is unacceptable.[81] This *midrash* adds nuance to our discussion of *ha'aramah* as entailing the flexibility needed to maintain relationships. In fact, there are times when its use undermines relationships.

Conclusion

This chapter explored the relationships between rabbinic legal theory and contemporary secular legal theory as refracted through the prism of *ha'aramah*.

Starting with Haim Tchernowitz's analysis of *ha'aramah* through the lens of Historical jurisprudence, I argued that other legal systems can offer new ideational frameworks through which to view rabbinic legal phenomena. I then introduced the analyses of several contemporary legal scholars of legal fictions, specifically relating to the reasons one might wish to change a fact rather than a rule: both because of the unacceptability or unpalatability of changing a rule and because of the unforeseen consequences of changing a rule. Scholars like Frederick Schauer and Alan Watson observe that the preference for changing fact over law explains why adjudication was such a prominent part of the history of Western lawmaking. Additionally, I presented Leo Katz's thesis that loopholes are not sustained by imperfect legislation but by needing and wanting to uphold the competing principles of the law itself. I noted that the rabbinic paradigm might challenge Katz, not on his thesis but on the latitude he gives regarding which loopholes are acceptable.

In the second half of the chapter, I moved beyond comparative theories of legal circumventions to more general discussions of how adjudication works. Using Ronald Dworkin's theory of law as integrity, I emphasized the role that legal principles play in understanding the law and how to apply it. Dworkin recognizes the duality of constraint and freedom that attends to this process, which is likewise applicable to *ha'aramah*. The duality of constraint and freedom cuts through a more binary way of thinking about law as either formalistic or realistic. Moreover, the role of subjectivity in developing the principles of the law highlights the porous boundary of what is internal to the law and what is external to it.

Carol Rose's work provided a second lens for comparison. She introduces the notion that the evolution of law is cyclical: first come the clear-cut laws and then the open-ended, flexible standards, and back again. Often, the more flexible standards speak to a relationship between the parties seeking to apply the laws to those transactions. A sense of trust undergirds a willingness to be flexible. I applied the same connection of relationship to legal flexibility in permitting *ha'aramah*: to keep people in relationship with Jewish law, it is important to maintain the possibility of using ambiguity to the advantage of those who attempt to stay faithful to the law. To dramatize this sense of relationship, I turned to later *midrashic* materials that place the use of circumvention in the context of maintaining relationships among people, between God and individuals, and between God and the collective Jewish people. Borrowing from rabbinic protest literature, I suggest that legal circumvention, by its very nature of being circumscribed by fealty to the legal system, is a way of managing the conflicts between God's law and human concerns. And viewing the way that rabbinic legal discourse evolved regarding *ha'aramah*, this paradigm is quite fitting: *ha'aramah* is consistently defined by attempting to hold both reverence for God's word and appreciation for human concerns as part and parcel of a healthy legal system. And yet the rabbis show deep reverence for the authority of Jewish law, setting boundaries where they thought that reverence might be undermined by *ha'aramah*. This makes the twin vectors in the *midrashic* accounts of God and *ha'aramah*—allowing its use in the Divine courtroom to save the Jewish people but challenging it in the Heavenly courtroom when used for destruction—a most fitting way to encapsulate rabbinic approaches to circumventing the law.

Epilogue

Ha'aramah and *Takkanot*

This book has focused on *ha'aramah*, a subset of rabbinic legal circumventions mostly defined as a private tool used by individuals to navigate difficult situations. However, we cannot conclude a study on rabbinic circumventions without discussing some well-known public rabbinic circumventions which shape Jewish life today. Many of these mechanisms are oriented toward public policy, originate in ancient rabbinic literature, but are not labeled *ha'aramah*. Some examples include retaining debts in the sabbatical year (*prosbul*), rendering a public space a shared private domain (*'eruv*), and a mechanism for cooking on a festival for the Sabbath (*'eruv tavshilin*). Rather than ad hoc private circumventions, the aforementioned are understood as explicit rabbinic enactments designed to ameliorate pervasive complications and to be adopted widely. We will also address here the sale of *ḥametz*, with which this book began, which first appears in rabbinic literature as a private ad hoc loophole and only became a widespread recommended practice much later in Jewish history. It merits discussion both because of its fame as a quintessential Jewish loophole and because its evolution challenges the binary between *ha'aramah* and *takkanah*. These four public policy circumventions fit in the Venn diagram of well-known and emerging from early rabbinic literature. There are of course, many other circumventions in Jewish life that are either less well-known or emerge after the close of the Talmud, which likewise merit study. However, this epilogue is intended only to begin the process of relating widespread *takkanot* that use circumventive strategies to our study of *ha'aramah*.

Moshe Silberg and Solomon Zeitlin disagree about the relationship between *ha'aramot* and *takkanot*.[1] Here, we will define *takkanot* not only as that which is referred to using the root *t.k.n.*, but as rabbinic legislation that is both additive to biblical law and meant to be adopted widely.² Silberg focuses on methodological similarities between *takkanot* and *ha'aramot* while Zeitlin emphasizes what we have already mentioned—the difference between the private nature of most *ha'aramot* and the public nature of *takkanot*. He also adds that rabbis specifically seek scriptural support for *takkanot*. However, it is indeed difficult to fully disentangle *ha'aramot* from *takkanot*, especially because some *ha'aramot* may be about pervasive public issues (*bekhor, ma'aser sheni*) and at least one is accompanied by the *hitknu* terminology and scriptural validation (*yMS* 4:4, 55a). At the same time, there are rabbinic texts that explicitly distinguish between *takkanot* and *ha'aramot*, as in the case of employing *'eruv tavshilin* rather than "accidentally" cooking leftovers on the festival (*yBetzah* 2:1, 61b; *bBetzah* 17b). Rather than making sweeping claims, in this Epilogue, we will examine similarities and differences between individual cases of public policy *takkanot* and *ha'aramah*.

Prosbul—Collecting Debts Even in the Sabbatical Year

Per biblical law, every seven years, debts between Jews are canceled. However, *prosbul* allows lenders to collect anytime, even in a sabbatical year.³ As *mGittin* 4:3 offers: "Hillel instituted (*hitkin*) *prosbul* in order to rectify society." *MShevi'it* 10:3 further offers Scriptural support:

> *Prosbul* does not get canceled (in the sabbatical year). This is one of the things that Hillel the elder instituted (*hitkin*): When he saw that the people refrained from lending money to each other, thus violating that which is written in the Torah: "Beware lest you harbor the base thought ('The seventh year, the year of remission is approaching' so that you are mean to your needy kinsfolk and given them nothing (Deut. 15:9))," Hillel instituted (*hitkin*) the *prosbul*.

Hillel imported *prosbul* (lit. "before the court") from Greek law, where it allowed a lender to forcibly sell their debtor's assets to collect loan payment. In rabbinic law, it likely gave lenders more power to collect always, and only later became used specifically for circumventing debt remission in the sabbatical year.⁴ *Prosbul* echoes *ha'aramah* in its negotiation of a law to uphold legal principle. But here that principle is scriptural, rare for *ha'aramah* cases, as explained above.

The biggest question in comparing *prosbul* and *ha'aramah* is whether *prosbul* actually uses circumventive methodology at all. *MShevi'it* 10:4 describes the *prosbul* mechanism:

> This is the text of *prosbul:* "I pass on to you, so and so and so and so the judges in such and such place, that every debt that I am owed, that I shall collect it whenever I wish." And the judges sign below, or the witnesses.

The Sabbatical *prosbul* may function like any Greek *prosbul*: the court has placed a lien on the debtor's assets, and therefore the loan is considered already collected.[5] However, that is questionable (a) because the *prosbul* language indicates that that collection is yet to come ("I shall collect whenever I wish"); and (b) because there is no indication that the lender can collect forcibly, as in Greek law.[6] Another option is that *prosbul* converts a private loan into a *ma'aseh bet din*, a court ruling. While private loans are canceled in the sabbatical year, court rulings are not (*mShevi'it* 10:2). In fact, *prosbul* itself is actually called a *ma'aseh bet din* in *tShevi'it* 8:7.[7]

Recently, some have argued that *prosbul* does not utilize circumvention at all: it is simply a declaration to the court that one intends to collect a debt despite the sabbatical year. On this thesis, Hillel observed two biblical values in tension—remitting debts and extending credit to lenders—and he decreed to prioritize the latter over the former. Because Hillel cited a biblical concern, and he himself was a rabbinic authority, his *takkanah* was deemed acceptable.[8] This thesis defines *prosbul* as an act of equity, backed by rabbinic authority, rather than using the formal rules of the law to circumvent it. This suggestion is part of a larger movement to challenge the view of rabbinic jurisprudence as formalistic, an issue which we examined broadly in Chapter 6.[9]

If *prosbul* uses a workaround, as is the more common understanding of how it works, it bears similarity to *ha'aramah*. It uses the letter of the law to uphold the important value of ensuring that the poor still receive loans. As *mShevi'it* 10:3 expresses, because loans were remitted in the sabbatical year, people were loath to loan money to the poor. Hillel worried about the undermining of a biblical value, and even direct command, that people not refrain from lending money to the poor because they worry that they will not be reimbursed due to the sabbatical remittance (Deut. 15:9). In response, he offered a circumvention in the form of a *takkanah* to keep (at least some loans) from being remitted. But rather than being a private use loophole, it is a public service meant to solve a widespread problem. However, if *prosbul* is an explicit rabbinic decree to change the law that does not use a workaround, but simply a declaration on the part of the lender, it differs from *ha'aramah*: this understanding of *prosbul* argues that it relies on rabbinic authority to legislate based on Torah values and what is needed in society.

Another dimension that should be considered in comparing *ha'aramah* and *prosbul* is the status of law that may be negotiated. In both cases, *amoraic* literature begins to distinguish between rabbinic and biblical law. A few sources presage (*yPes.* 3:3, 30a) or indicate a difference (*bShab.* 139b) between *ha'aramah* to circumvent rabbinic and biblical law, even as *tannaitic ha'aramot* circumvent biblical law. Regarding *prosbul*, both Talmuds are more explicit in debating whether *prosbul* can cancel biblically remitted debts or only rabbinically remitted debts.[10] This reflects *amoraic* developments regarding the distinction between biblical and rabbinic law.

'Eruv—Carrying on the Sabbath

Jewish law permits carrying items within a private domain (*reshut ha-yaḥid*) on the Sabbath, defined as a space at least four handbreadths or *tefaḥim* (about 1 foot) wide that is enclosed by a barrier at least 10 handbreadths high (30–40 inches).[11] However, multiple biblical passages indicate explicitly (or are understood by rabbinic tradition to mean) that carrying items between a *reshut ha-yaḥid* and a public domain (*reshut ha-rabim*) on the Sabbath is forbidden.[12] Carrying more than 4 *amot* (6–7 feet) within a *reshut ha-rabim* is likewise considered biblically forbidden on the Sabbath.[13] A *reshut ha-rabim* is defined as an unroofed public open space at least 16 *amot* (approximately 28 feet) wide, with fewer than 3 walls (and some require that 600,000 people pass through it daily to qualify).[14] In addition to these laws, which have the status of biblical prohibitions, there are further rabbinic prohibitions designed to distance people from transgressing biblical law: rabbinic law prohibits carrying (4 *amot*) in open public spaces that do not meet the criteria of *reshut ha-rabim* as well as carrying between such public spaces and private domains.[15] Moreover, rabbinic law prohibits carrying even from one *reshut ha-yaḥid* to another *reshut ha-yaḥid*, where their respective ownership differs, such as in the case of various homes that open to a joint enclosed courtyard.[16]

The mechanism known as *'eruv* (lit. "combination") circumvents these latter rabbinic restrictions: it permits Jews to carry items within (non-*reshut ha-rabim*) public space and between such spaces and private domains on the Sabbath, as well as between variably owned *reshuyot ha-yaḥid* (pl.). An *'eruv* does this by legally merging discrete spaces into a single shared private domain through (a) setting aside a portion of food (e.g., enough *matzah* for two meals' worth) kept in someone's home to represent join ownership of the space among all *'eruv*-observant Jews; (b) ensuring that public spaces are "enclosed" by symbolic "doorways" consisting of strings and poles (akin how a *reshut ha-yaḥid* is enclosed by actual walls);[17] and (c) renting any spaces within the desired area owned by non-Jews or even non-*'eruv*-observant Jews for a nominal sum from local authorities.[18] Thus, a Jew may carry items to synagogue on the Sabbath because their town has been transformed into a jointly owned Jewish private domain through a box of food, poles and string, and renting the public space from local authorities. As other *takkanot* are rooted in Scripture, the *amora* Shmuel attributes the *takkanah* of *'eruv* to King Solomon.[19]

The strategies of mimicking enclosure through string/pole doorways and symbolically joining ownership through foodstuffs are a type of legal fiction, and renting space owned by those not engaged in the *'eruv* is akin to *ha'aramah*.[20] Another similarity is the consideration that only rabbinic prohibitions can be circumvented by *'eruv*. However, unlike *ha'aramot*, the *takkanah* of *'eruv* may be part of a stricture rather than a leniency. It is possible that the *takkanah* of *'eruv* not only circumvents prohibitions but includes the extra prohibitions against carrying in and between certain spaces in the first place! If so, the *takkanah* of *'eruv* is actually what is often known as a "fence around the Torah" rather than solely a loophole. Commentators assert that when Solomon is credited with the innovation of *'eruvin* (pl.), he is actually being credited with decreeing that one may not carry between various *reshuyot ha-yaḥid* without an *'eruv ḥatzerot* (lit., "a merging of the courtyards").[21] Thus, rather than primarily being about getting around the law to uphold a value such as allowing people to enjoy the Sabbath by transporting what they need from place to place, the *'eruv* upholds the value of protecting biblical law itself: reminding people that they should not carry in a true *reshut ha-rabim* or between such a domain and a *reshut ha-yaḥid*.

Moreover, *'eruv* does much more than simply allowing items to be carried; it creates a map of Divine presence and religious community in a decentralized, post-Temple world. Previously, the Temple in Jerusalem was the sacred map of God's space; in the rabbinic world, people's residential areas were God's space on the Sabbath, and the *'eruv* made it so.[22] Charlotte Fonrobert further describes the rabbinic Jewish identity formation involved in *'eruv* in the rabbinic era: it separated Jew from non-Jew by requiring Jews to rent the property of non-Jews to include it in the *'eruv*, and also separated rabbinic Jews from those who did not believe in the *'eruv* by not allowing the latter to participate.[23] Thus, on the one hand *'eruv* exemplifies the role the legal circumventions can play in constructing the world and identity of adherents to Jewish law. But on the other hand, its impact is so qualitatively different from other circumventions that it seems reductionist to refer to *'eruv* as mere circumvention.[24]

'Eruv Tavshilin—Cooking on the Festival for Sabbath

When it comes to *'eruv tavshilin* (lit. "mixture of cooked foods") the Talmud itself differentiates using this rabbinic mechanism from simply using *ha'aramah* to cook "leftovers" on the festival for the Sabbath (*yBetzah* 2:1, 61a; *bBetzah* 17b). Moreover, rabbinic texts attempt to authorize *'eruv tavshilin* further by providing scriptural support for it[25] and even by claiming that Abraham himself set aside *'eruv tavshilin*.[26] As mentioned, this type of authorization is mostly absent from discussions of *ha'aramot*. After all, they make less of a widespread change to the way that Judaism is practiced. *Takkanot*, on the other hand, change how Judaism is practiced and thus require their authority (and rabbinic authority) to be bolstered.

Additionally, it is unclear whether *'eruv tavshilin* utilizes *ha'aramah* methodology. Given its name because it *combines* food prepared before the festival and food prepared on the festival, it is unclear how it works.[27] Perhaps only starting to cook on the festival for the Sabbath is prohibited, and therefore setting aside the *'eruv tavshilin* constitutes beginning to cook for Sabbath prior to the festival. Consequently, continued cooking on the festival for Sabbath is permitted.[28] Alternatively, setting aside cooked food as *'eruv tavshilin* prior to the festival supplies a cover: if one already has the *'eruv tavshilin* food for the Sabbath meal, cooking on the festival for the Sabbath will not be suspected.[29]

David Henshke suggests that *'eruv tavshilin* developed diachronically during the *tannaitic* and *amoraic* periods.[30] In stage 1 (beginning of *mBetzah*

2:1), cooking for the Sabbath on the festival is prohibited, as it downgrades the festival as just a preparatory day. At the same time, not having anything special for the Sabbath, but simply paltry festival leftovers would dishonor the Sabbath. *'Eruv tavshilin* solves both problems by providing a food cooked specifically for the Sabbath before the festival. Thus, one will not need to cook on the festival for Sabbath, and one will eat more than simply leftovers from the festival on the Sabbath. In stage 2 (second half of *mBetzah* 2:1), however *'eruv tavshilin* does more than simply provide food for the Sabbath: it allows one to cook on the festival for Sabbath. This is because cooking some food for the Sabbath before the festival means that the festival is not being used primarily as a preparation day for the Sabbath (which would be beneath the former's dignity) but cooking on the festival for Sabbath is simply a continuation of the cooking that one did prior to the festival.[31] It is at this stage that the term *'eruv tavshilin*, a mixture of foods, becomes significant: the cooked food set aside before the festival for Sabbath and the cooking that one does on the festival for the Sabbath, are considered one.[32] And in stage 3 (per second-generation *amoraim*), there is a different understanding of the prohibition to cook on the festival for the Sabbath.[33] The rabbis only prohibited cooking on the festival for the Sabbath because it might lead one to cook on the festival for a mundane day. The latter would be an actual transgression. The role of *'eruv tavshilin* in this case is simply to make it clear to people that they cannot simply cook on the festival for another day. After all, even to cook for the Sabbath, they have to do a special performance of setting aside cooked food before the festival.[34]

All three stages marshal a value of the law itself to justify *'eruv tavshilin*. However, only stage 2 parallels *ha'aramah*: changing the facts changes the legal consequences. Starting to cook for Sabbath before the festival makes cooking on the festival into mere continuation.[35] In contrast, stage 1 is to ensure that one has Sabbath food and not just festival leftovers. And stage 3 also styles *'eruv tavshilin* as stricture: though it is permissible to cook on the festival day for the Sabbath, the rabbis outlawed doing so to keep people from cooking on the festival for a mundane day. However, rather than making the stricture all-encompassing, they provided *'eruv tavshilin* as a reminder of the limitations. This parallels the view of *'eruv hatzerot* that describes it as part of a stricture rather than a leniency. And yet, stage 3 conforms to the pattern of *amoraim* and *stammaim* limiting *takkanot* and perhaps *ha'aramot* to circumventing rabbinic law. Additionally, the *Bavli* explicitly emphasizes that *'eruv tavshilin* can only override rabbinic law.[36]

Another final connection between *'eruv tavshilin* and *ha'aramah* is not the similarity between them, but the preference for one over the other. In both *yBetzah* 2:1, 61b and *bBetzah* 17b, the existence of the *takkanah* of *'eruv tavshilin* is contrasted with the private *ha'aramah* of "accidentally" cooking leftovers for the Sabbath suspect. This perhaps relates to preference for what Henshke called stage 3, wanting people to have a clear reminder in the *'eruv tavshilin* that they should not cook on the festival for a weekday. Perhaps using *ha'aramah* would not be enough. Alternatively, perhaps, as we have seen reflected specifically in the *Bavli* in other situations, the concern is that the *ha'aramah* would be too obvious. And third, perhaps banning *ha'aramah* in the presence of the availability of *'eruv tavshilin* speaks to the (il)legitimacy of private *ha'aramah* when it undermines a rabbinic *takkanah*. We discussed this issue in chapters 2 and 5.

Mekhirat Ḥametz—Selling Leaven Before Passover

Selling one's *ḥametz* prior to Passover and buying it back afterward to avoid owning *ḥametz* during Passover is a great example of something that began as an ad hoc circumvention and developed into a widespread Jewish practice. It is, as it were, a *ha'aramah*-turned-*takkanah*.

Tannaitic sources discuss the possibility of selling one's *ḥametz* before Passover, but *tPes.* 2:12–13 specifically discusses the possibility of buying it back afterward.[37] The passage narrates this scenario: a Jew and gentile are traveling together by boat just before Passover. The Jew may sell their *ḥametz* or give it to the gentile and buy it back after Passover, with this qualification: "so long as he gives it to him as a complete gift." This likely means that no explicit condition can be included that the gentile return the food after Passover.[38] This scenario is presented as happenstance emergency rather than annual practice, just like most cases of *ha'aramah*, though absent the terminology.

Yet, the next sentence reads: "A Jew may tell a gentile: 'Rather than buying [food somewhere else] for 100 *zuz*, buy it [from me] for two hundred *zuz*, for perhaps I may need it and come to buy it [back] from you after Passover.'" This allowance is repeated in *yPes.* 2:2, 28d.[39] It is unclear whether this is a blanket annual allowance or refers to the boat scenario only (or similarly extenuating circumstances).[40] It is also unclear whether the "perhaps" slyly means "definitely" or is just sharing the possibility that may make it worthwhile for a gentile to buy from a Jew before Passover.

Some medieval commentators indeed understood this as only meant for exigent ad hoc circumstances: they prohibited using this as a *ha'aramah* each year and forbade Jews from eating *ḥametz* that was sold this way.[41] However, others permitted it, given two limitations: (a) the transfer of ownership to the gentile could not be conditional on returning it after Passover, and (b) the *ḥametz* had to be removed from the Jew's property for the duration of Passover. The transfer was considered effective even if the gentile paid a very low sum for the food.[42] But the requirement of physically removing the *ḥametz* from the Jew's property fell away in the sixteenth century, as Eastern European Jews became more involved in manufacturing beer and many Jews kept large quantities of fermented grain. Rather than removing their supplies, they were permitted to sell the *ḥametz* and the room where it was located to a gentile so that it was technically not on Jewish property during Passover.[43]

The circumvention of selling *ḥametz* parallels *ha'aramah* in that it does not arise as an explicit rabbinic *takkanah* based on Scripture, nor is it said to be formulated or used by biblical characters. Moreover, it is clearly an example of using the letter of the law to uphold a value of ensuring that people do not lose meaningful sums of money or even their livelihood. It is likewise telling that some who allow this practice annually explain its viability and/or limit its use to circumventing rabbinic *ḥametz* prohibitions, citing the *ha'aramah* by a young Torah scholar in *bShab*. 139b as precedent.[44] *Mekhirat ḥametz* is an ad hoc *ha'aramah* that arises from particular individual circumstances, but eventually was recognized as necessary for many people because of changing circumstances. Its evolution marks an example of how circumventions can be expanded in their use. When done to prevent financial loss, it is the quintessential *ha'aramah*: upholding a principle of the legal system through technically legal means.

Conclusion

I have attempted to outline differences and similarities between some *takkanot* and *ha'aramah* generally. A few dimensions emerged: (a) a shared concern for using legal mechanisms to uphold important values; (b) parallel concerns in *amoraic* material about the difference between circumventing biblical and rabbinic law; (c) the broader impact on Jewish life intended by *takkanot*; (d) the role played by scriptural and other authorization for *takkanot* that is lacking in *ha'aramah* discussions; (d) the question of whether *takkanot* such as *prosbul* even use *ha'aramah* methodology at all. But the question itself of how *takkanot* and *ha'aramot* are related returns us to a core argument of this book: the rabbinic establishment saw (and continues to see) loopholes as affording the possibility of holding values and authorities in tension for the good of their two most precious clients, the law itself (perhaps a proxy for God) and Jews attempting to observe that law. And it is not the choice of whether or not to circumvent the law, but rather in what situations and how to circumvent the law that reveals the values of a given interpretive community.

Appendix

Comparing the *Yerushalmi*'s and the *Bavli*'s Use of *Ha'aramah* Terminology and Concept

Where both *Yerushalmi* and *Bavli* discuss circumvention, but the *Bavli* does not use the term *ha'aramah*:

- *YPe'ah* 6:1, 19b brings up *ha'aramah* in a case of making one's field legally ownerless (*hefker*) to avoid tithing; *bNed.* 44a, however, uses the term "tricksters" *rama'in* (רמאין) in all MSS and Eds.
- *YTer.* 2:3, 41c refers to drawing water with impure vessels on the festival in order to purify them as *ha'aramah*; *bBetzah* 18a, however, suffices without *ha'aramah* terminology. (It is noteworthy also that "*ha'aramah*" terminology is missing from the *toseftan* discussion in *tBetzah* 2:9/*tShab.* 16:12 as well. Thus, the choice to use the terminology in the *Yerushalmi* but not in the *Bavli* may say more about the *Yerushalmi*'s preoccupation with *ha'aramah* than the *Bavli*'s lack thereof.
- *YNed.* 5:6, 39b uses the term *ha'aramah* in describing the scenario known as the *Bet Ḥoron* sale; *bNed.* 48a does not use the term *ha'aramah*, even though it clearly discusses the same issue of circumventing the original vow.
- *YNaz.* 5:1, 54a terms conspiracy "*ha'aramah*" when a man divorces and remarries his wife to get back consecrated money from her *ketubah* payment; *b'Ar.* 23a, however, retains the *mishnaic* terminology of *kinunya* (conspiracy). At one point in

the passage, however, the redactor does suggest that Abaye would call such a person a *rasha 'arum*, a cunning rogue, but significantly Abaye does not mention this in his statement, where he gives the very advice to circumvent the law itself.

"Missing" Cases—where the *Bavli* does not mention a *ha'aramah* scenario included in the *Yerushalmi*:

- *YḤallah* 3:1, 59a discusses the workaround of snacking on unfinished dough before *ḥallah* is taken; the *Bavli* does not cite this case. This may be due to the paucity of Babylonian discussion on the agricultural order of the *Mishnah*, known as *Seder Zera'im*. Additionally, *bMen*. 67b does discuss avoiding the requirement of separating *ḥallah* by baking less dough than the amount that triggers a *ḥallah* requirement. However, the *Bavli* still does not use the term *ha'aramah*.
- *YPes*. 2:2, 29a discusses suspected *ha'aramah* where one declares their *ḥametz* ownerless (*hefker*) a few days before Passover; the *Bavli* does not cite this case.
- R. Tarfon's heroism in feeding three hundred women priestly food during a famine by betrothing them (*yYev*. 4:11, 6b) is absent from the *Bavli*.
- *YKid*. 3:5, 64a, in context of betrothal based on misunderstanding, discusses a case of *ha'aramah*: purposely appointing a penniless guarantor; *bKid*. 62a–63a, which also discusses such misunderstandings, does not cite this case at all.

Where *Bavli* seems unconcerned about *ha'aramah*:

- Both *yMK* 2:1, 81a and *yMK* 3:1, 82a offer distinct laws for *shiv'ah* and *ḥol ha-mo'ed*, because the latter is more subject to evasion. However, *bMK* 14a suggests that some rules for the festival and one's bereavement period should be identical. It does not mention suspected *ha'aramah*. (Where the *Bavli* does cite an instance of *ha'aramah* [of selling phylacteries to make a living, *bMK* 12a] on the *ḥol ha-mo'ed*, it is a *tannaitic* citation rather than *amoraic* or redactors' discussion.)

Notes

INTRODUCTION

1. Gilgamesh XI (Stephanie Dalley, *Myths from Mesopotamia: Creation, the Flood, Gilgamesh, and Others* [Oxford: Oxford University Press, 1989)], 110). My thanks to Professor Samuel Greengus for directing me to this citation. A parallel recounting in the myth of Atrahasis casts Enki as Ea, and Atrahasis as Utnapishtim. See W. G. Lambert and A. R. Millard, *Atrahasis: The Babylonian Story of the Flood* (Oxford: Clarendon Press, 1969), Tablet III, lines 15–25, 26–37: (88–89). William L. Moran suggested that earlier in Atrahasis, Enki uses a different loophole—a message in a dream—to inform Atrahasis of an earlier plague: "My god speaks to me, but being under oath, He must inform me in dreams" (Atrahasis II, iii). Moran, "Some Considerations of Form and Interpretation in Atrahasis," in *Language, Literature, and History: Philological and Historical Studies Presented to Erica Reiner*, ed. F. Rochberg-Halton (New Haven: American Oriental Society, 1987), 251.

2. See Aaron D. Panken, *The Rhetoric of Innovation: Self-conscious Legal Change in Rabbinic Literature* (New York: University Press of America, 2005), 1–8; Christine Hayes, *What's Divine About Divine Law?* (Princeton: Princeton University Press, 2015), 288–309; Moshe Bloch, *Sha'are Torat Ha-takkanot* (Jerusalem: Makor, 1970).

3. Whether rabbis consciously changed law through forced exegesis is debated among scholars. For academic discussions, see Moshe Halbertal, *Interpretive Revolutions in the Making: Values as Interpretative Criteria in Jewish Law* (Hebrew) (Jerusalem: Magnes Press, 1999); E. E. Urbach, "*Derashah* as the Foundation of *Halakhah*, and the Problem of the Scribes," *Tarbiz* 27:2–3 (1958): 166–82; H. Albeck, *Mavo La-Mishnah* (Tel Aviv: Dvir, 1967), 40–54; Benjamin De Vries, *Toldot Ha-halakhah Ha-talmudit* (Tel Aviv: Abraham Zioni Publishing House, 1962), 9–21; Menachem Elon, *Ha-mishpat Ha-'ivri: Toldotav Mekorotav 'Ekronotav* (Jerusalem: Magnes Press, 1982), 1:243–49. For a summary of traditional Jewish debates about this issue, see Jay M. Harris, *How Do We Know This? Midrash and the Fragmentation of Modern Judaism* (New York: SUNY Press, 1994).

4. Bryan A. Garner, ed., *Black's Law Dictionary*, 8th ed. (St. Paul, MN: Thomson/West, 2004), 962.

5. In coming chapters, we will contrast the obvious "local" intent of a statute with the "global" intent of the legal system as a whole.

6. See Lon L. Fuller, *Legal Fictions* (Stanford: Stanford University Press, 1967), 9; Pierre J. J. Olivier, *Legal Fictions in Practice and Legal Science* Vol. 2 (Rotterdam: Rotterdam University Press, 1975), 4; and Alan Watson, *The Spirit of Roman Law* (Athens: University of Georgia Press, 1995), 80. Some theorists have questioned the classification of fictions as false. See Douglas Lind, "The Pragmatic Value of Legal Fictions" and Maksymilian Del Mar,

"Legal Fictions and Legal Change in the Common Law Tradition," in *Legal Fictions in Theory and Practice*, ed. Maksymilian Del Mar and William Twining (New York: Springer International Publishing, 2015).

7. Thus, Henry Sumner Maine defined fictions as "any assumption which conceals, or affects to conceal, the fact that a rule of law has undergone alteration, its letter remaining unchanged, its operation being modified": *Ancient Law* (London: Oxford University Press, 1931), 22.

8. Fuller, *Legal Fictions*, 72. To some, fictions mask judicial activism; to others they afford new ways to apply existing law. Nonetheless, analogies and legal fictions are not the same, as the former rely upon a shared common denominator between that which is being compared while the latter do not.

9. *yYevamot* 10:5, 11a.

10. Leib Moscovitz, "Rabbinic Legal Fictions," in *Legal Fictions in Theory and Practice*, ed. Maksymilian Del Mar and William Twining (New York: Springer, 2015), 334–36.

11. *tMenaḥot* 11:14.

12. Christine Hayes, "Authority and Anxiety in the Talmuds: From Legal Fiction to Fact," in *Jewish Religious Leadership: Image and Reality*, ed. Jack Wertheimer (New York: Jewish Theological Seminary, 2004), 127–54. She notes, however, that the Talmud often attempts to "murder" fictions by offering realist explanations.

13. *yKiddushin* 4:1, 65c; *bYevamot* 78b.

14. See also Tzvi Novick, "They Come Against Them with the Power of the Torah: Rabbinic Reflections on Legal Fiction and Legal Agency," *Studies in Law, Politics and Society* 50 (2009): 1–17; idem, "The 'For I Say Presumption: A Study in Early Rabbinic Legal Rhetoric," *Journal of Jewish Studies* 61:6 (Spring 2010): 48–61. Scholars debate the relationship(s) between legal fictions and legal presumptions. See Raymundo Gama, "Presumptions and Fictions: A Collingwoodian Approach," in *Legal Fictions in Theory and Practice*, ed. Maksymilian Del Mar and William Twining (New York: Springer, 2015), 347–66. For more on the use of fictions in rabbinic jurisprudence, see Jacob Samuel Zuri, "Legal Equivalence in Jewish Law" (Hebrew), in *Festschrift in Honor of Dr. B. M. Lewin*, ed. Y. L. Fishman (Jerusalem: Mosad Ha-Rav Kook, 1939), 174–95; Samuel Atlas, *Pathways in Jewish Law* (Hebrew) (New York: Sefer Harmon, 1978), 228–36; Yitzhak Adler, *Lomdus: A Substructural Analysis* (Hebrew) (New York: Bet Sha'ar, 1989), 86–93; Haim Tchernowitz, *Toldot Ha-halakhah*, Vol. 1 (New York: Ha-Meḥaber, 1934), 182–83.

15. See Leib Moscovitz, "Legal Fictions in Rabbinic and Roman Law: Some Comparative Observations," in *Rabbinic Law in Its Roman and Ancient Near Eastern Context*, ed. Catherine Hezser (Tübingen: Mohr Siebeck, 2003), 131: "Fictions tend to develop and flourish in a particular type of legal and intellectual climate, which seems to have been shared by the Romans and rabbis—a frequently rigid and formalistic approach to law, at least insofar as explicit formulation and justification of the law are concerned."

16. See, e.g., Atlas, *Pathways*, 224.

17. See Eben Moglen, "Legal Fictions and Common Law Legal Theory: Some Historical Reflections," *Tel-Aviv University Studies in Law* 10 (1990): 33–52; Frederick Schauer, "Legal Fictions Revisited," in *Legal Fictions in Theory and Practice*, ed. Maksymilian Del Mar and William Twining (New York: Springer, 2015), 113–30.

18. Marcus Jastrow defines the causative verb form—*he'erim* הערים—as "to plan, act deliberately," but also "to act with subtlety," "ערם." *A Dictionary of the Targumim, the Talmud Babli and Yerushalmi, and the Midrashic Literature* (New York: Judaica Press, 1992).

19. For example, the word *pike'aḥ/pikaḥat* (פיקח(ת)) can refer to someone tactful enough to use the law to their advantage: see, e.g., *mKetubot* 12:2, 13:9; *tMenaḥot* 3:4; *Mekhilta d'R. Yishmael* 15; *yTerumot* 2:3, 41c; *bBava Metzi'a* 97a. For example, during a house fire on the Sabbath, by Jewish law, the homeowner may only retrieve food for three meals from the house. However, the homeowner may call others to take food for themselves. A *pike'aḥ/pikaḥat* retrieves food but sells it to the homeowner after the Sabbath (*mShabbat* 16:3). Tannaitic literature also has terminology for tricksters, *rama'in* רמאין (*mShekalim* 5:5; *tBava Metzi'a* 2:16), those who sneakily break the law.

20. Some examples will appear in Chapter 5.

21. We will explore some *takkanot* and the practice of selling *ḥametz* in the Epilogue.

22. The guidelines are available here: https://www.jjs-online.net/pdfs/SBL-Transl.pdf.

CHAPTER 1. (WHEN) DO CIRCUMVENTIONS DISRESPECT THE LAW?

1. See "חכם, חכמה" in Naphtali H. Tur-Sinai, *Encyclopedia Mikra'it*, vol. 3 (Jerusalem: Mosad Byalik, 1950–88), 128. See also 1 Sam. 23:22; Ps. 83:4. Brown, Driver, and Briggs define ערמה as "n.f. craftiness, prudence; 1- בערמה—craftily Ex. 21:14, Jos. 9:4, 2. ערמה in Pr., in good sense, *prudence* Pr. 1:4, 8:5, 12." Francis Brown, S. R. Driver, and Charles A. Briggs, eds., *A Hebrew and English Lexicon of the Old Testament: Based on the Lexicon of William Gesenius as Translated by Edward Robinson* (Boston: Houghton Mifflin, 1906).

2. See Prov. 8:5a, 12; 12:16b, 23; 13:16a; 14:8a, 15b, 18b; 15:5; 17:2; 19:25a; 22:3; 27:12. The positive use of *'ormah* contrasts with *mezimmah*, shrewdness, in Proverbs. The primary meanings of *mezimmah* are "hidden, private thinking," and "planning and scheming." The term can mean mischief (12:2, 14:7, 24:8); or discretion (2:11; 5:2; 8:12). A related term, *taḥbulot*—perhaps from *ḥovel*, a sailor who navigates the seas—is understood as evil (Prov. 12:5b). Michael V. Fox, *Proverbs 1–9: A New Translation with Introduction and Commentary*. 1st ed. Anchor Bible. Vol. 18A (New York: Doubleday, 2000), 34, 37.

3. Becoming "prudent" is likewise a theme in the Wisdom of Ben Sira 6:32: "My son, if you will, you shall be taught; and if you will apply your mind, you shall be prudent." The Rule of the Community also contains this language in discussing the point of view of the messianic figure known as the Master in 1QS 9.12ff.:

> With the counsel of salvation, I will conceal knowledge, and with prudent knowledge (*u-ve-'ormat da'at*) I will hedge (it) with a firm boundary, keeping faithfulness and strong judgment of God's righteousness. (1QS 24–25)

> My eyes beheld what shall be salvation which is hidden from humankind, knowledge and prudent discretion (*mezimmat 'ormah*) [which is hidden] from the Sons of Adam, a fountain of righteousness and a well of strength as well as a spring of glory (hidden) from the assembly of flesh. (1QS XI.6)

> God loves knowledge. Wisdom and prudence He has set up before Him. Craft (*'ormah*) and knowledge (*da'at*) shall serve Him (CD MS A 2.3–4).

Joshua Brand uses the terminology as an indication of the ancient provenance of the Damascus Document. Brand, "Megillat brit Damesek u-zemana," *Tarbiz* 28 (1959): 27–28.

(Translations from James H. Charlesworth, ed. *The Dead Sea Scrolls: Hebrew, Aramaic, and Greek Texts with English Translations*. Princeton Theological Seminary Dead Sea Scrolls Project. Tübingen: J. C. B. Mohr (Paul Siebeck), 1994.

4. Robert Alter, *The Wisdom Books: Job, Proverbs, and Ecclesiastes: A Translation with Commentary* (New York: W. W. Norton, 2011), 194n4.

5. Robert Alter translates *peti* as "dupe," from the root for seduction, which "suggests gullibility." Alter, *The Wisdom Books*, 190. LXX renders *peti* three different ways: (1) ἄφρων—fool; (2) ἄκακος—innocent; and (3) νήπιος—childlike innocence. Johann Cook, *The Septuagint of Proverbs: Jewish and/or Hellenistic Proverbs? Concerning the Hellenistic Colouring of LXX Proverbs*, Supplements to Vetus Testamentum, vol. 69 (Leiden: Brill, 1997), 52, 95.

6. Fox, *Proverbs 1–9*, 35–36.

7. There may be another mention of *'ormah*. According to the Septuagint, Proverbs 14:24 reads: "The crown of the wise is their shrewdness (*'ormah*)," whereas the received MT version reads: "The crown of the wise is their wealth (*'oshram*)." See Alter, *The Wisdom Books*, 256n24.

8. Fox, *Proverbs 1–9*, 61.

9. Michael V. Fox, "Words for Wisdom: '*Tevunah*' and '*Binah*'; '*Ormah*' and '*Mezimah*'; '*Ezah*' and '*Tushiyah*,'" *Zeitschrift für Althebräistik* 6:2 (1993): 159.

10. Fox, *Proverbs 1–9*, 61.

11. See Lev. 27:30–31; Deut. 14:22–27; *Sifra Beḥukotai* 12:2. For a straightforward explanation, see Maimonides *Mishneh Torah*, Laws of Secondary Tithes 5:1.

12. The parallel *Tosefta* explicitly states "to exempt him from the 25 percent."

13. לך, "for you," may indicate that the recipient is meant to keep the money, even as the sanctity of the fruit devolves upon the money, and it can therefore only be spent Jerusalem. However, the word is missing from Geniza MS of the *mishnah*, from all *toseftan* MSS, and from *bGittin* 65a. According to Lieberman, the word לך was emended based on the discussion *yMS* 4:4, 55a.

Saul Lieberman, *Tosefta Ki-feshutah: Be'ur Arokh La-Tosefta* (New York: Jewish Theological Seminary, 1955), 766.

14. *Sifra Beḥukotai* 12:2 stipulates that ḥomesh does not refer to 20 percent but 25 percent: the original value is divided into 4, and one who pays ḥomesh pays a fifth part, i.e, five quarters, or 125 percent.

15. A Hebrew indentured maid redeeming tithes is surprising, as they are minors (freed at age twelve). Therefore, *Ra'avad* and the *Meyuḥas Le-Rosh* suggest that there must have been a Sinaitic tradition that someone as young as nine years and one day old can redeem tithes; Maimonides (Laws of Secondary Tithes 5:8–9) writes that per rabbinic law, even minors may redeem tithes.

16. Consequently, they cannot own the money independently, and no transfer of money has taken place.

17. The prohibition of making the "redeemer" one's emissary is made clear in the *toseftan* version (*tMS* 4:3) of this *ha'aramah*: אבל לא יאמר לו פדה לי בהן את מעשר זה.

18. This phenomenon is known as a "man of straw" in British and German law, a "front man" in American law, and a "dummy" in Australian law. See David Daube, "Dodges and Rackets in Roman Law," *Proceedings of the Classical Association* 61 (1964): 29.

19. Both *Mishnah* and *Tosefta* are products of early third-century Palestine. While scholarly consensus is that *Mishnah* was edited first, the relationship between their respective content is debated. Some consider *Tosefta* a commentary on *Mishnah* (J. N. Epstein, *In-*

troduction to Tannaitic Literature: Mishnah, Tosefta, and Halakhic Midrashim [Hebrew] [Jerusalem: Magnes Press, 1959], 242–62; Abraham Goldberg, "The Tosefta—Companion to the Mishna," in *The Literature of the Sages: Part I*, ed. Shmuel Safrai [Assen: Van Gorcum, 1987], 283–302). Others consider each work to be a version of a shared ur-text. Others consider *Tosefta* a competing variation based on the same text as the one stylized by *Mishnah* (Martin Jaffee, *Torah in the Mouth: Writing and Oral Tradition in Palestinian Judaism, 200 BCE–400 CE* [New York: Oxford University Press, 2001], 39–61; Elizabeth Shanks Alexander, *Transmitting Mishnah: The Shaping Influence of Oral Tradition* [Cambridge: Cambridge University Press, 2006], 35–55; Judith Hauptman, *Rereading the Mishnah: A New Approach to Ancient Jewish Texts* [Tübingen: Mohr Siebeck, 2005]). Still others claim the *Tosefta* contains materials both antedating and postdating *Mishnah*: see Shamma Friedman, "Mishna-Tosefta Parallels" (Hebrew), *Proceedings of the Eleventh World Congress of Jewish Studies* (1994): 15–22; idem, "The Primacy of Tosefta to Mishnah in Synoptic Parallels," in *Introducing Tosefta: Textual, Intratextual, and Intertextual Studies*, ed. Harry Fox, Tirzah Meacham, and Diane Kriger (Hoboken, NJ: Ktav, 1999), 99–121.

20. This account about the evolution of this *ha'aramah* tracks with the *Tosefta* being more "anthropological" and "rooted in the concrete historical situations of ancient Palestine" than the *Mishnah* (Friedman, "The Primacy of *Tosefta*," 106).

21. See Peter J. Haas, *A History of the Mishnaic Law of Agriculture: Tractate Ma'aser Sheni* (Chico, CA: Scholars Press, 1980), 129. He discusses the relationship between the *mishnaic* and *toseftan* versions of this case and analyzes *tMS* 4:4–4:9, which further discuss avoiding the 25 percent tax.

22. See R. Ovadiah Bartenura's commentary. Maimonides (*Commentary to the Mishnah* ad loc.) explains that whether the owner gives only the *ma'aser sheni* produce or the larger bundle depends on whether *ma'aser sheni* produce is considered to be the possession of the owner or not. If it is not considered the possession of the owner (*mammon ba'alim*), the owner may not gift specifically *ma'aser sheni* produce to the straw person.

23. Per Jewish law, one can acquire produce by acquiring the space where it is found. The method of selling property might protect the field owner from defrauders, as the transferred land is elsewhere, so the second party would be less likely to run off and eat the produce. See Ridbaz on *yMS* 4:3, 55a.

24. This parallels the distinction in Proverbs 14:8 between the prudent *'arum* and the fool whose folly is *mirmah* (deceit).

25. MSS Moscow and London cite this as a *baraita* in the name of R. Yehoshua ben Korhah.

26. See Ridbaz, s.v. *R. Inya*.

27. The *stam* (anonymous editorial voice) in *bGit.* 65a suggests that this *mishnah* describes post-Temple times to explain the acquisitional power of a maidservant who is a minor.

28. See *tMS* 3:13. Significantly, the *Tosefta* itself makes the point that *ma'aser sheni* was no longer being taken to Jerusalem; see also *Sifre Re'eh* 106; *tSanhedrin* 5:6. *M'Eduyot* 8:6 presents an exception to this stance, citing R. Yehoshua that it remains appropriate to consume *ma'aser sheni* in Jerusalem even without a Temple or city walls. See also *tMS* 3:18, 4:4; *mMS* 2:7; and Shmuel Safrai, *Be-yeme Ha-bayit Ha-sheni U-ve'-yeme Ha-Mishnah: Meḥkarim Be-toldot Yisrael* (Jerusalem: Magnes Press, 1994), 379. Safrai casts doubt on a *baraita* cited in *bBetzah* 5a/*bRH* 31b that indicates that R. Eliezer actually took *ma'aser sheni* to Jerusalem based on Eliezer's own statements in *m'Eduyot* 8:6 regarding the status of Jerusalem without its

Temple infrastructure. For a survey of rabbinic application of the various Temple-era priestly and Levitical gifts after the Temple's destruction, see Gedaliah Alon, *The Jews in Their Land in the Talmudic Age, 70–640 C.E.* (Jerusalem: Magnes Press, 1980–84), chap. 12.

29. Once the coins redeemed produce, the coins were considered sacred and were useless because they would not be taken to Jerusalem. Given the ubiquity of such coins once people no longer ate secondary tithes in Jerusalem, rabbinic texts discuss whether found coins should be considered sacred or mundane (*mMS* 4:9).

30. Ephraim Elimelech Urbach reads this ruling as rabbinic capitulation to lax constituents. He suggests that the flight from the Land of Israel following the (132–35 CE) Bar Kokhba revolt produced laxity in tithing, as had happened after the Hasmonean revolt. The rabbis thus found a leniency. Urbach writes: "It would appear that evasion of the payment of the 'one-fifth' was widespread and the Sages realized that insistence on their part on the strict observance of the law could very well lead to the populace refraining altogether from bringing the redemption money to Jerusalem. The halakhic sanction they gave to the practice of evasion was, in a sense, a *takkanah* (rabbinic decree) to prevent the development of a situation in which 'the people refrained from bringing.'" Urbach, *The Halakhah: Its Sources and Development*. Trans. Raphael Posner. (Jerusalem: Yad le-Talmud, 1986), 252–53. I do not subscribe to this view. First, there is no textual indication of laxity in tithing as background for this *ha'aramah*, which is unusual given that tractate *Demai* openly discusses those who do not tithe. Second, *tannaitic* texts indicate that people were no longer supposed to bring secondary tithes or redemption money to Jerusalem. Third, it is unclear how much sway the rabbis had over other Jews. (See Seth Schwartz, *Imperialism and Jewish Society, 200 B.C.E. to 640 C.E.* [Princeton: Princeton University Press, 2001].) Additionally, discussions about how to minimize the financial burden of redeeming tithes post-Temple continued in later rabbinic literature. In *bBM* 57a, Samuel is cited asserting that one may redeem a very expensive consecrated item on a mere *perutah* (a coin of very little value).

31. The fact that both *mishnaic* instances affirm the use of *ha'aramah* probably led to Maimonides's assertion in his *Commentary to the Mishnah, Temurah 5:1* that the terminology *ha'aramah* is used whenever a circumvention is permissible, whereas the term *mirmah*—trickery—is used when such strategies are forbidden. He may also have been influenced by Proverbs 14:8. *Tiferet Yisrael* (commentary to *mTem.* 5:1) is more precise: *mirmah* is always negative, while *'ormah* is mixed, sometimes negative, sometimes positive.

32. Exod. 13:12; Num. 18:17–18.

33. See *mBekh.* chap. 2. But he may not use it for labor or shear it (*mBekh.* 3:3).

34. This takes for granted that its status as a firstling does not take hold until it is born. The *Sifra* (*Behukotai* 5, MS London) passage that justifies the ability to consecrate a *bekhor* in the womb based on a verse is challenging: "Might one suppose that one may not consecrate the firstling while it is still in the womb? Scripture says, 'which is a firstling belongs to the Lord, no man may dedicate'—once the beast has emerged as a firstborn, you may not consecrate it, but you may consecrate it when it is yet in the womb. From here sages said: they employ prudence (*ma'arimin*) in connection with the firstling."

The above follows MS London, which allows *ha'aramah* (and MS Oxford concurs), while MS JTS and Venice Ed. both read *en ma'arimin/m*, "people may not use *ha'aramah*." Furthermore, MSS Parma and Vatican 31 read instead *ma'arikhin*, meaning to promise the value of the animal. At any rate, the terminology of "From here sages said" indicates that the *midrash* is citing our *mishnah*. This is consistent with the perspective that the *midrashim* from R. Akiva's school, *Mekhilta d'R. Yishmael, Sifra, Sifre Deut.*, postdate the *Mishnah*. See Menahem Kahana, "The Halakhic Midrashim (Hebrew)," in *The Literature of the Sages: Second Part: Midrash and Targum, Liturgy, Poetry, Mysticism, Contracts, Inscriptions, Ancient Science and the Languages of Rabbinic Literature*, ed. Shmuel Safrai, Ze'ev Safrai, and Joshua Schwartz (Amsterdam: Fortress Press, 2006), 56.

35. *mKid.* 1:6.

36. *Bekhor* status does not apply to female animals; perhaps the female is included here due to the continuing *mishnayot* that deal with non-*bekhor* male and female animals that are consecrated in the womb. See Hanoch Albeck, *Shishah Sidre Mishnah* (Jerusalem: Mosad Byalik, 1952–58), vol. 5, notes on page 235.

37. Rashi, s.v. *ma'arimin*. See Lev. 7:16.

38. Urbach, *The Halakhah*, 254. The term "clean" is a synonym for kosher. Rabbi Zvi Hirsch Chajes suggests more broadly that all instances of *ha'aramah* reflect rabbinic capitulation to the likelihood that people would transgress the law under pressure unless they were offered a loophole. See Zvi Hirsch Chajes, *Darkhe Hora'ah* (Zolkiew: Saul Meyerhoffer, 1842), chap 2.

39. Even in Babylonia centuries after the Temple had fallen, rabbis still considered the firstborn consecrated, though the *kohen* could no longer offer it as a sacrifice (see *bBetzah* 27b, *bHullin* 44b, *bBekh.* 3b, and *bTem.* 8b). See, however, David Henshke, "The Firstborn of a Kosher Animal Outside the Land of Israel: From the Talmud to Maimonides and Back" (Hebrew), in *Meir Benayahu Memorial Volume, Vol. 1: Studies in Talmud, Halakhah, Custom, and Jewish History*, ed. M. Bar Asher, Y. Liebes, M. Assis, and Y. Kaplan (Jerusalem: Yad Ha-Rav Nissim, 2019), 241–74. Henshke discusses the possibility that some did not consider firstborn animals born outside the land of Israel (whether during Temple times or after its destruction) to be consecrated at all.

40. MS Erfurt and Ed. Princeps: אף מעשר שני, "also the secondary tithe," rather than simply ומעשר שני, "and the secondary tithe."

41. MS Erfurt and Ed. Princeps: לירושלים, to Jerusalem. I use this translation because it is grammatically correct.

42. Though the Hebrew ו is usually translated as "and," in this sentence, it pivots from the logic of the previous sentence. Consequently, I translate it as "but."

43. MS Erfurt and Ed. Princeps: לא יהא נאכל, "it should not be eaten" rather than אינו נאכל, "it is not eaten."

44. MS Erfurt: לא יהא אלא, presumably meaning "it should not be eaten except," but with the word "eaten" missing. Ed. Princeps: לא יהא נאכל אלא, "it should not be eaten except," rather than "it is not eaten."

45. See also *Sifre Deuteronomy* 106:4.

46. *mBekh.* 5 delineates which serious blemishes would permit eating the animal without sacrifice.

47. See *mBekh.* 4.

48. See *bTem.* 24b (and *bBekh.* 35a) where the *stam* (anonymous editorial voice) reconstructs R. Judah's comments as applying post-Temple, and the *mishnah* as relevant for when the Temple stood.

49. *Tur Shulḥan 'Arukh, Yoreh De'ah*, 320:6. *MBekh.* 2:1 rules that joint ownership between a Jew and a non-Jew of the mother animal or of the fetus exempts the fetus from *bekhor* status. It does not, however, recommend using partnership with a non-Jew as an avoidance mechanism. The fact that joint ownership might have been a useful workaround in the time of the *Mishnah* but it not mentioned may cast doubt on whether the workaround

of sanctifying the animal in utero is indeed post-Temple. After all, if the discussion is post-Temple, why not suggest joint ownership with a non-Jew to completely exempt the animal from any sanctity rather than turning it into a sacred animal that will not be sacrificed? On the other hand, perhaps there are other reasons why joint ownership with a gentile is not suggested at this point in rabbinic thought. Alternatively, the *mishnah* which mentions joint ownership exempting the *bekhor* and the *mishnah* describing *ha'aramah* regarding *bekhor* represent teachings from different time periods.

50. Alternatively (per *bTem.* 10b), the owner may sell the animal even unblemished and consecrate the funds. While this would not save the owner money, the animal could be used.

One indication that this *mishnah* relates to a post-Temple reality is how it differs from the *toseftan* version of this ruling. *TTem.* (Zuckermandel) 3:1 discusses consecrating any animal in utero, not only a firstborn. That the *mishnah* focuses on the firstborn animal is surprising, unless this animal is a particular cause for concern. This switch from any animal to a firstborn animal may also explain the imprecision of the *mishnah*: the *mishnah* describes a person declaring that if the firstborn is female, it will be given as a peace offering. However, there is no need for this because the laws of the firstborn animal do not apply to a female! It seems likely that the *mishnah* reworked an earlier tradition about consecrating any animal in utero and applied it to the problem of the firstborn. The Talmud (*bTem.* 24b) suggests that perhaps the section about the male firstborn and the section about the female firstborn in our *mishnah* refer to different situations. The beginning of the *mishnah* refers to the laws of the consecration of the firstborn animal, restricted to male animals, while the section about the female firstborn refers to consecrating *any* animal still in utero.

Tzvi Novick argues similarly about *mBekh.* M*Bekh.* 6 lists blemishes that render animals unfit for sacrifice. The list in the *mishnah*, unlike its *toseftan* parallel (*tBekh.* 4), focuses on major blemishes that permit animals to be eaten as a non-sacrifice, followed by an appended list of minor blemishes that bar animals from both sacrifice and consumption. T*Bekh.* 4, however, focuses on the difference between blemishes—whether minor or major—and non-blemishes. Novick argues that *tBekh.* represents an earlier erstwhile Temple tradition, where the key factor is fitness for sacrifice, while *mBekh.* represents a post-Temple tradition where sacrifice is no longer an option; in the latter case, the key issue is whether one may consume the animal on account of its blemish. See Tzvi Novick, "The Blemished First-Born Animal: A Case Study in Tannaitic Sources," *Hebrew Union College Annual* 76 (2005): 113–32. Novick, however, does not suggest that such a redactional relationship between *Mishnah* and *Tosefta* is ubiquitous, or that the *Mishnah* as a whole represents post-Temple traditions while *Tosefta* represents Temple traditions (130).

51. Per *ySotah* 3:4, 19a: a woman who is celibate and mocks the sex lives of biblical characters to show herself more virtuous than they are.

52. See Meir Minkovitz, "Ishah perushah u-tzevu'im she-domim le-perushim," *Hado'ar* 54 (1975): 136.

53. It is significant that the singular usage of *'arum* as bad in *Mishnah* is somehow connected to the sexually deviant woman. While Lady Wisdom in Proverbs is associated positively with *'ormah*, this *tannaitic* text suggests a negative association between women and *'ormah*. This lays groundwork for the later rabbinic rereading of *'ormah* from Proverbs in the verse "I am Wisdom who dwells in prudence (*'ormah*)" (8:12) to suggest that *'ormah* in women, contrary to the very clear meaning of Proverbs itself, is a negative attribute rather than a positive one (*bSotah* 21b). For a suggestion that this is the correct reading of Proverbs proper, see Claudia V. Camp, "Wise and Stranger: An Interpretation of the Female Imagery

in Proverbs in Light of Trickster Mythology," *Semeia* 42 (1988): 14–36. For more on women as tricksters and manipulators in rabbinic literature, see Rachel Adelman, ed., *The Journal of Textual Reasoning* 6:2 (March 2011); Dvora Weisberg, "Desirable but Dangerous: Rabbis' Daughters in the Babylonian Talmud," *Hebrew Union College Annual* 75 (2004): 121–61. For a suggestion that *tannaitic* material about the *sotah* woman accentuates the dangers of women, see Ishay Rosen-Zvi, *The Mishnaic Sotah Ritual: Temple, Gender and Midrash* (Leiden: Brill, 2012). This connection may also reflect an emerging link between *'ormah* and sexuality. See Genesis Rabbah *Vayeshev* 85, where the snake's character of *'ormah* is related to his seeing Adam and Eve copulating. This connotation is based on the linguistic similarity and biblical proximity of *'arum* as cunning (Gen. 3:1) and the description of Adam and Eve as *'arumim*, "naked" (Gen. 2:25).

54. Other definitions of *rasha 'arum* in *bSotah* 21b–22a include: one who explains their case to the judge before the other litigant arrives; one who gives advice to sell an estate which is inconsiderable (the law of inheritance is that where the estate is small, the daughters inherit "and the sons can go begging" [*bBava Batra* 140a]); one who counsels another to sell possessions with the following provision: "My property is yours and after you for So-and-so," because the second person only received what the first one does not consume; one who induces others to follow in their ways (by pretending to be pious, according to Rashi, s.v. *ha-makhri'a*); one who is lenient on oneself but strict with others; and one who learned Scripture and *Mishnah* but did not attend upon rabbinical scholars.

There is another explanation for "cunning rogue" as one who may cause his daughter to become a prostitute by delaying her marriage, cited by some MSS/Ed. in the name of Abaye: *bSan.* 76a–b:

R. Kahana said in the name of R. Akiva: There is no poorer man in Israel than a cunning rogue and one who delays his daughter as an adult. But is not one who delays his daughter as an adult not a cunning rogue? Abaye said: This is what he says: "Who is a poor man? This cunning rogue who delays his daughter as an adult."

Following Halivni, I do not believe this to be Abaye's statement: first, he is cited in several places in the *Bavli* asserting that the *rasha 'arum* is one who gives advice to a primary heir about how to fend off his secondary heir; second, this definition of *rasha 'arum* is excluded from the litany of explanations offered by *amoraim* on *bSotah* 21b. (See *Mekorot U-mesorot Sanhedrin-Horayot*, 139). Indeed MS Jerusalem (Yad HaRav Herzog) excludes his name, preferring *hakhi ka-amar* (so he said) with no attribution. It is possible that Abaye's name is there because he and Rava are the subjects of the beginning of the inquiry, and he is the one who has defined the *rasha 'arum* elsewhere in the *Bavli*.

55. Both *mMS* 4:4 and *mTem.* 5:1 contain cases that stand on their own, and both contain the term *ha'aramah* as an introduction to the cases. One might speculate that the cases and the introductory statements respectively represent different layers of transmission and/or editing. However, the opening lines of each *mishnah* that announce that this is how *ha'aramah* is employed begin to create the vocabulary of *ha'aramah* for the legal mechanism of loopholing.

56. Ranon Katzoff, "Judicial Reasoning in *P. Catt—Fraus Legi*," *Transactions and Proceedings of the American Philological Association* 101 (1970): 249.

57. Contra legem facit qui id facit quod lex prohibet, in fraudem vero qui salvis verbis legis sententiam eius circumvenit (*Digest* 1.3.29), translation by S. P. Scott, *The Civil Law II* (Cincinnati: Central Trust Company, 1932). In an earlier formulation: Lex non dubium est: in legem committere eum qui verba legis amplexus contra legis nititur voluntatem: nec poenas

insertas legibus evitabit, qui se contra iuris sententiam scaeva praerogativa verborum fraudulenter escusat. Fraus enim legi fit, ubi quod fieri noluit, fieri autem non vetuit, id fit. (Codex Th. I 14,5). For more on the topic, see Giovanni Rotondi, *Gli atti in Frode Alla Legge Nella Dottrina Romana E Nella Sua Evoluzione Posteriore* (Torino: Unione tipografico-editrice torinese, 1911).

58. See Chapter 3 for examples.

59. Because the relationship between *toseftan* and *mishnaic* material is unclear, it is difficult to know whether the omission of *toseftan* material in the *mishnah* is purposeful or not. Regarding the *toseftan* arguments between R. Eliezer and R. Yehoshua, or by R. Yose b. Yehudah, perhaps the *mishnaic* redactors (a) simply had no record of these arguments, (b) knew of them but chose to leave them out, or (c) the attributions in the *Tosefta* were mistaken or purposely changed and actually represent opinions from after the close of *Mishnah*.

60. Regarding the centrality of the Temple for biblical purity law, see Jacob Milgrom, *Leviticus 1–16: A New Translation with Introduction and Commentary*, 1st ed., Anchor Bible, vol. 3 (New York: Doubleday, 1991), 718–42.

61. See *mDemai* 2:2–3; *tDemai* 2:2–13. For more on the development and parameters of this group, see Yair Furstenberg, "Eating in a State of Purity in the Tannaitic Period: Tractate Taharot and Its Historical and Cultural Contexts" (PhD diss., Hebrew University, 2010).

62. Based on the translation of R. Samson of Sens, *mKelim* 16:2, which Lieberman prefers. See Saul Lieberman, *Tosefet Rishonim Perush Meyusad 'al Kitve Yad Ha-Tosefta Ve-sifre Rishonim U-midrashim Be-khitve Yad U-defusim Yeshanim* (Jerusalem: Mosad Ha-Rav Kook, 1939).

63. The continuation of this passage, not cited here, notes that this leniency does not apply to reed baskets. Reed baskets are susceptible to ritual impurity once they are usable, while twig baskets are only susceptible to impurity when their user has determined that they have been completed.

64. For other examples, see *tTaharot* 10:3, 10:12; *tOhalot* 8:4; *tHagigah* 3:10/*tParah* 4:10.

65. Vered Noam, *From Qumran to the Rabbinic Revolution: Conceptions of Impurity* (Hebrew) (Jerusalem: Yad Ben Zvi Press, 2010), 226, 247–48. For example, *tannaim* distinguish between the biblical categories of *ohel* (shelter, has at least one opening), which does not transfer impurity to someone who touches its walls on the outside, and *kever* (tomb, has no openings), which even transfers impurity to one who touches its walls on the outside. This distinction reflects a realistic conception, as impurity can drain to the opening of an *ohel*, while it bursts forth through the walls of a sealed *kever*. Nonetheless, appended to this realistic view is a nominalistic footnote: if the *kever* has a doorframe, even if the frame is completely plugged up, the frame suffices as a doorway and can render a construction an *ohel*.

66. The extent to which it had waned was contested. According to Jacob Neusner, during the *mishnaic* period, purity practices were refocused from everyday life such as eating practices to overall abstract questions about reality. Yair Furstenburg, however, citing Ya'akov Sussman, maintains that purity practices remained relevant to everyday eating in Palestine even during the post-*mishnaic* period, though their observance was indeed decreasing. See Neusner, *A History of the Mishnaic Law of Purities* (Leiden: Brill, 1977); Furstenberg, "Eating," 1n2; and Ya'akov Sussman, "Babylonian Sugyot for Zerai'm and Tohorot" (Hebrew) (PhD diss., Hebrew University, 1969), 310n16. Mira Balberg is agnostic on the issue, maintaining that rabbinic texts suggest more about what the rabbis thought than about what they did (Balberg, *Purity, Body and Self in Early Rabbinic Literature* [Berkeley: University of Cali-

fornia Press, 2014]). For archaeological evidence of the decline in observance of ritual purity law, see Ronny Reich, "*Miqwa'ot* (Jewish Ritual Immersion Baths) in Eretz-Israel in the Second Temple and the Mishnah and Talmud Periods" (Hebrew) (PhD diss., Hebrew University, 1990), 143. For textual evidence thereof, see H. Birenboim, "Observance of the Laws of Bodily Purity in Jewish Society in the Land of Israel During the Second Temple Period" (PhD diss., Hebrew University, 2006), 66–67; Furstenberg, "Eating," 254–62.

67. See Michael Newton, *The Concept of Purity at Qumran and in the Letters of Paul*, SNTSMS 53 (Cambridge: Cambridge University Press, 1985), 52–116; Louis William Countryman, *Dirt, Greed, and Sex: Sexual Ethics in the New Testament and Their Implications for Today* (Philadelphia: Fortress Press, 1988), 97–123. For Countryman's critique of Newton, see 98n2.

68. Balberg, *Purity*. Admittedly, though, it is then strange that *Mishnah*, which may focus on *ha'aramot* for a post-Temple reality, does not discuss *ha'aramah* for ritual im/purity law. If it is so important specifically for a post-Temple world that the self be a true subjective self, why not include the rejection of *ha'aramah* to underscore that point? On the other hand, one might argue that the same point about the subjective self is made by not bringing up the possibility of *ha'aramah* at all in this realm. And furthermore, both *mishnaic* cases of *ha'aramah* relate to *kodashim* and financial loss. Ritual im/purity law does not fit that theme. It is also possible that *Mishnah* is not discussing post-Temple reality.

69. See Exod. 22:24; Lev. 25:36–37; Deut. 23:20.

70. This prohibition includes five separate transgressions distributed among all parties involved (see *mBM* 5:12), and it is considered a trait of the wicked, in *tBM* 4:9. Christianity and Islam know of similar prohibitions. See Ian Harper and Lachlan Smirl, "Usury," in *The Oxford Handbook of Christianity and Economics*, ed. Paul Oslington (New York: Oxford University Press, 2014), 564–80.

71. MS Erfurt: הערמת רבית; Venice Ed.: ערמית רבית.

72. Lieberman changes the term סאה from the MSS and printed editions, to מאה, suggesting that such a switch occurs with regularity (*Tosefta Ki-feshutah*, 89n37). MS Erfurt: עשרים סאה של חיטין.

73. This is not found in MS Vienna, but because it is found in the otherwise identical line above, Lieberman adds it (*Tosefta Ki-feshutah*, 196).

74. One *maneh* is equivalent to 100 *zuz*.

75. Twenty-four *sela* is only 96 *zuz*, whereas twenty-five *sela* would be 100 *zuz*.

76. See Naḥmanides (Ramban) *Novellae bBM* 62b.

77. See Maimonides, *Mishneh Torah*, Laws of Lender and Borrower 5:15.

78. I use the term "festival" to refer to the part of the holiday that has labor restrictions similar, but not identical, to the Sabbath. Parts of a holiday that do not have these restrictions are known as *ḥol ha-mo'ed*, "the mundane of the holiday." These we term "the intermediate days of the festival/holiday."

79. Per *yShab.* 16:3, 18d, the problem is preparing for a weekday on the Sabbath or festival by saving food. Per *bShab.* 117b, one might become so determined to save more food that one will extinguish the fire.

80. For a discussion about whether this refers to food for minors on Yom Kippur or breakfast for adults after Yom Kippur ends, see Lieberman, *Tosefta Ki-feshutah*, 210.

81. *bShab.* 117b: ומצילין מיום הכפורים לשבת. This may be related to a debate between R. Akiva and R. Yishmael in *mShab.* 15:3 about other preparation on Yom Kippur for the Sabbath.

82. The parallel *mShab*.16:2 does not mention inviting guests but does mention asking others to take food for themselves. It is unclear whether this means that the *mishnah* is opposed to inviting guests to save more food or if the situation is simply too time pressured to do so. *BShab*. 117b cites the argument about inviting guests in the context of saving liquid spilling from a broken barrel on the Sabbath rather than saving food from a house fire.

83. MS Erfurt: אין צריך. Lieberman suggests that the term צריך (must) here means רשאי (may) (*Ha-Yerushalmi Ki-feshuto: Perush Meyusad 'al Kitve Yad shel Ha-Yerushalmi Ve-sifre Rabotenu Ha-rishonim U-midrashim*. 3rd ed. [New York: Jewish Theological Seminary, 1934], 252; *Tosefet Rishonim*, vol. 1, 155; *Tosefta Ki-feshutah, Shabbat*, 210).

84. MS Erfurt: בהן. This change reflects both the *Yerushalmi* and the *Bavli*'s readings of the *baraita*. *YShab*. 16:3, 18d cites two opposing *baraitot* about inviting guests before saving the food and explains them in light of the debate about *ha'aramah*. *BShab*. likewise relates אין מערימין to inviting guests. By changing אין מערימין בהן to אין מערימין בכך, MS Erfurt suggests that the אין מערימין debate is about both inviting guests and saving coarse bread. *BMo'ed Katan* 12b, however, cites only the end of this *tosefta*, using אין מערימין בכך, and does not discuss which part of the *tosefta* this clause refers to.

85. While the *mishnah* discusses how many meals to save from a burning home on the Sabbath (*mShab*. 16:2), only the *tosefta* raises the possibility of *ha'aramah* by saving coarse bread first "by accident" in order to save extra bread.

86. Many *toseftan* cases seem to engage circumventions of rabbinic law rather than biblical law, though Benjamin De Vries has suggested that the parameters of biblical and rabbinic law, respectively, evolved from the *tannaitic* to the *amoraic* period, with expansion of the rabbinic category specifically among Babylonian *amoraim*. On the difference between rabbinic law and biblical law, see De Vries, *Toldot Ha-halakhah Ha-talmudit*, 69–95; Yitzchak D. Gilat, "Issur shevut be-Shabbat ve-hishtelshelutam," *Perakim Be-hishtalshelut Ha-halakhah* (Ramat Gan: Bar Ilan University, 1992); H. Albeck, *Mavo La-Mishnah* (Jerusalem: Mosad HaRav Kook/Tel Aviv: Dvir, 1967), 49–53; Urbach, *The Halakhah*, 111–14; Elon, *Ha-mishpat Ha-'ivri*, 1:185–98; Joel Roth, *The Halakhic Process: A Systematic Approach* (New York: Jewish Theological Seminary, 1986), 13–48.

87. Exod. 12:16. Jewish law permits food preparation on festivals, including cooking and slaughtering, which are otherwise forbidden on those days. For a brief discussion of *halakhic* literature concerning the *muktzeh* status of pets, see Howard Jachter, "Halachic Perspectives on Pets," *Journal of Halacha & Contemporary Society*, no. 23 (Spring 1992): 49–53.

88. See Lev. 22:28.

89. There is no parallel in *Mishnah* (or *Midrash Halakhah*) to this *toseftan* passage. Instead *mBetzah* 3:4 deals only with the case of a *bekhor* (firstborn) animal that falls into a pit on the festival (also in *tBetzah* 3:3): if the animal had been maimed prior to the festival it may be retrieved from the pit for slaughter, as it is not *muktzeh*. Though the case of a non-*bekhor* animal falling into a pit on the festival is not found in *Mishnah* some assume that the ruling would be the same: because it is edible, it may be retrieved, but only to be slaughtered for that day's food (*Or Zarua, Laws of the Festival*, 2:355). Others have argued unconvincingly that one can retrieve a single non-*bekhor* animal from a pit on the festival even without planning to slaughter or slaughtering it (*Magen Avraham Oraḥ Ḥayyim* 498:10).

90. MS Erfurt, MS London, and Venice Ed. add: על מנת לשחוט.

91. Thus, MSS Vienna and Erfurt. But MSS Leiden, London, Venice Ed.: רצה לשחוט רצה שלא לשחוט אחד מהן הרשות בידו (see *'Ittur, Laws of Festivals*, Part III, 140; *Shibbole Ha-leket Ha-shalem* Laws of *'Atzeret* chap. 252).

92. This case parallels Matthew (12:11–12) and Luke (14:5), where Jesus charges the Pharisees with being unwilling to save a person on the Sabbath, though they would find a way to save their own sheep if it fell into a pit on the Sabbath. Interestingly, *tShab.* 14:3 unanimously and anonymously forbids one from lifting an animal that falls into a pit on the Sabbath. The Damascus Document records the same ruling about the animal that falls into the pit on the Sabbath (CD 11:13–14). However, on the festival, even R. Eliezer, who is stricter, allows the retrieval of one animal from the pit. Perhaps R. Eliezer's strictness is animated by kinship to the Qumranic position, albeit more lenient on the festival because there is a licit way to handle the animal on that day while there is no such option on the Sabbath. Scholars have posited an affinity between R. Eliezer's legal outlook and rulings and those of Qumran. See Aharon Shemesh, *Halakhah in the Making: The Development of Jewish Law from Qumran to the Rabbis*, Taubman Lectures in Jewish Studies (Berkeley: University of California Press, 2009), 39, 46; Vered Noam, "Traces of Sectarian Halakhah in the Rabbinic World," in *Rabbinic Perspectives: Rabbinic Literature and the Dead Sea Scrolls: Proceedings of the Eighth International Symposium of the Orion Center for the Study of the Dead Sea Scrolls and Associated Literature*, ed. Steven G. Fraade, Aharon Shemesh, and Ruth A. Clements (Leiden: Brill, 2006), 69; Yitzchak D. Gilat, *R. Eliezer Ben Hyrcanus: A Scholar Outcast*, Bar-Ilan Studies in Near Eastern Languages and Culture (Ramat Gan: Bar Ilan University Press, 1984), 12, 60; and Jacob Neusner, *Eliezer ben Hyrcanus: The Tradition and the Man* (Leiden, Brill 1973), 2:277. R. Yehoshua's position is interesting in light of his condemnation of the cunning rogue in *mSotah* 3:2. And while one might wish to connect R. Yehoshua's permissive position to the talmudic oven of Akhinai story (*bBM* 59b/*yMK* 3:1, 81c) where R. Yehoshua's position is that Torah "is not in Heaven" and is instead a matter of human creativity, much of that story consists of later *amoraic*/redactional editorializing.

CHAPTER 2. BEING EXPLICIT ABOUT LEGAL VALUES AND INTEGRITY

1. That is, a prohibition to see and own leaven during Passover.
2. Venice Ed.: אני.
3. *Or Zarua*: שורף without כ.
4. Lieberman, *Ha-Yerushalmi Ki-feshuto: Perush Meyusad ʻal Kitve Yad shel Ha-Yerushalmi Ve-sifre Rabotenu Ha-rishonim U-midrashim*. 3rd ed. (New York: Jewish Theological Seminary, 1934), 366: לר' יושע.
5. MS Leiden and Venice Ed., *y'Er.* 10:13: מוטב לעבור על מצות לא תעשה שלא באת לידך ממצות לא תעשה שבאת לפניך—Better to transgress a negative commandment that has not come to your hand than a negative commandment that has come before you.
6. *Yerushalmi* translations are variations on Jacob Neusner, *The Talmud of the Land of Israel: An Academic Commentary to the Second, Third, and Fourth Divisions* (Atlanta: Scholars Press, 1998).
7. This part of the discussion between R. Yehoshua and R. Eliezer is found also in *tPes.* 3:7.
8. See commentaries to *mḤallah* 2:3, 7 and *tḤallah* 1:8. Shamma Friedman points out that R. Akiva is the one who requires separation of *ḥallah* from impure dough while the earlier law was to obviate the requirement for *ḥallah* from impure dough by preparing it in smaller quantities than that from which *ḥallah* must be separated. As such, R. Eliezer, Ben Beterah, and R. Yehoshua, all of whom predated R. Akiva, must be discussing a case in which the dough only became impure once it had already been kneaded; for if not, they would

have simply suggested that one prepare the dough in smaller baskets to exempt it from the separation of *ḥallah* altogether. And, in fact, this *Yerushalmi* passage explicitly includes the provision that "our source discusses the case where it became impure after its kneading, but if it had become impure before its kneading, one should make it in smaller quantities." See Friedman, *Tosefta 'Attiqta: Masekhet Pesaḥ Rishon: Makbilot Ha-Mishnah Ve-ha-Tosefta* (Ramat Gan: Bar Ilan University Press, 2002), 278.

9. The unstated assumption is that separating pure dough from a batch being prepared on the festival is permissible. See *mBetzah* 1:6; see also *tBetzah* 1:14 where this is permissible for dough—both ritually pure and impure—so long as it is kneaded on the festival. If, however, it was kneaded the day before, the dough offering may not be separated from it on the festival.

10. See Exod. 12:16; *mShab.* 2:1; *tShab.* 2:1.

11. In Israel, Passover has one festival day at the beginning of the holiday and one at the end of the holiday, with *ḥol ha-mo'ed* in between. Outside of Israel, Passover has two festival days to start the holiday and two to end it, with *ḥol ha-mo'ed* in between.

12. Moreover, one may not burn the dough or feed it to dogs because impure *kodashim* may not be burned on the Sabbath or festival (*tShab.* 2:1).

13. Gilat bases this on the biblical qualification "And no leaven shall be seen *to you*," i.e., one may not see their own *ḥametz* but may see *ḥametz* that belongs to others or to God (*Mekhilta d'R. Shimon b. Yohai* 13:7/*Sifre* Deuteronomy 131). While "to others" is usually understood as belonging to gentiles, Gilat suggests that because the *ḥallah* belongs to someone else (the priest), there is no violation. One could equally argue it belongs to God as a commanded offering to the priest. (Gilat, "'Al ḥametz shel aḥerim ve-shel gavohah," *Tarbiz* 33 [1963]: 20–27.) Rashi (*bPes.* 46b, s.v. *lo zehu*) connects this to how the *Bavli* explains R. Yehoshua's position.

Shamma Friedman explains R. Yehoshua differently, based on *tPes.* 3:7 (cited by this *Yerushalmi*), where he indicates that owning risen *ḥallah* is a violation, but at least is done only passively rather than actively placing dough in the oven. Friedman suggests that "this is not the leaven about which we are warned" still indicates transgression, but the lesser of two evils. He cites parallel language in *mTer.* 8:11, where an action is prohibited generally, but in that specific case should be done because it is less egregious than other options. Friedman's preference for the *tosefta*'s version of R. Yehoshua accords with his general position that *Tosefta* represents earlier sources than the later, redacted *Mishnah* (Friedman, *Tosefta 'Attiqta*, 279–80, 288).

David Weiss Halivni suggests that R. Yehoshua is committed to both reasons—that the prohibition of owning *ḥametz* does not apply to *ḥallah* and that the passive rising of the dough is less problematic than placing dough into the oven. Halivni cites *mZev.* 8:10 as precedent, where R. Yehoshua offers two conflicting explanations for a single position within the same *mishnah*: (David Weiss Halivni, *Mekorot U-mesorot: 'Eruvin U-Pesaḥim.* (Jerusalem: Jewish Theological Seminary of America, 1982), 413). See *Tos. bShab.* 14a s.v., *tanna*, who discuss why one might offer two reasons for a ruling. Gilat, however, suggests that in *tPes.* 3:7, R. Yehoshua is specifically offering not his own opinion, but an argument that R. Eliezer might accept, given that the latter believes owning risen *ḥallah* violates a prohibition.

Lieberman suggests that each Talmud reads R. Yehoshua's *mishnaic* opinion differently. The *Bavli* reads it as being exempt from violation due to lack of ownership, while the *Yerushalmi* reads it as stating that one need not burn risen *ḥallah* on the festival because it is forbidden to burn food that rises on the festival (*Tosefta Ki-feshutah, Betzah*, 502).

14. MS Leiden and Venice Ed., *y'Er.* 10:13: שלא חישב לשחוט אחד מהן 'א'ע'פ. Both Dov Baer Ratner, *Ahavat Tziyon Ve-Yerushalayim* (Jerusalem, 1966) and Lieberman, *Tosefta Kifeshutah*, *Betzah* 3:4 consider the *'Eruvin* version errant.

15. The language of requiring a sin offering on the festival is problematic, given the fact that one incurs lashes only for violating the festival (*yBetzah* 1:3), while sin offerings are reserved for Sabbath violations. However, perhaps an infraction being a *ḥiyuv ḥatat*, an obligation of a sin offering, refers to the status of the transgression: it has that status because if one committed it on the Sabbath, one would be obligated to bring a sin offering. (*Pene Moshe*, s.v. *amar R. Idi* states that the language is imprecise, and *Korban Ha-'edah*, s.v. *ve-kan ḥiyuv ḥatat* offers a different explanation.)

16. The category of *shevut* applies to both Sabbath and festivals. The category of *ḥiyuv ḥatat*, however, is more complicated: on the Sabbath, one who violates one of the thirty-nine forbidden labors by accident is liable to bring a sin offering, while on the festival, one is exempt from such an offering. Again, the term *ḥiyuv ḥatat* is being used to delineate the severity of a transgression, whether committed on the Sabbath or the festival, rather than suggesting that one would bring a sin offering for committing said transgression on the festival. A transgression defined as a *ḥiyuv ḥatat* is more severe than one defined as a *shevut*.

17. This approach omits the possibility that there may also be a violation in the animal/offspring case: causing harm to animals. *BBM* 32b records a debate about whether causing an animal harm constitutes a biblical or a rabbinic prohibition. Moreover, in the parallel discussion of *ha'aramah* parameters on *bShab*. 117b, the *stam* suggests that R. Yehoshua is lenient in the livestock case because leaving the animal in the pit causes it pain. That the *Yerushalmi* omits the possibility of causing animals pain as justifying *ha'aramah* indicates that: (a) causing pain to animals does not violate Jewish law; (b) causing pain to animals is an insufficient violation of Jewish law to warrant *ha'aramah*; or (c) the animal can be protected even in the pit.

18. Gilat ("Issur shevut," 87–108) traces the development of the term *shevut*, which becomes synonymous with rabbinic rather than biblical transgression. He notes that in the early legal *midrash*, *shevut* refers to a Sabbath transgression not explicitly indicated in Scripture and thus does not carry the death penalty, the default punishment for Sabbath desecration. These more leniently punished offenses take their label from the term *shabbaton*, a rest, used to describe the Sabbath throughout the Pentateuch (Exod. 16:23, 31:15; Lev. 23:3, 35:2). See also *Sifra Aḥare Mot* 7:9; *Mekhilta d'R. Shimon b. Yohai* 20; *Mekhilta d'R. Yishmael, Bo* 9; *Mekhilta d'R. Yishmael, Mishpatim, Kaspa* 20; *Mekhilta d'R. Yishmael Ki Tisa* 1. However, in the *amoraic* period, the term *shevut* evolved from referring to a biblical prohibition that does not incur the death penalty to referring to a rabbinic prohibition, resulting in other leniencies as well (Gilat, "Issur shevut," 105).

19. *ySan.* 4:1, 22a; *yPes.* 1:8, 28a; or "not to make Israel lose money," in *yGit.* 1:5, 43d.

20. See Leviticus 14.

21. MS Parma 2596 renders the spelling טפיו.

22. There is another example where the *Yerushalmi* compares contradictory opinions about something that it calls *ha'aramah*. However, it seems that the notion of *ha'aramah* as circumvention does not fit there. *Y'Eruvin* 26d (MS Leiden) discusses two cases related to ritual impurity in the Temple. One case (*mEruvin* 10:14) discusses what to do if an impure reptile (*sheretz*) is found in the Temple. R. Yohanan ben Berokah allows the priest to carry it in his belt to remove it quickly, even though doing so multiplies the impurity by making the belt impure as well. R. Yehudah, however, wishes to limit impurity and allows the priest to

find a wooden tong that will not contract impurity, with which to remove the reptile, even though this may take longer. The second case regarding impurity in the Temple discusses how the recovering *metzora* who comes to the Temple for expiation but may not fully enter the sanctum due to their impurity should place their body parts that need blood applied to them by the priest for expiation into the sanctum (*mNega'im* 14:9). According to the anonymous first opinion, the *metzora* separately and sequentially places their head inside and pulls out again, then their hand and pulls back out again, and then their foot and pulls back out again. R. Yehudah, however, allows the *metzora* to place all three body parts into the sanctum at once. *Y'Eruvin* asserts a contradiction between these two opinions of R. Yehudah, as in the case of the *sheretz*, he wants to limit the impurity in the sanctum, while in the case of the *metzora*, he permits multiple impurities in the sanctum at once. Strangely, the passage describes the contradiction as follows: מחלפה שיטת ר' יהודה תמן הוא אוסר להערים וכא או' מותר, "R. Yehudah's opinion has switched: there he says one may not use cunning, while here he says it is permitted to use cunning." The passage does the same in the reverse for the non–R. Yehudah opinion in the respective *mishnayot*. It is odd to use "cunning" with regard to these actions. There is nothing that is cunning about them. Thus, I do not think this is about *ha'aramah* at all. Rather, the language is copied from the comparison of the two *ha'aramah* cases in *yPes.* 3:3, 30a. This is further buttressed by the fact that the preceding lines in the *Yerushalmi* passage actually discuss the case of *ha'aramah* for impure *ḥallah* on Passover. It is also supported by the fact that the passage asserts מחלפה שיטת דרבנן, "the opinion of the sages is switched," which is surprising given that the first *mishnaic* example is cited in the name of R. Yohanan ben Berokah. (See Lieberman, *Ha-Yerushalmi Ki-feshuto*, 367.)

23. Jewish law requires two stages of marriage: betrothal (*kiddushin*) and marriage (*nisu'in*). Unlike engagement in our day, *kiddushin* can only be undone by a writ of divorce (known as a *get*). In the ancient world, betrothal took place up to a year before marriage.

24. MS Darmstadt 407 הן.

25. There are various ways to understand this *ha'aramah*. *Korban Ha-'edah* explains it as tricking a *levir* into marrying a sister-in-law whom he does not want to marry by telling him he is forbidden to reject her. I, however, read this case as parallel to R. Tarfon's precedent: that is, the *levir* would like to betroth several of the women in order to support them.

26. Predictably, the *Korban Ha-'edah* reads this line differently: there (= in the case of R. Tarfon), each woman could not eat *terumah* without R. Tarfon's *ha'aramah*, but here (= in the case of the *levir*), the *levir* is allowed to marry whomever he wishes. In other words, it should be up to the *levir* whether he performs levirate marriage on a particular woman rather than up to the court.

27. The final line describing the experience of R. Yudan son of R. Yishmael challenges the previous distinction between R. Tarfon's case and levirate marriage. *Ridbaz* (s.v., *u-mahu*) suggests that others duped R. Yudan (ערמו אותו), while *Pene Moshe* (s.v., *'avdin le khen*) suggests that R. Yudan himself committed the *ha'aramah*.

28. Deut. 25:5–10.

29. See *Pene Moshe*, s.v. *u-mahu le-ha'arim*. Parenthetically, this would delay his marriage to any one of them.

30. *mKetubot* 5:2; in *tKetubot* 5:1, R. Tarfon states that one may feed a betrothed woman completely from *terumah* food once twelve months have passed and the couple has not married. Lieberman suggests the groom in this case could stipulate that he would feed those whom he betrothed immediately, and he could fulfill that stipulation by giving them priestly food (*Tosefta Ki-feshutah*, ad loc.)

31. Though R. Tarfon's case is mentioned in *tKet.* 5:1, it is the *Yerushalmi* that suggests using it as a paradigm for circumvention in cases of levirate marriage.

32. The concern with the obviousness of a ruse will be central to the *Bavli*'s treatment of *ha'aramah*.

33. This echoes R. Yonah in *yMS* 4:3, 55a about giving his money wholeheartedly to R. Inya to affect the latter's acquisition.

34. MS Vatican: אבין.

35. On this point, I have been able to find only one explicit example of *ha'aramah* within *Midrash Halakhah*, which underscores just how disconnected the phenomenon of *ha'aramah* is from the authority of the Bible and how much it rests on rabbinic logic and authority. See Chapter 1, n34 above.

36. The *Yerushalmi* also cites earlier *tannaitic* cases—e.g., taking interest through evasion, *yBM* 5:1, 10a–b; saving extra bread through avoision, *yShab.* 16:3, 18d.

37. MS Darmstadt: רב כהנא בר בא.

38. See Exod. 12:16.

39. The Epilogue will discuss these rationales.

40. Later rabbis understand the *mishnah*'s guidance to be an official rabbinic enactment. See the *Yerushalmi* text a few lines before R. Kahana's statement, and *bBetzah* 16a–b. Thus, R. Kahana may be concerned about someone undermining the authority of the rabbis by using their own dodge rather than following a rabbinic decree. On *bBetzah* 17b, Rav Ashi appears concerned about the use of this *ha'aramah* and perhaps about (misused) *ha'aramah* in general.

41. See *Korban Ha-'edah*, s.v. *mole'ah hu*.

42. See *Pene Moshe*, s.v. R. Aha.

43. See Deut. 16:15; *Sifre* Deut. 142; *yShab.*15:3, 15a.

44. Additionally, in the previous section of that very same chapter of the *Yerushalmi* (*yBetzah* 1:5, 60c; *yShab.* 12:1, 13c) not wanting to prevent holiday celebration properly is named as the reason for additional leniencies on the festival. Significantly, R. Aha is featured there as well. *MBetzah* 1:5 cites the Bet Hillel as permitting one to reattach shutters onto a closet or chest on the festival, though this appears to transgress a festival prohibition on construction. Bet Hillel does not want people to refrain from getting food out of shuttered cabinets for fear of being unable to protect the rest of their food by resealing the shutters that day. (See Albeck, *Shishah Sidre Mishnah*, 288.) The framing given is: "They permitted the matter in the end (i.e., re-sealing the shutters) out of consideration for the outset (i.e., that people will take food to eat on the festival."

45. This is how R. Shlomo ibn Aderet differentiates between cooking for Sabbath and salting meat on the festival: in the first instance, one was negligent in not setting aside *'eruv tavshilin*, while in the second instance, one is trying to celebrate the festival properly with a meal (Rashba *Novellae*, *bBetzah* 11b).

46. Alternatively, he knew that the guarantor would run away. See *Korban Ha-'edah*, s.v. *ifarsan Levi* and *Shiyare Ha-korban*.

47. See *Pene Moshe*, s.v. *be-she-lo 'asu be-ha'aramah*.

48. There are also situations in which the rabbis explicitly do not suspect *ha'aramah*, e.g., *yPe'ah* 6:1, 19b (MS Leiden), where rabbis do not worry that one who declares their field ownerless does so merely to evade having to tithe it. However, the phrasing raises an additional possibility: some versions read: לא חשו על הערמה while others read הדא אמרה לא חשו להערמה. The difference between להערמה and על הערמה may be the difference between not

being suspicious that *ha'aramah* is being used and not caring even if it is used. However, in other passages, such as *yPes.* 2:2, 29a, להערמה is used in all versions.

49. See *m'Arakhin* 6:1.

50. The parallel *t'Arakhin* 4:3 puts the debate differently: R. Eliezer and R. Yehoshua agree that he must forswear the woman he divorces from future benefit, but they argue over whether he may remarry her after they divorce.

51. I presume that this is not a situation in which the man could argue that he became so destitute that, had he known this would happen, he would not have vowed to the Temple treasury in the first place. In that situation, one might nullify the vow before a sage rather than having to resort to ruses. See *bHagigah* 10a for a discussion about the origins of the practice of nullifying vows.

52. The *ketubah* is a rabbinic prenuptial agreement stipulating the financial requirements of a husband to his wife, including the requirement to pay her a lump sum, should they get divorced.

53. There are other examples of suspecting *ha'aramah*, e.g., *yPesahim* 2:2, 29a, where R. Yohanan and Resh Lakish argue whether someone who declared their *hametz* ownerless before Passover (rather than otherwise disposing of it) may reclaim it after Passover. R. Yohanan forbids it, while Resh Lakish permits it. Their argument is interpreted by the editors as an argument over suspecting *ha'aramah*: R. Yohanan suspects that the person is employing *ha'aramah* just to get their food back after Passover, while Resh Lakish does not suspect it. I address this example further in the Epilogue.

54. The seven-day period's many restrictions are meant to keep a mourner focused on their mourning.

55. Constantinople Ed.: נזרעת.

56. Though MSS Leiden reads יודה, we emend based on the Constantinople Ed.'s דרבי יוסה for the sake of coherence.

57. See *Pene Moshe*, s.v. *u-manu ameru lo*. On this reading, R. Yose, on the other hand, would have likely permitted doing everything as usual for the mourner rather than waiting until the following week.

58. This distinction about when people are or are not likely to use *ha'aramah* is absent from the parallel Babylonian passage (*bMK* 11b). Moreover, a *baraita* cited in the *Bavli* (*bMK* 12b) as permitting *ha'aramah* to make beer on *hol ha-mo'ed* for after the holiday is at odds with this cautionary *Yerushalmi* passage about the need to rein in potential *ha'aramah* on *hol ha-mo'ed*.

59. This is known in *mMK* 2:3 as one who יכוין מלאכתו במועד, who purposely plans their labor for the intermediate days of the festival.

60. This tracks with the explanation of Ridbaz. Other traditional commentators, however, interpret this *ha'aramah* differently. *Korban Ha-'edah*, s.v. *u-meshani shenaya*, suggests that *ha'aramah* means lying about wanting to plant flax rather than a plant that can be sowed later in the season. This interpretation of *ha'aramah* as bald lying, I assert in later chapters, is a feature of the later Babylonian Talmud. Perhaps *Korban Ha-'edah* is influenced in his reading here by the use of the terminology of *ha'aramah* in the *Bavli*. *Pene Moshe* asserts that *ha'aramah* here refers to the farmer fully pressing olives on the holiday under guise of only doing the initial pressing. This too understands *ha'aramah* as lying.

The Ridbaz also does recognize a relationship between subterfuge and lying, as the farmer may misrepresent the situation as unavoidable rather than planned. However, even this misrepresentation is somewhat of a circumvention in that it recognizes that the law does not actually provide criteria for assessing whether a farmer's need to work during *ḥol ha-mo'ed* is unavoidable.

The same concern about people employing *ha'aramah* during the *ḥol ha-mo'ed* recurs in *yMK* 3:1, 82a. The context is likely the prohibition to shave during *sheloshim* as on *ḥol ha-mo'ed*. Once again, the rabbis suspect subterfuge with regards to *ḥol ha-mo'ed* but not with regard to mourning. One might purposely orchestrate "not having had time" to shave prior to the festival by keeping oneself busy. (See *Korban Ha-'edah* s.v., *be-she-yesh sham ha'aramah*.) Similar to his read of *ha'aramah* in the olive-pressing case above, *Pene Moshe* (s.v., *be-she-yesh sham ha'aramah*) asserts that the *ha'aramah* here would be that a person would "accidentally" shave his entire beard rather than just trimming his moustache. His reading of *ha'aramah* does not comport with the idea of legal circumvention per se but is more akin to lying or trickery.

61. The amount varies based on the produce. See *mMa'aserot* 1:5.

62. The difference between a snack and a meal may be determined by the amount that one eats, whether one eats on a regular weekday or on Sabbath, and/or whether people or animals are eating the food. See Maimonides *Mishneh Torah*, Laws of Tithing 3:19–20 and *bBetzah* 34b.

63. See *mMa'aserot* chaps. 1–3; *mTerumot* 8:3; *yMa'aserot* 1:5, 4b; this applies to the separation of *terumah* as well.

64. MSS Paris and London add the words ומאכיל לבהמתו, "and feed his animal," at the end of R. Hoshaya's teaching.

65. See R. Elazar Ezkari, *Sefer Ḥaredim*, s.v. *tani R. Hoshaya*, who interprets this passage in light of *Bavli* parallels that read: מכניסה במוץ שלה, brings it inside in its chaff.

66. See *Pene Moshe*, s.v. *marbeh adam dagan ba-teven* and *Ḥiddushe R. Yonah* 22a (of the Rif).

67. Those who wish to reconcile the two Talmuds, such as *Pene Moshe*, assume that the purpose is to feed one's animals food that has not yet been tithed, as the *Bavli* reads "so that his animal can eat it, and it will be exempt from tithing." MSS Paris and London add the words "and feed his animal" at the end of R. Hoshayah's teaching. Louis Ginzberg points out that the *Yerushalmi* version is more lenient than the *Bavli* version in that it permits people to eat too. (Ginzberg, *Perushim Ve-ḥiddushim Be-Yerushalmi* [New York: JTSA, 1961], 120–21.) According to one opinion in Rashba's Novellae (*bBerakhot* 31a), restricting consumption to animals prevents misusing the loophole. However, a second opinion there allows people to eat the food as well. See likewise *bMen*. 67b *Tos.*, s.v. *kede*.

68. This would differ from the *Bavli*, which specifically permits rabbis to avail themselves of *ha'aramah* even where others should not. See Chapter 5.

69. Regarding whether rabbinic exegesis creates novel law or upholds preexisting traditions, see E. E. Urbach, "Derashah as the Foundation of Halakhah, and the Problem of the Scribes," *Tarbiz* 27:2–3 (1958): 166–82. H. Albeck, *Mavo La-Mishnah* (Tel Aviv: Dvir, 1967), 40–54; DeVries, *Toldot Ha-halakhah Ha-talmudit*, 9–21; and Elon, *Ha-mishpat Ha-'ivri*, 1:243–49. For a summary of traditional debates about this issue over the last two millennia, see Harris, *How Do We Know This?*

70. For example, to execute their child, his parents must sound alike, look alike, and be the same height (*bSan*. 71a), based on the biblical clause: "he does not listen to *our voice*." See Rachel Leigh Rosenthal's study of rabbinic approaches to balancing rabbinic moral concerns with fealty to Scripture regarding the rebellious son: "Rebel with a Clause: Interpretation,

Pedagogy, and the Problem of the Stubborn and Rebellious Son" (PhD diss., Jewish Theological Seminary, 2019).

71. See *Sifre* Deut. 220, where R. Yose questions the harshness of the law of the wayward son. However, other rabbinic sources justify this law as preventing a terrible future of crime and havoc—which is good for the child and for society (*Sifre* Deut. 220; *bSan.* 72a).

72. See Halbertal, *Interpretive Revolutions*, chaps. 1 and 8. See also Aaron Kirschenbaum, *Equity in Jewish Law: Halakhic Perspectives in Law: Formalism and Flexibility in Jewish Civil Law* (Hoboken, NJ: Ktav, 1991), who writes: "equitable interpretations of statute are not regarded as intrusions or 'reinterpretations' of the text based upon extrinsic considerations. On the contrary, many equitable interpretations are the products of the interpreter's search for the 'true,' original, and authentic meaning of the passage" (29). See also Abraham Isaac Kook, *Iggerot Ha-Re'ayah* (Jerusalem: Mosad Ha-Rav Kook, 1977), letter #90, 103. Rabbi Kook argues that Torah itself contains multiple interpretations, and different generations merely find a different refraction of the truth internal to the Torah's meaning. Mark D. Rosen, "Beyond Interpretation: The 'Cultural Approach' to Understanding Extra-Formal Change in Religious and Constitutional Law," *Journal of Law, Religion and State* 2.2 (2013): 200–233; Elon, *Ha-mishpat Ha-'ivri*.

73. See Hayes, *What's Divine*, 318–23; and Amnon Bazak, *To This Very Day: Fundamental Questions in the Study of Oral Law* (Hebrew) (Rishon Le-Tziyon: Miskal-Yedioth Ahronoth Books and Chemed Books, 2020).

CHAPTER 3. ROMANS AS JURISTS, RABBIS AS LAWYERS

1. Gaius discusses fictions in book four of his second-century tract *Institutes of Gaius* (*Institutiones*, in Latin). The *Institutes* was used as a textbook to train law students.

2. Clifford Ando, "Fact, Fiction and Social Reality in Roman Law," in *Legal Fictions in Theory and Practice*, ed. Maksymilian Del Mar and William Twining (New York: Springer International Publishing, 2015), 295–324. For more on Roman legal fictions, see J. S. Richardson, "The Roman Mind and the Power of Fiction," in *The Passionate Intellect: Essays on the Transformation of Classical Traditions Presented to Professor I. G. Kidd*, ed. L. Ayres, Rutgers University Studies in Classical Humanities 7 (New Brunswick: Transaction, 1995), 117–30; Yan Thomas, "Fictio legis: L'empire de la fiction romaine," *Droits: Revue française de théorie juridique* 21 (1995): 17–63; Ernesto Bianchi, *Fictio iuris: Ricerche sulla finzione in diritto romano dal periodo arcaico all'epoca augustea* (Padova: CEDAM, 1997); Clifford Ando, *Law, Language and Empire in the Roman Tradition* (Philadelphia: University of Pennsylvania Press, 2011), esp. 1–18, 115–31; and Nicolas Cornu Thénard, "La notion de fait dans la jurisprudence classique: Étude sur les principes de la distinction entre fait et droit" (PhD diss., University of Paris, 2011).

3. This example is cited in Justinian's *Digest* (*Digesta*, in Latin), an anthology of Roman jurists' writings from the first to third centuries CE. It was commissioned by Emperor Justinian and published in 533 CE. The example cited here is attributed to Ulpian, a Roman jurist who lived in the late second to early third century CE. See *Digest* 29.1.3. Reinhard Zimmerman discusses this and other examples in *The Law of Obligations: Roman Foundations of the Civilian Tradition* (New York: Oxford University Press, 1996), 684.

4. See, for instance, *Rhetorica ad Herennium* (in English, *Rhetoric for Herennius*) 1.11.19. It is the oldest extant Latin book of rhetoric, and it is dated to an unknown author at the

beginning of the first century BCE. It is addressed to the otherwise unknown Gaius Herrenius.

5. See W. W. Buckland, *Equity in Roman Law: Lectures Delivered in the University of London, at the Request of the Faculty of Laws* (London: University of London Press, 1911): "Attempts to evade the rules of law by keeping the letter while breaking the spirit were as common in Rome, as they have been in our courts" (112); Bertram B. Benas, "The Legal Device in Jewish Law," *Journal of Comparative Legislation and International Law*, 3rd ser., 11:1 (1929): 75–80; Katzoff, "Judicial Reasoning," esp. 250; Fritz Schulz, *History of Roman Legal Science* (London: Oxford University Press, 1946), 24–30.

6. Zimmerman, *The Law of Obligations*, 703.

7. David Daube, "Fraud No. 3," in *Collected Studies in Roman Law*, ed. David Daube, David Cohen, and Dieter Simon (Frankfurt am Main: V. Klostermann, 1991), 1410.

8. Some *ha'aramot* work similarly: e.g., the *interposita persona* for *ma'aser sheni*; nominal status change in R. Tarfon's betrothal of three hundred women during a famine; sanctifying an animal in utero to evade *bekhor* status. There is even a near exact Roman parallel to the attempted loophole of divorcing one's wife and remarrying her to acquire property. In the Roman system, gifts between husbands and wives were void. The circumvention arose as early as the first century BCE whereby the husband would divorce his wife, give her a gift, and then remarry her (Katzoff, "Judicial Reasoning," 251n38). See *Digest* 24.1.64 where a string of jurists is cited condemning this loophole. The list includes Trebatius (first centry BCE) and Labeo (first century CE), making this among the earliest recorded instances of a jurist rejecting a loophole that does not violate the literal wording of a statute. It is noteworthy, though, that he does not use *fraus legi* nomenclature, which seems to not yet have been developed.

9. John W. Vaughn, "Law and Rhetoric in the *Causa Curiana*," *Classical Antiquity* 4:2 (October 1985): 208–22.

10. See Tamás Nótári, "*Summum Ius Summa Iniuria*—Comments on the Historical Background of a Legal Maxim of Interpretation," *Acta Juridica Hungarica* 42:1–2 (2004): 301–3. He finds earlier iterations of this concept in the works of Terence (*Heautontimoroumenos* 792. *Sqq*), Hieronymus (*Epistulae* 1, 44), and Columella (*De re rustica* 1.7.1 *Sq*). See also Johannes Stroux, "Summum ius summa iniuria—Ein Kapitel in der Geschichte der interpretatio iuris" (A Chapter in the History of Legal Interpretation), in *Romische Rechtswissenschaft und Rhetorik* (Potsdam: Stichnote, 1949), 7–66.

11. *De Officiis* 1.33 (trans. Walter Miller [London: W. Heinemann, 1921]).

12. *Digest* 40.9.7.1. At the end of the Roman Republic and the beginning of the Roman Empire, manumissions were so common that they threatened the socioeconomic fabric of Rome. At the end of the first century BCE, Emperor Augustus passed law to stem the practice. See Kathleen M. T. Atkinson, "The Purpose of the Manumission Laws of Augustus," *Irish Jurist*, n.s., 1 (1966): 356–74.

13. T. A. J. McGinn, "The 'SC' from Larinum and the Repression of Adultery at Rome," *Zeitschrift fuer Papyrologie und Epigraphik* 93 (1992): 284n59. In addition to closing loopholes, it was in this era that the praetor outlawed the enforceability of any contracts made under duress (*exceptio metus*) or by virtue of fraud (*exceptio doli*), indicating a relaxation of rigid formalism. See Peter Stein, *The Character and Influence of the Roman Civil Law: Historical Essays* (London: Hambledon Press, 1988), 25–26. And see 27–28 for a nuanced description of the law where the contract was made in error.

14. *Digest* 48.5.11.2.

15. *Tacitus Annals* 15.19. The *Annals* (in Latin, *Annales*) are an account of the Roman Empire from 14 to 68 CE, written by Roman senator and historian Tacitus. See also Katzoff, "Judicial Reasoning," 249.

16. As Roman legal historian W. W. Buckland notes, "the two tendencies, to rigidity and to equitable relaxation, will be found existing side by side." Buckland, *The Main Institutions of Roman Private Law* (Cambridge: Cambridge University Press, 1931), 9.

17. And, for members of the highest class, only male Roman citizens. See Stein, *The Character and Influence of the Roman Civil Law*, 23–24.

18. Fideicommissum comes from the Latin *fides* (trust) and *committere* (to commit).

19. Dio Cassius, *Roman History* (in Latin, *Historiae Romanae*) 55.5.4.

20. *Annals* 2.30.3.

21. It was in this century (160 CE) that Gaius's *Institutes* was written. See A. D. E. Lewis and David J. Ibbetson, "The Roman Law Tradition," in *The Roman Law Tradition* (Cambridge: Cambridge University Press, 1994), 1–14; Stephen A. Stertz, "Appendix: Roman Legal Codification in the Second Century," in *The Mishnah in Contemporary Perspective: Part I*, ed. Alan J. Avery-Peck and Jacob Neusner (Leiden: Brill, 2002), 149; Boaz Cohen, *Jewish and Roman Law: A Comparative Study*, Vol. 1 (New York: Jewish Theological Seminary of America, 1966), 15.

22. *Digest* 1.1.1.1.

23. *Digest* 1.3.17.

24. Significantly, however, Celsus allowed at least one exception, permitting a father to collect debt against his son (not ordinarily permitted) by installing his son as a loan guarantor rather than the debtor (*Digest* 1.6.7). Julian, however, outlawed this practice on grounds of violating the spirit of the law.

25. Katzoff, "Judicial Reasoning," 249.

26. See Chapter 1, note 56.

27. And yet second-century examples of legislators attempting to outlaw *fraus legi* within a given statute exist as well. See, for example, *Institutiones* 1.46, where Gaius writes "the *Lex Fufia Caninia*, as well as other special Decrees of the Senate, have declared all testamentary provisions devised for the purpose of evading the law to be void" (*The Institutes of Gaius*, parts 1 and 2, *Text with Critical Notes and Translation*, ed. Francis de Zulueta [Oxford: Clarendon Press, 1946]). This is still more sophisticated than trying to write a statute that is so comprehensive that it can prevent loopholes; here, the notion of legal fraud is included in the statute. See also Ulpian's statement that the praetor will not allow contracts that employ fraud to stand (*Digest* 2.14.7).

28. The jurist Julian (110–170 CE) is credited with consistent application of *fraus legi*, e.g.:

- During Celsus's era, according to the *senatus consultum* (senate decree) *Macedonianum*, loans made to *filiifamilias* could not be collected. A circumvention developed whereby the *filiusfamilias* would be written in the document as a guarantor rather than the debtor, and a non-family member would be written in as the debtor (see note 24). While Celsus permitted this, Julian ruled against it as "*fraus senatusconsulto facta*." He ruled the same way for a *filiusfamilias* who brought in a second person as his co-debtor (*Digest* 14.6.7).
- According to the *lex Papia Poppaea*, the patron of a freedman was entitled to a share of the freedman's estate equivalent to that of his children, so long as the freedman had fewer than three children and the estate was worth at least

100,000 HS. Julian wrote that an attempt by the freedman to alienate some of his property to get below 100,000 HS was considered *in fraudem legis* and was thus legally ineffective (*Digest* 37.14.16).

- A husband-to-be who tried to offer his undowered bride a gift that she would then return to him as a dowry would not get away with it. If the marriage was terminated, she would not receive the dowry money in return (*Digest* 12.1.20).

Following Julian, the concept of *fraus legi* became more and more widespread among jurists (Katzoff, "Judicial Reasoning," 248).

29. Zimmerman, *The Law of Obligations*, 704. Greek rhetoric was brought to Rome in the second century BCE (see Cohen, *Jewish and Roman Law*).

30. The pre-Socratic philosopher Protagoras (fifth century BCE) is credited with first contrasting διάνοια (meaning) and ὄνομα (word) (*Diogenes Laertius* XI.51). See Boaz Cohen, "Letter and Spirit in Jewish and Roman Law," in *Jewish and Roman Law*, vol. 1 (Piscataway, NJ: Georgias Press, 2018), 38n41. Cohen suggests that the terms "letter" and "spirit" probably come from Jewish sources, as the apostle Paul wished to preach to Jews as well—e.g., Isaiah 28:5–6. He cites rabbinic use of the letter of the law as: (1) the literal (as opposed to allegorical) interpretation of the law; (2) the ability of the omission of any single letter to change an entire law; (3) the interpretive significance of every letter in a word. See Cohen, *Jewish and Roman Law*, 37.

31. Aristotle, *Rhetoric* I.13–I.15.

32. Aristotle, *Nichomachean Ethics* 5.10.3–7, trans. H. Rackham, Loeb Classical Library.

33. See Cohen, "Letter and Spirit," 39; Robert J. Bonner and Gertrude Smith, *The Administration of Justice from Homer to Aristotle* (Chicago: University of Chicago Press, 1930), 1:75.

34. Cohen, "Letter and Spirit," 40.

35. See *Inst. Or.* III.6.61. *Institutio Oratoria*, as it was known in Latin, was a textbook on the philosophy and practice of rhetoric.

36. See *Inst. Or.* III.6.46.

37. Cohen, "Letter and Spirit," 41.

38. I use H. E. Butler's translation, published by Loeb Classical Library in 1920. He also mentions a preference for the *voluntas* of the law over the *scriptum* in cases that must logically be considered an exception to a particular law. For example, if the law states, "Whatever son has not defended his father shall be disinherited," does this mean any son, without exception? As Quintilian writes: "Suppose that a son who was but an infant, or one who was sick, or one who was out of the country, or in the army, or on an embassy, did not defend his father. Would he be disinherited?" (*Inst. Or.* VII.1.50).

39. See Cohen, "Letter and Spirit," 45; Leopold Wenger, *Institutes of the Roman Law of Civil Procedure*, rev. ed., trans. Otis Harrison Fisk (New York: Veritas Press, 1940), 140 18a, 195n16; J. Himmelschein, "Studien Zu Der Antiken Hermeneutica Iuris," in *Symbolae Friburgenses in Honorem Ottonis Lenel* (Leipzig: B. Tauchnitz, 1931), 398–417; Alvaro D'Ors Perez-Peix, "La Actitud Legislativa del Emperador Justiniano," *Orientalia Christiana Periodica* 13:1–2 (1947): 125–32; and H. Schmidt, "Einfluss Der Rhetorik Auf Die Gestaltung Der Richterlichen Entscheidung in Den Papyri," *Journal of Juristic Papyrology* 4 (1950): 165–77.

40. *Digest* 1.3.30.

41. See Cohen, "Letter and Spirit," 47; Fritz Schulz, *Principles of Roman Law* (Oxford: Clarendon Press 1936) 210n2; Carl Wium Westrup, *Introduction to Early Roman Law: Comparative*

Sociological Studies, the Patriarchal Joint Family, vol. 3 (Copenhagen: Levin & Munksgaard, 1934), 21–22.

42. "Why some dodges pass and others do not, or why the same dodge succeeds at a certain time and place and not at another, I leave unexplored" (Daube, "Fraud No. 3," 1417). Daube notes that many circumventions (some accepted, some rejected) were altruistic, done on behalf of the elite's inner circle, as part of their obligations to one another. See David Daube, *Roman Law: Linguistic, Social and Philosophical Aspects* (Edinburgh: Edinburgh University Press, 1966), 92. For example, an insolvent debtor (from among the Roman elite) who owed one hundred *aurei* and only had ten would do the following: He handed the creditor ten *aurei*, and the creditor accepted it and handed it back as a gift. The debtor again handed over ten *aurei* to the creditor, who again accepted it, and again handed it to the debtor as a gift. This continued until the debtor had handed ten *aurei* to the creditor ten times, and in the end (having left the ten *aurei* with the creditor on the final exchange), the creditor was considered fully repaid (*Digest* 46.3.67). This was to save the debtor from the infamy of not paying a debt or even of getting a creditor to accept less money than he was owed (see *Tab. Heracl.* 114g). Another was used by masters who wished to release many or all of their slaves upon their deaths but were forbidden to do so due to a limitation placed by Augustus in 2 BCE (Daube, *Roman Law*, 94). An owner of four slaves who was permitted to release only two slaves would bequeath the remaining two to a friend with instructions to free them (*Digest* 35.1.37). A third illustration is the origin of the *fideicommissa* (mentioned above): because a testator could not pass on his property to non-Romans (or women, if he was of the highest class), he would bequeath his land to a Roman male and instruct him in the will to hand the land over to whichever woman or non-Roman the testator had really wanted to inherit him. Augustus legalized this method, though there was strict oversight and local decision making by the consuls over whether the non-Roman was worthy and should get the land (*Digest* 18.1.36; *Institutes of Gaius* 2.285). At the end of the first century, Hadrian outlawed the *fideicommissa* for non-citizens.

43. Cohen, "Letter and Spirit," 55.

44. The extent of rabbinic awareness of Roman ideas and the latter's influence upon rabbinic thought are debated. Some argue that rabbinic thought is clearly influenced by Roman thought: Peter Schaefer and Catherine Heszer, eds., *The Talmud Yerushalmi and Graeco-Roman Culture*, vols. 1–3 (Tübingen: Mohr Siebeck, 1998–2002); Saul Lieberman, *Greek in Jewish Palestine; Hellenism in Jewish Palestine* (New York: Jewish Theological Seminary of America, 1941); idem, "Roman Legal Institutions in Early Rabbinics and in the Acta Martyrum," *Jewish Quarterly Review* 35:1 (1944): 1–57; Cohen, *Jewish and Roman Law*; Tzvi Novick, "The *Borer* Court: New Interpretations of mSan 3," *Zutot* 5:1 (2008): 1–8; Richard Hidary, *Rabbis and Classical Rhetoric: Sophistic Education and Oratory in the Talmud and Midrash* (Cambridge: Cambridge University Press, 2017). Others note that direct influence is impossible to prove and that the rabbis had every reason to reject Roman influence: Bernard S. Jackson, "On the Problem of Roman Influence on the Halakhah and Normative Self-Definition in Judaism," in *Jewish and Christian Self-Definition*, ed. E. P. Sanders, A. I. Baumgarten, and Alan Mendelson (London: SCM Press, 1981), 2:157–203; Schwartz, *Imperialism*. Here I compare Roman and rabbinic rhetoric about circumventions without claiming any clear direct influence or purposeful resistance.

45. Boaz Cohen compares the rabbis to both magistrates and jurists: "The magistrates at Rome formulated, adapted, corrected, extended and interpreted the Laws. The jurists organized and classified the means by which every legal problem could be brought to a solu-

tion. This applies with equal force to the Tannaim and Amoraim who were both magistrates and jurists. It was they who expounded, expanded and transmuted the Pentateuchal law into a theoretical and applied science of law. It may be truly said of the rabbis of the Talmud, that they resembled 'the Roman jurists who were admirable casuists and admitted neither a priori theses nor cumbersome generalizations, relying on their subtle genius to discover in each case the adequate, or as they called it, the "elegans" solution' (Declaureuil, *Le Quatrieme Centenairs de Cujas*, 1922, 9)" (Cohen, "Some Remarks on the Law of Persons in Jewish and Roman Jurisprudence," *Proceedings of the American Academy for Jewish Research* 16 [1946–47]: 37).

46. See *Mekhilta d'R. Yishmael, Kaspa* 20; *Mekhilta d'R. Shimon bar Yohai, Mishpatim* 23:1; and *mAvot* 1:8. See also Eliezer Segal, *Holidays, History, and Halakhah* (Northvale, NJ: Aronson, 2001). The appointment of an advocate, *apotropos* (from the Greek ἐπίτροπος, meaning guardian or curator), to represent those (such as minors) who cannot handle their own affairs is an exception (e.g., *mGit.* 5:4).

47. See *mSan.* 3:6.

48. See Yuval Sinai, *The Judge and the Judicial Process in Jewish Law* (Hebrew) (Jerusalem: Hebrew University, 2010), 398–413.

49. Paul Mandel suggests that the judges' lawyerly deliberation prevents "transforming the trial into an actual 'inquisition' . . . completely directed towards proving the charges against the accused." See Mandel, "'Al 'pataḥ ve-'al ha-petiḥa: 'Iyun ḥadash," in *Higayon Le-Yonah* (Jerusalem: Magnes Press, 2006), 79n114. This excerpt follows Hidary's translation (Hidary, *Rabbis and Classical Rhetoric*, 232–33).

50. Hidary, *Rabbis and Classical Rhetoric*, 239.

51. *ySan.* 4:1, 22a; *bSan.* 17a.

52. Lev. 11:29–30. In suggesting that rabbinic judges used rhetoric when deliberating a case like Greek and Roman advocates argued a case before judges in court, Hidary differs with Boaz Cohen. Cohen ("Letter and Spirit," 161) argued that the rabbis did not develop the Greek science of rhetoric (Hidary, *Rabbis and Classical Rhetoric*, 234n78).

53. Meira Z. Kensky notes that rabbinic images of the Divine courtroom are often used exegetically, to explain God's past actions as recorded in Scripture, thereby attesting to Divine justice. God is not capricious but instead is "engaged in a particular process that seeks to channel his understandable anger appropriately." This imagery also suggests that God is reflective and dynamic. See Kensky, *Trying Man, Trying God: The Divine Courtroom in Early Jewish and Christian Literature* (Tübingen: Mohr Siebeck, 2010), 311 and chap. 8. For more on God's "personality" and "inner dynamism" in these instances, see David Stern, "*Imitatio Hominis*: Anthropomorphism and the Character(s) of God in Rabbinic Literature," *Prooftexts* 12 (1992): 151–74; and Michael Fishbane, *Biblical Myth and Rabbinic Mythmaking* (Oxford: Oxford University Press, 2003).

54. See *mAvot* 4:111; *Sifre* Deuteronomy 343; *tPe'ah* 1:1, *yTa'anit* 2:4, 65b; *yTa'anit* 1:1; 63c, Leviticus *Rabbah* 6:1. The image is drawn out further in later *midrashim* such as Song of Songs *Rabbah* 6:3; Lamentations *Rabbah* 1:13; Ecclesiastes *Rabbah* 4:1; Exodus *Rabbah* 43; and Numbers *Rabbah* 19:33. For an overview, see Kensky, *Trying Man, Trying God*.

55. Hidary, *Rabbis and Classical Rhetoric*, 251. Hidary points out that such rabbinic passages specifically used the imagery, tools, and terminology of Greco-Roman courts.

56. Kensky, *Trying Man, Trying God*.

57. It is fruitful to consider rabbinic lawyering in light of Christine Hayes's research on the place of truth in rabbinic perspectives on Divine law. Through a study of the term "truth" (אמת) in rabbinic corpora, she finds that "Mosaic Law is not portrayed in rabbinic

texts as *necessarily* allied with the truth." She contrasts this approach with a Greco-Roman orientation to Divine law, which requires that it comport with rational truth and be unchanging and universal. Hayes, *What's Divine*, 167, chap. 5; see also idem, "Legal Truth, Right Answers and Best Answers: Dworkin and the Rabbis," *Diné Israel: Studies in Halakhah and Jewish Law* 25 (2008): 73–121.

CHAPTER 4. *HA'ARAMAH* AND INTENTION

1. See Shmuel Shilo, "Circumvention of the Law in Talmudic Literature," *Israel Law Review* 17:2 (1982): 153; and idem, "Evasion of the Law in the Talmud," in *Authority, Process and Method: Studies in Jewish Law*, ed. Hanina Ben-Menahem and Neil Hecht (Amsterdam: Harwood Academic Publishers, 1998).

2. See Samuel Atlas, "Ha'aramah Mishpatit Ba-Talmud (Fictions in the Talmud)," in *Louis Ginzberg: Jubilee Volume on the Occasion of His Seventieth Birthday* (New York: American Academy for Jewish Research, 1945), 2n3.

3. See Moshe Silberg, *Kakh Darko shel Talmud (Principia Talmudica)* (Hebrew) (Jerusalem: Mif'al Ha-shikhpul, 1961), 30.

4. On this *tosefta* see Chapter 1, notes 89–91.

5. See *mShab.* 22:3 for *kavvanah*; see *mOhalot* 7:3 for *maḥshavah*.

6. *tKeritot* 2:14.

7. Vienna and Erfurt MSS of this *tosefta*: הרשות בידו מהן אחד לשחוט שלא רצה, "If he wished to slaughter neither of them, he has permission." While one might be tempted to read this as permission only to slaughter one and not the other, this is unlikely, as biblically he is forbidden to slaughter both anyway. The Leiden and London MSS and the Venice Ed. of the *Yerushalmi* are unambiguous: בידו הרשות אחד מהן לשחוט שלא רצה לשחוט—If he wishes to slaughter, he may, and if he wishes not to slaughter (either) one, he may.

8. See Michael Sokoloff, *A Dictionary of Jewish Palestinian Aramaic of the Talmudic and Geonic Periods* (Ramat Gan: Bar Ilan University Press, 2002), חשב, where he translates it as "to think, to calculate, to plan."

9. Some defang this by suggesting that even though the owner had not planned to slaughter the animals *before* they fell into the pit, once they fell in, he may retrieve both *so long as he slaughters one of them* (see *Shitat Kadmonim*, s.v. *af 'al pi, Shiyare Korban*; this parallels the usage of *lo ḥishev* regarding ritual impurity in *tOhalot* 8:4.) Others suggest this means that only *after* removing them from the pit it is permissible to decide not to slaughter either of them (see *Korban Ha-'edah*).

10. Atlas, *"Ha'aramah Mishpatit*,*"* 2n3.

11. See Michael Higger, "Intention in Talmudic Law" (PhD diss., Columbia University, 1927), 15; and Howard Eilberg-Schwartz, *The Human Will in Judaism: The Mishnah's Philosophy of Intention*, Brown Judaic Studies no. 103 (Atlanta: Scholars Press, 1986).

12. Thus, Tchernowitz, *Toldot Ha-halakhah*, 4:307n3.

13. The implied audience for *mar'it 'ayin* (presumed by traditional commentators) is challenged by Rav's dictum that "every situation in which the sages prohibited due to appearance is prohibited even in the most private room" (*bShab.* 64b, 146b; *bBetzah* 9a). Commentators suggest that the prohibition remains because someone still may witness and misinterpret the deed (viz. Maimonides, *Laws of the Sabbath* 22:20) or to keep law uniform (*Mishnah Berurah* 301:165). But perhaps for Rav, *mar'it 'ayin* is not about the onlooker but about oneself. One

must keep the law in a manner that objectively is beyond scrutiny. See Nahum Rakover, *Matarah Ha-mekadeshet et Ha-emtza'im (The End That Justifies the Means)* (Jerusalem: Office of the Judiciary, 2000), 16. Abraham Arzi ("Mipnei mar'it ha-'ayin," *Sinai* 74 [1974]: 161–70) discusses whether Rav's dictum was accepted by medieval *halakhists*.

14. *mShekalim* 3:2 explains the logic behind *mar'it 'ayin*.

15. *tShevi'it* 2:2, 2:11, 2:15; *tShab.* 5:9; *tYoma* 4:1; *tBM* 5:8, 8:10; *tBekhorot* 5:2.

16. *bYoma* 78b cites the shoe ban without mentioning *mar'it 'ayin*. The *stam* first suggests *mar'it 'ayin* as the reason but concludes that it is forbidden because children do not need leather shoes for their health, unlike washing (Lieberman, *Tosefta Ki-feshutah*, 808–11).

17. Rashi *bYoma* 78b s.v., *inshe 'avdu le* explains that people will think an adult put the shoes on the child, which constitutes directly giving something forbidden to a minor.

18. Although sometimes *ha'aramah* is the stricter position, e.g., using *ha'aramah* by "intending" to eat each piece of meat on the festival, thereby justifying salting it rather than just salting all their meat at once (*yBetzah* 1:5, 60c; Chapter 2).

19. Adam B. Seligman, "Ritual, the Self, and Sincerity," *Social Research* 76:4 (Winter 2009): 1073–1106.

20. As Ruth Anna Putnam writes, "I want to draw attention to the role of convention in religious ritual. Even if intention is required (at a minimum the awareness that one participates in a religious ritual), intention is not enough. Just as one cannot make one's words mean what one likes, so one cannot turn any behavior one chooses into a religious ritual. Religious ritual is irreducibly social, even if it is practiced by oneself" (Putnam, "Must We Mean What We Do?" *S'vara* 2:2 [1991]: 55).

21. It is unclear whether a person is meant to say anything to this effect aloud or otherwise indicate these intentions.

22. Per Gilat, R. Eliezer and R. Yehoshua represent the schools of Shammai and Hillel, respectively, regarding intention: for R. Eliezer, deed is primary whereas for R. Yehoshua, intention defines (e.g., *mKer.* 4:3, *tKer.* 2:9, where R. Yehoshua requires intention to define sinful action) (Gilat, *R. Eliezer*, 44; idem, "Kavvanah u-ma'aseh be-mishnat ha-tannaim," *Bar Ilan Annual* 4–5 [1967]: 104–16; see also Noam, "Traces," 73). Consequently, perhaps R. Yehoshua is inconsistent by allowing "fake" intention in this *ha'aramah*. But perhaps R. Yehoshua is consistent because if intention is definitive, then intent to slaughter—whether performative or subjective—defines the action of lifting the animal as licit. R. Eliezer's position is more complex: the deed is primary, so intent to slaughter is insufficient. But the deed here may be defined by potential: the animal must have the potential to be slaughtered that day, which applies to only one animal. Alternatively, R. Yehoshua and R. Eliezer do not debate intention versus deed but performative versus subjective intention. Or maybe both R. Yehoshua and R. Eliezer license performed intention, but R. Eliezer thinks this ruse is too obvious. (Neusner challenges Gilat's thesis about R. Eliezer and the House of Shammai and argues that R. Eliezer maps onto the opinions of the House of Shammai regarding intention only in some areas of law and not others: Neusner, *Eliezer ben Hyrcanus*, 2:284. Tchernowitz and Yitzhak Baer analyze the position of the House of Shammai differently in the first place. See Tchernowitz, *Toldot Ha-halakhah*, 4:307; and Baer, *Yisra'el Ba-'amim: 'Iyunim Be-toldot Yeme Ha-bayit Ha-sheni U-tekufat Ha-Mishnah U-vi-yesodot Ha-halakhah Ve-ha-emunah* [Jerusalem: Bialik Institute, 1955], 100.)

23. As Michael Higger writes: "in many cases in Jewish Religious Law where the commission of the act may involve purposes which are permitted or prohibited, it is the

purpose proper that decides the validity of the act" ("Intention in Talmudic Law," 18.) He uses the term "purpose" as distinct from "intention," as intention is the *conscious* choice to act, whereas purpose is about *why* someone acts. In this book, I use both terms to refer to "purpose." See Eilberg-Schwartz, *The Human Will in Judaism*, chap. 2, for more on the distinction between intention and purpose.

24. For a distinction between *kavvanah* and *maḥshavah*, see Higger, "Intention in Talmudic Law," 247–49; Eilberg-Schwartz, *The Human Will in Judaism*, chap. 3; and Vered Saydon, "A Syntactic, Semantic and Pragmatic Study of the Hebrew Verb xašav 'Think' and Other Related Verbs from Biblical Hebrew to Contemporary Hebrew" (PhD diss., Tel Aviv University, 2012), 134–215.

25. Ishay Rosen-Zvi, "The Mishnaic Mental Revolution: A Reassessment," *Journal of Jewish Studies* 66:1 (Spring 2015): 56.

26. See Jacob Bazak, "The Element of Intention in the Performance of 'Mitsvot' Compared to the Element of Intention in Current Criminal Law," *Jewish Law Association Studies: The Jerusalem 2002 Conference Volume* 14 (2004), 10–11; Shalom Albeck, "Ha-im kayam ha-musag 'kavvanah' be-mishpat ha-pelili ba-Talmud?" *Kovetz Ha-tziyonut Ha-datit* 5 (2002/5762): 460–71.

27. See Sacha Stern, *Time and Process in Ancient Judaism* (Oxford: Littman Library of Jewish Civilization, 2003), 16–18, with gratitude to Professor Elisheva Carlebach for bringing this comparison to my attention.

28. Rosen-Zvi (in "Mishnaic Mental Revolution") limits his assertion to legal conceptions rather than homiletical/*midrashic* conceptions.

29. Lawrence Rosen argues that even the Greeks did not have that sense of the individual self: Rosen, *Law as Culture: An Invitation* (Princeton: Princeton University Press, 2006), 53.

30. Rosen-Zvi, "Mishnaic Mental Revolution," 54. Additionally, he notes that scholars disagree over the degree to which Stoic thought parallels our post-Cartesian understanding of interiority. See, for example, Christopher Gill, *Personality in Greek Epic, Tragedy and Philosophy: The Self in Dialogue* (Oxford: Clarendon Press, 1996).

31. For paradigmatic examples, see *mTohorot* 8:6 and *mKelim* 22:2.

32. On this *tosefta* see Chapter 1, notes 62–63.

33. Vered Noam, "Ritual Impurity in Tannaitic Literature: Two Opposing Perspectives," *Journal of Ancient Judaism* 1:2 (2010): 102–3.

34. For more on nominalism and realism, see Gonzalo Rodriguez-Pereyra, "Nominalism in Metaphysics," in *The Stanford Encyclopedia of Philosophy*, ed. Edward N. Zalta (2011); Paul Vincent Spade and Claud Panaccio, "William of Ockham," in *The Stanford Encyclopedia of Philosophy*, ed. Edward N. Zalta (2011); Peter King, "Peter Abelard," in *The Stanford Encyclopedia of Philosophy*, ed. Edward N. Zalta (2011). For how nominalism and realism may be used to analyze rabbinic law, including how Jewish studies scholars misuse the terminology, see Hayes, *What's Divine*, chap. 5; Daniel Schwartz, "Law and Truth: On Qumran-Sadducean and Rabbinic Views of Law," in *The Dead Sea Scrolls: Forty Years of Research*, ed. D. Dimant and U. Rappaport (Leiden: Brill, 1992), 229–40; Jeffrey L. Rubenstein, "Nominalism and Realism in Qumranic and Rabbinic Law: A Reassessment," *Dead Sea Discoveries* 6:2 (July 1999): 157–83; and Christine Hayes, "Legal Realism and the Fashioning of Sectarians in Jewish Antiquity," in *Sects and Sectarianism in Jewish History*, ed. Sacha Stern (Leiden: Brill, 2010), 119–46. Aryeh Amihay has suggested the move to the terminology of legal essentialism versus legal formalism for these discussions. He cites Jane Wong to define essentialism

as follows: "that the characteristics used to define a thing are thought to inhere in its very essence and, thus, to be unchangeable" (Wong, "The Anti-Essentialism v. Essentialism Debate in Feminist Legal Theory: The Debate and Beyond," *William and Mary Journal of Women and the Law* 5:2:2 [1999]: 275). Amihay defines legal formalism as offering "a plan for action of adjudicators. The emphasis is on the form of law: so long as it is maintained, it should also be obeyed. Questions regarding the legislator's intent or the spirit of the law can lead to a shaky ground of interpretation, and thus undermine the rule of law. In the face of this instability supposedly caused by realists, legal formalists propose to conform to the letter of the law" (Amihay, "Law and Society in the Dead Sea Scrolls" [PhD diss., Princeton University, 2013], 25–26).

35. Balberg suggests that this shift to the self already emerged during Temple times. She sees the shift to the self as "the result of a very gradual evolvement and change of social, intellectual, and ideological concerns and interests that converged in the encounter between the rabbis, the traditions they interpreted, and the greater cultural context in which this interpretation was taking place" (*Purity*, 5). Eric Ottenjeim locates focus on the self in purity law within Jesus's critique in Mark 7:14–15: "There is nothing outside the man which defiles him, but those things coming out of the man are what defile him" ("Impurity Between Intention and Deed," in *Purity and Holiness*, ed. M. J. H. M. Poorthius and J. Schwartz [Leiden: Brill, 2000], 129–48.

36. Balberg, *Purity*, 90.

37. E.g., *tKelim (batra)* 1:2–3.

38. Balberg, *Purity*, 150.

39. Joshua Levinson, "From Narrative Practise to Cultural Poetics: Literary Anthropology and the Rabbinic Sense of Self," in *Homer and the Bible in the Eyes of Ancient Interpreters*, ed. Maren R. Niehoff, 345–67, (Leiden: Brill, 2012). While he recognizes the consideration of intention prior to the rabbinic period, including at Qumran, he argues that it undergoes a transformation and major expansion in the *tannaitic* period. For instance, though the Bible distinguishes between willful murder and accidental manslaughter, intention only determines the punishment's severity. For the rabbis, however, the absence of intention may fully exempt a person from prosecution. One methodological challenge of Levinson's argument, however, is that he blends *tannaitic* and *amoraic* material, as well as legal and homiletical material, making it difficult to track the evolution of rabbinic ideas or their variation within different genres.

40. For more on intention and subjectivity in early rabbinic literature, see Robert Goldenberg, "Commandment and Consciousness in Talmudic Thought," *Harvard Theological Review* (1975): 261–71; idem, "Law and Spirit in Talmudic Religion," in *Jewish Spirituality, Vol. I: From the Bible Through the Middle Ages*, ed. A. Green (New York: Crossroads, 1986), 232–52; Jonathan Wyn Schofer, "Self, Subject, and Chosen Subjection: Rabbinic Ethics and Comparative Possibilities," *Journal of Religious Ethics* 33:2 (June 2005): 255–91; Ron Naiweld, "L'anti-sujet: Le rapport entre l'individu et la loi dans la littérature rabbinique classique" (PhD diss., l'École des hautes études en sciences sociales, 2009); Jacob Neusner, "A History of the Mishnaic Law of Purities," *SJLA* 6:22 (1977): 182–89; Martin S. Jaffee, "Mishnaic Literary History and the History of a Mishnaic Idea: On the Formation of the Mishnah's Theory of Intention, with Special Reference to Tractate Ma'aserot," *AJS Review* 11 (1986): 135–55; Jonathan Klawans, *Impurity and Sin in Ancient Judaism* (Oxford: Oxford University Press, 2000); Albeck, *Shishah Sidre Mishnah, Hashlamot Le-Seder Zera'im: Kila'im*, 369–72; Yonatan Sagiv, "'Iyunim be-darkhe ha-midrash shel ha-tannaim 'al pi parshiot nivḥarot ba-Sifra."

(PhD diss., Hebrew University, 2008), 89–91; David Daube, "Error and Ignorance as Excuses in Crime," in *Ancient Jewish Law: Three Inaugural Lectures* (Leiden: Brill, 1981), 49–69; Bernard S. Jackson, "Liability for Mere Intention in Early Jewish Law," *Hebrew Union College Annual* 42 (1971): 197–225; Urbach, *The Halakhah*, 177–205; Solomon Zeitlin, "Studies in Tannaitic Jurisprudence: Intention as a Legal Principle," *Journal of Law and Philosophy* 1 (1919): 297–311; Menachem Lorberbaum, "Theories of Action in the Halakhah: Intention in Mitzvot" (Hebrew) (MA thesis, Hebrew University, 1988); and Ron Margolin, *Inner Religion: The Phenomenology of Inner Religious Life and Its Manifestation in Jewish Sources* (From the Bible to Hasidic Texts) (Hebrew) (Ramat Gan: Bar Ilan University, 2011), 76–90, 379–82.

CHAPTER 5. *HA'ARAMAH* IN THE *BAVLI*: DISCOMFORT WITH RITUALIZED INTENTION

1. The *Bavli* duplicating *ha'aramah* parameters of the *Yerushalmi* corresponds to a general trend of Palestinian material appearing among fourth-century Babylonian *amoraim*. See Zvi Dor, *Torat Eretz Yisrael Be-Bavel* (Tel Aviv: Dvir, 1971), 11–84; and Richard Lee Kalmin, *Jewish Babylonia Between Persia and Roman Palestine: Decoding the Literary Record* (Oxford: Oxford University Press, 2006).

2. Additionally, the *Bavli* suggests that wealthy landowners would be too ashamed to use public *ha'aramot* to save money on tithing (*bMen.* 67a–b). This may be to save face because it is in poor taste for the wealthy to try to save money by skimping on tithes or because it is embarrassing for people to know that they actually need to save the money.

3. In *bBetzah* 37a (MS Munich) R. Yosef compares two cases of leniency with one another: using *ha'aramah* to retrieve the animal pair from the pit on the festival with permission to bring dried fruit in through the skylight on the festival so that it will not get wet, though doing so is a strenuous activity considered improper on the festival. The comparison suggests that circumvention is just another leniency. Moreover, the response to this comparison focuses on *ha'aramah* as a last resort: "Perhaps R. Eliezer bars the use of *ha'aramah* there (i.e., in the case of the animal pair in the pit on the festival) because it is possible to make provisions. But here [in the case of letting fruit down through the skylight on the festival so that it will not get ruined outdoors], R. Eliezer would permit leniency because there is no way to make provisions [for the fruit without it]."

4. *bShab.* 65b, for example, asks if a woman may circumvent the Sabbath prohibition of carrying outside the private domain by using the nut she wishes to bring to her infant child as her cloak fastener. One consideration offered is whether the woman will violate the Sabbath by carrying the nut outside directly if *ha'aramah* is not permitted. See also *mShab.* 6:7, which discusses using objects to tie one's clothing on the Sabbath. There is no *ha'aramah* indicated there, only a discussion about *muktzeh* (in context of clothing worn even where there is no *'eruv*).

5. The very rare *Bavli* case (*bBM* 90a–b) of suspecting *ha'aramah* involves an early Babylonian *amora* answering a query from the land of Israel. The context is animal castration, a violation that Jewish law applies only to Jews, not to Gentiles (Lev. 22:24; *bḤag.* 14b). While *bSan.* 56b suggests that this prohibition applies to non-Jews as well, *bBM* 90a–b does not: "They sent [a question] to Shmuel's father: These oxen that the Arameans steal and spay, what is the law regarding them? He sent to them: something cunning has been done with them הערמה איתעביד בהו. Do something cunning to *them* עלייהו ערימו and sell them (i.e., the

animals)" (MS Vatican 115). The texts suggest that non-Jews were "stealing" animals, spaying them, and returning them to their original Jewish owners. Shmuel's father suspects cunning and wants the animals to be sold so their owners cannot benefit from this inappropriate circumvention.

6. Most mentions of *ha'aramah* as legal dodge in the *Bavli* come from *tannaitic* literature or have parallels in the *Yerushalmi*.

7. See also *bMK* 12a; *bShab*. 139b. Alternatively, where it is no *tannaitic* citation, it may come from an early *amoraic* source, as in *bBetzah* 18a, which cites *ha'aramah* in the name of Rav.

8. A case of conceptual absence of *ha'aramah* will be discussed in this chapter regarding cooking on a festival: where the *Yerushalmi* uses the lens of *ha'aramah* to analyze a *tannaitic* case, the *Bavli* uses a different legal concept to analyze the same case. For more cases where the *Bavli* diverges from the *Yerushalmi* by excluding *ha'aramah* terminology, cases, or suspicion, see the Appendix.

9. Alyssa Gray discusses this issue in her introduction to *A Talmud in Exile: The Influence of Yerushalmi Avodah Zarah on the Formation of the Bavli* (Providence: Brown Judaic Studies, 2020), 1–40.

10. See Rashi, s.v. *ma'arim*, and *bShab*.138a. *MShab*. 20:1 records an argument between R. Eliezer and the sages, with the former permitting setting up a strainer on the festival and the latter prohibiting it. Our passage seems to follow the sages.

11. While MS Munich reads שעורים, I replace it with שמרים, dregs, which appears in other MSS and editions.

12. Commentators are troubled by the similarity between the strainer and beer cases. After all, drinking some of the new beer on the holiday and using the strainer for pomegranates both concretely change the situation. Most distinguish between the two cases in that Rav Ashi requires that the strainer be used for pomegranates first, while one may brew new beer even if one has old beer, i.e., the new beer is not needed. And once the beer is brewed one should drink some of the holiday (Ritva *s.v. ha de-amar*; Nahmanides *s.v. ha de-amar*).

13. In a related *sugya*, *bMK* 12b, the *stam* indicates a *tannaitic* perspective that outlaws *ha'aramah* altogether. It is, to my knowledge, the only source to definitively suggest that a *tanna* might outlaw *ha'aramah* under all circumstances. Both *bShab*. 117b and 124a offer that possibility as an initial suggestion only to reject it.

14. Two *Yerushalmi* passages may reflect the concern with transparency of the circumvention. One involves immersing a vessel on the festival by drawing water because immersing a vessel to purify it on the festival is prohibited (*yPes*. 2:2, 61b). The dispensation is for small vessels only. Lieberman suggests that using large vessels to draw water would be too obviously a ruse meant primarily for the purpose of immersing the vessel (*Tosefta Ki-feshutah*, *Shabbat* chap. 16). (Alternatively, perhaps larger vessels would not fit down the well.) Yet the *Yerushalmi* does not explicitly mention a concern for how obvious the ruse is, while the *Bavli* redactors do. Another *Yerushalmi* example that may relate to transparency of the ruse is R. Tarfon betrothing multiple women during a famine to feed them priestly food. As we saw in Chapter 2, the *Yerushalmi* is explicit that a *ha'aramah* must have the potential to come to fruition: it is only valid because R. Tarfon could potentially marry all those women. Such *ha'aramah* could not be used, however, if one could not marry all the betrothed women, as in levirate marriage. This too may be about believability. However, it also may reflect a procedural concern that betrothals that cannot lead to marriage are too legally flimsy to effect circumvention.

15. MS Kaufmann reads בתו, "his daughter."

16. Or perhaps daughter, based on the Kaufmann Mishnah manuscript.

17. MS Munich and the *editio princeps* offer the most cogent version. I use MS Munich but translate based on a combination of the two versions.

18. See *bGit.* 66a/*bḤul.* 39b for usage of "its end proves its beginning." David Weiss Halivni asserts that if the man had said, "This is yours *only* so that father may eat," it would be a case of "its *beginning* proves its beginning" rather than "its *end* proves its beginning." Instead, the man must have said "And they are yours *until* father comes" (והן בפניך עד שיבא אבא), as in the *mishnah MS Parma*. If he says, "*until* father comes," the gift only belongs to the third party until the father eats from the food. In other words, it is a temporary gift given on the condition that it will be returned. And when the man later protests the consecration of the food, he makes his true motivations known. It is the protest against consecrating the gift at the end that proves that the terms at the beginning were a legal dodge (Halivni, *Mekorot U-mesorot*: Nashim, Tel Aviv: Dvir, 1968, 315–16).

19. Halivni suggests that though the redactors rendered it "*until* father comes" (עד שיבא אבא), Rava seems to be using the version "*so* that father will come" (כדי שיבא אבא). He infers this from the fact that Rava later (48b) compares the Bet Ḥoron gift to giving a gift so the recipient will give it to someone else, which is similar to giving the gift so the recipient will share it with one's father (Halivni, *Nashim*, 315–16).

20. See Rashba Novellae, s.v. *ve-enan lefanekha*. The man has made feeding his father a condition on the gift, which makes the transfer ineffective. The Venice Ed. of *tAZ* 7:7 mentions a similar situation of *'ormah* related to the prohibition of drinking wine handled by a gentile. The *tosefta* states that if a Jew prepared a gentile's wine, and the gentile writes a note that he has been paid for the wine even if no money has been transferred, the wine is permissible for Jews to drink even if the wine is yet in the gentile's domain. This is because the note indicated that the wine belonged to the Jew already, and therefore it is assumed that the gentile would not and did not touch it. If, however, the gentile wrote the note but would not allow the Jew to remove the wine from the gentile's domain until the Jew pays, the wine is forbidden for Jews to drink. No MSS of the *mishnah*'s version of this case (*mʿAvodah Zarah* 4:12) mention *'ormah*. The *toseftan* version, however, calls this latter scenario *'ormah*: the note was just a trick to make the wine permissible to the Jew. But because the gentile will not allow the Jew to remove the wine without giving money, clearly the wine does not actually belong to the Jew. This parallels the Bet Ḥoron case.

21. This statement is difficult to parse, and all textual witnesses need emending. I have chosen to translate the sentence based on my understanding of the text, having viewed all witnesses.

22. Per Maimonides, the abundance of the meal betrays his purpose in giving the food away (Commentary to *Mishnah*; *Mishneh Torah* Laws of *Nedarim* 7:15); Halivni suggests that handing over a ready-made meal for his father to eat proves his motives (*Mekorot U-mesorot: Nashim*, 315).

23. The concern that a matter is obvious also appears in situations that do not involve *haʾaramah* terminology. For example, *b'Er.* 39a distinguishes between two cases involving preparation on the festival/Sabbath for afterward based on which is obvious and which is not; *bBekh.* 31b distinguishes between two cases of circumventing laws about exchanging money for sacred items based on which is obvious and which is not; *bTem.* 8b distinguishes between two cases involving a *kohen* potentially inappropriately giving benefits to a non-priest based on which is obvious and which is not.

24. *yNedarim* 5:7, 39b describes the following: a father forswore his son any benefit from his possessions and gave them instead to an *interposita persona*. This third party sold some of the possessions, consecrated others, and gave others to the forsworn son. The third party argued that anyone who challenges his ability to give the possessions to the son should also challenge his ability to sell the items or consecrate them: once the possessions are his, he has a right to do with them what he pleases. The discussion ends by clarifying that "any gift which is like the gift of Bet Ḥoron which was done as a subterfuge, that may not be consecrated, is an invalid gift." In other words, the father cannot constrain the ability of the third party to do what he wishes. Anything less would not be considered a true transfer of ownership. While commentators (*Pene Moshe*, s.v. *Rabbi Yirmiyah ba'e*; *Korban Ha-'edah*, s.v. *R"Y ba'e*) suggest that any condition on what the third party can do with the gift reveals that the gift-giver never intended to transfer ownership, the issue of intention is not explicit in the *Yerushalmi*. Instead, a straightforward reading suggests that such a gift is simply ineffective. Regardless of how noble the motives are, the means are insufficient. As Moshe Silberg writes, "the *ha'aramah* of Bet Ḥoron was . . . not forbidden, but ineffective" (*Principia*, 37).

25. MSS Munich 95, Munich 6, JTS 1608, JTS 1623, Columbia, and Lunzer-Sassoon cite Rava, but I render it Rabbah due to other instances where R. Hisda and Rabbah debate the concept of *ho'il*, "since."

26. See *Sifra Dibura De-nedavah* 5:3 (MS Vatican 66) for the expanded derivation of this principle from Leviticus 1:3.

27. See *bBava Batra* 48a, where this logic is used to explain why a coerced sale is legally binding. Commentators argue whether this logic can be applied to coercion to make a purchase as well (e.g., *Sefer ha-'ittur, ot kuf kiddushin, ḥelek bet, ot mem moda'ah*).

28. Spanish Ed. adds: "for we see that it is satisfactory to him in his heart" just like the case of the compelled sacrifice.

29. See *Rashi* s.v. *de-mitzvah*.

30. My thanks to Shalhevet Schwartz for this second interpretation. Maimonides in *Mishneh Torah* Laws of Divorce 2:20 offers logic that seems to straddle both interpretations. He argues that, on the one hand this person subjectively does not wish to give the divorce. However, on the other hand, this person does subjectively wish to be a member of the Jewish people. Thus, the wrongful internal protest against the divorce is considered a type of the coercion, while the external coercion that allows the person to finally state "I want to" grant the divorce liberates his true desire to be part of the Jewish people. Maimonides in *Mishneh Torah* Laws of Sale 10:1 is much more straightforward regarding compelled consent to sell: due to coercion, the seller resolves to sell the object.

31. For how the notion of compelled consent evolved after the close of the *Bavli*, see Yehiel Kaplan, "*Kofin oto 'ad she-yomar rotzeh ani*—The Quality of the Principle and Its Application in Our Time," in *'Iyun Be-mishpat 'Ivri U-ve-halakhah: Dayan Ve-diyun*, ed. Ya'akov Habba and Amihai Radziner (Ramat Gan: Bar Ilan University Press, 2007), 189–248.

Nonetheless, *bGit.* 37b problematizes our thesis that the *Bavli* dislikes obvious ruses. The passage cites the requirement for a lender to declare their loan canceled at the end of the sabbatical year. But if the borrower says, "Nonetheless [I'd like to repay the loan]," the borrower may take the money. One opinion cited suggests that the borrower can be compelled to say, "Nonetheless [I'd like to repay the loan]." Even if this compelled consent also indicates subjective intention, it is a surprisingly obvious workaround to be accepted in the *Bavli*. Simultaneously, it still perhaps requires more of the lender than the *Yerushalmi*, which states: One who returns a loan in the Sabbatical year, the lender says, "I waive [the payment]." Rav

Huna said: [Do so] in a soft voice with one's right hand outstretched to accept [payment] (*yShevi'it* 10:8, 39d).

32. See all textual witnesses for *bBetzah* 37a, *bShab.* 117b and 124a.

33. I subscribe to Shamma Friedman's understanding that divergences between *Bavli baraitot* and *toseftan* passages may not reflect two traditions; instead, the *Bavli* actively expands, reworks, and changes *tannaitic* material to suit its own assumption and theories. Friedman, "Uncovering Literary Dependencies in the Talmudic Corpus," in *The Synoptic Problem in Rabbinic Literature*, ed. S. J. D. Cohen (Providence: Brown Judaic Studies, 2000), 35–57; idem, "The Baraitot in the Babylonian Talmud and Their Parallels in the Tosefta" (Hebrew), in *Atara Le-Haim, Studies in the Talmud and Medieval Rabbinic Literature in Honor of Professor Haim Zalman Dimitrovsky* (Jerusalem: Magnes Press, 2000), 163–201; idem, "Towards a Characterization of Babylonian Baraitot: Ben Tema and Ben Dortai," in *Neti'ot Ledavid: Jubilee Volume for David Weiss Halivni*, ed. Y. Elman et al. (Jerusalem: Orhot Press, 2007), 195–274.

34. The *Bavli*'s editors similarly redact the *baraita* about evading tithes. *YBerakhot* 5:1, 8d cites R. Hoshaya: "One may increase one's grain with straw and be prudent in its regard to exempt it from tithes." As explained in Chapter 2, mixing processed grains with unprocessed grain before bringing the produce into one's home exempts it from tithing because only produce that has been fully processed when it "sees the face of the house" requires tithing. When straw, which is not fully processed, is placed on the outside of the bundle, the processed grain does not "see the face of the house." Also, the straw on the outside makes the entire package seem like animal food, which does not require tithing (*bNid.* 51a; *yHallah* 4:4, 60b). The *baraita* as quoted in the *Yerushalmi* does not limit who can eat this food, but every extant manuscript and printed edition of the *Bavli* (*bBer.* 31a; *bPes.* 19a; *b'AZ* 41b; *bMen.* 67b; *bNid.* 15b) specifies that the grains be used only as animal food. In adding this requirement, the *Bavli*'s redactors express their unwillingness to allow a presentation of produce as animal food (straw) unless it will be used that way. (The limitation on eating likewise may be related to the question of snacking versus eating a proper meal. Snacking is permitted for food that has not been tithed whereas eating a proper meal is not. Animal food is defined as a snack while human consumption would be defined as a proper meal. See *bMen.* 67b Tos., s.v. *kede she-tehe behemto okhelet u-poteret min ha-ma'aser*.)

35. MSS Munich 6, JTS 1608, 1623, Columbia, Oxford, Lunzer-Sassoon: רבא; MSS Vatican 109, Vatican 125, Vatican 134, Venice Ed., Vilna Ed.: רבה.

36. *Tos. bPes.* 46b, s.v. "Rabbah." Meiri, *Bet Ha-behirah bPes.* 46b cites on behalf of most traditional medieval commentators that even R. Hisda agrees that if household members have not eaten yet, there is no punishment for cooking the food because they may eat it. Rabbah's innovation is that he permits this even once household members have eaten. Yet commentators debate whether Rabbah still prohibits such cooking but does not punish it or whether he completely permits it. (R. Zerahiah Halevi, *Ba'al Ha-ma'or bPes.* and *Shittah Mekubetzet bBetzah* 21a, s.v. *ho'il*.)

37. Commentators explain how each piece of dough individually can be eaten that day even though some part of the dough must be separated as *hallah* and will therefore be inedible: (a) perhaps each piece individually might not be the *hallah* portion (R. Samson of Sens cited in *Tos. bPes.* 46b, s.v. *ho'il*), or (b) one may break off a small portion of each piece of bread as *hallah* rather than designating any single piece *hallah*. Even if a portion of a piece of dough will end up being *hallah*, the rest of that piece of dough will be edible and thus legitimate to bake (Rashi *bPes.* 48a, s.v. *mahloket*).

38. Traditional commentators debate whether Rabbah would penalize one who explicitly admits to baking for after the festival if there is still time for guests to arrive (Meiri, *Bet Ha-behirah bPes.* 46b).

39. Some interpret the *Bavli*'s version of mixing straw with processed grain to avoid tithing this way as well: lie about the grain, suggesting it is animal food even if it will be consumed by humans. See Nahmanides *Novellae b'AZ* 41b; Tos. *bMen.* 67b, s.v. כדה.

40. This is known in rabbinic parlance as *nikhse melug*, possessions that a bride brings to the marriage from her father's house. She continues to own the principal (*keren*) of these possessions while her husband gains the profits (known as "fruits") of these possessions. These possessions are returned to her upon divorce or the death of the husband.

41. All others: היה.

42. MSS St. Petersburg, Vatican 130, Vatican 487.11, Soncino Ed., Vilna Ed. add אם כן.

43. The names "Rava" and "Rabbah" were originally spelled identically, and after the close of the Babylonian Talmud, two different spellings emerged to minimize confusion. Shamma Friedman, "The Spelling of the Names רבה and רבא in the Babylonian Talmud," *Sinai* 110 (Spring–Summer 1992): 140–57, esp. 144–45; R. Hai Gaon's comments at the end of *b'AZ*; Elyakim Weissberg, "The Writing of the Names Rabbah and Rava: Rav Hai Gaon's Perspective and Conflicting Opinions," *Mehkarim Be-lashon* 5–6 (1992): 181–214; Aharon Shweka, "Studies in the *Halakhot Gedolot*: Text and Redaction" (PhD diss., Hebrew University of Jerusalem, 2008), 71–73.

Here I am convinced that this is indeed Rava rather than Rabbah because Abaye, Rava's older colleague, speaks first whereas Abaye's teacher Rabbah would have spoken first. On this phenomenon, see R. Isaiah di Trani *Responsum #93*; Nahmanides, *Novellae BM* 52a.

44. Perhaps the redactors attribute this terminology to Rava because he issues a similar (though not identical) warning to a naïve R. Nahman in *bSan.* 25a.

45. See also *bSan.* 30a.

46. See *tMS* 5:11, in which a father tricks his children into thinking that certain money is consecrated for *ma'aser sheni* or the following examples in the *Yerushalmi*: the high priest Yehoshua b. Gamla tricks a woman into marrying him: "*ha'aramah 'asah*," he did something cunning (*yYev.* 6:4, 7c); those who devise a method of invisible ink are known as '*arimin sagin*—"very clever people (*yShab.* 12:4, 13d; *yGit.* 2:3, 44b)"; tricking one who has been instigating others to serve idolatry (known as a *mesit*) into doing so in front of witnesses is introduced by the question: "What can they do to trick (*le-ha'arim*) him?" (*yYev.* 16:6, 15d; *ySan.* 7:12, 25d); meat salesmen taking advantage of a prohibition to weigh *bekhor* meat and charge based on appearance rather than by actual size are described as *ma'arimin 'alav u-mokhrin oto be-yoker*, they are tricky about it and sell it for a higher price (*yMK* 2:3, 81b). There are likewise sources in *Midrash Halakhah* that use '*.r.m.* similarly: e.g., *Mekhilta d'R. Yishmael Masekhta De-shirah* 6; *Sifre Bemidbar Naso* 7.

47. See also *bGit.* 54b; *bKet.* 52a, 80a.

48. Sokoloff, *Dictionary of Jewish Babylonian Aramaic of the Talmudic and Geonic Periods*. In his dictionary of Jewish Palestinian Aramaic, he defines ערמו as "wile."

49. See Shana Strauch Schick, *Intention in Talmudic Law: Between Thought and Deed* (Boston: Brill, 2021). New concepts relating to intention introduced by these *amoraim* include Sabbath law concepts regarding unintended secondary consequences (*davar she-eno mitkaven*) and deliberate thought (*melekhet mahshevet*), as well as civil law concepts, such as doing an action almost on purpose (*shogeg karov le-mezid*). (See also Alona Lisista, "'Intent' and 'Thought' as Halakhic Concepts in Talmudic Literature" [MA thesis, Jewish

Theological Seminary, 2004]; Aharon Shemesh, "Shogeg karov le-mezid," *Hebrew University Annual* 20 [1996]: 342–99; and Shaul Kolcheim, "Davar she-en mitkaven be-safrut ha-tanna'it U-ve-Talmud" [PhD diss., Bar Ilan University, 2002], 18.) Additionally, fourth-generation *amoraim* first generalize the question whether one requires intention to fulfill a commandment (*mitzvot tzerikhot kavvanah*) rather than asking piecemeal about individual commandments.

50. Unlike Levinson, who asserts the existence of a subjective self among *tannaim*, Palestinian *midrash*, and Babylonian *amoraim* (in "From Narrative Practise to Cultural Poetics"), Ayelet Hoffman Libson sides with Ishay Rosen-Zvi about the flatness of the *tannaitic* legal self while recognizing the subjectivity displayed in Palestinian *midrash* and Babylonian legal texts (Libson, *Law and Self-Knowledge in the Talmud* [Cambridge: Cambridge University Press, 2018], chap. 1). Libson argues that the *amoraic* ideas of subjectivity are reflected in increased legal recognition of the individual's sense of their own needs. She demonstrates that while *tannaitic* material does not recognize the authority of individuals to understand their own needs better than others do—e.g., when their bodies urgently need food on Yom Kippur—Babylonian *amoraim* do grant this subjective knowledge authority. However, as Shana Strauch Schick has challenged, Libson's examples revolve around recognizing bodily sensations that one might only know about their own body, and this may be different than acknowledging the interior self (*Intention in Talmudic Law: Between Thought and Deed* [Boston: Brill, 2021], 155).

51. Scholarly literature on the Sassanian context of the Talmud is too vast to list here. For general impressions, see Yaakov Elman, "Middle Persian Culture and Babylonian Sages: Accommodation and Resistance in the Shaping of Rabbinic Legal Tradition," in *Cambridge Companion to Rabbinic Literature*, ed. Charlotte Elisheva Fonrobert and Martin S. Jaffe (Cambridge: Cambridge University Press, 2007), 165–97; Carol Bakhos and Rahim Shayegan, eds., *The Talmud in Its Iranian Context* (Tübingen: Mohr Siebeck, 2010); Shai Secunda, *The Iranian Talmud: Reading the Bavli in Its Sassanian Context* (Philadelphia: University of Pennsylvania Press, 2014); Uri Gabbay and Shai Secunda, eds., *Encounters by the Rivers of Babylon: Scholarly Conversations Between Jews, Iranians and Babylonians in Antiquity* (Tübingen: Mohr Siebeck, 2014); Geoffrey Herman and Jeffrey L. Rubenstein, eds., *Aggadah of the Bavli and Its Cultural World* (Providence: Brown Judaic Studies, 2018); Shaul Shaked and Amnon Netzer, eds., *Irano-Judaica: Studies Relating to Jewish Contacts with Persian Culture Throughout the Ages*, vols. 5–6 (Jerusalem: Ben-Zvi Institute for the Study of Jewish Communities in the East, 2008); and Julia Rubanovich and Geoffrey Herman, eds., *Irano-Judaica: Studies Relating to Jewish Contacts with Persian Culture Throughout the Ages*, vol. 7 (Jerusalem: Ben-Zvi Institute for the Study of Jewish Communities in the East, 2019).

52. For general impressions about relationships, polemics, and mutual influence among Jews and Christians in Babylonia, see Michal Bar-Asher Siegal, *Early Christian Monastic Literature and the Babylonian Talmud* (Cambridge: Cambridge University Press, 2013); Adam H. Becker et al., *The Ways That Never Parted: Jews and Christians in Late Antiquity and the Early Middle Ages* (Tübingen: Mohr Siebeck, 2003); Kalmin, *Jewish Babylonia*; Adiel Schremer, "The Christianization of the Roman Empire and Rabbinic Literature," in *Jewish Identities in Antiquity: Studies in Memory of Menahem Stern*, ed. Lee Levine et al. (Tübingen: Mohr Siebeck, 2009); Holger M. Zellentin, *Rabbinic Parodies of Jewish and Christian Literature* (Tübingen: Mohr Siebeck, 2011); and Peter Schäfer, *The Jewish Jesus: How Judaism and Christianity Shaped Each Other* (Princeton: Princeton University Press, 2012).

53. Bar-Asher Siegal, *Early Christian Monastic Literature*, 19.

54. Shaul Shaked, "Religious Actions Evaluated by Intention: Zoroastrian Concepts Shared with Judaism," in *Shoshannat Yaakov: Jewish and Iranian Studies in Honor of Yaakov Elman*, ed. Shai Secunda and Steven Fine, Brill Reference Library of Judaism, vol. 35 (Leiden: Brill, 2012), 413. See also Strauch Schick, *Intention*; Yishai Kiel, "Cognizance of Sin and Penalty in the Babylonian Talmud and Pahlavi Literature: A Comparative Analysis," *Oqimta* 1 (2013): 1–49; M. Macuch, "On the Treatment of Animals in Zoroastrian Law," in *Iranica Selecta: Studies in Honour of Professor Wojciech Skalmowski on the Occasion of His Seventieth Birthday*, ed. A. van Tongerloo, Silk Road Studies 8 (Turnhout: Brepols, 2003), 129; and Yaakov Elman, "Toward an Intellectual History of Sasanian Law: An Intergenerational Dispute in Hērbedestān 9 and Its Rabbinic Parallels," in *The Talmud in Its Iranian Context*, ed. Carol Bakhos and Rahim Shayegan (Tübingen: Mohr Siebeck, 2010), 21–57.

55. See Elman, "Middle Persian Culture."

56. See *bBB* 16a and 164b; *bShab.* 64a–b; *bBer.* 12b and 20b; *bKid.* 40a; *bYoma* 28b–29a.

57. Ron Naiweld, "Purity of Body, Purity of Self: *Hirhur* in Rabbinic Literature," *Judaïsme ancien* 2 (2014): 223.

58. Bernard Jackson rejects the assertion that early rabbinic law prosecutes for intention alone. One illustration is that the prohibition to covet was interpreted as a prohibition to steal (Exod. 20:17; Deut. 5:21). Jackson, "Liability," 197–207. David Brodsky locates this notion about the punishability of thoughts among Palestinian *amoraim* as well. He claims that they imported Babylonian ideas (Brodsky, David. "'Thought Is Akin to Action': The Importance of Thought in Zoroastrianism and the Development of a Babylonian Rabbinic Motif," in *Irano-Judaica: Studies Relating to Jewish Contacts with Persian Culture Throughout the Ages*, ed. Julia Rubanovich and Geoffrey Herman, vol. 7 [Jerusalem: Ben-Zvi Institute for the Study of Jewish Communities in the East, 2019], 187–88).

59. Vilna Ed. adds that the angel saw that R. Katina was accustomed to wearing a linen wrap in the summer and a cloak in the winter.

60. Rashi explains that the winter cloak has rounded edges rather than corners, so it does not require *tzitzit*. The wrap does not require *tzitzit* because it is linen. The Bible prohibits wearing clothing made of both wool and linen (Deut. 22:11). An exception, however, is made for *tzitzit*, where the torso of the clothing may be made of linen and the blue dyed string (*tekhelet*) attached may be made of wool (*bYev.* 4a–b). However, people also wore linen sleepwear, and there is no requirement to wear *tzitzit* at night. Therefore, someone wearing linen garb with the wool *tekhelet* at night would violate the prohibition of wearing wool and linen. To keep people from mistakenly doing this, some ruled not to wear fringes even on linen clothing worn during the day (*mMen.* 40b and Rashi, s.v. *h"g Rabbi Zera amar*).

61. They claim the same for *bBava Kamma* 56a, where the term refers to the measures that animals will take to escape if they are trapped in a sunny place.

62. Cited by Yishai Kiel, "Redesigning Tzitzit in the Babylonian Talmud in Light of Literary Depictions of the Zoroastrian Kustig," in *Shoshannat Yaakov: Jewish and Iranian Studies in Honor of Yaakov Elman*, ed. Shai Secunda and Steven Fine, Brill Reference Library of Judaism, vol. 35 (Leiden: Brill, 2012), 190–92.

63. Perhaps specifically an angel would have access to R. Katina's innermost thoughts whereas human beings would not.

64. Christine Hayes, "Rabbinic Contestations of Authority," *Cardozo Law Review* 28:1 (2006): 134; Novick, "The 'For I Say' Presumption," 61. Pierre J. J. Olivier explains that while legal fictions make presumptions that are known to be untrue, legal presumptions do not make deliberately false assumptions, nor are they maintained after their falsity has been

proven. See Olivier, *Legal Fictions in Practice and Legal Science*, 42; and Novick, "'They Come Against Them,'" 10.

65. Novick, "'They Come Against Them,'" 10.

66. Hayes borrows the categories of rejection and redefinition from Lon Fuller's description of how legal fictions die over time—either by being cast off or through changes in the meaning of the words that made the fiction fictive in the first place (Fuller, *Legal Fictions*, 14). But whereas Fuller describes the possibility of redefinition as the natural of evolution of language, Hayes points out that people can also consciously choose to redefine a word or scenario precisely to narrow the gap between law and reality.

67. Hayes, *What's Divine*, 212–22, 229–43.

68. Hayes also suggests that the prominence of the Roman praetorian edict may have influenced rabbinic comfort with *takkanot* that modify Torah law in *tannaitic* and even earlier Palestinian *amoraic* literature (Hayes, *What's Divine*, 306–9).

69. Yitzhak D. Gilat, "Bet din matnin la'akor davar min ha-Torah," in *Perakim Behishtalshelut Ha-halakhah* (Jerusalem: Bar Ilan University, 1992), 191–204.

70. See *bYev.* 89b–90b for the third. Note that R. Hisda continues to hold that rabbis may decree to abrogate a Torah law.

71. E.g., *mTerumot* 1:4, 2:2; *mGit.* 4:2, 8:5; *mYev.* 10:1; *bBer.* 9:5.

72. See Gilat, "Bet din matnin," 191–20; and idem, "The Halakhah and Its Relationship to Social Reality," *Tradition: A Journal of Orthodox Jewish Thought* 13–14:1 (Spring–Summer 1973): 68–87.

73. While the *Yerushalmi* occasionally dulls the boldness of a rabbinic modification of Torah law, it also contains about a dozen cases of unanimous acceptance that rabbinic enactments may contradict Torah law.

74. On whether this passage refers solely to festivals or also to Sabbath, see Halivni, *Mekorot U-mesorot Mo'ed*, 298–300. Clothing and vessels may not be immersed for purification on a festival/Sabbath because (1) (on Sabbath) one might carry the vessel/clothing to the ritual bath, (2) one might wring out the water from the clothing (not immersing vessels prevents immersing clothing), (3) one might wait until the festival/Sabbath to immerse the vessel and use it before it has been immersed, or (4) it resembles repairing a vessel on the festival/Sabbath because now it is usable. Regardless of the reason, the *explicit* suggestion that a person may utilize *ha'aramah* only because its strangeness reminds her not to violate or forget the law in the future is a feature of the *Bavli*. A few lines earlier in the same passage in *bBetzah* 18a, the redactors suggest this about drawing water from a well with an impure vessel to purify it on the Sabbath. While in the *Yerushalmi*, that case is discussed using the terminology of *ha'aramah* (*yTer.t* 2:3, 41c), its *Bavli* counterpart does not use the term *ha'aramah*, though the example is the same.

75. The fuller context of this passage is enlightening. The passage goes on to state that Rav Ada bar Ahava saved his meat from spoiling by using *ha'aramah* to salt one piece at a time. The precise process is not described, though presumably it parallels other examples of *ha'aramah*: salt each piece "in order" to eat it, but then do not eat it. (This is Rashi's interpretation.) Presenting Rav Ada bar Ahava's position as a foil for the too-obvious hanging of the meat on pegs indicates that this *ha'aramah* is not considered obvious. This echoes the discussion about how making new beer that one "needs" but is really for after the festival is not an obvious *ha'aramah* in the part of *bShab.* 139b presented above. It seems that eating choices are not considered obvious *ha'aramah*.

At the same time, Rav Ada bar Ahava's *ha'aramah* is surprising because presumably he advocates ritualizing intention to eat each piece, which the *Bavli* generally dislikes. But maybe the Rav Ada bar Ahava cited here is the first-/second-generation *amora* (rather than the later *amora* by that name), who retains an understanding of intention that need not be subjective. Relatedly, this *ha'aramah* is attributed to early *amora* Rav Aha in the name of Rav in *yBetzah* 1:5, 60c, which means it predates the later Babylonian *amoraim*. Alternatively, because Rav Ada bar Ahava is a rabbi, he is more trusted to use intention-oriented *ha'aramah*, just as Rav Ashi trusts R. Huna bar Hilvon in the citation below from *bShab.* 139b.

76. The Vilna and Soncino editions, and MS Venice, indicate concern for the one circumventing the law:

אתי למימ' מ"ט שרו לי רבנן כי היכי דלא לסרח מה לי למשטחינהו מה לי לממלחינהו

One will say: why did the rabbis permit *me* to do this? To keep the meat from spoiling. And what difference does it make to me to hang the meat or to salt it?

But MSS Gottingen, Oxford, Munich, Vatican 109b, and Vatican 134 read slightly differently:

אתי למימר מאי טעמ' שרו ליה רבנן כי היכי דלא ליסרח מה לי משטחינהו מה לי ממלחינהו

One will say: why did the rabbis permit *him* to do this? To keep the meat from spoiling. And what difference does it make to me to hang the meat or to salt it?

Nonetheless, this latter reading may still be about the one circumventing, i.e., he will ask himself why the rabbis allowed *him* to do this.

77. Note: The term *ha'aramah* is not used in this passage.

78. This loophole is not labeled *ha'aramah*, but the *Bavli* often leaves out *ha'aramah* terminology. Concern that people will exploit loopholes emerges earlier than the *Bavli* regarding the wrongly suspected *sotah*, to whom Scripture (Num. 5:28) promises children as recompense for her ordeal. In *Sifre* Numbers 19, one *tanna* objects to this recompense because women who want children will purposely get themselves wrongfully suspected of adultery. This concern is repeated in *ySotah* 3:4, 18d. In the *Bavli*, an additional layer is added by suggesting that Hannah's famous prayer for a child (1 Sam. 1:10–3) involved "threatening" God that if she did not get pregnant, she would purposely get herself wrongfully suspected as a *sotah* to force God to give her a child, per Scripture's promise (*bBer.* 31b; *bSotah* 26a). It is noteworthy that alongside the rabbinic normativization of Hannah's biblical prayer as the model of the rabbinic *'amidah*, the *Bavli* in this instance implies that Hannah did something wrong by trying to force God's hand with the threat of becoming a *sotah*. For analysis of rabbinic approaches to Hannah's prayer, see Judith R. Baskin, "Rabbinic Reflections on the Barren Wife," *Harvard Theological Review* 82:1 (1989): 101–14; and Ishay Rosen-Zvi, "The Standing Woman: Hannah's Prayer in Rabbinic Exegesis," in *Jewish Culture in the Eye of the Storm, a Jubilee Book in Honor of Yosef Ahituv*, ed. N. Ilan and A. Sagi ('Ein Zurim: Hakibbutz Hameuchad and the Jacob Herzog Center, 2002), 675–98.

79. MS Oxford: הערמה מ(ד)רבנן היא.

80. For this prohibition, see *mShab.* 12:1; *bBetzah* 34a; and *b'Er.* 103a.

81. See *mBetzah* 5:2. See also Rashi, s.v. *ve-omer*: the boat belongs to a non-Jew whom the young scholar knows will surely use it to cross the river. Hence, the ferry travels as the young scholar sleeps.

82. Based on MS Oxford היא מדרבנן הערמה, *ha'aramah* is a rabbinic transgression; see *Sefer Ra'avyah* chap. 296.

83. The language of MS Vatican, היא בדרבנן הערמה, it is the circumvention of a rabbinic law, became, for traditional commentaries, a source for a position that *ha'aramah* is only permitted when circumventing rabbinic laws. See R. Alexander Shor's commentary to *bPes.* 21b in *Bekhor Shor 'al Ha-Shas*. (*BGit.* 65a offers similar support for *ha'aramah* as a phenomenon used specifically to circumvent rabbinic, as opposed to biblical, law.) Crossing a river passively by ferry on the Sabbath is only rabbinically prohibited. As for the case of the garlic in the barrel, perhaps this would only be rabbinically prohibited because it may not be a permanent way to fix the barrel. (There are opinions in this case as well, that such temporary fixing would not amount to any transgression at all. This is the subject of debate relating to *bShab.* 113a.)

84. MS Oxford: היא מרבנן הערמה, *ha'aramah* is from the rabbis.

85. The *Ra'avyah* indicates that perhaps R. Ashi's comments permit *ha'aramah* generally (at least on festivals) to Torah scholars, even if it is forbidden for the average person. See R. Eliezer Yoel Halevi of Bonn, *Laws of the Festival*, chap. 752; *Laws of Ḥol ha-mo'ed*, chap. 827.

86. *yNazir* 5:1, 54a (Chapter 2) discusses the concern that a man might divorce his wife to make her marriage contract (*ketubah*) money available and then remarry her to acquire said money. In *b'Arakhin* 23a, Abaye advises R. Huna, a young scholar in financial straits, and his wife to perform this ruse with his father, the guarantor of the marital contract. Clearly, Abaye sympathizes with the couple's plight. The redactors question Abaye's leniency, as he is specifically cited elsewhere as condemning those who encourage such ruses as *rasha 'arum*. Therefore, the redactors posit a distinction between one's child and others, as well as between a young scholar and others.

Traditional commentators (R. Gershom; R. Elijah of Vilna, *Hagahot U-be'urim Merabenu Ha-gadol Ha-Gra Mi-Vilna*) argue R. Huna is exceptional because he is *both* the son of the guarantor *and* a young scholar: he doubly deserves financial support. However, perhaps R. Huna can do this specifically because as the son and Torah scholar, we do not expect him to use this loophole unless it is necessary.

87. The term *tzurba me-rabanan* is often used to indicate someone beginning their studies rather than a full scholar (*bBer.* 33b; *bBetzah* 16b; *bGit.* 37b; et al.). In such examples, it is used to denote the inferiority of a young scholar and can even be condescending in tone.

88. Richard Lee Kalmin, *The Sage in Jewish Society of Late Antiquity* (London: Routledge, 1999), 27. See also Jeffrey L. Rubenstein, *The Culture of the Babylonian Talmud* (Baltimore: Johns Hopkins University Press, 2003), though Rubenstein attributes the phenomenon to stammaitic pseudepigraphy (130). Kalmin attributes the difference between Palestinian and Babylonian rabbis to (a) cultural differences between a more egalitarian structure in Roman Palestine and a more hierarchical culture in Zoroastrian Babylonia, and (b) the weaker station of Palestinian rabbis, which led to their dependence on non-rabbis, as compared to the more stable and powerful position of Babylonian rabbis, allowing them to be aloof (see *The Sage in Jewish Society of Late Antiquity*, introduction and conclusion). And while Kalmin has suggested that the rabbis became more integrated beginning in the fourth century due to Roman

influence, this does not necessarily mean that they no longer distinguished between the religious commitments of rabbis and non-rabbis. It simply means that they were more willing to interact with non-rabbis socially, and even to marry them (Kalmin, *Jewish Babylonia*, 173–86).

89. Rava: *bBB* 22a, 168a; *bBer.* 15a; (*bYoma* 26a—not about differences in attitudes but about differences in lineage); *bTa'anit* 4a (about the *tzurba me-rabanan*'s passion for Torah); et al. R. Ashi: *bYev.* 121a (but this is not about rabbinic elitism, just a difference in law based on realities within the culture); *bShevuot* 41a (interlocutor of R. Ashi). Redactors: e.g., *bBM* 19a, 42a; *bBB* 168a; *bBer.* 19a; *bBekh.* 35a; *bKet.* 20a–b.

90. Rashi, s.v. *shani ha'aramah* suggests that the difference between the reaction to purposeful transgression and *ha'aramah* relates to the respective outcomes: one who purposely transgresses is unlikely to influence others and will perhaps even repent herself, due to an awareness of having done something wrong. One who employs *ha'aramah*, however, believes herself to be in the right. Thus, she will influence others, and the notion of *'eruv tavshilin* will "be uprooted." Rav Ashi's screed against *ha'aramah* stands out when compared to the parallel *Yerushalmi* passage (*yBetzah* 2:1, 61a). There, Rabbi Ḥiyya bar Ba simply states that one should not use *ha'aramah* where *'eruv tavshilin* is available, but he does not talk about *ha'aramah* as worse than intentional outright transgression.

CHAPTER 6. *HA'ARAMAH* AND CONTEMPORARY LEGAL THEORY

1. Haim Tchernowitz, known as *Rav Tza'ir* (lit. "Young Rabbi"), was born in 1871 in Vitebsk, Russia. Ordained at twenty-five by the leading Russian rabbinical authority, R. Isaac Elhanan Spektor, he also trained in more academic, critical methods of Jewish study. In Odessa, he founded and/or became headmaster of a yeshiva that would be a rabbinical seminary in 1907. His yeshiva used the critical methods of academia known as *Wissenschaft des Judentums* in reading classical Jewish texts. This was rare for a rabbinic school. See Benjamin Hoffseyer, "Ha-Rav Chaim Tchernowitz, 'Rav Tza'ir,' ve-ha-yeshiva be-Odessa" (PhD diss., Yeshiva University, 1967); Zvi Gitelman, *A Century of Ambivalence: The Jews of Russia and the Soviet Union, 1881 to the Present* (New York: Schocken Books, 1988), 35–41.

2. See Friedrich Carl von Savigny, *Of the Vocation of Our Age for Legislation and Jurisprudence*, trans. Abraham Hayward (London: Littlewood & Co., 1831). This essay, originally written in German, was published in response to German professor of Roman law A. F. J. Thibaut when he suggested in 1814 that Germany adopt a civil code similar to the French civil code established in 1804.

3. He asserts that even the Bible, which he believes to be the word of God, mirrors Jewish *Volksgeist*. Tchernowitz, *Toldot Ha-halakhah*, 135; idem, *Be-sha'are Tziyon: Kovetz Ma'amarim Be-'inyane Eretz Yisra'el Ve-ha-tziyonut* (New York: Schulsinger Bros., 1936), 12–13; idem, *Masekhet Zikhronot: Partzufim Ve-ha'arakhot* (New York: Va'ad ha-Yovel, 1945), 257–62. See also Allan Arkush, "Biblical Criticism and Cultural Zionism Prior to the First World War," *Jewish History* 21:2 (June 2007): 121–58.

4. Tchernowitz, *Toldot Ha-halakhah*, 180.

5. For more on Tchernowitz's theory, see Elana Stein Hain, "Secular Legal Paradigms and Talmudic Law: Rav Tsa'ir on Legal Loopholes," in *Swimming Against the Current: Reimagining Jewish Tradition in the Twenty-First Century*, ed. Shaul Seidler-Feller and David N. Myers (Brookline, MA: Academic Studies Press, 2020), 94–113.

6. Frederick Schauer, "Legal Fictions Revisited," in *Legal Fictions in Theory and Practice*, ed. Maksymilian Del Mar and William Twining (New York: Springer International Publishing, 2015), 113–29.

7. See, for example, Hayes, *What's Divine*, chap. 7; Gilat, "Bet din matnin"; and idem, "The Halakhah."

8. For other examples of the *ḥomesh* requirement, see Lev. 5:16, 24, 27:13; Num. 5:7.

9. I noted above, for example, that *ma'aser sheni* and *bekhor* are linked in early Jewish thought, and the linkage results in rulings that affect both. How might this linkage with *ma'aser sheni*, or others within rabbinic legal thought, be affected by a change in the ruling of *ma'aser sheni*?

10. Moglen, "Legal Fictions." He does recognize, however, that in the thirteenth, sixteenth, and twentieth centuries, "the primary onus for the making of rules shifted into the legislature. For more on adjudication versus legislation in the Common Law tradition, see Alan Watson, *Failures of the Legal Imagination* (Philadelphia: University of Pennsylvania Press, 1988), esp. 37–40.

11. Leo Katz, *Why the Law Is So Perverse* (Chicago: University of Chicago Press, 2011), especially part 2. Katz applies a classic voting paradox to understanding loopholes, but we will not delve into the details of that here. He also suggests that loopholes comport with human beings' innate rule-based sense of morality. So long as the means are indirect, they are usable to achieve otherwise unachievable ends. He fleshes this out further in another book, *Ill-Gotten Gains: Evasion, Blackmail, Fraud, and Kindred Puzzles of the Law* (Chicago: University of Chicago Press, 1996), esp. 52–59. See also Elana Stein, "Rabbinic Legal Loopholes: Formalism, Equity and Subjectivity" (PhD diss., Columbia University, 2014), 250–55., where I discuss the possible evolution of moral theories in rabbinic texts about *ha'aramah*.

12. Katz goes a step further than rabbinic *ha'aramah*, suggesting that any time one uses a loophole, a relevant legal principle applies. Katz has been criticized for failing to distinguish between good loopholes and bad loopholes and for giving lawyers free reign to exploit any loopholes they wish. See, for example, Peter H. Huang, review of *Why the Law Is So Perverse, by Leo Katz, Journal of Legal Education* 131 (2013): 131–60.

13. W. Bradley Wendel, *Lawyers and Fidelity to Law* (Princeton: Princeton University Press, 2010), 71.

14. See David A. Green, "Balancing Ethical Concerns Against Liberal Discovery: The Case of Rule 4.2 and the Problem of Loophole Lawyering," *Georgetown Journal of Legal Ethics* 8 (1995): 283–312.

15. Wendel, *Lawyers and Fidelity to Law*, 176.

16. He borrows this terminology from legal positivist H. L. A. Hart, who distinguishes between someone who is coerced to follow a law and someone who follows a law out of a sense of obligation to legal norms. The latter acts from the "internal point of view" (Hart, *The Concept of Law*, 2nd ed. [New York: Oxford University Press, 1994], 82–83, 88–89).

17. Daniel T. Ostas, "Legal Loopholes and Underenforced Laws: Examining the Ethical Dimensions of Corporate Legal Strategy," *American Business Law Journal* 46:4 (Winter 2009): 487–529. For a more affirmative approach than "self-restraint," see Don Mayer, "Legal Loopholes, Business Ethics, and Corporate Legal Strategy: A Reply to Professor Ostas," *American Business Law Journal* 48:4 (Winter 2011): 713–63.

18. See Steven M. Quevedo, "Formalist and Instrumentalist Legal Reasoning and Legal Theory," *California Law Review* 73:1 (January 1985): 119–57.

19. See Christopher Columbus Langdell, a major proponent of Formalism, "Harvard Celebration Speeches (Nov. 5, 1886)," *Law Quarterly Review* 3 (1887): 123–24.

20. Thomas C. Grey, "Langdell's Orthodoxy," *University of Pittsburgh Law Review* 45 (1983): 5.

21. Grey, "Langdell's Orthodoxy," 11.

22. Frederick Schauer, "Formalism," *Yale Law Journal* 97:4 (1988): 510n1 offers a wide array of definitions for the term "Legal Formalism" over the years.

23. S. Levinson, "What Do Lawyers Know (and What Do They Do with Their Knowledge)? Comments on Schauer and Moore," *Southern California Law Review* 58 (1985): 441, 445; Schauer points out ("Formalism," 521n42) that this definition has parallels in literary theory. See, for example, W. B. Michaels, "Against Formalism: The Autonomous Text in Legal and Literary Interpretation," *Poetics Today* 1 (1979): 23.

24. Schauer describes two other versions of formalism in depth, both revolving around the denial of choice: either

> (a) the denial of choice within the interpretation of a norm—per H. L. A. Hart, who attacks formalism for its refusal to acknowledge choice as it relates to the "open texture" of legal language. Hart claims that legal terms have a core of settled meaning but also a penumbra of debatable meaning that may be useful in questionable cases and that formalists refuse to acknowledge the penumbra in cases of questionable application of a word and instead remain pure literalists (Schauer, "Formalism," 511–514); or (b) the denial of choice about whether to apply a norm (Schauer, "Formalism," 515–17).

25. Schauer, "Formalism," 535.

26. Schauer, "Formalism," 537.

27. Also, he posits "presumptive formalism" in which decisions are made formalistically by a lower court but may be reviewed by a higher court taking "less locally applicable norms," including the reason behind the rule in question, into account, should there be a pressing reason to do so (Schauer, "Formalism," 547).

28. Ernest Weinrib, "Legal Formalism: On the Immanent Rationality of Law," *Yale Law Journal* 97 (May 1988): 949–1016.

29. Suzanne Last Stone, "Halakha and Legal Theory," *Journal of the Society for Textual Reasoning* 6:1 (December 2010).

30. See Elizabeth Mertz, Stewart Macaulay, and Thomas Mitchell, *The New Legal Realism: Translating Law and Society for Today's Legal Practice*, vols. 1 and 2 (Cambridge: Cambridge University Press, 2016), and especially Mertz's introduction to that volume, "Law and Social Science in the New Millennium."

31. Brian Z. Tamanaha, "Legal Realism in Context," in *The New Legal Realism: Translating Law and Society for Today's Legal Practice*, vols. 1 and 2, eds. Elizabeth Mertz, Stewart Macaulay, and Thomas W. Mitchell, 147–168 (Cambridge: Cambridge University Press, 2016).

32. Karl N. Llewellyn, "A Realistic Jurisprudence—The Next Step," *Columbia Law Review* 30 (1930): 443–44.

33. Llewellyn, "A Realistic Jurisprudence," 449, 452–53.

34. Oliver Wendell Holmes Jr., "Law in Science and Science in Law," *Harvard Law Review* 12:17 (1899): 460; see also idem, "Codes and the Arrangement of the Law," *American Law Review* 5 (1870): 1, reprinted in *Harvard Law Review* 44 (1931): 728.

35. For further development of this notion, see Katherine R. Kruse, "The Jurisprudential Turn in Legal Ethics," *Arizona Law Review* 53 (2011): 498–505.

36. Stephen Pepper, "Lawyers' Amoral Ethical Role: A Defense, a Problem and Some Possibilities," *American Bar Foundation Research Journal* 11:14 (1986): 624–26.

37. See Quevedo ("Formalist and Instrumentalist Legal Reasoning and Legal Theory"), who outlines two approaches to their debates: the first from Professor David Lyons, over whether the law has gaps in it and/or the degree to which the law has "open texture," that is, gray area (as in Hart, *The Concept of Law*, 121–25). The first is Quevedo's own approach, which sees their divide as being about how "old" the concepts they use are: Formalists are prone to hold onto old concepts even in the face of new cases while instrumentalists are prone to abandon the old concepts in the face of new cases.

38. See Pierre Schlag, "Formalism and Realism in Ruins (Mapping the Logics of Collapse)," *Iowa Law Review* 95 (2009): 195.

39. For a Formalistic characterization of Jewish law, see J. David Bleich's volumes of *Contemporary Halakhic Problems*, vol. 1 (Ktav, 1976), vol. 4 (1995), and vol. 5 (Targum Feldheim, 2005); Joseph B. Soloveitchik, *Shiurei Ha-Rav: A Conspectus of the Public Lectures of Rabbi Joseph B. Soloveitchik* (Hoboken, NJ: Ktav, 1974), 97–110; and Aaron Kirschenbaum, *A Historical Sketch of the Sources of Jewish Law*, in *Equity in Jewish Law: Halakhic Perspectives in Law: Formalism and Flexibility in Jewish Civil Law* (Hoboken, NJ: Ktav, 1991). For Realist perspectives, see Halbertal, *Interpretive Revolutions*; Avinoam Rosenak, *Halakhah as an Agent of Change* (Hebrew) (Jerusalem: Magnes, 2009); Eliezer Berkowitz, *Not in Heaven: The Nature and Function of Halakhah* (New York: Ktav, 1983); Yair Lorberbaum and Haim Shapira, "Maimonides' Epistle on Martyrdom in Light of Legal Philosophy," *Diné Israel: Studies in Halakhah and Jewish Law* 25 (2008): 123; Hanina Ben-Menahem and Neil S. Hecht, *Judicial Deviation in Talmudic Law: Governed by Men, Not by Rules* (New York: Harwood Academic Press, 1991), Hanina Ben-Menahem, "Is Talmudic Law a Religious Legal System? A Provisional Analysis," *Journal of Law and Religion* 24 (September 2008): 379–402; idem, "The Myth of Formalism: (Mis)Readings of Jewish Law from Paul to the Present," Hebrew University Legal Research Paper no. 17-5, December 2016; and Daniel Statman, "Halakha and Morality: A Few Methodological Considerations," *Journal for the Society of Textual Reasoning* 6:1 (December 2010). For ways in which rabbinic law does not perfectly match any secular theory of law, see Bernard S. Jackson, "Secular Jurisprudence and the Philosophy of Jewish Law: A Commentary on Some Recent Literature," *Jewish Law Annual* 6 (1987): 3–44; and Suzanne Last Stone, "In Pursuit of the Counter-Text: The Turn to the Jewish Legal Model in Contemporary American Legal Theory," *Harvard Law Review* 106 (1993): 813–94.

40. Many have discussed whether *halakhah* should be considered formalistic and have come to the same conclusion. See Statman, "Halakha and Morality": "The argument . . . that halakhic interpretation is non-formalistic, namely that it relies on human judgment or human discretion, in contrast to formalistic interpretation . . . is simply trivial. To be sure, halakhic interpretation is not 'a simple act of applying the written law to reality,' but this is the case with all legal interpretation, and, in fact, with *any* kind of interpretation. . . . Whereas the claim that the halakhic interpretation is non-formalistic is trivial, the opposing claim which describes halakhic interpretation as a 'simple act of applying the written law to reality' is so embarrassing that it is hard to believe that anyone seriously upholds it." Benjamin Brown has similarly suggested that rabbinic law is somewhere on the continuum between formalism and values-based jurisprudence. Brown, "Formalism and Values: Three

Models (Hebrew)," in *New Streams in the Philosophy of Halakhah*, ed. Aviezer Ravitzky and Avinoam Rosenak (Jerusalem: Magnes Press and Van Leer Institute, 2008), 253. See also Noam Zohar, "Developing a Halakhic Theory as a Necessary Basis for a Philosophy of the Halakhah (Hebrew)," in *New Streams in Philosophy of Halakhah*, ed. Aviezer Ravitzky and Avinoam Rosenak (Jerusalem: Magnes Press and Van Leer Institute, 2008), 48.

41. Chaim Saiman, "Is Jewish Law Formalistic: A Survey of the Dispute and Why It Matters," in *Oxford Handbook of Jewish Law*, ed. Zev Eleff, Roberta Kwall, and Chaim Saiman (New York: Oxford University Press, forthcoming). My thanks to Chaim for the advance copy of the chapter.

42. Ronald Dworkin, "The Model of Rules," in *Taking Rights Seriously* (London: Duckworth, 1977), 24.

43. Dworkin, "The Model of Rules," 22. For a view of the difference between rules and principles as being about their respective levels of abstraction, see Joseph Raz, "Legal Principles and the Limits of Law," *Yale Law Journal* 81 (1972): 823.

44. Riggs v. Palmer, 115 N.Y. 506, 22 N.E. 188 (1889).

45. Riggs v. Palmer, at 189.

46. Ronald Dworkin, *Law's Empire* (Cambridge, MA: Harvard University Press, 1986), 19. Finding out what a statute really says, according to Dworkin, does not mean what exactly the lawgiver had in mind when writing the legislation. Rather, it is a question of how the lawgiver would want it to be interpreted in light of their entire legal project. Halbertal applies Dworkin's thought to rabbinic exegesis (*Interpretive Revolutions*, 186–87).

47. Dworkin, *Law's Empire*, 20.

48. Jackson, "Secular Jurisprudence," 22.

49. Dworkin himself notes his perspective as a compromise position between "conventionalism" and "pragmatism": *A Matter of Principle* (Cambridge, MA: Harvard University Press, 1985), chaps. 4 and 5.

50. Michel Rosenfeld, "Dworkin and the One Law Principle: A Pluralist Critique," *Revue Internationale du Philosophie* 59:233 (2004): 385.

51. Dworkin, *Law's Empire*, 233.

52. A major exception to this is the *Yerushalmi*'s Scriptural support for using *ha'aramah* to avoid the *ma'aser sheni* redemption tax (Chapter 2). This differs from other cases because it describes the intention of the Divine legislator regarding the law in question rather than principles that can be read into the legal system as a whole.

53. For applications of Dworkin's paradigm to rabbinic law, see Hayes, "Legal Truth, Right Answers and Best Answers"; Benjamin Brown, "From Principles to Rules and from Musar to Halakhah: The Hafetz Hayim's Rulings on Libel and Gossip," *Diné Israel: Studies in Halakhah and Jewish Law* 25 (2008): 171–256; Shraga Bar-On, "The Art of the Chain Novel in b.Yoma 35b: Reconsidering the Social Values of the Babylonian Yeshivot," *Hebrew Union College Annual* 88 (2017): 55–88; Yaakov Elman, "Hercules Within the Halakhic Tradition," *Diné Israel: Studies in Halakhah and Jewish Law* 25 (2008): 7–41; and Azzan Yadin-Israel, "The Chain Novel and the Problem of Self-Undermining Interpretation," *Diné Israel: Studies in Halakhah and Jewish Law* 25 (2008): 43–71.

54. MS Parma: שכרני.

55. See e.g., *bKet.* 11a, 39b; *bGit.* 55b; *bMen.* 6b; *bSotah* 15a; *bBK* 39a.

56. Carol M. Rose, "Crystals and Mud in Property Law," *Stanford Law Review* 40 (1987–88): 577, with gratitude to Chaim Saiman for showing me this article.

57. Rose, "Crystals and Mud," 578.

58. Rose cites examples: Swinton v. Whitinsville Savings Bank, 311 Mass. 677, 42 N.E.2d 808 (1942); Levy v. C. Young Constr. Co., 46 NJ. Super. 293, 134 A.2d 717 (NJ. Super. Ct. App. Div. 1957), aff'd, 26 N.J. 330, 139 A.2d 738 (1958) (overruled in McDonald v. Mianecki, 159 N.J. Super. 1, 386 A.2d 1325 (1978), aff'd, 79 NJ. 275, 398 A.2d 1283 (1979)).

59. Rose writes that in California, this doctrine took special force with cases involving landfill—e.g., Clauser v. Taylor, 44 Cal. App. 2d 453, 112 P.2d 661 (1941); Rothstein v. Janss Inv. Corp., 45 Cal. App. 2d 64, 68, 113 P.2d 465, 467 (1941). Now, however, the doctrine extends to "material" defects of all kinds. See, e.g., Lingsch v. Savage, 213 Cal. App. 2d 729, 29 Cal. Rptr. 201 (1963).

60. See Lingsch v. Savage, 209.

61. Throughout the article (esp. part 2), Rose lists theorists who prefer crystalline rules and others who prefer mud when it comes to property law.

62. Rose, "Crystals and Mud," 608–9.

63. *mYev.* 6:6.

64. This phrase alludes to Song of Songs 1:4, the scriptural anchor for this *midrash*. The verse describes the union of lovers, which rabbinic interpretation reads as the union between God and the People Israel.

65. See Exodus 32.

66. The term *sanegor* comes from the Greek συνήγορος; *synégoros*, lit. "co-speaker." This person adds arguments on behalf of one litigant or against another once each party has presented their own case. "Synegoros," in *Brill's New Pauly*, ed. Hubert Cancik and Helmuth Schneider, trans. Christine F. Salazar and Francis G. Gentry (2005).

67. Likely this actually refers to אני י-י א-להיכם in either Lev. 25:38 or Num. 15:41.

68. The word אתמהא may simply add an exclamation point to the end of Moses's sentence rather than having the distinct meaning of "Strange!" See Jastrow, "אתמהא."

69. For humor within this *midrash*, see Hershey H. Friedman, "He Who Sits in Heaven Shall Laugh: Divine Humor in Talmudic Literature," *Thalia* 17:1 (January 1, 1997): 36–50; and Don Waisanen, Hershey H. Friedman, and Linda Weiser Friedman, "What's So Funny About Arguing with God? A Case for Playful Argumentation from Jewish Literature," *Argumentation* 29 (2015): 57–80.

70. There are likewise *midrashim* in which God explicitly teaches the Jewish people what arguments to mount in the Divine courtroom to win their case—e.g., *Pesikta d'Rav Kahana* 23:7.

71. Exodus *Rabbah* 47:9 cites a similar argument but focuses on relationship and character: "Moses said before God: Why are You angry at them? That they did idolatry about which You never commanded them?! God said to him: In the second commandment, did I not say, 'You shall not have [other gods before Me]?' Moses said before God: You did not command them; You only commanded me. Did you say to them, you (plural) shall not have [other gods]? You commanded me! If I committed idolatry, erase me from Your book. When God saw that Moses was willing to sacrifice himself for them, God said: For your sake, I give them the Torah, as it is said, 'Write for *yourself* (sing.) these words' (Ex. 34:27)." In this case, God is moved not by Moses's clever statutory interpretation but by his devotion to the Israelites.

72. Moshe Silberg suggests this as the logic of all *ha'aramah*: the omniscient Lawgiver gave permission for dodges by leaving gaps in the law for people to use (*Principia*, 30–31). His thesis is difficult to sustain given the rabbinic distinctions between proper and improper *ha'aramot*.

73. *bBer.* 32b contains a parallel source where Moses releases God from God's vow, using the legal format of *hatarat nedarim* (*mḤag.* 1:8 and *bḤag.* 10a). *Hatarat nedarim* is found in this *midrash* as well, but we focus on the part of the *midrash* that relates to lawyerly interpretation. For further analysis of these scenes in the heavenly court, see Hidary, *Rabbis and Classical Rhetoric*, chapter 7.

74. Dov Weiss, *Pious Irreverence: Confronting God in Rabbinic Tradition* (Philadelphia: University of Pennsylvania Press, 2013), 170–71.

75. Weiss, *Pious Irreverence*, chap. 3.

76. The respective evolutions of protest and *ha'aramah* move in opposite chronologies: *tannaitic* and early Palestinian *amoraic* texts accept *ha'aramah* as a tool and engage in developing parameters for its use. Later, the Babylonian Talmud tries to contain how radically *ha'aramah* should be used. According to Weiss's study, however, earlier sources object to protest while later rabbinic sources reflect comfort with protest.

77. Weiss, *Pious Irreverence*, 119–20. And see Chapter 3 for fuller explication.

78. See also Genesis *Rabbah* 49:9.

79. As above, the word אתמהא may simply add an exclamation point to the end of Abraham's sentence rather than having the distinct meaning of "Strange!" See Jastrow, "אתמהא."

80. On protesting collective punishment in Genesis *Rabbah*, see Gilad Sasson, "She-elat ha-'anishah ha-kibutzit be-derashot amora'e Eretz Yisrael she-be-Bereshit Rabbah parashat 49," *Sidra* 29 (5774): 161–77.

81. This citation conforms to Meira Kensky's observation noted in Chapter 3 that in rabbinic heavenly courtroom scenes, it is God's justice that is on trial.

EPILOGUE. *HA'ARAMAH* AND *TAKKANOT*

1. Silberg, *Principia*, 40–41; Solomon Zeitlin, "The Need for a New Code," *Jewish Quarterly Review*, n.s., 52:3 (January 1962): 203–15.

2. As discussed below, sometimes rabbinic literature ascribes a given *takkanah* to a biblical character as well.

3. Deut. 15:1–2; *mShevi'it* 10:3–4; *mGit.* 4:3; *Sifre Deuteronomy* 113:3; *tShevi'it* 8:9–10; *Midrash Ha-gadol* Deuteronomy 15:3; *yShevi'it* 10:2, 39c; *yGit.* 4:3, 45c–d; *bGit.* 36a–37a.

4. *Prosbul* is used in contexts that need not be only about the sabbatical—e.g., *mPe'ah* 3:6; *mMK* 3:3; *mKetubot* 9:9. Thus, Hillel would have enacted the use of *prosbul* because lenders were having trouble collecting their debts, so they were no longer willing to lend money even if the sabbatical year was far off. On the evolution of *prosbul* for use in the sabbatical year, see David Bigman, "Be'ayah hilkhatit oh tikkun ḥevrati? 'Al mashma'ut ha-prosbul," *Akdamot* 20 (2008): 155–66.

5. See L. Blau, "Prosbol im Lichte der griechischen Papyri und Rechtsgeschichte," in *Festschrift zum 50 jahrigen Bestehen der Franz-Joseph Landesrabbinerschule in Budapest* (Budapest: Alexander Kohut Memorial Foundations, 1927), 96–151.

6. See Atlas, *Pathways*, 278n21; and Hanoch Albeck, *Shishah Sidre Mishnah*, Vol. 1, *Seder Zera'im*, 383.

7. "Just as an actual court ruling which would have come out about these debts (e.g., if the borrower denied owing, and the court ruled that he was actually obligated to pay) would have been removed from [the application of] sabbatical [law], for this is a *ma'aseh bet din*, likewise the *prosbul* is considered a 'court ruling(פסק דין) ' regarding the lender's loans (similar to

the Greek *prosbul*), and court rulings are not remitted [by the sabbatical year] (David Henshke, "How Does Prosbul Work? A History of the Explanation of Hillel's Takkanah," 97)." *Shenaton Ha-mishpat Ha-'ivri* 22 (April 5761): 71–106. Others compare *prosbul* to another *mishnaic* workaround: depositing a loan deed to the court (*mShevi'it* 10:2). Such deeds are not canceled by the sabbatical: either because the debtor's property is considered collected, as it is mortgaged, or because courts may collect debts during the sabbatical year, though individuals may not. For those who make this comparison, *prosbul* still differs from depositing loan deeds with the court: perhaps in that the lender need not physically deposit the deed with the court (Solomon Zeitlin, "Prosbol: A Study in Tannaitic Jurisprudence," *Jewish Quarterly Review*, n.s., 37:4 [April 1947]: 341–62); or in that the lender acts as an emissary of the court to collect on the *prosbul*, while court personnel collect the money promised in deposited deeds (see Dahlia Hoshen, "Ha-prosbul: Ben fictziah mishpatit le-drama hilkhatit: Shinui oh dinamikah parshanit," *Akdamot* 15 [5765]: 165–92).

8. See Elisha S. Ancselovits, "The Prosbul—A Legal Fiction?" *Jewish Law Annual* 19 (2011): 1–16.

9. See especially n39.

10. *yShevi'it* 10:2, 39c; *yGit.* 4:3, 45c–d; *bGit.* 36a–b. Henshke links this debate with how the authority for *prosbul* is both derived and defined. Some suggest that *prosbul* is authorized by a careful reading of Deut. 15:3 which specifies that the sabbatical year cancels "that which you have (אשר יהיה לך)," whereas loan documents handed over to the *bet din* will not be canceled. On this explanation, *prosbul* entails handing over loan documents to the *bet din* so that debt remission will not apply. This does not uproot Torah law, but simply follows a careful reading thereof. Thus, even where the sabbatical year is biblical in authority, *prosbul* is effective. However, others define *prosbul* not as handing over documents, but simply as the lender declaring intention to collect loans despite the sabbatical year, and having that intention ratified by the *bet din*. Those who define *prosbul* thusly consider it to be a rabbinic innovation based on their authority to make *takkanot*. Thus, it is only effective when the sabbatical year is considered rabbinic in status (Henshke, "How Does Prosbul Work?" esp. 82–88).

11. *tShabbat* 1:1; *bShabbat* 6a. For conversions of rabbinic measurements into today's western measurement standards for *'eruv* see Eliezer Melamed, *Laws of Shabbat*, Vol. 2, trans. Yocheved Cohen (Jerusalem: Maggid Books, 2015), chap. 21; Chaim Jachter with Ezra Frazer, *Gray Matter: Ve-zot Li-Yehudah*. (Teaneck: C. Jachter, 2000). They disagree somewhat in their conversion ratios.

12. For an explicit biblical prohibition, see Jer. 17:19–27; Neh. 13:15–21. There are texts to this effect outside the biblical canon as well, such as Jubilees 2:30 (forbidding carrying from house to house) and 50:8 (forbidding carrying anything out of one's tent or one's home). Additionally, rabbinic interpretation (*yShab.* 1:1, 2b; *bShab.* 96b) suggests that Moses's command to the people to cease bringing materials for the construction of the Tabernacle and its vessels (Ex. 36:6) is in fact a warning not to carry items from their private domains to the public domain on the Sabbath. The Talmud there also states the inverse—carrying from a public to a private domain as a logical extension of the prohibition of carrying from a private to a public domain.

13. See again *bShab.* 96b which states that this prohibition has been passed down by tradition rather than citing an express biblical source.

14. *Shulḥan 'Arukh Oraḥ Ḥayyim* 345:7. See Melamed, 115–17 for fuller discussion of the 600,000-person requirement.

15. Such an area is known as a *karmelit* and can also include places that have enclosures, but said enclosures are shorter than ten *tefaḥim* (*bShab*. 6a, 7a-b; Maimonides *Mishneh Torah* Laws of the Sabbath 14:4). For contemporary arguments over what constitutes a *reshut ha-rabim*, see Chaim Jachter, *Zikhron Shmuel Walking the Line: Hilchot Eruvin from the Sources to the Streets* (Teaneck: C. Jachter, 2020).

16. This latter prohibition is attributed to King Solomon. See *b'Er*. 21b Rashi s.v., *Shlomo tikken*

17. There are in fact a number of legal mechanisms that fall under the broad category of *'eruv*: *'eruv hatzerot* designed for carrying from *reshut ha-yaḥid to reshut ha-yaḥid*; *shittuf mevo'ot* (lit., "partnership of alleys") designed to carry from courtyards into the somewhat enclosed street that adjoins those courtyards; and what we talk about today simply as *'eruv*, that which creates joint ownership and symbolic enclosures in non-enclosed areas. Today, it is generally this latter and widest sense of *'eruv* that is used, that which transforms large unenclosed public spaces into jointly owned private and symbolically enclosed spaces and includes all of the *reshuyot ha-yaḥid* found within those spaces as well.

18. This latter practice is known as *sekhirat reshut*, where the Jewish community rents the entire area from local authorities. *Shulḥan 'Arukh Oraḥ Ḥayyim* 391:1 records this practice. For contemporary discussion of how this works in democratic societies, see Jachter, *Walking the Line*, 51–65.

19. *bShab*. 14b/*b'Er*. 21b.

20. On the difference between legal fictions and legal loopholes, see the Introduction.

21. See Maimonides *Mishneh Torah* Laws of *'Eruvin* 1:2–5. See also Rashi *bShab*. 14b, s.v. *Shlomo gazar* (and *b'Er*. 21b *Shlomo tikken*) who interprets Solomon's decree as making a fence around the Torah. See also Yehuda HaLevi, *Kuzari* 3:50–51; Maimonides Laws of *'Eruvin* 1:1–2. This whole system may have been a way to distinguish rabbinites from Qumranites who did not carry at all on the Sabbath. This may explain the repeated authorization and celebration of *'eruv* as central: e.g., Rabba bar Rav Hanan expresses shock at scholars who do not put up an *'eruv* (*b'Er*. 68a); *mShab*. 2:7 lists *'eruv* on the final pre-Sabbath checklist before lighting Sabbath candles; *Y'Er*. 3:2, 20d/7:9, 24c describes how *'eruv* can bring peace among people; rabbis Ami and Asi prefer to start their Sabbath meal using the bread from the *'eruv* "because it has already been used to fulfill a *mitzvah* (*bBer*. 39b)"; a heavenly echo emerged when Solomon initiated *'eruv*, approving the decree (*bShab*. 14b/*b'Er*. 21b). This last example also speaks to Zeitlin's point about scriptural support for *takkanot*.

22. David Kraemer, *Rabbinic Judaism: Space and Place* (New York: Routledge, 2016), chap. 5. He also applies this logic to *'eruv teḥumin*, which extends the boundaries beyond which a Jew may walk on the Sabbath.

23. *M'Eruvin* 6:1–2. (See also *t'Er*. 5:18 for a discussion of the exclusion of Sabbath desecrators from some participation.) Charlotte E. Fonrobert, "From Separatism to Urbanism: The Dead Sea Scrolls and the Origins of the Rabbinic *'Eruv*," *Dead Sea Discoveries* 11:1 (2004): 43–71. She contrasts this with Qumran. While the Qumran sectarians walled themselves off in the wilderness through physically sharing property (known as ערב in their literature; 1QS 5:1–2), rabbinic Jews created community among mixed urban Palestinian space through the use of sharing property in the form of *'eruv*.

24. Though many do read *'eruv* this way (e.g., Gilat, R. Eliezer, 219).

25. From Ex. 16:23. See *yBetzah* 2:1, 61a–b; *bBetzah* 15b.

26. *bYoma* 28b.

27. See e.g., *Ra'avad*'s gloss to Maimonides *Mishneh Torah* Laws of Festival Rest, 6:2. Others suggest that the 'eruv earns its name by making the festival and the Sabbath as if into a single day, as one may cook on one for the other (see e.g., *Rashba, 'Avodat Ha-kodesh, Bet Mo'ed* 4:1). This gloss is less convincing because of the word *tavshilin*, cooked items.

28. Albeck, *Shishah Sidre Mishnah* Vol. II, *Seder Mo'ed*, 291.

29. See, e.g., Mordechai Breuer, "'Eruv Tavshilin," *Sinai* 91:3–4 (5742): 113–21; *Lekah Tov* Exodus 16:23; Ritva Novellae *bBetzah* 15b, s.v. *rav ashi*.

30. David Henshke, "'Eruve tavshilin—le-toledotehah shel takkanah," *Sinai* 101 (5748): 53–81.

31. Henshke breaks *mBetzah* 2:1 into two parts. Stage 1 corresponds to the following lines: "When a festival falls out on Friday, one should not cook on the festival for Sabbath, but instead may cook for the festival [on the festival] and if one has leftovers, the leftovers may be used for the Sabbath. And one should make a cooked item before the festival and depend on it [as food] for the Sabbath." Stage 2 corresponds to the end of the *mishnah*: "If one ate it (= the cooked item) or it was lost, one may not begin cooking [based] on it. If one left over any of it (= the cooked item), one may depend on it [to cook] for the Sabbath."

32. See e.g., the explanation of *Piske Ha-Rid* (*bBetzah* 15b): "What is the language of the mixture of cooked items? That one combines the completion of cooking that one does on the festival with the beginning of cooking that one does prior to the festival, and it is as though all was done prior to the festival."

33. This appears in both *Yerushalmi* and *Bavli* sources: *yBetzah* 2:1, 61a; *bBetzah* 15b and *bPes*. 46b.

34. On this explanation, the term 'eruv tavshilin, seems to be less relevant. However, Maimonides (*Mishneh Torah* Laws of Festival Rest 6:1–2) explains that the term 'eruv is used for this in parallel to the 'eruv that allows people to carry outside on the Sabbath, as it too serves as a reminder of a prohibition, that carrying in(to) a *reshut ha-rabim* is prohibited.

35. As mentioned above, there are those who understand the idea of not starting to cook on the festival for the Sabbath as being related to how obvious it is that one is cooking for the Sabbath. The logic is that if one already has food for Sabbath in the form of 'eruv tavshilin, it is no longer obvious that one is cooking for the Sabbath. (This seems to be the explanation the *stam* offers to explain a position of Rava in *bBetzah* 22a. This tracks with what we have seen about the *stam*'s concern with the concept of *mukheha milta*, something being obvious, in Chapter 5.) The notion that 'eruv's purpose is to hide something from view parallels some explanations of *ha'aramah* that we examined in Chapters 4 and 5 about whether it is about truly making change or simply covering something up. Perhaps, in the case of cooking on the festival, however, the two are intertwined: obviously spending festival time cooking for the Sabbath denigrates the festival, but doing so inconspicuously does not.

36. *bPes*. 46b.

37. *mPes*. 2:1; *tPes*. 1:7.

38. See Maimonides *Mishneh Torah* Laws of Leaven and Matzah 4:6–7; and Lieberman, *Tosefta Ki-feshutah*.

39. In *yPes*. 2:2, 29a R. Yohanan and Resh Lakish also debate whether *hametz* that was declared ownerless (*hefker*) a couple of days before Passover may be eaten after Passover. The *Yerushalmi* explains their debate as being about whether declaring food ownerless is just *ha'aramah* to take it back following Passover, as the proximity to Passover makes it unlikely that anyone will take possession of the *hametz*. Instead, the original owner will just retrieve it following the holiday (Menahem Meiri, *Bet Ha-behirah* comments to *bPes*. 9a). Some (*Or*

Zarua 1:748, 2:246; R. Asher b. Yehiel, *Piskei Ha-Rosh, bPes.* 2:4; R. Yeruham, *Toldot Adam ve-Ḥava*, 5:5; *Pene Moshe*, s.v. *enah ken*; *Korban Ha-'edah*, s.v. *hayish le-ha'aramah*) read this as a concern that one will not even declare the food ownerless but will just pretend to have done so. How *ha'aramah* impacts the declaration of ownerlessness is unclear: perhaps the declaration itself is invalid (See *Pene Moshe yPe'ah* 6:1, 19b, s.v. *lishnah de-matnita*). Alternatively, perhaps the declaration is valid, but Rabbi Yohanan calls to discount it because it does not look right.

40. E.g., *Rabenu Manoah* commentary to Maimonides *Mishneh Torah* Laws of Leaven and *Matzah* 4:6–7.

41. E.g., Ritva, Novellae, *bPes.* 21a. He and others may have thought the clause ובלבד שלא יערים, "so long as one does not practice cunning," was in the original *toseftan* text. This distinction between selling and buying back *hametz* occasionally in exigencies and doing so annually is already found in the writings of Rav Amram Gaon. See *Otzar Ha-geonim Pesaḥim*, section 48.

42. See, e.g., fourteenth-century *Shulḥan 'Arukh Oraḥ Ḥayyim* 448:3 and fifteenth-century Responsa *Terumat Ha-deshen* I:120. In the latter case, the question already presumes that the *hametz* will be removed from the Jew's property.

43. See R. Yoel Sirkes, *Bayit Ḥadash Oraḥ Ḥayyim* 448.

44. For this reason, R. Alexander Schorr permitted selling *hametz* but forbade selling one's animals to a non-Jew so they can be fed *hametz* for the duration of Passover (see *Bekhor Shor Pesaḥim* 21b): the latter circumvents the biblical prohibition of deriving benefit from *hametz* (bPes. 21b), while the former only circumvents a rabbinic prohibition: biblically, declaring one's *hametz* null and void (i.e., *bitul hametz*) is sufficient for ridding oneself of *hametz* (bPes. 4b); rabbinically, however, one must actually search for and destroy one's *hametz*. Therefore, selling *hametz* circumvents only the added rabbinic requirement of destroying one's *hametz* before Passover. Others forbade selling actual *hametz* (e.g., bread) but permitted selling foods made mostly of non-*hametz* but that had some *hametz* in them because there is only a rabbinic prohibition to own such mixtures during Passover (per Rabbenu Tam in Tos. *bPes.* 42a, s.v. *ve-eilu*). See, e.g., Herschel Schachter's citation of R. Joseph Dov Soloveitchik, *Nefesh Ha-Rav* (Jerusalem: Reshit Yerushalayim, 5754 [1994]), 177. A written anthology of the practices of the Vilna Gaon allows the sale of *hametz* only if it permanent (*Ma'aseh Rav*, 180).

Bibliography

Adelman, Rachel, ed. *Journal of Textual Reasoning* 6:2 (March 2011).
Adler, Yitzhak. *Lomdus: A Substructural Analysis* (Hebrew). New York: Bet Sha'ar, 1989.
Albeck, Hanoch. *Mavo La-Mishnah*. Tel Aviv: Dvir, 1967.
———. *Mavo La-Talmudim*. Tel Aviv: Dvir, 1969.
———. *Meḥkarim Bi-veraita Ve-Tosefta Ve-yaḥasan La-Talmud*. Jerusalem: Mosad Ha-Rav Kook, 1969.
———. *Shishah Sidre Mishnah*. Vols. 1–6. Jerusalem: Bialik Institute, 1952–58.
Albeck, Shalom. "Ha-im kayam ha-musag 'kavvanah' be-mishpat ha-pelili ba-Talmud?" *Kovetz Ha-tziyonut Ha-datit* 5 (2002/5762): 460–71.
Alexander, Elizabeth Shanks. *Transmitting Mishnah: The Shaping Influence of Oral Tradition*. Cambridge: Cambridge University Press, 2006.
Alon, Gedaliah. *The Jews in Their Land in the Talmudic Age, 70–640 C.E.* Jerusalem: Magnes Press, 1980–84.
Alter, Robert. *The Wisdom Books: Job, Proverbs, and Ecclesiastes: A Translation with Commentary*. 1st ed. New York: W. W. Norton, 2011.
Amihay, Aryeh. "Law and Society in the Dead Sea Scrolls." PhD diss., Princeton University, 2013.
Ancselovits, Elisha S. "The Prosbul: A Legal Fiction?" *Jewish Law Annual* 19 (2011): 1–16.
Ando, Clifford. "Fact, Fiction and Social Reality in Roman Law." In *Legal Fictions in Theory and Practice*, ed. Maksymilian Del Mar and William Twining, 295–324. New York: Springer International Publishing, 2015.
———. *Law, Language and Empire in the Roman Tradition*. Philadelphia: University of Pennsylvania Press, 2011.
Arkush, Allan. "Biblical Criticism and Cultural Zionism Prior to the First World War." *Jewish History* 21:2 (June 2007): 121–58.
Arzi, Abraham. "Mipne mar'it ha-'ayin." *Sinai* 74 (1974): 161–70.
Atiyah, P. S. *The Rise and Fall of Freedom of Contract*. New York: Oxford University Press, 1979.
Atkinson, Kathleen M. T. "The Purpose of the Manumission Laws of Augustus." *Irish Jurist*, n.s., 1 (1966): 356–74.
Atlas, Samuel. "Ha'aramah mishpatit ba-Talmud (Fictions in the Talmud)." In *Louis Ginzberg: Jubilee Volume on the Occasion of His Seventieth Birthday*, 1–24. New York: American Academy for Jewish Research, 1945.
———. *Pathways in Jewish Law* (Hebrew). New York: Sefer Harmon, 1978.
Baer, Yitzhak. *Yisra'el Ba-'amim: 'Iyunim Be-toldot Yeme Ha-bayit Ha-sheni U-tekufat Ha-Mishnah U-ve-yesodot Ha-halakhah Ve-ha-emunah*. Jerusalem: Bialik Institute, 1955.

Bakhos, Carol, and Rahim Shayegan, eds. *The Talmud in Its Iranian Context*. Tübingen: Mohr Siebeck, 2010.

Balberg, Mira. *Purity, Body and Self in Early Rabbinic Literature*. Berkeley: University of California Press, 2014.

Barak, Aharon. *Parshanut Ba-mishpat*. Jerusalem: Nevo, 1994.

Bar-Asher Siegal, Michal. *Early Christian Monastic Literature and the Babylonian Talmud*. Cambridge: Cambridge University Press, 2013.

Bar-On, Shraga. "The Art of the Chain Novel in b.Yoma 35b: Reconsidering the Social Values of the Babylonian Yeshivot." *Hebrew Union College Annual* 88 (2017): 55–88.

Baskin, Judith R. "Rabbinic Reflections on the Barren Wife." *Harvard Theological Review* 82:1 (1989): 101–14.

Bazak, Amnon. *Fundamental Questions in the Study of Oral Law*. Rishon Le-Tziyon: Miskal-Yedioth Ahronoth Books and Chemed Books, 2020.

Bazak, Jacob. "The Element of Intention in the Performance of 'Mitsvot' Compared to the Element on Intention in Current Criminal Law." *Jewish Law Association Studies: The Jerusalem 2002 Conference Volume* 14 (2004): 9–15.

Becker, Adam H. and Annette Y. Reed. *The Ways That Never Parted: Jews and Christians in Late Antiquity and the Early Middle Ages*. Tübingen: Mohr Siebeck, 2003.

Benas, Bertram B. "The Legal Device in Jewish Law." *Journal of Comparative Legislation and International Law*, 3rd ser., 11:1 (1929): 75–80.

Ben-Menahem, Hanina. *Authority, Process and Method Studies in Jewish Law*. Jewish Law in Context. Vol. 2. Australia: Harwood Academic, 1997.

———. "Is Talmudic Law a Religious Legal System? A Provisional Analysis." *Journal of Law and Religion* 24 (September 2008): 379–402.

———. "The Myth of Formalism: (Mis)Readings of Jewish Law from Paul to the Present." Hebrew University Legal Research Paper no. 17-5, December 2016.

Ben-Menahem, Hanina, and Neil S. Hecht. *Judicial Deviation in Talmudic Law: Governed by Men, Not by Rules*. New York: Harwood Academic Press, 1991.

Berkowitz, Beth A. *Execution and Invention: Death Penalty Discourse in Early Rabbinic and Christian Cultures*. New York: Oxford University Press, 2006.

Berkowitz, Eliezer. *Not in Heaven: The Nature and Function of Halakhah*. New York: Ktav, 1983.

Berman, Harold. "The Origins of Western Legal Science." *Harvard Law Review* 90 (March 1977): 894–943.

Bianchi, Ernesto. *Fictio iuris: Ricerche sulla finzione in diritto romano dal periodo arcaico all'epoca augustea*. Padova: CEDAM, 1997.

Bigman, David. "Be'ayah hilkhatit oh tikkun ḥevrati? 'Al mashma'ut ha-prosbul." *Akdamot* 20 (2008): 155–66.

Birenboim, H. "Observance of the Laws of Bodily Purity in Jewish Society in the Land of Israel During the Second Temple Period." PhD diss., Hebrew University, 2006.

Blau, L. "Prosbol im Lichte der grieschischen Papyri und Rechtsgeschichte." In *Festschrift zum 50 jahrigen Bestehen der Franz-Joseph Landesrabbinerschule in Budapest*, 96–151. Budapest: Alexander Kohut Memorial Foundations, 1927.

Bleich, J. David. *Contemporary Halakhic Problems, Volumes 1, 4 and 5*. New York: Ktav, 1976, 1995, and 2005.

Bloch, Moshe. *Sha'are Torat Ha-takkanot*. Jerusalem: Makor, 1970.

Bonner, Robert J., and Gertrude Smith. *The Administration of Justice from Homer to Aristotle.* Vol. 1. Chicago: University of Chicago Press, 1930.
Bove, Lucio. "Frode, Diritto Romano." *Noviss. Dig. Ital.* 7 (1961): 630–31.
Brand, Joshua. "Megillat brit Damesek u-zemanah." *Tarbiz* 28 (1959): 18–39.
Breuer, Mordechai. "'Eruv tavshilin." *Sinai* 91:3–4 (5742): 113–21.
Brodsky, David. "'Thought Is Akin to Action': The Importance of Thought in Zoroastrianism and the Development of a Babylonian Rabbinic Motif." In *Irano-Judaica: Studies Relating to Jewish Contacts with Persian Culture Throughout the Ages.* Vol. 7, ed. Julia Rubanovich and Geoffrey Herman, 145–96. Jerusalem: Ben-Zvi Institute for the Study of Jewish Communities in the East, 2019.
Brown, Benjamin. "Formalism and Values: Three Models (Hebrew)." In *New Streams in the Philosophy of Halakhah,* ed. Aviezer Ravitzky and Avinoam Rosenak. Jerusalem: Magnes Press and Van Leer Institute, 2008.
———. "From Principles to Rules and from Musar to Halakhah: The Hafetz Hayim's Rulings on Libel and Gossip." *Diné Israel: Studies in Halakhah and Jewish Law* 25 (2008): 171–256.
Brown, Francis, S. R. Driver, and Charles A. Briggs, eds., *A Hebrew and English Lexicon of the Old Testament: Based on the Lexicon of William Gesenius as Translated by Edward Robinson.* Boston: Houghton Mifflin, 1906.
Buckland, W. W. *Equity in Roman Law: Lectures Delivered in the University of London, at the Request of the Faculty of Laws.* London: University of London Press, 1911.
———. *The Main Institutions of Roman Private Law.* Cambridge: Cambridge University Press, 1931.
Camp, Claudia V. "Wise and Strange: An Interpretation of the Female Imagery in Proverbs in Light of Trickster Mythology." *Semeia* 42 (1988): 14–36.
Casavola, Franco. *"Lex Cincia": Contributo All Storia Delle Origini Della Donazio Romana.* Naples: Jovene, 1960.
Cassius, Dio Cocceianus. *Dio Cassius Roman History.* Trans. Earnest Carey, on the basis of the version of Herbert Baldwin Foster. London: W. Heinemann, 1914–27.
Chajes, Zvi Hirsch. *Darkhe Hora'ah.* Zolkiew: Saul Meyerhoffer, 1842.
Charlesworth, James H., ed. *The Dead Sea Scrolls: Hebrew, Aramaic, and Greek Texts with English Translations.* Princeton Theological Seminary Dead Sea Scrolls Project. Tübingen: J. C. B. Mohr (Paul Siebeck), 1994.
Cicero, Marcus Tullius. *Cicero De Officiis.* Trans. Walter Miller. London: W. Heinemann, 1921.
Cohen, Boaz. *Jewish and Roman Law: A Comparative Study.* New York: Jewish Theological Seminary of America, 1966.
Cohen, S. J. D., ed. *The Synoptic Problem in Rabbinic Literature.* Providence: Brown Judaic Studies, 2000.
Cook, Johann. *The Septuagint of Proverbs: Jewish and/or Hellenistic Proverbs? Concerning the Hellenistic Colouring of LXX Proverbs.* Supplements to Vetus Testamentum. Vol. 69. Leiden: Brill, 1997.
Cornu Thénard, Nicolas. "La notion de fait dans la jurisprudence classique: Étude sur les principes de la distinction entre fait et droit." PhD diss., University of Paris, 2011.
Countryman, Louis William. *Dirt, Greed, and Sex: Sexual Ethics in the New Testament and Their Implications for Today.* Philadelphia: Fortress Press, 1988.

Dagan, Hanoch. "The Realist Conception of Law." *University of Toronto Law Journal* 57 (2007): 607–60.
Dalley, Stephanie, trans. *Myths from Mesopotamia: Creation, the Flood, Gilgamesh, and Others.* Oxford: Oxford University Press, 1989.
Daube, David. "Dodges and Rackets in Roman Law." *Proceedings of the Classical Association* 61 (1964): 28–30.
———. "Error and Ignorance as Excuses in Crime." In *Ancient Jewish Law: Three Inaugural Lectures*, 49–69. Leiden: Brill, 1981.
———. "Fraud No. 3." In *Collected Studies in Roman Law*, ed. David Daube, David Cohen, and Dieter Simon, 1409–24. Frankfurt am Main: V. Klostermann, 1991.
———. "Fraud on Law for Fraud on Law." *Journal of Legal Studies* 1:1 (Spring 1981): 51–60.
———. *Roman Law: Linguistic, Social and Philosophical Aspects.* Edinburgh: Edinburgh University Press, 1966.
———. "Summum Ius Summa Iniuria." In *Studies in Biblical Law*, 190–313. Cambridge: Cambridge University Press, 1947.
Del Mar, Maksymilian. "Legal Fictions and Legal Change in the Common Law Tradition." In *Legal Fictions in Theory and Practice*, ed. Maksymilian Del Mar and William Twining, 225–54. New York: Springer International Publishing, 2015.
De Vries, Benjamin. *Toldot Ha-halakhah Ha-talmudit.* Tel Aviv: Abraham Zioni Publishing House, 1962.
Dimant, Devorah, and Uriel Rappaport. *The Dead Sea Scrolls. Forty Years of Research.* Studies on the Texts of the Desert of Judah. Vol. 10. New York: E. J. Brill, 1992.
Dor, Zvi. *Torat Eretz Yisrael Be-Bavel.* Tel Aviv: Dvir, 1971.
D'Ors Perez-Peix, Alvaro. "La Actitud Legislativa del Emperador Justiniano." *Orientalia Christiana Periodica* 13:1–2 (1947): 119.
Dundes, Alan. *The Shabbat Elevator and Other Sabbath Subterfuges: An Unorthodox Essay on Circumventing Custom and Jewish Character.* New York: Rowman and Littlefield, 2002.
Dworkin, Ronald. *Law's Empire.* Cambridge, MA: Belknap Press, 1986.
———. *A Matter of Principle.* Cambridge, MA: Harvard University Press, 1985.
———. *Taking Rights Seriously.* London: Duckworth, 1977.
Eilberg-Schwartz, Howard. *The Human Will in Judaism: The Mishnah's Philosophy of Intention.* Brown Judaic Studies no. 103. Atlanta: Scholars Press, 1986.
Elman, Yaakov. "Hercules Within the Halakhic Tradition." *Diné Israel: Studies in Halakhah and Jewish Law* 25 (2008): 7–41.
———. "Middle Persian Culture and Babylonian Sages: Accommodation and Resistance in the Shaping of Rabbinic Legal Tradition." In *Cambridge Companion to Rabbinic Literature*, ed. Charlotte Elisheva Fonrobert and Martin S. Jaffe, 165–97. Cambridge: Cambridge University Press, 2007.
———. "Toward an Intellectual History of Sasanian Law: An Intergenerational Dispute in Hērbedestān 9 and Its Rabbinic Parallels." In *The Talmud in Its Iranian Context*, ed. Carol Bakhos and Rahim Shayegan, 21–57. Tübingen: Mohr Siebeck, 2010.
Elon, Menachem. *Ha-mishpat Ha-'ivri: Toldotav Mekorotav 'Ekronotav.* Vol. 1. Jerusalem: Magnes Press, 1982.
Epstein, J. N. *Introduction to Tannaitic Literature: Mishnah, Tosefta, and Halakhic Midrashim* (Hebrew). Jerusalem: Magnes Press, 1959.
———. *Mavo Le-nusaḥ Ha-Mishnah.* 3rd ed. Jerusalem: Magnes Press, 1964.

Fishbane, Michael A. *Biblical Interpretation in Ancient Israel*. Oxford: Clarendon Press, 1985.
———. *Biblical Myth and Rabbinic Mythmaking*. Oxford: Oxford University Press, 2003.
Fonrobert, Charlotte E. "From Separatism to Urbanism: The Dead Sea Scrolls and the Origins of the Rabbinic 'Eruv." *Dead Sea Discoveries* 11:1 (2004): 43–71.
Fox, Michael V. *Proverbs 1–9: A New Translation with Introduction and Commentary*. 1st ed. Anchor Bible. Vol. 18A. New York: Doubleday, 2000.
———. "Words for Wisdom: 'Tevunah' and 'Binah'; 'Ormah' and 'Mezimah'; 'Ezah' and 'Tushiyah.'" *Zeitschrift für Althebräistik* 6:2 (1993): 149–69.
Fraade, Steven D., Aharon Shemesh, and Ruth A. Clements, eds. *Rabbinic Perspectives: Rabbinic Literature and the Dead Sea Scrolls: Proceedings of the Eighth International Symposium of the Orion Center, 7–9 January 2003*. Studies on the Texts of the Desert of Judah. Vol. 62. Orion, Center for the Study of the Dead Sea Scrolls and Associated Literature. Leiden: Brill, 2006.
Friedman, Hershey H. "He Who Sits in Heaven Shall Laugh: Divine Humor in Talmudic Literature." *Thalia* 17:1 (January 1, 1997): 36–50.
Friedman, Shamma. "The Baraitot in the Babylonian Talmud and Their Parallels in the Tosefta." In *Atara Le-Haim, Studies in the Talmud and Medieval Rabbinic Literature in Honor of Professor Haim Zalman Dimitrovsky*, 163–201. Jerusalem: Magnes Press, 2000.
———. "Mavo kelali 'al derekh ḥeker ha-sugya." In *Meḥkarim U-mekorot*, ed. H. Z. Dmitrovsky, 283–321. New York: Jewish Theological Seminary of America, 1978.
———. "Mishna-Tosefta Parallels." *Proceedings of the Eleventh World Congress of Jewish Studies* (1994): 15–22.
———. "The Primacy of Tosefta to Mishnah in Synoptic Parallels." In *Introducing Tosefta: Textual, Intratextual and Intertextual Studies*, ed. Harry Fox and Tirzah Meacham, 99–121. Hoboken, NJ: Ktav, 1999.
———. "The Spelling of the Names רבה and רבא in the Babylonian Talmud." *Sinai* 110 (Spring–Summer 1992): 140–64.
———. *Tosefta 'Attiqta: Masekhet Pesaḥ Rishon: Makbilot Ha-Mishnah Ve-ha-Tosefta*. Ramat Gan: Bar Ilan University Press, 2002.
———. "Towards a Characterization of Babylonian Baraitot: Ben Tema and Ben Dortai." In *Neti'ot LeDavid: Jubilee Volume for David Weiss Halivni*, ed. Y. Elman et al., 195–274. Jerusalem: Orhot Press, 2007.
Fuller, Lon L. *Legal Fictions*. Stanford: Stanford University Press, 1967.
Furstenberg, Yair. "Eating in a State of Purity in the Tannaitic Period: Tractate Taharot and Its Historical and Cultural Contexts." PhD diss., Hebrew University, 2010.
Gabbay, Uri, and Shai Secunda, eds. *Encounters by the Rivers of Babylon: Scholarly Conversations Between Jews, Iranians and Babylonians in Antiquity*. Tübingen: Mohr Siebeck, 2014.
Gaius. *The Institutes of Gaius*. Parts One and Two. *Text with Critical Notes and Translation*. Ed. Francis de Zulueta. Oxford: Clarendon Press, 1946.
Gama, Raymundo. "Presumptions and Fictions: A Collingwoodian Approach." In *Legal Fictions in Theory and Practice*, ed. Maksymilian Del Mar and William Twining, 347–66. New York: Springer International Publishing, 2015.
Gamoran, Hillel. "The 'Prozbul': Accommodation to Reality." *Jewish Law Association Studies* 22 (2012): 103–11.
———. "The Tosefta in Light of the Law Against Usury." *Jewish Law Association Studies* 9 (1997): 57–78.

Garner, Bryan A., ed. *Black's Law Dictionary*. 8th ed. St. Paul, MN: Thomson/West, 2004.
Gilat, Yitzchak D. "Bet din matnin la'akor davar min ha-Torah." In *Perakim Be-hishtalshelut Ha-halakhah*, 191–204. Jerusalem: Bar Ilan University, 1992.
———. "The Halakhah and Its Relationship to Social Reality." *Tradition: A Journal of Orthodox Jewish Thought* 13–14:1 (Spring–Summer 1973): 68–87.
———. "Issur shevut be-Shabbat ve-hishtalshelutam." *Perakim Be-hishtalshelut Ha-halakhah*. Ramat Gan: Bar Ilan University Press, 1992.
———. "Kavvanah u-ma'aseh be-mishnat ha-tannaim." *Bar Ilan Annual* 4–5 (1967): 104–16.
———. "'Al ḥametz shel aḥerim ve-shel gavohah." *Tarbiz* 33 (1963): 20–27.
———. *R. Eliezer Ben Hyrcanus: A Scholar Outcast*. Bar-Ilan Studies in Near Eastern Languages and Culture. Ramat-Gan: Bar Ilan University Press, 1984.
Gill, Christopher. *Personality in Greek Epic, Tragedy and Philosophy: The Self in Dialogue*. Oxford: Clarendon Press, 1996.
Ginzberg, Louis. "'Al ha-yaḥas she-ben ha-Mishnah ve-ha-Mekhilta (On the Relationship Between the Mishnah and the Mekhilta)." In *Studies in Memory of Moses Schorr*, ed. Louis Ginzberg and Abraham Weiss, 57–95. New York: Professor Moses Schorr Memorial Committee, 1944.
———. *Perushim Ve-ḥiddushim Be-Yerushalmi*. New York: JTSA, 1961.
———. *Tamid: The Oldest Treatise of the Mishnah*. Cincinnati: Ark, 1919.
Gitelman, Zvi. *A Century of Ambivalence: The Jews of Russia and the Soviet Union, 1881 to the Present*. New York: Schocken Books, 1988.
Goldberg, Abraham. "The Palestinian Talmud." In *The Literature of the Sages: Part I*, ed. Shmuel Safrai. Assen, Netherlands: Van Gorcum, 1987.
———. "The Tosefta—Companion to the Mishna." In *The Literature of the Sages: Part I*, ed. Shmuel Safrai. Assen: Van Gorcum, 1987.
Goldenberg, Robert. "Commandment and Consciousness in Talmudic Thought." *Harvard Theological Review* (1975): 261–71.
———. "Law and Spirit in Talmudic Religion." In *Jewish Spirituality, Vol. I: From the Bible Through the Middle Ages*, ed. A. Green, 232–52. New York: Crossroads, 1986.
Gray, Alyssa. *A Talmud in Exile: The Influence of Yerushalmi Avodah Zarah on the Formation of the Bavli*. Providence: Brown Judaic Studies, 2020.
Gray, Alyssa, and Bernard Jackson, eds. *Studies in Mediaeval Halakhah in Honor of Stephen M. Passamaneck*. Jewish Law Association Studies 17. England: Jewish Law, 2007.
Green, David A. "Balancing Ethical Concerns Against Liberal Discovery: The Case of Rule 4.2 and the Problem of Loophole Lawyering." *Georgetown Journal of Legal Ethics* 8 (1995): 283–312.
Grey, Thomas C. "Langdell's Orthodoxy." *University of Pittsburgh Law Review* 45 (1983): 1–53.
Haas, Peter J. *A History of the Mishnaic Law of Agriculture: Tractate Ma'aser Sheni*. Chico, CA: Scholars Press, 1980.
Hadot, Pierre. *The Inner Citadel: The Meditations of Marcus Aurelius*. Cambridge, MA: Harvard University Press, 1998.
Halberstam, Chaya T. *Law and Truth in Biblical and Rabbinic Literature*. Bloomington: Indiana University Press, 2010.
Halbertal, Moshe. *Interpretive Revolutions in the Making: Values as Interpretative Criteria in Jewish Law* (Hebrew). Jerusalem: Magnes Press, 1999.
Halivni, David Weiss. *Mekorot U-mesorot: Bava Kamma*. Jerusalem: Magnes Press, 1993.

———. *Mekorot U-mesorot: Bava Metzi'a*. Jerusalem: Magnes Press, 2003.
———. *Mekorot U-mesorot: 'Eruvin U-Pesaḥim*. Jerusalem: Jewish Theological Seminary of America, 1982.
———. *Mekorot U-mesorot: Mi-Yoma 'ad Ḥagigah*. Jerusalem: Jewish Theological Seminary of America, 1975.
———. *Mekorot U-mesorot: Nashim*. Tel Aviv: Dvir, 1968.
———. *Mekorot U-mesorot: Shabbat*. Jerusalem: Jewish Theological Seminary of America, 1975.
———. *Midrash, Mishnah, and Gemara: The Jewish Predilection for Justified Law*. Cambridge, MA: Harvard University Press, 1986.
Harper, Ian, and Lachlan Smirl. "Usury." In *The Oxford Handbook of Christianity and Economics*, ed. Paul Oslington, 564–80. New York: Oxford University Press, 2014.
Harris, Jay M. *How Do We Know This? Midrash and the Fragmentation of Modern Judaism*. New York: SUNY Press, 1994.
Hart, H. L. A. *The Concept of Law*. 2nd ed. New York: Oxford University Press, 1994.
Haskell, Paul G. "The Case for an Implied Warranty of Quality in Sales of Real Property." *Georgetown University Law Journal* 53 (1965): 633.
Hauptman, Judith. *Rereading the Mishnah: A New Approach to Ancient Jewish Texts*. Tübingen: Mohr Siebeck, 2005.
Hayes, Christine. "Authority and Anxiety in the Talmuds: From Legal Fiction to Fact." In *Jewish Religious Leadership: Image and Reality*, ed. Jack Wertheimer, 127–54. New York: Jewish Theological Seminary, 2004.
———. "Legal Realism and the Fashioning of Sectarians in Jewish Antiquity." In *Sects and Sectarianism in Jewish History*, ed. Sacha Stern, 119–48. Leiden: Brill, 2011.
———. "Legal Truth, Right Answers and Best Answers: Dworkin and the Rabbis." *Diné Israel: Studies in Halakhah and Jewish Law* 25 (2008): 73–121.
———. "Rabbinic Contestations of Authority." *Cardozo Law Review* 28:1 (2006): 123–41.
———. "What Is (the) Mishnah? Concluding Observations." *AJS Review* 32:2 (2008): 291–97.
———. *What's Divine About Divine Law?* Princeton: Princeton University Press, 2015.
Hecht, N. S. *An Introduction to the History and Sources of Jewish Law*. Publication of the Institute of Jewish Law, Boston University School of Law no. 22. New York: Clarendon Press, 1996.
Henshke, David. "'Eruve tavshilin—le-toldotehah shel takkanah." *Sinai* 101 (5748): 53–81.
———. "The Firstborn of a Kosher Animal Outside the Land of Israel: From the Talmud to Maimonides and Back" (Hebrew). In *Meir Benayahu Memorial Volume, Vol. 1: Studies in Talmud, Halakhah, Custom, and Jewish History*, ed. M. Bar Asher, Y. Liebes, M. Assis, and Y. Kaplan, 241–74. Jerusalem: Yad Ha-Rav Nissim, 2019.
———. "How Does Prosbul Work? A History of the Explanation of Hillel's Takkanah (Hebrew)." *Shenaton Ha-mishpat Ha-'ivri* 22 (April 5761): 71–106.
———. *Mishnah Rishonah Be-talmudam shel Tannaim Aḥaronim: Sugyot Be-dine Shomrim*. Ramat Gan: Bar Ilan University Press, 1997.
Herman, Geoffrey, and Jeffrey L. Rubenstein, eds. *Aggadah of the Bavli and Its Cultural World*. Providence: Brown Judaic Studies, 2018.
Hezser, Catherine, ed. *Rabbinic Law in Its Roman and Near Eastern Context*. Texte und Studien Zum Antiken Judentum. Vol. 97. Tübingen: Mohr Siebeck, 2003.

———. "Roman Law and Rabbinic Legal Composition." In *The Cambridge Companion to the Talmud and Rabbinic Literature*, ed. Charlotte E. Fonrobert and Martin S. Jaffee, 144–64. Cambridge: Cambridge University Press, 2007.

Hidary, Richard. *Rabbis and Classical Rhetoric: Sophistic Education and Oratory in the Talmud and Midrash*. Cambridge: Cambridge University Press, 2017.

Higger, Michael. "Intention in Talmudic Law." PhD diss., Columbia University, 1927.

Himmelschein, J. "Studien Zu Der Antiken Hermeneutica Iuris." In *Symbolae Friburgenses in Honorem Ottonis Lenel*, 398–417. Leipzig: B. Tauchnitz, 1931.

Hirschman, Albert. *Shifting Involvements*. Princeton: Princeton University Press, 1982.

Hoffseyer, Benjamin. "Rabbi Haim Tchernowitz, 'Rav Tza'ir,' and the Yeshiva of Odessa (Hebrew)." PhD diss., Yeshiva University, 1967.

Holderness, Clifford G. "A Legal Foundation for Exchange." *Journal of Legal Studies* (1985): 321–44.

Holmes, Oliver Wendell, Jr. "Codes and the Arrangement of the Law." *American Law Review* 5 (1870): 1–13.

———. "Law in Science and Science in Law." *Harvard Law Review* 12:7 (1899): 443–63.

———. "The Path of the Law." *Harvard Law Review* 10:8 (1897): 457–78.

Hoshen, Dahlia. "Ha-prosbul: ben fictziah mishpatit le-dramah hilkhatit: Shinuy oh din-amikah parshanit." *Akdamot* 15 [5765]: 165–92.

Huang, Peter H. Review of *Why the Law Is So Perverse*, by Leo Katz. *Journal of Legal Education* 131 (2013): 131–60.

Jachter, Chaim with Ezra Frazer, *Gray Matter: Ve-zot Li-Yehudah*. Teaneck: C. Jachter, 2000.

Jachter, Chaim. *Zikhron Shmuel Walking the Line: Hilchot Eruvin from the Sources to the Streets*. Teaneck: C. Jachter, 2020.

Jachter, Howard. "Halachic Perspectives on Pets." *Journal of Halacha & Contemporary Society*, no. 23 (Spring 1992): 33–62.

Jackson, Bernard S. *Essays in Jewish and Comparative Legal History*. Leiden: Brill, 1975.

———. "History, Dogmatics and Halakhah." In *Jewish Law in Legal History and the Modern World*, ed. Bernard S. Jackson, 1–26. Leiden: Brill, 1980.

———. "Liability for Mere Intention in Early Jewish Law." *Hebrew Union College Annual* 42 (1971): 197–225.

———. "On the Problem of Roman Influence on the Halakhah and Normative Self-Definition in Judaism." In *Jewish and Christian Self-Definition*, ed. E. P. Sanders, A. I. Baumgarten, and Alan Mendelson, 2:157–203. London: SCM Press, 1981.

———. "Secular Jurisprudence and the Philosophy of Jewish Law: A Commentary on Some Recent Literature." *Jewish Law Annual* 6 (1987): 3–44.

Jaffee, Martin S. "Mishnaic Literary History and the History of a Mishnaic Idea: On the Formation of the Mishnah's Theory of Intention, with Special Reference to Tractate Ma'aserot." *AJS Review* 11 (1986): 135–55.

———. *Torah in the Mouth: Writing and Oral Tradition in Palestinian Judaism, 200 BCE–400 CE*. New York: Oxford University Press, 2001.

Jastrow, Marcus. *A Dictionary of the Targumim, the Talmud Babli and Yerushalmi, and the Midrashic Literature*. New York: Judaica Press, 1992.

Kahana, Menahem. "The Halakhic Midrashim." In *The Literature of the Sages, Second Part: Midrash and Targum, Liturgy, Poetry, Mysticism, Contracts, Inscriptions, Ancient Science and the Languages of Rabbinic Literature*, ed. Shmuel Safrai, Ze'ev Safrai, and Joshua Schwartz, 1–105. Amsterdam: Fortress Press, 2006.

Kalmin, Richard Lee. *Jewish Babylonia Between Persia and Roman Palestine*. Oxford: Oxford University Press, 2006.
———. *The Sage in Jewish Society of Late Antiquity*. London: Routledge, 1999.
Kaplan, Yehiel. "*Kofin oto 'ad she-yomar rotzeh ani*—The Quality of the Principle and Its Application in Our Time." In *'Iyun Be-mishpat 'Ivri U-ve-halakhah: Dayan Ve-diyun*, ed. Ya'akov Habba and Amihai Radziner, 189–248. Ramat Gan: Bar Ilan University Press, 2007.
Katz, Leo. *Ill-Gotten Gains: Evasion, Blackmail, Fraud, and Kindred Puzzles of the Law*. Chicago: University of Chicago Press, 1996.
———. *Why the Law Is So Perverse*. Chicago: University of Chicago Press, 2011.
Katzoff, Ranon. "Judicial Reasoning in *P. Catt—Fraus Legi*." *Transactions and Proceedings of the American Philological Association* 101 (1970): 241–52.
Kensky, Meira Z. *Trying Man, Trying God: The Divine Courtroom in Early Jewish and Christian Literature*. Tübingen: Mohr Siebeck, 2010.
Kiel, Yishai. "Cognizance of Sin and Penalty in the Babylonian Talmud and Pahlavi Literature: A Comparative Analysis." *Oqimta* 1 (2013): 1–49.
———. "Redesigning Tzitzit in the Babylonian Talmud in Light of Literary Depictions of the Zoroastrian Kustig." In *Shoshannat Yaakov: Jewish and Iranian Studies in Honor of Yaakov Elman*. Vol. 35, ed. Shai Secunda and Steven Fine, Brill Reference Library of Judaism, 185–202. Leiden: Brill, 2012.
King, Peter. "Peter Abelard." In *The Stanford Encyclopedia of Philosophy*, ed. Edward N. Zalta. 2011. https://plato.stanford.edu/entries/abelard/
Kirschenbaum, Aaron. *Equity in Jewish Law: Halakhic Perspectives in Law: Formalism and Flexibility in Jewish Civil Law*. Hoboken, NJ: Ktav, 1991.
———. "A Historical Sketch of the Sources of Jewish Law." In *Equity in Jewish Law: Halakhic Perspectives in Law: Formalism and Flexibility in Jewish Civil Law*. Hoboken, NJ: Ktav, 1991.
Kirschenbaum, Aaron, and Norman Lamm. "Freedom and Constraint in the Jewish Judicial Process." *Cardozo Law Review* 1 (1979): 99–133.
Klawans, Jonathan. *Impurity and Sin in Ancient Judaism*. Oxford: Oxford University Press, 2000.
Kolcheim, Shaul. "Davar she-en mitkaven be-safrut ha-tanna'it u-ve-Talmud." PhD diss., Bar Ilan University, 2002.
Kook, Abraham Isaac. *Iggerot Ha-Re'ayah*. Jerusalem: Mosad Ha-Rav Kook, 1977.
Kraemer, David. *Rabbinic Judaism: Space and Place*. New York: Routledge, 2016.
Kruse, Katherine R. "The Jurisprudential Turn in Legal Ethics." *Arizona Law Review* 53 (2011): 493–531.
Lambert, W. G., and A. R. Millard. *Atrahasis: The Babylonian Story of the Flood*. Oxford: Clarendon Press, 1969.
Langdell, Christopher Columbus. "Harvard Celebration Speeches (Nov. 5, 1886)." *Law Quarterly Review* 3 (1887): 123–26.
Levinson, Joshua. "From Narrative Practise to Cultural Poetics: Literary Anthropology and the Rabbinic Sense of Self." In *Homer and the Bible in the Eyes of Ancient Interpreters*, ed. Maren R. Niehoff, 345–67. Leiden: Brill, 2012.
Levinson, Sanford. "What Do Lawyers Know (and What Do They Do with Their Knowledge)? Comments on Schauer and Moore." *Southern California Law Review* 58 (1985): 441, 445.

Lewis, A. D. E., and David J. Ibbetson, eds. *The Roman Law Tradition*. Cambridge: Cambridge University Press, 1994.

Libson, Ayelet Hoffman. *Law and Self-Knowledge in the Talmud*. Cambridge: Cambridge University Press, 2018.

Lieberman, Saul. *Greek in Jewish Palestine; Hellenism in Jewish Palestine*. New York: Jewish Theological Seminary of America, 1941.

———. *Ha-Yerushalmi Ki-feshuto: Perush Meyusad 'al Kitve Yad shel Ha-Yerushalmi Ve-sifre Rabotenu Ha-rishonim U-midrashim*. 3rd ed. New York: Jewish Theological Seminary, 1934.

———. "Roman Legal Institutions in Early Rabbinics and in the Acta Martyrum." *Jewish Quarterly Review* 35:1 (1944): 1–57.

———. "*Talmudah shel Kisrin*: Yerushalmi Masekhet Nezikin." Supplement to *Tarbiz II 4*, (1931): 1–108.

———. *Tosefet Rishonim Perush Meyusad 'al Kitve Yad Ha-Tosefta Ve-sifre Rishonim U-midrashim Be-khitve Yad U-defusim Yeshanim*. Jerusalem: Mosad Ha-Rav Kook, 1939.

———. *Tosefta Ki-feshutah: Be'ur Arokh La-Tosefta*. Volumes 1–10. New York: Jewish Theological Seminary, 1955–1988.

Lind, Douglas. "The Pragmatic Value of Legal Fictions." In *Legal Fictions in Theory and Practice*, ed. Maksymilian Del Mar and William Twining, 83–112. New York: Springer International Publishing, 2015.

Lisista, Alona. "'Intent' and 'Thought' as Halakhic Concepts in Talmudic Literature." MA thesis, Jewish Theological Seminary, 2004.

Llewellyn, Karl N. "A Realistic Jurisprudence—The Next Step." *Columbia Law Review* 30 (1930): 431–65.

Lorberbaum, Menachem. "Theories of Action in the Halakhah: Intention In Mitzvot" (Hebrew), MA thesis, Hebrew University, 1988.

Lorberbaum, Yair. "Halakhic Realism." NYU Halakha and Reality Conference, Fall 2012.

———. *Tzelem Elohim: Halakhah Va-aggadah*. Jerusalem: Schocken, 2004.

Lorberbaum, Yair, and Haim Shapira. "Maimonides' Epistle on Martyrdom in Light of Legal Philosophy." *Diné Israel: Studies in Halakhah and Jewish Law* 25 (2008): 123–69.

Macuch, M. "On the Treatment of Animals in Zoroastrian Law." In *Iranica Selecta: Studies in Honour of Professor Wojciech Skalmowski on the Occasion of His Seventieth Birthday*, ed. A. van Tongerloo, 109–29. Silk Road Studies 8. Turnhout: Brepols, 2003.

Maine, Henry Sumner. *Ancient Law*. London: Oxford University Press, 1931.

Maloney, Robert P. "Usury in Greek, Roman and Rabbinic Thought." *Tradition* 27 (1971): 79–109.

Mandel, Paul. "'Al pataḥ ve-'al ha-petiḥa: 'iyun ḥadash." In *Higayon Le-Yonah*, 49–82. Jerusalem: Magnes Press, 2006.

Manuščihr. *Dādestān Ī Dēnīg*. Paris: Association pour l'avancement des études iraniennes, 1998.

Margolin, Ron. *Inner Religion: The Phenomenology of Inner Religious Life and Its Manifestation in Jewish Sources* (From the Bible to Hasidic Texts) (Hebrew). Ramat Gan: Bar Ilan University, 2011.

Mayer, Don. "Legal Loopholes, Business Ethics, and Corporate Legal Strategy: A Reply to Professor Ostas." *American Business Law Journal* 48:4 (Winter 2011): 713–63.

McGinn, T. A. J. "The 'SC' from Larinum and the Repression of Adultery at Rome." *Zeitschrift fuer Papyrologie und Epigraphik* 93 (1992): 273–95.

Melamed, Eliezer. *Laws of Shabbat*. Vol. 2, trans. Yocheved Cohen. Jerusalem: Maggid Books, 2015.

Mertz, Elizabeth, Stewart Macaulay, and Thomas Mitchell. *The New Legal Realism: Translating Law and Society for Today's Legal Practice*. Vols. 1 and 2. Cambridge: Cambridge University Press, 2016.

Michaels, W. B. "Against Formalism: The Autonomous Text in Legal and Literary Interpretation." *Poetics Today* 1 (1979): 23–34.

Milgrom, Jacob. *Leviticus 1–16: A New Translation with Introduction and Commentary*. 1st ed. Anchor Bible. Vol. 3. New York: Doubleday, 1991.

Minkovitz, Meir. "Ishah perusha u-tzevu'im she-domim le-perushim." *Ha-do'ar* 54 (1975): 136.

Moglen, Eben. "Legal Fictions and Common Law Legal Theory: Some Historical Reflections." *Tel-Aviv University Studies in Law* 10 (1990): 33–52.

Moran, W. L. "Some Considerations of Form and Interpretation in Atrahasis." In *Language, Literature, and History: Philological and Historical Studies Presented to Erica Reiner*, ed. F. Rochberg-Halton, 245–56. New Haven: American Oriental Society, 1987.

Moscovitz, Leib. "Legal Fictions in Rabbinic and Roman Law: Some Comparative Observations." In *Rabbinic Law in Its Roman and Ancient Near Eastern Context*, ed. Catherine Hezser, 105–32. Tübingen: Mohr Siebeck, 2003.

———. "Rabbinic Legal Fictions." In *Legal Fictions in Theory and Practice*, ed. Maksymilian Del Mar and William Twining, 334–36. Cham: Springer, 2015.

———. *Talmudic Reasoning: From Casuistics to Conceptualization*. Tübingen: Mohr Siebeck, 2002.

Naiweld, Ron. "L'anti-sujet: Le rapport entre l'individu et la loi dans la littérature rabbinique classique." PhD diss., l'École des hautes études en sciences sociales, 2009.

———. "Purity of Body, Purity of Self: 'Hirhur' in Rabbinic Literature." *Judaïsme ancien* 2 (2014): 209–35.

Neusner, Jacob. *Ancient Israel After Catastrophe: The Religious World View of the Mishnah*. Charlottesville: University Press of Virginia, 1983.

———. "Aristotle's Economics and the Mishnah's Economics: The Matter of Wealth and Usury." *Journal for the Study of Judaism* 21:1 (1990): 41–59.

———. *Eliezer Ben Hyrcanus: The Tradition and the Man*. Studies in Judaism in Late Antiquity v. 3–4 Leiden: Brill, 1973.

———. *A History of the Mishnaic Law of Purities*. Leiden: Brill, 1977.

———. *The Talmud of the Land of Israel: An Academic Commentary to the Second, Third, and Fourth Divisions*. Atlanta: Scholars Press, 1998.

Newton, Michael. *The Concept of Purity at Qumran and in the Letters of Paul*. SNTSMS 53. Cambridge: Cambridge University Press, 1985.

Noam, Vered. *From Qumran to the Rabbinic Revolution: Conceptions of Impurity* (Hebrew). Jerusalem: Yad Ben Zvi Press, 2010.

———. "Ritual Impurity in Tannaitic Literature: Two Opposing Perspectives." *Journal of Ancient Judaism* 1:2 (2010): 65–103.

———. "Traces of Sectarian Halakhah in the Rabbinic World." In *Rabbinic Perspectives: Rabbinic Literature and the Dead Sea Scrolls: Proceedings of the Eighth International Symposium of the Orion Center, 7–9 January 2003*. Studies on the Texts of the Desert of Judah. Vol. 62. Orion, Center for the Study of the Dead Sea Scrolls and Associated Literature, ed. Steven G. Fraade, Aharon Shemesh, and Ruth A. Clements, 67–85. Leiden: Brill, 2006.

Noegel, Scott B. "Sex, Sticks and the Trickster: A New Look at an Old Crux." *Journal of Ancient Near Eastern Society* 25 (1997): 7–17.

Nótári, Tamás. "*Summum Ius Summa Iniuria*—Comments on the Historical Background of a Legal Maxim of Interpretation." *Acta Juridica Hungarica* 42:1–2 (2004): 301–22.

Novick, Tzvi. "The Blemished First-Born Animal: A Case Study in Tannaitic Sources." *Hebrew Union College Annual* 76 (2005): 113–32.

———. "The *Borer* Court: New Interpretations of mSan 3." *Zutot* 5:1 (2008): 1–8.

———. "The 'For I Say' Presumption: A Study in Early Rabbinic Legal Rhetoric." *Journal of Jewish Studies* 61:1 (Spring 2010): 48–61.

———. "'They Come Against Them with the Power of the Torah': Rabbinic Reflections on Legal Fiction and Legal Agency." *Studies in Law, Politics and Society* 50 (2009): 1–17.

Olivier, Pierre J. J. *Legal Fictions in Practical and Legal Science.* Vol. 2. Rotterdam: Rotterdam University Press, 1975.

Ostas, Daniel T. "Legal Loopholes and Underenforced Laws: Examining the Ethical Dimensions of Corporate Legal Strategy." *American Business Law Journal* 46:4 (Winter 2009): 487–529.

Ottenjeim, Eric. "Impurity Between Intention and Deed." In *Purity and Holiness*, ed. M. J. H. M. Poorthius and J. Schwartz, 129–48. Leiden: Brill, 2000.

Panken, Aaron D. *The Rhetoric of Innovation: Self-conscious Legal Change in Rabbinic Literature.* New York: University Press of America, 2005.

Pepper, Stephen. "Lawyers' Amoral Ethical Role: A Defense, a Problem and Some Possibilities." *American Bar Foundation Research Journal* 11:4 (1986): 613–35.

Pound, Roscoe. "Common Law and Legislation." *Harvard Law Review* 21:6 (April 1908): 383–407.

———. *The Ideal Element of Law.* Ed. Stephen Presser. Indianapolis: Liberty Fund, 2002.

———. "The Scope and Purpose of Sociological Jurisprudence: I. Schools of Jurists and Methods of Jurisprudence." *Harvard Law Review* 24:8 (June 1911): 591–619.

Putnam, Ruth Anna. "Must We Mean What We Do?" *S'vara* 2:2 (1991): 52–60.

Quevedo, Steven M. "Formalist and Instrumentalist Legal Reasoning and Legal Theory." *California Law Review* 73:1 (January 1985): 119–57.

Rakover, Nahum, *Matarah Ha-mekadeshet et Ha-emtza'im.* Jerusalem: Office of the Judiciary, 2000.

———. "Violation of the Law in Order to Preserve It." Ed. B. S. Jackson and S. M. Passmaneck. *JLAS: The Jerusalem 1990 Conference Volume* 6 (1990): 107–23.

Ratner, Dov Baer. *Ahavat Tziyon Ve-Yerushalayim.* Jerusalem, 1966.

Raz, Joseph. "Legal Principles and the Limits of Law." *Yale Law Journal* 81 (1972): 823–54.

Reich, Ronny. "*Miqwa'ot* (Jewish Ritual Immersion Baths) in Eretz-Israel in the Second Temple and the Mishnah and Talmud Periods." PhD diss., Hebrew University, 1990.

Richardson, J. S. "The Roman Mind and the Power of Fiction." In *The Passionate Intellect: Essays on the Transformation of Classical Traditions Presented to Professor I. G. Kidd*, ed. L. Ayres, 117–30. Rutgers University Studies in Classical Humanities 7. New Brunswick: Transaction, 1995.

Riles, Annelise. *Rethinking the Masters of Comparative Law.* Portland: Hart Publishing, 2001.

Rodriguez-Pereyra, Gonzalo. "Nominalism in Metaphysics." In *The Stanford Encyclopedia of Philosophy*, ed. Edward N. Zalta. 2011. https://plato.stanford.edu/entries/nominalism-metaphysics/

Rose, Carol M. "Crystals and Mud in Property Law." *Stanford Law Review* 40 (1987–88): 577–610.
Rosen, Lawrence. *Law as Culture: An Invitation.* Princeton: Princeton University Press, 2006.
Rosen, Mark D. "Beyond Interpretation: The 'Cultural Approach' to Understanding Extra-Formal Change in Religious and Constitutional Law." *Journal of Law, Religion and State* 2:2 (2013): 200–233.
Rosen, Yisrael. "Ha'aramot hilkhatiot ke-takkanot tzibur." *Tehumin* 21 (2003): 209–22.
Rosenak, Avinoam. *Ha-halakhah Ke-meholelet Shinui: 'Iyunim Bikorti'im Ba-filosofiah shel Ha-halakhah.* Jerusalem: Magnes Press, 2009.
Rosenfeld, Michel. "Dworkin and the One Law Principle: A Pluralist Critique." *Revue International du Philosophie* 59:233 (2004): 363–92.
Rosenthal, Eliezer Shimshon. *Yerushalmi Nezikin.* Jerusalem: Hebrew University Press, 2008.
Rosenthal, Rachel Leigh. "Rebel with a Clause: Interpretation, Pedagogy, and the Problem of the Stubborn and Rebellious Son." PhD diss., Jewish Theological Seminary, 2019.
Rosen-Zvi, Ishay. "The Mishnaic Mental Revolution: A Reassessment," *Journal of Jewish Studies* 66:1 (Spring 2015): 36–58.
———. *The Mishnaic Sotah Ritual: Temple, Gender and Midrash.* Leiden: Brill, 2012.
———. "Orality, Narrative, Rhetoric: New Directions in Mishnah Research." *AJS Review* 32:2 (2008): 235–49.
———. "The Standing Woman: Hannah's Prayer in Rabbinic Exegesis." In *Jewish Culture in the Eye of the Storm, a Jubilee Book in Honor of Yosef Ahituv*, ed. N. Ilan and A. Sagi, 675–98. 'En Tzurim: Ha-kibbutz Ha-me'uhad and the Jacob Herzog Center, 2002.
Roth, Joel. *The Halakhic Process: A Systematic Approach.* New York: Jewish Theological Seminary, 1986.
Rotondi, Giovanni. *Gli Atti in Frode Alla Legge Nella Dottrina Romana E Nella Sua Evoluzione Posteriore.* Torino: Unione tipografico-editrice torinese, 1911.
Rubanovich, Julia, and Geoffrey Herman, eds. *Irano-Judaica: Studies Relating to Jewish Contacts with Persian Culture Throughout the Ages.* Vol. 7. Jerusalem: Ben-Zvi Institute for the Study of Jewish Communities in the East, 2019.
Rubenstein, Jeffrey L. *The Culture of the Babylonian Talmud.* Baltimore: Johns Hopkins University Press, 2003.
———. "Nominalism and Realism in Qumranic and Rabbinic Law: A Reassessment." *Dead Sea Discoveries* 6:2 (July 1999): 157–83.
Safrai, Shmuel. *Be-yeme Ha-bayit Ha-sheni U-ve-yeme Ha-Mishnah: Mehkarim Be-toldot Yisrael.* Jerusalem: Magnes Press, 1994.
Sagiv, Yonatan. ""Iyunim be-darkhei ha-midrash shel ha-tannaim 'al pi parshiot nivharot ba-Sifra." PhD diss., Hebrew University, 2008.
Saiman, Chaim. "Is Jewish Law Formalistic: A Survey of the Dispute and Why It Matters." In *Oxford Handbook of Jewish Law*, ed. Zev Eleff, Roberta Kwall, and Chaim Saiman. New York: Oxford University Press, forthcoming.
Sasson, Gilad. "She'elat ha-'anishah ha-kibutzit be-derashot amora'e Eretz Yisrael she-be-Bereshit Rabbah parshat 49." *Sidra* 29 (5774): 161–77.
Saydon, Vered. "A Syntactic, Semantic and Pragmatic Study of the Hebrew Verb xašav 'Think' and Other Related Verbs from Biblical Hebrew to Contemporary Hebrew." PhD diss., Tel Aviv University, 2012.

Schäfer, Peter. *The Jewish Jesus: How Judaism and Christianity Shaped Each Other.* Princeton: Princeton University Press, 2012.

Schäfer, Peter, and Catherine Hezser, eds. *The Talmud Yerushalmi and Graeco-Roman Culture.* Vols. 1–3. Tübingen: Mohr Siebeck, 1998–2002.

Schauer, Frederick. "Formalism." *Yale Law Journal* 97:4 (1988): 509–48.

———. "Legal Fictions Revisited." In *Legal Fictions in Theory and Practice*, ed. Maksymilian Del Mar and William Twining, 113–30. New York: Springer International Publishing, 2015.

Schlag, Pierre. "Formalism and Realism in Ruins (Mapping the Logics of Collapse)." *Iowa Law Review* 95 (2009): 195–244.

Schmidt, H. "Einfluss Der Rhetorik Auf Die Gestaltung Der Richeterlichen Entscheidung in Den Papyri." *Journal of Juristic Papyrology* 4 (1950): 165–77.

Schofer, Jonathan Wyn. "Self, Subject, and Chosen Subjection: Rabbinic Ethics and Comparative Possibilities." *Journal of Religious Ethics* 33:2 (June 2005): 255–91.

Schremer, Adiel. "The Christianization of the Roman Empire and Rabbinic Literature." In *Jewish Identities in Antiquity: Studies in Memory of Menahem Stern*, ed. Lee Levine et al. Tübingen: Mohr Siebeck, 2009.

Schulz, Fritz. *History of Roman Legal Science.* London: Oxford University Press, 1946.

———. *Principles of Roman Law.* Oxford: Clarendon Press, 1936.

Schwartz, Daniel. "Law and Truth: On Qumran-Sadducean and Rabbinic Views of Law." In *The Dead Sea Scrolls: Forty Years of Research*, ed. D. Dimant and U. Rappaport, 229–40. Leiden: Brill, 1992.

Schwartz, Seth. *Imperialism and Jewish Society, 200 B.C.E. to 640 C.E.* Princeton: Princeton University Press, 2001.

Scott, S. P. *The Civil Law II.* Cincinnati: Central Trust Company, 1932.

Secunda, Shai. *The Iranian Talmud: Reading the Bavli in Its Sassanian Context.* Philadelphia: University of Pennsylvania Press, 2014.

Segal, Eliezer. *Holidays, History, and Halakhah.* Northvale, NJ: Aronson, 2001.

Seligman, Adam B. "Ritual, the Self, and Sincerity." *Social Research* 76:4 (Winter 2009): 1073–1106.

Shaked, Shaul. "Religious Actions Evaluated by Intention: Zoroastrian Concepts Shared with Judaism." In *Shoshannat Yaakov: Jewish and Iranian Studies in Honor of Yaakov Elman*, ed. Shai Secunda and Steven Fine, 403–14. Brill Reference Library of Judaism, vol. 35. Leiden: Brill, 2012.

Shaked, Shaul, and Amnon Netzer, eds. *Irano-Judaica: Studies Relating to Jewish Contacts with Persian Culture Throughout the Ages.* Vols. 5–6. Jerusalem: Ben-Zvi Institute for the Study of Jewish Communities in the East, 2008.

Shakespeare, William. *The Merchant of Venice.* Ed. John Russell Brown. London: Methuen, 1969.

Shemesh, Aharon. *Halakhah in the Making: The Development of Jewish Law from Qumran to the Rabbis.* Taubman Lectures in Jewish Studies. Berkeley: University of California Press, 2009.

———. "Shogeg karov le-mezid." *Hebrew University Annual* 20 (1995): 342–99.

Shilo, Shmuel. "Circumvention of the Law in Talmudic Literature." *Israel Law Review* 17:2 (1982): 151–68.

———. "Evasion of the Law in the Talmud." In *Authority, Process and Method: Studies in Jewish Law*, ed. Hanina Ben-Menahem and Neil S. Hecht, 171–229. Amsterdam: Harwood Academic Publishers, 1998.

Shweka, Aharon. "Studies in the *Halakhot Gedolot*: Text and Redaction." PhD diss., Hebrew University, 2008.
Silberg, Moshe. *Kakh Darko shel Talmud (Principia Talmudica)*. Jerusalem: Mifʻal ha-shikhpul, 1961.
———. "The Order of Holy Things as a Legal Entity." *Sinai* 52 (1962): 8–18.
Silman, Y. "Halakhic Determinations of a Nominalistic and Realistic Nature: Legal and Philosophical Considerations." *Diné Israel: Studies in Halakhah and Jewish Law* 12 (May 1984): 249–66.
Sinai, Yuval. *The Judge and the Judicial Process in Jewish Law* (Hebrew). Jerusalem: Hebrew University, 2010.
Sokoloff, Michael. *A Dictionary of Jewish Babylonian Aramaic of the Talmudic and Geonic Periods*. Ramat Gan: Bar Ilan University Press, 2002.
———. *A Dictionary of Jewish Palestinian Aramaic of the Byzantine Period*. Dictionaries of the Talmud, Midrash and Targum 2. Ramat Gan: Bar Ilan University Press, 1990.
Soloveitchik, Joseph B. *Shiure Ha-Rav: A Conspectus of the Public Lectures of Rabbi Joseph B. Soloveitchik*. Ed. Joseph Epstein. Hoboken, NJ: Ktav, 1974.
Spade, Paul Vincent, and Claud Panaccio. "William of Ockham." In *The Stanford Encyclopedia of Philosophy*, ed. Edward N. Zalta. 2011. https://plato.stanford.edu/entries/ockham/
Statman, Daniel. "Halakha and Morality: A Few Methodological Considerations." *Journal for the Society of Textual Reasoning* 6:1 (December 2010). https://jtr.shanti.virginia.edu/volume-6-number-1/a-reply/
Stein, Elana. "Rabbinic Legal Loopholes: Formalism, Equity and Subjectivity." PhD diss., Columbia University, 2014.
Stein, Peter. *The Character and Influence of the Roman Civil Law: Historical Essays*. London: Hambledon Press, 1988.
Stein Hain, Elana. "Secular Legal Paradigms and Talmudic Law: Rav Tsaʾir on Legal Loopholes." In *Swimming Against the Current: Reimagining Jewish Tradition in the Twenty-First Century*, ed. Shaul Seidler-Feller and David N. Myers, 94–113. Brookline, MA: Academic Studies Press, 2020.
Stern, David. "*Imitatio Hominis*: Anthropomorphism and the Character(s) of God in Rabbinic Literature." *Prooftexts* 12 (1992): 151–74.
Stern, Sacha. *Time and Process in Ancient Judaism*. Oxford: Littman Library of Jewish Civilization, 2003.
Stertz, Stephen A. "Appendix: Roman Legal Codification in the Second Century." In *The Mishnah in Contemporary Perspective: Part I*, ed. Alan J. Avery-Peck and Jacob Neusner. Leiden: Brill, 2002.
Stone, Suzanne Last. "Halakha and Legal Theory." *Journal of the Society for Textual Reasoning* 6:1 (December 2010). https://jtr.shanti.virginia.edu/volume-6-number-1/halakha-and-legal-theory/
———. "In Pursuit of the Counter-Text: The Turn to the Jewish Legal Model in Contemporary American Legal Theory." *Harvard Law Review* 106 (1993): 813–94.
Strauch Schick, Shana. *Intention in Talmudic Law: Between Thought and Deed*. Boston: Brill, 2021.
Stroux, Johannes. "*Summum Ius Summa Iniuria*—Ein Kapitel in Der Geschichte Der Interpretatio Iuris" (A Chapter in the History of Legal Interpretation). In *Roemische Rechtswissenschaft und Rhetorik*, 7–66. Potsdam: Stichnote, 1949.

Sussman, Ya'akov. "Babylonian Sugyot for Zerai'm and Tohorot (Hebrew)." PhD diss., Hebrew University, 1969.
———. *Talmudic Reasoning: From Casuistics to Conceptualization*. Tübingen: Mohr Siebeck, 2002.
———. *Tamid: The Oldest Treatise of the Mishnah*. Cincinnati: Ark, 1919.
———. "Ve-shuv le-Yerushalmi Nezikin." *Mehkarei Talmud* 1 (1990): 55–133.
"Synegoros." In *Brill's New Pauly*, ed. Hubert Cancik and Helmuth Schneider. Trans. Christine F. Salazar and Francis G. Gentry. 2005. https://referenceworks.brillonline.com/entries/brill-s-new-pauly/synegoros-e1127120
Tacitus, Cornelius. *The Annals*. Trans. John Jackson. Cambridge, MA: Harvard University Press; London: W. Heinemann, 1962–69.
Tamanaha, Brian Z. "Legal Realism in Context." In *The New Legal Realism: Translating Law and Society for Today's Legal Practice*. Vols. 1 and 2, eds. Elizabeth Mertz, Stewart Macaulay, and Thomas W. Mitchell, 147–168. Cambridge: Cambridge University Press, 2016.
Tchernowitz, Haim. *Be-sha'are Tziyon: Kovetz Ma'amarim Be-'Inyane Eretz Yisrael Ve-hatziyonut*. New York: Schulsinger Bros., 1936.
———. *Masekhet Zikhronot: Partzufim Ve-ha'arakhot*. New York: Va'ad ha-Yovel, 1945.
———. *Toldot Ha-halakhah: Kolel Shalshelet Ha-kabalah Ve-hitpathut Ha-Torah She-be'al Peh, Mi-tokh Shorashehah Ve-mekorotehah Mi-reshitah 'ad Ḥatimat Ha-Talmud*. New York: n.p., 1934–50.
Thomas, Yan. "Fictio legis: L'empire de la fiction romaine." *Droits: Revue française de théorie juridique* 21 (1995): 17–63.
Tur-Sinai, Naphtali H., ed. *Encyclopedia Mikra'it*. Vol. 3. Jerusalem: Bialik Institute, 1950–88.
Urbach, Ephraim Elimelech. "*Derashah* as the Foundation of *Halakhah*, and the Problem of the Scribes," *Tarbiz* 27:2–3 (1958): 166–82.
———. *The Halakhah: Its Sources and Development*. Trans. Raphael Posner. Jerusalem: Yad le-Talmud, 1986.
———. *The Sages, Their Concepts and Beliefs*. Jerusalem: Magnes Press, 1975.
Vaughn, John W. "Law and Rhetoric in the *Causa Curiana*." *Classical Antiquity* 4:2 (October 1985): 208–22.
Von Savigny, Friedrich Carl. *Of the Vocation of Our Age for Legislation and Jurisprudence*. Trans. Abraham Hayward. London: Littlewood & Co., 1831.
Waisanen, Don, Hershey H. Friedman, and Linda Weiser Friedman. "What's So Funny About Arguing with God? A Case for Playful Argumentation from Jewish Literature." *Argumentation* 29 (2015): 57–80.
Walfish, Avraham. "Megamot ra'ayoniot be-te'ur ha-Mikdash va-'avodato be-masekhet Tamid u-ve-masekhet Middot." *Mehkere Yehudah Ve-Shomron* 7 (1997): 79–92.
———. "Shitat ha-'arikhah ha-sifrutit ba-Mishnah 'al pi masekhet Rosh Ha-shanah." PhD diss., Hebrew University, 2001.
Watson, Alan. *Failures of the Legal Imagination*. Philadelphia: University of Pennsylvania Press, 1988.
———. *The Spirit of Roman Law*. Athens: University of Georgia Press, 1995.
Weinrib, Ernest. "Legal Formalism: On the Immanent Rationality of Law." *Yale Law Journal* 97 (May 1988): 949–1016.
Weisberg, Dvora. "Desirable but Dangerous: Rabbis' Daughters in the Babylonian Talmud." *Hebrew Union College Annual* 75 (2004): 121–61.

Weiss, Dov. *Pious Irreverence: Confronting God in Rabbinic Tradition*. Philadelphia: University of Pennsylvania Press, 2016.

Weissberg, Elyakim. "The Writing of the Names Rabbah and Rava: Rav Hai Gaon's Perspective and Conflicting Opinions (Hebrew)." *Meḥkarim Be-lashon* 5–6 (1992): 181–214.

Wendel, W. Bradley. *Lawyers and Fidelity to Law*. Princeton: Princeton University Press, 2010.

Wenger, Leopold. *Institutes of the Roman Law of Civil Procedure*. Rev. ed. New York: Veritas Press, 1940.

Westbrook, Raymond. "Good as His Word: Jacob Manipulates Justice." *Biblical Archaeology Review* 35:3 (2009): 50–55, 64.

———. *A History of Ancient Near Eastern Law*. Handbook of Oriental Studies. Vol. 72. Leiden: Brill, 2003.

Westrup, Carl Wium. *Introduction to Early Roman Law: Comparative Sociological Studies, the Patriarchal Joint Family*. Vol. 3. Copenhagen: Levin & Munksgaard, 1934.

Wong, Jane. "The Anti-Essentialism v. Essentialism Debate in Feminist Legal Theory: The Debate and Beyond." *William and Mary Journal of Women and the Law* 5:2:2 (1999): 273–96.

Yadin-Israel, Azzan. "The Chain Novel and the Problem of Self-Undermining Interpretation." *Diné Israel: Studies in Halakhah and Jewish Law* 25 (2008): 43–71.

Zeitlin, Solomon. "The Need for a New Code." *Jewish Quarterly Review*, n.s., 52:3 (January 1962): 203–15.

———. "Prosbol: A Study in Tannaitic Jurisprudence." *Jewish Quarterly Review*, n.s., 37:4 (April 1947): 341–62.

———. "Studies in Tannaitic Jurisprudence: Intention as a Legal Principle." *Journal of Law and Philosophy* 1 (1919): 297–311.

Zellentin, Holger M. *Rabbinic Parodies of Jewish and Christian Literature*. Tübingen: Mohr Siebeck, 2011.

Zimmerman, Reinhard. *The Law of Obligations: Roman Foundations of the Civilian Tradition*. New York: Oxford University Press, 1996.

Zohar, Noam. "Developing a Halakhic Theory as a Necessary Basis for a Philosophy of the Halakhah (Hebrew)." In *New Streams in Philosophy of Halakhah*, ed. Aviezer Ravitzky and Avinoam Rosenak, 43–64. Jerusalem: Magnes Press and Van Leer Institute, 2008.

Zuri, Jacob Samuel. "Legal Equivalence in Jewish Law" (Hebrew). In *Festschrift in Honor of Dr. B. M. Lewin*, ed. Y. L. Fishman, 174–95. Jerusalem: Mosad Ha-Rav Kook, 1939.

Index

Abraham, 130–131, 140, 193n79
actio Serviana, 53–54
adjudication, 109–110, 113, 116–117, 132
  fraus legi and, 22, 57
aggadic rabbinic discussion, 62–63, 123
Aha, R., 163n44
  on Divine loopholes, 131
  on food preparation, 42, 184n75
  on loan fraud, 43
Akiva, R., 48, 155n54, 157n81, 159n8
Alter, Robert, 10–11
Amihay, Aryeh, 174n34
Ando, Clifford, 54
Aristotle, 57–58, 117
Asher, Jacob ben, 20
Ashi, R., 80, 102–106, 163n40, 187n90
Asi, R., 93, 195n21
Atlas, Samuel, 67, 70
Augustus, 56
avoidance, 1, 20, 26–27, 36, 153n49. *See also* avoison; evasion; *ha'aramah*
  ha'aramah as, 9, 10, 16, 31, 34, 79
  in the *Yerushalmi*, 40, 43, 51
avoison, 1. *See also* avoidance; evasion; *ha'aramah*
  ha'aramah as, 26–30, 36
  in the *Yerushalmi*, 31–32, 40, 43–44, 51
Avun, R., 39

Balberg, Mira, 24, 75–77, 175n35
Bavli, 78–106
  coerced consent in, 88–89, 179n31
  contrasted with *Yerushalmi* texts, 79, 112, 145–146
  deception in, 92–94
  'eruv tavshilin and, 141–142
  filtering of wine in, 80–82

food preparation in, 86–88
future adherence to law and, 102, 104–105, 112
gift of Bet Horon and, 82–85
ha'aramah in, 78–82, 85, 90–95, 97–99, 101–106, 112, 142, 145–146, 163n32, 176n2, 176n5, 177n6
livestock handling in, 90
loopholes in, 185n78
Passover dough in, 90–92
protest-affirming theology and, 129
realism in, 99–100
"sincere self" in, 78
subjective intent and, 78, 80, 82, 85–86, 88–90, 95–97, 105
tatzdeke/tatzreke in, 98–99
tithing in, 39, 47–49, 109, 145, 180n34
Zoroastrianism and, 95–97, 106
beer-brewing, 81–82
bekhor behemah tehorah, 17–20, 36, 152n34, 153n36, 153n39, 153n49, 154n50
  ma'aser sheni and, 188n9
ben sorer u-moreh (wayward son), killing of, 50, 165n70, 166n71
Bet Horon, gift of, 82–85, 145, 178nn18–19
biblical exegesis, 4–5, 147n3
biblical law
  animal sacrifice and, 17
  contrasted with rabbinical law, 50, 138, 158n86, 186n83
  debts and, 136
  'eruv and, 138–139
  ha'aramah and, 138, 186n83
  livestock handling and, 28
  marriage and, 38
  takkanot and, 135–136
  tithes and, 12, 109
Brodsky, David, 97

Index

Causa Curiana, 55
Celsus, 57, 168n24
Christianity, 95, 106
   intention and, 78
   Jewish-Christian relations, 95
   ritual purity and, 24
   sinful thoughts and, 97
   understanding of self in, 72, 97
Cicero, 55–56
circumvention, 6–9, 36, 65, 135, 144, 152n31. *See also* financial circumvention; *ha'aramah*
   altruistic, 170n42
   in the *Bavli*, 79, 97–99, 101, 105
   as deceit, 164n60
   destructive potential of, 130–131
   'eruv as, 140
   festival observance and, 42, 81–82, 86, 176n3
   fraudem legis and, 22
   gift of Bet Horon and, 84, 179n24
   goals of, 36
   ha'aramah as, 7–8, 11, 17–18, 29–30, 31, 36, 79, 105, 135, 152n31, 161n22, 186n83
   hametz and, 3, 142–143
   human-Divine relationship and, 123, 129, 132
   legal fiction and, 6
   loans and, 137
   ma'aser sheni and, 14
   marriage and, 38, 51, 167n8, 177n14
   performative intent and, 76
   prosbul and, 137
   ritual purity and, 24
   Roman concepts, 53–54, 56–57, 168n28
   Roman vs. rabbinic concepts of, 53, 63–64, 170n44
   Sabbath restrictions and, 27
   salting of meat and, 42, 185n76
   temporary betrothal and, 38–39, 167n8
   tithing and, 39–40, 47–49
   in *toseftan* cases, 158n86
   in the *Yerushalmi*, 51, 177n14
Cohen, Boaz, 60, 169n30
consent, coerced, 88–89, 106, 179nn30–31
conversion, 54
cunning rogues (*rasha 'arum*), 20–21, 145–146, 155n54, 186n86
   hametz foods and, 197n41
   trickiness, 181n46

Daube, David, 170n42
De Officiis (*On Duties*), 55–56
Digest (Justinian), 21–22, 166n3, 168n28
divorce, 44, 88–89, 92–93, 100–101, 123–125, 145, 179n30, 186n86. *See also* marriage
Dworkin, Ronald, 116–119, 132

Elazar, R., 6, 39
Eliezer, R.
   on animal handling, 29, 35, 66, 159n92
   on "cunning rogues," 21, 44
   on intention, 173n22
   on marriage settlements, 44, 164n50
   on Passover dough, 32–34, 90–92, 105–106, 159n8
Elman, Yaakov, 95
Epstein, J. N., 99
equity, 57–59, 109, 117, 137
'eruv, 3, 139–140, 194nn11–12, 195n17, 195nn21–23, 196n34
'eruv tavshilin, 41, 61, 104–105, 136, 140–142, 163n45
   Sabbath restrictions and, 41, 61, 104–105, 136, 140–142, 163n45, 196nn34–35
evasion, 9–10, 51. *See also* avoidance; avoison; *ha'aramah*
   in the *Bavli*, 98–99
   festival observance and, 146, 456–457
   ha'aramah as, 11, 22–26, 31, 34, 44, 46
   rasha 'arum and, 21
   of ritual obligations, 98–99
   takkanah and, 152n30
Exodus Rabbah, 123–131

festivals, 163n44, 176n3. *See also* food preparation on festival days; Sabbath restrictions
   animal handling on festival days, 28–29, 34–37, 65–67, 157n78, 158n59, 164nn59–60, 176n3
   food preparation and. *See* food preparation on festival days
   ha'aramah and, 35–37, 40–42, 45–46, 51, 65–66, 76–77, 80–82, 101–102, 118, 135–136, 145–146, 164n60, 173n17, 176n3, 177n8, 177n14, 184nn74–75, 186n85, 196n35
   house fires on festival days, 26–27
   inner self and, 76
   intent and, 71, 77, 173n18

ritual purity and, 102, 145, 177n14, 184n74
shevut and, 161n16
sin offerings and, 35, 161nn15–16
working during *ḥol ha-mo'ed*, 45, 47, 51, 81, 146, 157n78, 160n11, 164n58, 164n60
fiction, 99–100, 148n15, 148nn7–8. See also legal fictions
ha'aramah and, 8, 64, 65, 108–110
fideicommissum, 56
filtering of wine, 80–82
financial circumvention, 11–12, 18, 26, 31, 36, 49, 157n68
load fraud and, 43
making profit and, 11, 26, 30, 118–120
saving money and, 11–21, 28, 36–37, 143, 152n30
Fonrobert, Charlotte, 140
food preparation on festival days, 40–43, 51, 86–88, 91–92, 102, 158n87, 160n9, 163nn44–45, 180n36, 196n32. See also *'eruv tavshilin*
dough preparation and, 160n9
Sabbath and, 32–33, 36, 41–42, 51, 61, 105, 135, 140–142, 157nn78–79, 161n16, 163n45, 196n27, 196n31, 196n35
salting of meat and, 42, 102, 163n45, 173n18, 184n75
straining of wine, 80–82, 177n10
Fox, Michael V., 11
fraudem legis, 22, 30, 57
fraus legi, 57–60, 63
adjudication and, 22, 57
application of, 168n28
attempts to outlaw, 168n27
Friedman, Shamma, 159n8, 160n13

Gamliel, R., 5–6
Genesis, 10, 131
Genesis *Rabbah*, 129–131, 154n53, 193n79
Gilat, Yitzhak, 100
Gilgamesh, Epic of, 1–2
God, 123–129
fertility and, 124–125
as Judge, 62–64, 130–131
loopholes and, 4, 110, 127, 130–131
love language and, 65
morality and, 50
relationship with Jewish people, 122–123, 126–129, 132
golden calf, sin of, 127–129

gomer be-libo, 86, 94, 106
Greek legal conventions, 57–58, 137
Grey, Thomas C., 113

ha'aramah, 7–9, 30, 31, 69, 132–133. See also circumvention; loopholes
as avoidance, 9, 10, 16, 31, 34, 79
as avoision, 26–30, 36
in the *Bavli*, 78–82, 85, 90–95, 97–99, 101–106, 112, 142, 145–146, 163n32, 176n2, 176n5, 177n6
beer-brewing and, 81–82
biblical justification for, 39–40
biblical roots of term, 10–11
as circumvention, 7–8, 11, 17–18, 29–30, 31, 36, 79, 105, 135, 152n31, 161n22, 186n83
condemnation of, 20–21
contrasted with *fraus legi*, 59–60, 63–64
contrasted with purposeful transgression, 187n90
contrasted with *takkanah/takkanot*, 8, 16, 61–62, 136
contrasting *Yerushalmi* and *Bavli* texts, 100–101, 112, 180n33
crop planting and, 164n60
cunning rogues and, 20–21, 145–146, 155n54
as deceit, 92–94, 164n60
decline in observance and, 101, 104–106
destructive potential of, 130–131
developing parameters of, 32–38
'eruv tavshilin and, 105, 140–142, 163n45, 187n
as evasion, 11, 22–26, 31, 34, 44, 46
festivals and, 35–37, 40–42, 45–46, 51, 65–66, 76–77, 80–82, 101–102, 118, 135–136, 145–146, 164n60, 173n17, 176n3, 177n8, 177n14, 184nn74–75, 186n85, 196n35
filtering of wine and, 80–82
financial loss and, 37–38
firstborn animals (*bekhor behemah teḥorah*) and, 17–20, 36, 152n34, 153n49
food preparation and, 40–43, 61, 86–88, 102, 120
as historical jurisprudence, 107–108
ḥol ha-mo'ed and, 45, 47, 51, 81, 146, 157n78, 164n58, 164n60
house fires and, 26–28, 158nn84–85

ha'aramah (continued)
  intention and, 7, 22, 24, 60, 65–68, 69–77, 80, 92, 94–95, 103, 173n18, 173n22, 177
  labor restrictions and, 45–47
  lamenting of, 47–49
  legal fiction and, 64, 65, 108–110, 132
  legal flexibility vs. rigidity, 120–123, 132
  legal formalism vs. realism, 112, 116, 132
  legal integrity and, 118–120
  livestock handling and, 28–30, 34–36, 65–67, 70, 90, 161n17, 174n22, 176n3
  loan fraud and, 43
  logic of, 192n72
  as lying, 92, 94, 164nn60–61
  mar'it 'ayin and, 68–69
  marriage and, 39, 162nn25–26, 177n14
  in the *Mishnah*, 12–21, 155n55, 157n68
  misuse of, 43–49
  obviousness and, 82, 142, 163n32, 178n23
  ownership and, 122
  Passover dough and, 34–35, 90–92, 105–106
  performance and, 69–73
  performative intention and, 70, 73, 76, 79–82, 105
  prosbul and, 136–138
  protest and, 129–130, 132, 193n76
  for rabbinical scholars, 102–105
  redeeming of tithes (*ma'aser sheni*) and, 12–17, 70–71, 109, 121, 191n52
  restrictions on labor and, 45–47
  ritual impurity and, 22–24, 73–76, 145, 161n22
  in Roman context, 21–22, 167n5
  Sabbath restrictions and, 26, 176n4
  salting of meat and, 42, 102, 173n18, 184n75, 185n76
  selling of *ḥametz* foods and, 2–3, 7, 34–35, 142–143, 146, 160n13, 164n53, 196n39, 197n41
  setting aside of dough and, 32–34
  sin and, 35, 37, 79
  subjective intent and, 66–67, 74, 80–82, 85–86, 94, 97, 106
  takkanah/takkanot and, 8, 16, 61–62, 135–144
  Talmudic reasons for rejection or acceptance of, 35–36
  tatzdeke/tatzreke and, 98–99
  temporary betrothal and, 38–39
  in the *Tosefta*, 13–14, 16, 22–30, 34, 71, 102, 158n85
  translations of, 9
  usury and, 25–26
  in the *Yerushalmi*, 31–33, 38–49, 51–52, 79, 145–146, 161n22, 191n52
Halivni, David Weiss, 155n54, 160n13
ḥallah, 33, 90–92, 120, 146, 159n8, 180n37
ḥametz foods, selling of, 2–3, 7, 34–35, 142–143, 146, 160n13, 164n53, 196n39, 197n44
  cunning and, 197n41
Hayes, Christine, 99, 101
Henshke, David, 140–141
Heter 'iska, 12
Hidary, Richard, 62–63
Higger, Michael, 173n23
Hillel, 136–137, 163n44, 173n22, 193n4
Hisda, R., 86–87, 91, 180n36
ḥishev, 67
ho'il, 91, 96, 180n37
ḥol ha-mo'ed, 45, 47, 51, 81, 146, 157n78, 160n11, 164n58, 164n60
Holmes, Oliver Wendell, 115
ḥomesh, 109, 150n14
homiletic rabbinic discussion, 62–63, 123
Hoshaya, R., 48–49, 180n34
house fires, 26–28, 149n19, 157n79
Huna, R., 80, 106, 186n86

Idi, R., 35–36, 124
immigration law, 111
infertility, 123–125, 129
inner self concept, 76, 175n35
intention, 65–67, 69–77, 105–106, 173n23. *See also* performative intention; subjective intention
  in the *Bavli*, 79–82, 88–91, 95, 97, 101, 105
  consent and, 88–89, 179n31
  fraus legi and, 57
  gift of Bet Horon and, 84–85, 179n24
  ha'aramah and, 7, 22, 24, 60, 65–68, 71, 73–74, 76–77, 80, 92, 94–95, 103, 173n18, 173n22, 177
  kavvanah as, 67, 70–71, 76, 181n49
  loopholes and, 61
  maḥshavah and, 67, 71, 75
  in the *Mishnah*, 71–72
  performative. *See* performative intention
  prosbul and, 194n10

prosecution for, 183n58
purpose and, 173n23
ritualization of, 69–71, 77, 78, 81, 173n20, 184n75
ritual purity and, 24, 76
Roman legal conventions and, 54–55, 58–60, 63
Sabbath restrictions and, 27, 67, 71, 76–77, 181n49
sin and, 67, 95, 97
subjective. *See* subjective intention
in *tannatic* period, 175n39
Zoroastrianism and, 95, 99
interposita persona, use of, 16, 55, 66, 81–82, 167n8, 179n24

judges, 62, 114–119, 155n54, 171n49, 171n52
God as judge, 62–64, 130–131
loopholes and, 120–121
prosbul and, 137
Riggs vs. Palmer and, 117–118
Roman jurists, 22, 57
Julian, 168n28
Justinian, 21–22, 166n3. *See also Digest*

Kahana bar R. Hiyya bar Ba, R., 41, 155n54, 163n40
karmelit, 195n15
Katina, R., 98–99, 183n59
Katz, Leo, 110–111, 188nn11–12
kavvanah, 67, 70–71, 76, 181n49
Kensky, Meira, 62–63
kinunya, 145
Kohut, Alexander, 99
Korban ha-'edah, 162nn25–26, 164n60

labor restrictions, 45–47
Langdell, Christopher Columbus, 113
lawyers, 111–112, 114, 171n49, 171n57
biblical characters as, 62–63
loopholes and, 188n12
rabbis as, 62–64, 65
legal essentialism, 174n34
legal fictions, 5–7, 99, 108–109, 148n8, 183n64
evolution of, 184n66
ha'aramah and, 64, 65, 108–110, 132
legal formalism and, 6
loopholes and, 6–7, 108
in Roman law, 53–54
legal flexibility, 120–123

legal formalism, 6, 112–116, 132, 137, 189n24
contrasted with essentialism, 174n34
contrasted with instrumentalism, 190n37
contrasted with realism, 114–115
halakhah and, 190n40
"presumptive formalism," 189n27
legal realism, 108, 112, 114–115, 174n34
legal values, 49–51
letter vs. spirit of the law, 8, 57–61, 167n5, 168n24, 169n30, 174n34. *See also fraus legi*
animal handling and, 37
ha'aramah and, 65, 108
Levinson, Joshua, 76–77, 175n39
Libson, Ayelet Hoffman, 182n50
Lieberman, Saul, 157n72, 158n83, 160n13, 162n30, 177n14
livestock handling, 28–30, 34–36, 65–67, 70, 90, 158n89, 161n17, 172n7, 172n9
ha'aramah and, 28–30, 34–36, 65–67, 70, 90, 161n17, 174n22, 176n3
intent and, 173n22
New Testament parallels, 159n92
Llewellyn, Karl, 114–115
loan fraud, 43, 168n24
loopholes, 1–4, 110–111. *See also ha'aramah*
animal feeding and, 165n67
author's experience of, 2–3
in the *Bavli*, 185n78
in differing Talmuds, 79
divorce law and, 123–125
failure to close, 47–49
fraudem legis and, 57
in Gilgamesh, 1–2
God and, 4, 110, 127, 130–131
ha'aramah as, 70–71, 108, 111
Katz on, 188nn11–12
lawyers and, 111–112
legal fiction and, 6–7, 108
legal formalism and, 6
Roman and rabbinic cultures contrasted, 60–63
in Roman legal traditions, 22, 53–60
in Shakespeare, 2
sin of the golden calf and, 127–129
temporary betrothal, 38–39, 167n8

ma'arim, 15, 152n34, 177n12
ma'aserot, 47–48

ma'aser sheni, 12–17, 36, 40, 66, 70–71, 109, 121, 151n22, 151n28, 191n52
   bekhor and, 188n9
   ḥomesh and, 109, 150n14
maḥshavah, 67, 71, 75
Maimonides, 150n15, 151n22, 152n31, 178n22, 179n30, 196n34
Mana, R., 44
manumissions, 56, 167n12, 170n42
mar'it 'ayin, 68–69, 172n13, 173n16
marriage, 101, 162n23. *See also* divorce
   fraus legi and, 168n28
   ha'aramah and, 39, 162nn25–26, 177n14
   legal fiction and, 5
   levirate marriage, 38–39, 162nn26–27, 163n31, 177n14
   marriage settlements, 44, 93–94, 164nn50–52
   nikhse melug and, 181n40
   rasha 'arum and, 186n86
   R. Tarfon and, 38–39, 146, 162n27, 162n30, 167n8, 177n14
   temporary betrothal, 38–39, 167n8
mBekhorot, 19–20, 154n50
Mekhilta d'R. Yishmael, 152n34
Merchant of Venice (Shakespeare), 2
mezimmah, 152n34
midrashim, 62–63, 123–129, 152n34, 192n64, 192n70
   aggadic, 123–127
   amoraic, 130–131
   ha'aramah and, 131, 133, 163n35
   legal, 161n18, 193n73
   Palestinian, 182n50
mirmah, 151n24, 152n31
Mishnah, 12–21, 30, 150n19, 163n40
   condemnation of cunning in, 20–21
   contrasted with *Tosefta*, 154n50, 156n59, 158n85, 160n13
   firstborn animals (*bekhor behemah tehorah*) and, 17–20, 153n49, 154n50
   gifts of food and, 83
   ha'aramah and, 157n68
   intention and, 71–72
   redeeming of tithes (*ma'aser sheni*) and, 12–17
   sexuality and, 154n53
   understanding of self in, 72
Moglen, Eben, 109
Moscovitz, Leib, 5

Moses, 126–129, 192n68, 192n71, 193n73, 194n12
muktzeh, 28–29, 68

Naiweld, Ron, 97
New Testament, 159n92, 175n35
Noam, Vered, 24
nominalism, 99–100, 174n34
Novick, Tzvi, 99, 154n50
Numbers *Rabbah*, 127–129

ormah, 10–11, 149n2, 150n7, 154n53, 178n20

Palmer, Elmer, 117–118
Passover, 160n11
   hametz foods and, 2–3, 7, 34–35, 142–143, 146, 160n13, 164n53, 196n39, 197n41, 197n44
   loopholing and, 2–3
   setting aside of dough and, 32–34, 90–92, 105–106, 159n8, 180n37
Paul (Roman Jurist), 57
Pene Moshe, 162n27, 164n60, 165n67
performative intention, 70, 73, 76, 79–82, 92, 105, 177n12
   subjective intention and, 80–82, 88, 90, 105, 173n22
pike'aḥ/pikahat, 149n19
prosbul, 3, 135–138, 144, 193n4, 193n7, 194n10
Protagoras, 169n30
protest theology, 129–130, 132, 193n76
Proverbs, 10–11, 30, 149n2, 150n7, 151n24, 154n53

Quintilian, 58–59

Rabbah (b. R. Huna), 80, 86, 91–92, 179n25
Rabbah (text), 123–131
   Exodus, 126–127, 192n71
   Genesis, 129–131, 154n53, 193nn79–80
   Numbers, 127–129
   Song of Songs, 123–125
rabbinical scholars
   ha'aramah and, 102–105
rabbinic law
   circumvention and, 8, 103, 144, 150n86, 186n83
   contrasted with biblical law, 138, 141, 158n16
   'eruv and, 138, 141
   ha'aramah and, 7–8, 22, 103, 116, 141

intention and, 183n58
prosbul and, 136
rabbinical lawyering, 171n57
realism vs. formalism in, 116, 174n34, 190n40
tithing and, 47, 150n15
rama'in (tricksters), 15, 145, 149n19
Rami b. Hama, 91–92
rasha 'arum, 20–21, 146, 155n54, 186n86
Rashba, 165n67, 178n20
Rashi, 155n54, 160n13, 173n17, 177n10, 177n12, 183n60, 184n75, 187n90
Rav, 5, 42, 97
Rava, 89, 93–94, 98, 102, 181n43
  gift of Bet Horon and, 84–85, 178n19
  on Passover dough, 91
realism/nominalism, 99–100
Ridbaz, 162n27, 164n60
Riggs vs. Palmer (1882), 117–119
ritual purity, 22–24, 73–76, 145, 156n66
  baskets and, 23, 74, 156n63
  ha'aramah and, 157n68, 161n22
  hallah and, 120, 159n8
  shelters and, 156n65
  subjective intent and, 74–75
Ritva, 197n41
Roman legal conventions, 53–64
  contrasted with rabbinic legal cultures, 60–64, 170nn44–45, 171n57, 184n68
  fraus legi and, 59–60, 63
  ha'aramah and, 21–22, 167n5
  loopholing and, 53–63
  summum ius summa iniuria, 55
Rose, Carol, 121–122, 130, 132
Rosen-Zvi, Ishay, 71–73, 75–77

Sabbath restrictions, 103, 158n82, 194n12. *See also* festivals
  ati le-i'arume and, 94
  'eruv, 3, 138–140, 195n17, 195nn21–23, 196n34
  'eruv tavshilin and, 41, 61, 104–105, 136, 140–142, 163n45, 196n45, 196nn34–35
  festival food preparations and, 32–33, 41–42, 51, 61, 105, 135, 140–142, 157nn78–79, 161n16, 163n45, 196n27, 196n31, 196n35
  ha'aramah and, 26, 176n4
  house fires and, 26–28, 149n19, 157n79, 158n82, 158nn84–85

intention and, 27, 67, 71, 76–77, 103, 181n49
livestock handling, 28–29, 159n92
lying and, 94
ritual purity and, 184n74
shevut, 35, 161n16, 161n18
sin offerings and, 35, 161nn15–16
Sabbatical year, 3, 135–137, 179n31, 193n4, 193n7, 194n10
Saiman, Chaim, 116
Savigny, Friedrich Carl von, 107
Schauer, Fredrick, 109, 113–114, 132
scriptum vs. voluntas, 59–60, 63–64, 169n38
scriptural exegesis, 4–5, 147n3, 165n69
sekhirat reshut, 195n18
self, 7, 72–77, 175n35
  in the *Bavli*, 78
  Christian understanding of, 72, 97
  festivals and, 76
  ha'aramah and, 8
  inner self concept, 76, 175n35
  in the *Mishnah*, 72
  ritual purity and, 24, 75
  ritual vs. sincere, 69–70, 77, 78
  subjective, 24, 66, 72, 75–77, 88, 97, 99, 101, 157n68, 182n50
Seligman, Adam, 69
serpent, 10–11, 26, 30, 131
Shaked, Shaul, 95
Shakespeare, 2
Shammai, 41, 173n22
shema, 71
shevut, 35, 161n16, 161n18
Shimon ben Yohai, R., 37, 124–126
Shisha, R., 91–92
shiv'ah, 45, 47, 146
Siegal, Michal Bar-Asher, 95
Sifra, 150n14, 152n34
Silberg, Moshe, 135–136, 179n24, 192n72
sin, 11, 68, 70, 79
  ha'aramah and, 35, 37, 79
  intention and, 67, 95, 97
  sin offerings, 35, 161nn15–16
  sin of golden calf, 125, 129
sincerity, 66–67, 69–70
Sodom and Gomorrah, tale of, 130–131
Solomon, 139, 195n16, 195n21
  solomonic circumvention, 11, 26, 29–30
Song of Songs *Rabbah*, 123–124, 171n54

spirit of the law. *See* letter vs. spririt of the law
Stone, Suzanne Last, 114
Strauch Schick, Shana, 181n49, 182n50
straw man. *See interposita persona*
subjective intention, 85–90, 100
 in the *Bavli*, 78, 80, 82, 85–86, 88–90, 95–97, 105
 consent and, 88–89, 179n31
 gift of Bet Horon and, 82–85
 ha'aramah and, 66–67, 74, 80–82, 85–86, 94, 97, 106
 performative intention and, 73, 80–82, 88, 90, 100, 105, 173n22, 177n12
 ritual purity and, 74–75
 Zoroastrianism and, 95–97
subjective self, 24, 66, 72, 75–77, 88, 97, 99, 101, 157n68, 182n50
summum ius, summa iniuria (more law, more injury), 55
Sumner Maine, Henry, 148n7

takkanah/takkanot, 4, 61, 135–144
 'eruv and, 139–140
 'eruv tavshilin and, 104–105, 140–142
 ha'aramah and, 8, 16, 61–62, 105, 135–144
 intention and, 71
 prosbul and, 136–138, 144
 selling of *ḥametz* foods and, 142–143
Tarfon, R., 38–39, 146, 162n30, 167n8, 177n14
tatzdeke/tatzreke, 98–99
Tchernowitz, Haim, 107–108, 132, 187n1
Temple, 5, 16–19, 140
 destruction of, 16–18, 23
 notion of self and, 175n35
 post-temple context, 16–17, 19–20, 23–24, 30, 109, 140, 151nn27–28, 152n30, 153n49, 154n50, 157n68
 ritual purity and, 23–24, 74–75, 82, 161n22
 temple treasury, 44, 51, 118, 164n51
temple treasury refunds, 44
temporary betrothal, 38–39
terumah foods, 38, 72, 74, 162n26, 162n30
Tiberius, 56
tithing, 39, 47–49, 109, 145, 180n34. *See also ma'aser sheni*
 animal feeding and, 165n67
 in the *Bavli*, 165n67, 176n2, 180n34, 181n39
 circumvention and, 48–49

ha'aramah and, 12–17, 60, 70–71, 109, 121, 145, 152n30
 by minors, 150n15
 sacred coins and, 152n29
Tosefta, 150n19
 circumvention in, 36
 contrasted with the *Mishnah*, 154n50, 156n59, 158n85, 160n13
 ha'aramah in, 13–14, 16, 22–30, 34, 71, 102, 158n85
 livestock handling in, 28–29, 66–67, 172n7
 ma'aser sheni in, 19, 151n28
 mar'it 'ayin in, 68
 ormah in, 178n20
 ritual impurity and, 23–24, 73–74
tzitzit, 98–99, 183n60
tzurba me-rabanan (young rabbinic scholar), 104, 186n87, 187n89
 ha'aramah and, 102–105

Ulla, 48
Ulpan, 59
Urbach, Ephraim, 18, 152n30
usury, 25–26

voluntas, 59–60, 63–64, 169n38

Watson, Alan, 132
wayward sons, killing of, 50, 165n70, 166n71
Weiss, Dov, 129–130
Wendell Holmes, Jr., Oliver, 115

Yehoshua, R.
 on "cunning rogues," 21, 44
 on intention, 71, 173n22
 on livestock handling, 29, 35, 66–69, 79, 90, 102
 mar'it 'ayin and, 69
 on marriage settlements, 44, 164n50
 on money transfers, 14
 on Passover dough, 32–34, 90–92, 106, 160n13
Yehudah, R.
 on labor restrictions, 45–46
 on Passover dough, 32
 on ritual purity, 37, 161n22
 on tithing, 48
Yerushalmi, 31–32, 51–52
 avoision in, 31–32, 40, 43–44, 51
 circumvention in, 177n14

contrasted with *Bavli* texts, 79, 100–101, 145–146
festival celebration and, 40–43, 45–46, 163n44
ha'aramah and, 31–33, 38–49, 51–52, 79, 145–146, 191n52
livestock handling and, 161n17
loan fraud and, 43–44
Passover dough and, 32–35, 90–92, 159n8
temple treasury refunds and, 44
temporary betrothal and, 38–39
tithing and, 39, 48–49, 60
trickiness in, 181n46
Yohanan, R., 22–24, 145, 161n22
Yose, R.
on bread retrieval, 27
on *ha'aramah*, 36
on labor restrictions, 45–46
on livestock handling, 35
on tithing, 39, 48–49

Zeitlin, Solomon, 135–136, 195n21
Zoroastrianism, 95–97, 99, 106, 186n88

Acknowledgments

It is hard to separate my gratitude upon publishing this book from my gratitude at living a life suffused with Torah study. I feel blessed to have inherited a talmudic tradition of such depth and breadth, to have family, teachers, and community who encourage/d my Torah pursuits, and to live at a time when such study is accessible to me. And even when I express my gratitude for those who have helped me with this project, I must recall back about two decades. For this is where the project began.

Three people laid the foundation for this book project. Twenty years ago, Professor David Weiss Halivni *z"l* (obm) introduced me to the critical study of Talmud, and simply put, my life has never been the same. He modeled brilliance, kindness, and integrity all wrapped into one, and I am forever grateful for having studied with him and having developed such a rich personal connection with him. I only wish I could bring this book to his apartment in Jerusalem to see his beaming smile. Around the time that I began my graduate work, Suzanne Last Stone opened a fellowship program at Cardozo Law School to familiarize Jewish Studies doctoral students with western legal theory. Her vision and leadership in shaping the dialogue between law and rabbinics over the past twenty years has profoundly impacted the field of Jewish Studies. My own foray into comparative jurisprudence motivated me to think about legal loopholes as a research theme and gave me the foundations to consider its significance for jurisprudence beyond the field of rabbinics. A third transformative guide during my doctoral work was Barry Wimpfheimer. He selflessly gave of his time, energy, and insight not only to guide my dissertation but to train me further as a scholar, pushing me to problematize my findings and to hone more technical methodological skills that I lacked. He read each draft of my dissertation and offered useful feedback out of his own generosity.

During my graduate years, my thinking was deepened through my traditional *yeshiva* learning in the Graduate Program in Advanced Talmudic

Studies at Yeshiva University, where I was blessed with inspired *hevrutot* and teachers, including my brother-in-law Shmuel Hain. My work as clergy at both the Jewish Center and Lincoln Square Synagogue during and beyond those years allowed me to share my evolving thinking about the various legal loopholes used in Jewish life. (Don't ask how many times I taught on the topic of selling *ḥametz* before Passover!) During this time, I was also blessed to learn with Moshe Sokolow, analyzing many if not all *ha'aramah* examples in both the *Yerushalmi* and the *Bavli*.

During my years at the Shalom Hartman Institute of North America, I discovered a whole new community of support. Shaul Magid reviewed multiple drafts of this monograph and encouraged me to submit my manuscript to this series. I could not have gotten to this point without him. Christine Hayes, from whose mentorship I have benefitted in too many ways to count, offered extensive notes on my dissertation, along with advice on how to transform it into a book. Additionally, the Institute provided me with wonderful interns to help with the book—Elizabeth Kirshner and Elliot Salinger—each of whom contributed to my thinking through their research and through our conversations. My colleague Shalhevet Schwartz—whose books I hope to read someday—reviewed my treatment of the rabbinic material in this book, offering invaluable suggestions. Additionally, simply being in the thoughtful, collaborative, and rigorous intellectual environment of the Kogod Research Center and Hartman North America more generally helped me sharpen my ideas. I express my gratitude to Yehuda Kurtzer and Rachel Jacoby Rosenfield of Hartman, for their tireless efforts in maintaining such a powerful environment and also for giving me a writing furlough to finish an earlier draft of the manuscript, as well as to my many colleagues who supported me and cheered me along throughout this process. Notably, Tamara Mann Tweel not only encouraged me when I was flagging, but also strategized with me about how to carve out time to get the work done.

There are others—both longtime and newer friends—who helped me along the way as well, outside of an institutional context: Anne Gordon edited an earlier version of this manuscript, bringing her writing abilities and her rabbinics expertise to bear in ways that helped me tremendously. More recently Gillian Steinberg edited the manuscript and offered constructive stylistic and technical suggestions. Artemis Brod brought her proficiency in classics to editing Chapter 3 of the book. Chaim Saiman provided thoughtful feedback from his blended expertise in law and rabbinics, and Lynn Kaye offered helpful suggestions for how to improve the book's overall conceptual coherence. Aaron Koller was on hand for advice as I thought through how to transliterate in a manner that both academics and Jewish practitioners might appreciate, and Elli Fischer offered comments on the Epilogue. And it has been a joy to work with the very professional and supportive (!) Penn Press editorial team, especially Elisabeth Maselli and Lily Palladino.

And now, on to family. For years, my children have made me promise to include their loopholing exploits in this book. While I have not done so in the body of the book, I will share one example from each here: When Azzan was a toddler, I once asked him to put the caps on his Crayola markers so they would not dry out. After refusing multiple times, he finally placed the caps on the *back* of each marker, leaving the ink tips exposed. He smiled at me and said, "There, I did it. I put the caps on." Navon's example comes from his role as a Little League catcher. When he was eight, one of the interventions of the league meant to help developing players was that a runner could only steal a base if the catcher caught the pitch. So, Navon decided to make a habit of purposely letting pitches drop out of his mitt. As any reader can tell, I am simply overmatched by these two. As they age, their loopholes mature with them, consistently bringing a smile to my face. And in their maturity, they have given up so much time over the years to let me write and rewrite, edit and reedit this book, inspiring me along the way.

I am blessed to have in my spouse both a best friend and *hevruta*. He has always been my greatest ally and my greatest goad. A talmudist himself, Yonah has lovingly offered detailed suggestions about the book, but also about my general thinking on this topic. And the hours that he has given me and the responsibilities that he has taken on to support my work are too many to count. I am eternally grateful. And this line is just for him: I love you.

I end with the gratitude that inspires my Torah study: reaching for a connection to the Almighty. I feel blessed by the conditions of my life that have brought me to this point. ברוך אתה ה' חונן הדעת—Blessed are You, God, Who graciously grants knowledge.

www.ingramcontent.com/pod-product-compliance
Lightning Source LLC
Chambersburg PA
CBHW031435160426
43195CB00010BB/736